JUSTIFYING PRIVATE LAW REMEDIES

In August 2006 the third Australian Obligations Conference was hosted in Brisbane by the TC Beirne School of Law. The theme of the Conference was 'Justifying Private Law Remedies'. This book contains a number of the papers delivered at that Conference, presented under several categories but all dealing with the fundamental issue of justification: General Concepts; Performance; Compensation; Punishment; and Restitution and Disgorgement. The authors are largely drawn from the legal academy, and include Canadian, Australian, British and New Zealand scholars. The collection will be of interest to all those concerned with the role, nature and place of remedies in the private law of the common law world.

Justifying Private Law Remedies

Edited by Charles EF Rickett

·HART·
PUBLISHING

OXFORD AND PORTLAND, OREGON
2008

Published in North America (US and Canada) by
Hart Publishing
c/o International Specialized Book Services
920 NE 58th Avenue, Suite 300
Portland, OR 97213-3786
USA
Tel: +1 503 287 3093 or toll-free: (1) 800 944 6190
Fax: +1 503 280 8832
E-mail: orders@isbs.com
Website: www.isbs.com

Hart Publishing, 16C Worcester Place, Oxford, OX1 2JW
Telephone: +44 (0)1865 517530 Fax: +44 (0) 1865 510710
E-mail: mail@hartpub.co.uk
Website: http//:www.hartpub.co.uk

British Library Cataloguing in Publication Data

Data Available

ISBN: 978-1-84113-814-5

Typeset by Forewords, Oxford
Printed and bound in Great Britain by
Lightning Source UK Ltd

Contents

List of Contributors

Kit Barker, Associate Professor of Law, The University of Queensland

Allan Beever, Reader in Law, University of Durham

Michael Bryan, Professor of Law, The University of Melbourne

John W Carter, Professor of Commercial Law, The University of Sydney

Ralph M Cunnington, Lecturer in Law, University of Birmingham

James Edelman, Fellow and Tutor in Law, Keble College, Oxford

Darryn Jensen, Lecturer in Law, The University of Queensland

The Hon Justice P de Jersey, Chief Justice of Queensland

The Hon Justice Susan Kiefel, High Court of Australia

Elisabeth Peden, Associate Professor of Law, The University of Sydney

Charles EF Rickett, Sir Gerard Brennan Professor of Law and Dean of Law, TC Beirne School of Law, The University of Queensland

Struan Scott, Associate Professor of Law, University of Otago

Duncan Sheehan, Senior Lecturer in Law, University of East Anglia

Stephen A Smith, Professor of Law, McGill University

Graham Virgo, Professor in Law and Fellow of Downing College, Cambridge

Ernest J Weinrib, University Professor and Cecil A Wright Professor of Law, University of Toronto

Table of Cases

Antigua and Barbuda

Australia

Bahamas

Canada

European Court of Human Rights

Germany

Hong Kong

Israel

Jamaica

Malaysia

New Zealand

Trinidad

United Kingdom

United States of America

Table of Legislation

Australia

Germany

International

New Zealand

United Kingdom

Statutory Instruments

Restatements

Part I

General Concepts

1

Two Conceptions of Remedies

ERNEST J WEINRIB*

I THE TWO CONCEPTIONS

IN THIS PAPER I explore two ways of conceptualising the relationship between the basis of the defendant's liability and the remedy, that is, between what Peter Birks termed the 'causative event' and the response.[1] In the first way, originally formulated in Aristotle's account of corrective justice and later elaborated in the philosophical tradition of natural right, the causative event is the reason for the remedial response. In the second way, paradigmatically set out in Kelsen's pure theory of law, the causative event is the condition of the remedial response. For each of these two ways the causative event enters into the practical reasoning about the response in a different manner. In the first, the causative event is a condition of the response because it is the reason for it. In the second, the causative event is the reason for the response because it is a condition of it.

Consider first the following observations by Aristotle about the function of the judge in a civil action.

> [P]eople have recourse to a judge when they are engaged in a dispute. To go to a judge means to go to the just, for to be a judge means, as it were, to be the embodiment of what is just . . . The judge restores equality. As though there were a line divided into two unequal parts, he takes away the amount be which the larger part is greater than half the line and adds it to the smaller. Only when the whole has been divided into two equal parts can a man say that he has what is properly his, i.e., when he has taken an equal part.[2]

Aristotle represents what properly belongs to each of the disputing parties as an equal segment of a line. The injustice—the causative event—consists of the defendant's having taken part of the segment that properly belongs to the plaintiff, thereby destroying the underlying equality. The judge

* University Professor and Cecil A Wright Professor of Law, University of Toronto. I am grateful to Arthur Ripstein and Ben Zipursky for discussion of some of the issues dealt with in this paper.

1 P Birks, *Unjust Enrichment* 21 (2nd edition, 2005).

2 Aristotle, *Nicomachean Ethics*, V, 1132a19–29 (M Ostwald trans, 1962).

remedies this injustice by reattaching to the plaintiff's segment the amount by which the defendant's part exceeds the half-line that each should have.

In this representation, the causative event is the reason for the particular response. What the defendant has done *to* the plaintiff determines what the judge requires the defendant to do *for* the plaintiff. The defendant is now obligated to return what the defendant unjustly took from the plaintiff. Because justice between the parties obtains when the line is divided equally between them, the disturbance of the equality counts as an injustice, which the judge undoes by restoring the initial equality. Just as the causative event for liability is the defendant's taking a segment of the plaintiff's line, so the remedy is the retaking of that segment from the defendant and reattaching it to the plaintiff's part of the line. If one were to ask Aristotle's judge why he redivided the line in this way, he would answer that this was the only just response to the defendant's action.

The point of Aristotle's account is to draw attention to the relationship between the particular injustice of the causative event and the particular response ordered by the judge. One might think, following through on the representation of the parties' relative positions in terms of equal segments of a line, that one could restore the equality in a number of different ways. The shortening of the plaintiff's segment of the line, for example, might lead the judge to somehow arrange to extend the plaintiff's line by twice the length of the segment that the defendant took, thus leaving both parties with an equal share of a larger line. Conversely, the lengthening of the defendant's segment might lead the judge to order that the defendant's line be shortened by twice the length of the taken segment, thus leaving both parties with an equal share of a shorter line. These methods of restoring equality, however, do not reflect the nature of the injustice committed by the defendant. The injustice did not consist in the plaintiff's ending up with a shorter segment, to be remedied by lengthening the plaintiff's segment while leaving the defendant's increased segment intact. Nor did the injustice consist in the defendant's committing an unjust act that augmented his segment, to be remedied by shortening that segment while doing nothing for the plaintiff. Rather, the injustice simultaneously shortened the plaintiff's line and lengthened the defendant's; indeed, it shortened the plaintiff's line through its lengthening of the defendant's. Accordingly, the remedy to this injustice must similarly implicate both parties, restoring the equality by simultaneously relengthening the plaintiff's segment and reshortening the defendant's.

Aristotle's point is that only through this bipolarity can the injustice of the causative event be a fully adequate reason for a response that links the defendant to the plaintiff. For, if the injustice provided a reason for operating on the segment of merely one of the parties, there would be a puzzle as to why it also operated on the segment of the other. And if the response was motivated by two separate reasons, one applicable to the plaintiff's segment and the other to the defendant's, there would be a similar puzzle as to why these reasons, being separate, have to operate simultaneously.

Aristotle takes it for granted that a bipolar injustice provides the reason for the bipolar remedy. This is what makes the form of justice manifested by the judge's action corrective, *diorthotikon*, literally 'righting' a wrong. His concern is structural: how does the structure of the remedy reflect the structure of the injustice that it corrects? What he notices is that the both the remedy and the injustice involve a direct relationship between the plaintiff and the defendant. If the remedy operated on only one of the parties, either by shortening the defendant's segment of the line or by lengthening the plaintiff's, it would leave the relational aspect of the injustice unremedied. Accordingly, the remedy has to replicate the structure of the injustice, retracing and reversing the movement between the parties. In noticing this, Aristotle does not, of course, resolve any specific remedial problem, but he tells what it means for a remedy to correct an injustice.

One can contrast Aristotle's conception of the remedy with the one formulated by Hans Kelsen. For Kelsen, the legal order stipulates the conditions under which certain coercive acts function as sanctions that react against illegal acts or omissions. What counts as a wrong, or delict, is an act or omission that the legal order makes the condition of the coercive act; conversely, what counts as the sanction is the coercive consequence that the legal order attaches to that act or omission. Thus, the relationship between causative event and remedy is solely that of condition and consequence:

> Given, as condition, behaviour opposite that which the norm establishes, then a coercive act is to be forthcoming as consequence.[3]

Aristotle and Kelsen link the wrong to the remedy in entirely different ways. For Aristotle, the wrong is a reason for the remedy because it is an injustice that the judge, as the embodiment of justice, must reverse. For Kelsen, the notion that 'a moral value element is immanent in the concepts of delict and sanction'[4] is untenable, because only the positive legal order imbues an act or omission with the character of a delict. To put the point another way: for Aristotle, the causative event is the condition of a remedy because of the kind of event it is, whereas for Kelsen, the event counts as causative only because it is the condition of a remedy. In Kelsen's words:

> [A] definite action or refrainment is not—as traditional jurisprudence assumes—connected with the coercive act because this action or refrainment is a

[3] H Kelsen, *Introduction to the Problems of Legal Theory* (B Litschewski Paulson and SL Paulson, trans) 30.

[4] H Kelsen, *Pure Theory of Law* (M Knight, trans), 111.

> delict, but a definite act or refrainment is a delict because it is connected with a coercive act, that is, with a sanction as its consequence. No immanent quality, no relation to a meta-legal natural or divine norm is a reason for qualifying a specific human behaviour as a delict; but only and exclusively the fact that the positive legal order has made this behaviour the condition of a coercive act—of a sanction.[5]

This juxtaposition of Aristotle and Kelsen brings out the contrast between what we may call the 'reason conception' and the 'condition conception' of remedies. Aristotle and Kelsen are led to these differing conceptions by the differences in their projects. Aristotle's interest is in presenting the form of justice that is immanent in the relationship between the parties in private law. Integral to this form of justice is the idea that the direct relationship of the parties characterises both the causative event and the remedy, indeed, that it characterises the remedy because it characterises the causative event. Thus, the reason for thinking that the defendant's act is an injustice to the plaintiff is also a reason for thinking that the remedy that corrects the injustice has to have the same relational structure as the injustice. Kelsen, in contrast, is concerned not with justice but with the posited nature of law. Because a norm can be legally valid even if it is thought to be unjust, the connection between the causative event and the remedy must be understood in terms of condition and consequence with respect to the coercion that the positive law mandates. Whereas Aristotle views the relationship of causative event to remedy as immanent to the structure of justice between the parties, Kelsen regards that relationship as exhibited through 'an analysis of the immanent meaning of the legal order'[6] as a system of positive law. The injustice that is paramount for Aristotle is therefore irrelevant to Kelsen.

The sections of this paper that follow develop some of the implications of each of these conceptions of remedies. I first elaborate, in section II, the 'reason conception' by sketching a composite, drawn from the work of Aristotle, Kant and Hegel, of this conception's elements. Each of these thinkers mentions some of these elements and does not mention others, and they formulate the common elements in divergent ways. But for our purposes these differences are not as important as the overall picture that emerges about the relationship between the causative event and the remedy. In this picture the causative event is construed as an injustice that both grounds and limits the remedy that responds to it. This conception, I contend, provides the tightest possible rendition of what it is for a causative event to be the reason for a remedy in private law. Indeed, to the extent that one deviates from this picture, one slips into treating the causative event as a condition rather than a reason.

5 *Ibid.*
6 *Ibid*, 112.

I then turn to the 'condition conception'. Kelsen's account of this conception is part of his elucidation of what it is for a norm to have the form of positive law regardless of the norm's content. This indifference to content means that one cannot extrapolate from his account anything that would address the lawyer's interest in what the legal system should look like. In this respect there is an asymmetry between Kelsen's account and Aristotle's. For, as we saw in Aristotle's treatment of the segmented line, Aristotle thinks that the remedy has to match the bipolar structure of the injustice that it corrects; accordingly, his approach reproduces, although at a very high level of abstraction, the lawyer's concern for the normative intelligibility of the law's content. For Kelsen, in contrast, the law is a posited order that can have any content. Kelsen allows that actual legal systems do have remedies that purport to right the wrong by requiring the defendant to repair the damage illegally inflicted upon the plaintiff,[7] but he considers these to exemplify a kind of logical error in which the way a person behaves (a statement of what is) is mistakenly taken to contradict a norm (an statement of what ought to be).[8] In Kelsen's view, from the standpoint of positive law, the illegal act means nothing more than that the sanction ought to be forthcoming. Inasmuch as the sanction is an operation of the legal order, the illegal act should therefore be understood not as the negation of law but as its condition.

From the lawyer's standpoint, Kelsen's observations may suggest an unpromising framework for considering the role of remedies within a system of private law. Sophisticated legal systems, after all, are not indifferent to their own content. Rather, they view that content as the thing that makes at least incipient sense from a suitably defined moral point of view. Within private law, events are causative of liability because they are thought to work some sort of injustice toward the plaintiff. Nonetheless, torn from its context within Kelsen's pure theory, the idea of the causative event as a condition of the remedy is no stranger to contemporary discussions of remedies. It surfaces whenever the remedy is seen not as normatively continuous with what makes the causative event an injustice, but as the locus of an independent enquiry. By breaking the normative connection that might exist between the remedy and the causative event, such an enquiry treats the latter as a condition but not a reason for the former.

To the extent that remedies exemplify the condition conception, they ignore or go beyond the injustice that calls them into being. Such remedies are not concerned—or at least not concerned only—with responding to whatever aspect of the parties' interaction forms the basis for liability. In the language of the old remoteness cases, what goes to culpability is

[7] *Ibid*, 109.
[8] *Ibid*, 113.

viewed as distinguishable from what goes to compensation (or to other remedial impositions).[9] This disjunction between the injustice of the causative event and the remedial response creates a tension in which the injustice occasions the remedy without grounding it. On the one hand, the causative event is seen as some sort of injustice that requires a remedy; but on the other, the remedy's operation is independent of the reason for thinking of that the causative event was an injustice to begin with. Thus, so far as the remedy is concerned, the injustice of the causative event is both indispensable and superfluous.

Section III explores the problematic nature of the condition conception by reference to a conspicuous example of it: the indemnified injunction. This kind of injunction allows the plaintiff to bring a nuisance to an end but only if the defendant is compensated for costs imposed by the injunction. Although absent from the traditional corpus of remedies and rarely invoked in practice, the indemnified injunction has received extensive attention in the economic analysis of law. It is sometimes even regarded as suggesting a new 'grand theory of remedies'[10]: by breaking the 'sensible convention' of 'not asking those in the right to pay when they are wronged,'[11] it is supposed to contribute to a more unified theory of remedies that combines rights, remedies and bargains around those rights and remedies. Whatever its virtues on that score, the remedy operates independently of the injustice that lies at the root of the determination of liability, as its breach of the 'sensible convention' shows. Indeed, the remedy obscures the very nature of the injustice that gives birth to it. In these respects it is characteristic of the condition conception of remedies.

Finally, section IV aligns the distinction between the reason and the condition conception of remedies with the recent contrast made by remedies scholars between monistic and dualistic approaches to remedies. The focus within the reason conception on the normative ground of the remedy may cast light on the tension—present in both monism and dualism—between the centrality of the infringed right to the remedy and the introduction of new considerations at the remedial stage. The reason conception reconciles this tension by situating the right within the system of rights, thereby allowing systemic considerations to be introduced at the remedial stage. In this way, I shall suggest, the reason conception may narrow the gap between these two approaches.

9 The distinction between what 'goes to culpability' and what 'goes to compensation' was current in the law of negligence until overruled in *Overseas Tankship (UK) v Morts Dock & Engineering (The Wagon Mound, No 1)* [1961] AC 388 (PC).

10 S Levmore, 'Unifying Remedies: Property Rules, Liability Rules, and Startling Rules' (1997) 106 *Yale Law Journal* 2149.

11 *Ibid*, 2150.

II THE REASON CONCEPTION OF REMEDIES

In the reason conception of remedies, the reason for the law's regarding something as a causative event is also the reason for the law's awarding the remedy. The injustice to be corrected determines the nature of the remedy that corrects it. The reason conception thus presupposes not only a particular relationship between remedy and causative event, but also a conception of what counts as a causative event. Taken as a sequence that extends from the specification of the causative event to the determination of the remedy, the reason conception has the following aspects.

A The Relationship between the Parties

The parties, as participants in the regime of private law, are understood to be interacting directly with each other through a causative event in which the defendant does the plaintiff an injustice. This causative event is conceived not as two separate occurrences (an action done by the defendant and an injury suffered by the plaintiff) that happen to come together in the phenomenon of liability, but as a single normative sequence that situates the parties correlatively as doer and sufferer of the same injustice, so that the ground of liability is equally applicable to both parties. This understanding of the parties' relationship is mirrored in the structure of the remedial response, for in the absence of the parties' being directly linked through the event that causes liability, the law would have no reason to respond with a remedy that also directly links them. This is nothing more than Aristotle's point about the line: the defendant's taking of part of the plaintiff's segment is an injustice that links the parties directly and that is remedied by the judge's requiring the defendant to restore the segment to the plaintiff.

The directness of the injustice between the parties presupposes that the law treats them as being in a relationship of will to will. From the perspective of private law, they are regarded solely as persons who interact with each other through their self-determining capacity to set and pursue their own ends, rather than as subject to obligatory ends set by personal morality or social goals.[12] Private law makes no judgement about worth or value of the particular ends that the parties might pursue, because any such judgement would undermine the normative character either of the relationship or of its directness. For example, if the law insisted that the parties each act to promote their own moral goodness, then the normative relevance of the act would refer only to the virtue of either party singly rather than to the relationship between them. Similarly, if the law insisted

12 I Kant, *The Metaphysics of Morals*, M Gregor, ed, 24 [6:230].

that the parties act to advance some social good in which they would both participate, then the conception of social good would mediate the parties' relationship so that they would be connected not directly to each other but indirectly through the social good that they and others would share. Accordingly, private law regards each person as free to exercise the capacity for purposive action toward whatever purposes he or she chooses. In this, sense private law is a domain of interaction between parties on the basis of the freedom of each.

The self-determining capacity for purposive activity imbues the parties' interaction with the possibility of adherence to appropriate norms. It endows them with the status of persons who, in their relations with others, can never count as mere means but must at the same time be ends for them.[13] Having this status, they can assert themselves in relation to each other by insisting that they enjoy their self-determining freedom equally and that any constraints on its exercise must be reciprocal.[14] In this way they can regard each other both as self-authenticating sources of valid claims[15] and as bearers of responsibility for the effects that the execution of one's chosen purposes has on the other. Thus, their self-determining capacity links the interacting parties as potential plaintiff and defendant.

B The Role of Rights

In the relationship of will to will, both parties are equal. Private law neither regards the particular purposes of the parties nor has any particular purposes of its own; it therefore has no basis for preferring or subordinating either party to the other. Because the relationship is between the parties who are both self-determining actors, their equality consists in the compatibility of each person's action with the self-determining freedom of the other. Although private law does not require the parties to act positively for any particular goals, it does embody the negative principle that the action of one party ought not to be inconsistent with the other party's freedom.[16] The freedom of the other is not a goal that the actor must promote but is, rather, a limit on freedom of action that is implicit in the equality of the interacting parties as self-determining persons. The exercise of self-determining freedom is rightful when it operates within this constraint.

Because private law deals with the relationship between wills, the normative categories that actualise this constraint have to bear on the

13 *Ibid*, 29 [6:236] (rightful honor); see also GWF Hegel, *Elements of the Philosophy of Right*, AW Wood, ed (1991), s 36 (the commandment of abstract right to be a person).

14 Kant, above n 12, 29–30 [6:237–8].

15 The phrase is from J Rawls, *Justice as Fairness: A Restatement* (2001), 23.

16 Kant, above n 12, 24 [6:631] (the universal principle of right)

parties' action and freedom in a directly relational way. This requirement excludes categories that focus on moral virtue and social goals: as noted above, the former is not relational and the latter is not directly relational. As a determinant of liability, the appropriately relational normative category is that of a right; a right is inherently relational because its existence immediately implies that another is under a duty not to infringe it. Rights mark out legally secured spheres of freedom within which the holder of the right can exercise the capacity to pursue self-chosen ends. They also, through the duties that are correlative to them, act as constraints on the actions of others. They are thus the devices through which private law actualises the principle that the action of one party ought not to be inconsistent with the freedom of another.

Rights are the juridical expressions of self-determining freedom. They arise either (as in the case of bodily integrity) from the very existence of the person as a locus of self-determining activity or (as in the case of proprietary and contractual entitlements) from acts of acquisition that are expressive of one's self-determination in a way that is consistent with the freedom of others.[17] Once a person has a right to something, that thing is available for whatever use the holder of the right chooses to make of it in the exercise of his or her self-determining freedom, provided that this use is consistent with the rights of others. If the right in question is an acquired right, the thing can be abandoned, waived or alienated in the exercise of one's self-determining freedom. Thus, the subject matter of one's rights is permeated by the capacity of the holder of the right to set and pursue one's goals. In a sophisticated legal system, the law gives this conception of rights determinate content by working out in specific detail the scope of various rights, their modes of acquisition and the uses that impermissibly trench on the equal freedom of others.

Understood in this way, rights are the normatively decisive components of the relationship between the parties in private law. One does not have a right to something merely because (as Kelsen postulated) the courts grant a remedy for conduct that contravenes it; rather, the court grants a remedy because what the conduct contravenes is a right. The right, in other words, functions as the reason for the remedy, not merely as its condition.

From this it follows that an event that is causative of liability is an inconsistency on the defendant's part with the right of the plaintiff. Such an inconsistency constitutes an injustice by the defendant directly against the plaintiff, thus having the structure appropriate for a remedy that corrects this injustice by operating on the relationship between the parties.

[17] Kant, above n 12 at 30 [6:237] (contrasting innate and acquired right).

C The Remedy

The remedy for injustice so conceived is the elimination of this inconsistency with the plaintiff's rights. To put it in Hegelian terms, if the injustice is a negation of right, the remedy is a negation of the negation.[18] To eliminate the inconsistency, the remedy has to replicate the inconsistency's structure. Because the inconsistency is in the relationship between the plaintiff's right and what the defendant has or has done, the remedy must operate not merely on one party or the other but on the relationship between them. Just as the inconsistency directly links the parties as the active and passive poles of an injustice, so the remedy treats the parties as the active and passive poles in the removal of that injustice.

The structure of the relationship remains constant because the right and the correlative duty survive the injustice.[19] Suppose that the defendant has tortiously destroyed an object belonging to the plaintiff. Prior to the tortious act, the defendant was under a duty of care with respect to the object, because the object embodied the plaintiff's right. The defendant's breach of this duty destroyed the object as a physical entity, but it did not destroy the plaintiff's right as a normative entitlement. Even after the object's destruction the plaintiff is linked to the defendant through a right that pertains to the object as an undamaged thing, so that the right now takes the form of an entitlement to the cost of replacing it. Thus, although the defendant's action has modified the physical condition of the object embodying the plaintiff's right, the right remains intact as the normative marker of the relationship between them with respect to that object. This just follows from the nature of a right as a domain of freedom for its holder, for a right would not be a domain of freedom if the law did not secure that freedom from wrongful destruction by others. Accordingly, the defendant can wrongfully destroy the embodiment of the right as something that physically exists in the world, but the defendant cannot wrongfully destroy the normative connection that the plaintiff's right in the object creates.

The survival of the right means that the duty correlative to it also survives. The defendant's breach of the duty not to destroy the embodiment of the plaintiff's right did not, of course, bring to an end the duty with respect to that right, for if it did, the duty—absurdly—would have been discharged by its breach. Just as the plaintiff's right continues, so the duty correlative to that right continues. As with the right, the content of the duty has been transformed by the defendant's tort. Just as the plaintiff's right is no longer embodied in the specific object, which has been destroyed, but in an entitlement to receive the object's equivalent

[18] Hegel, above n 13, s 82.

[19] For an elaboration of this point see A Ripstein, 'As If It Had Never Happened' (2007) 48 *William and Mary Law Review* 1957.

from the defendant, so the defendant's duty is no longer to abstain from its destruction, which has already taken place, but to provide the plaintiff with the object's equivalent. Like Descartes's famous piece of wax that remains the same piece of wax despite its different qualities when heated and cooled,[20] the same duty is continuously correlative to the same right before and after the tort. One might say that, once the defendant destroys the plaintiff's object, the specific action that the duty requires is different, but it is not a different duty. This is because, from a juridical point of view, what determines the nature of the duty is not the action that the duty requires but the right to which the duty is correlative. Therefore, as the right continues after the tortious destruction, so does the duty.[21]

In awarding a remedy the law aims to remove the inconsistency with the plaintiff's rights by having the defendant restore to the plaintiff (in Aristotle's words) 'what is properly his [*to hautou*].'[22] This restoration can take two forms: the qualitative and the quantitative. The qualitative form restores to the plaintiff the very thing that is the subject matter of the right, thereby allowing the plaintiff to have and enjoy 'its specific qualitative character'.[23] In such cases the law gives specific relief, for example, specific delivery of a unique or unusual chattel, specific performance of a contractual obligation, or an injunction against a private nuisance. The quantitative form restores to the plaintiff, through an award of damages, the monetary value of the subject matter of the right, thereby treating the subject matter of the right as something that is quantitatively equivalent to other things. The task of the law of remedies is to work out the mechanics of the restoration of the plaintiff's right by addressing such issues as the method of computing the value of the right, the concurrence (or not) of remedies when the defendant's action infringes more than one kind of

20 R Descartes, *Meditations on First Philosophy*, Meditation II.

21 For objections to this view, see BC Zipursky, 'Rights, Wrongs, and Recourse in the Law of Torts' (1998) 51 *Vanderbilt Law Review* 1, 74. Zipursky has three criticisms. 'First, it is highly implausible that one is discharging the duty to refrain from wrongdoing someone by compensating her ex post for the harm she has suffered in consequence of being wronged.' Of course, paying compensation for an injury is not a discharge of the duty not to inflict the injury, because if it were, the inflicting of the injury would retroactively not be a wrong. Indeed, it is because there was a wrong that the duty correlative to the plaintiff's right continues to exist for the wrongdoer and requires the kind of performance appropriate to the this stage of the parties' relationship. 'Second, Weinrib's account does not explain why a tortfeasor might not owe a duty of repair even to those whose right was not violated.' The violation of a right is necessary for the duty to repair because the injury must come under the description of a normative concept that positions the parties correlatively to each other. 'Third, and more generally, Weinrib appears to be mixing categories. The question of how one is obligated to conduct oneself toward another is different from the question of what one ought to do if one harms another through breach of that obligation.' Of course, the specific action required of the defendant before and after the wrong is different. But the issue is whether the different actions required at these two stages are disconnected or whether they are moments in a single normative sequence organised under the idea of a duty on the defendant that is continuously correlative to the plaintiff's ongoing right.

22 Above n 2.

23 Hegel, above n 13, s 98R.

right, and the circumstances in which the subject matter of the right is so distinctive that it must be restored qualitatively rather than quantitatively.

In this conception of remedies, the nature of the plaintiff's infringed right defines the nature of the remedy. The only point of the remedy is to remove the inconsistency between the plaintiff's right and what the defendant has or has done. Accordingly, the determination of the appropriate remedy depends on an appreciation of the nature of the infringed right. Assume, for example, that one is considering whether to award damages that reflect the defendant's gain rather than the plaintiff's loss. Here the crucial factor is not the attractiveness of the moral sentiment that one should not profit from one's wrongdoing, for this sentiment does not specifically tie the defendant's gain to an entitlement of the plaintiff. The issue, rather, is whether the potential for the gain that the defendant realised is an incident of the plaintiff's right, therefore placing the defendant under a correlative duty with respect to it. This explains the salience for gain-based damages of the defendant's wrongful dealing with the defendant's property, for a right in property carries with it a right to the gains from the use or alienation of the property. In contrast, one would not be able to recover the gains that a negligent defendant made by not undertaking the proper precautions. The negligently injured plaintiff has a right not to be injured through the materialisation of an unreasonable risk created by the defendant, but does not have a right to the specific precautions that are the contingent means of avoiding that risk.[24] A similar argument applies to the gains from breach of a contract: because the plaintiff's right is to the defendant's performance rather than to the property that the performance would transfer, the plaintiff has no right to gains from that property that the defendant realises through breach of the contract.[25] Thus, in defining the remedy, the right also limits it. Anything beyond the scope of the plaintiff's right does not belong to the remedy, because the defendant cannot be under a correlative duty to restore something that is not rightfully the plaintiff's.

In restoring the plaintiff's right, the law exercises a double function. The first function is that, from the standpoint of the parties, the remedy eliminates the injustice between them by removing the inconsistency between what the defendant has or has done and what is rightfully the plaintiff's. There is, however, also a second function. The granting of the remedy by a court provides public and authoritative confirmation both of the injustice and of its bipolar nature. These two functions are intertwined because, on the one hand, the public confirmation presupposes the injustice that it confirms; and on the other, the injustice would remain spectral—and the

24 For a fuller treatment of these issues, see EJ Weinrib, 'Restitutionary Damages as Corrective Justice' (2000) 1 *Theoretical Inquiries in Law* 2.

25 EJ Weinrib, 'Punishment and Disgorgement as Contract Remedies' (2003) 78 *Chicago-Kent Law Review* 55.

plaintiff's right correspondingly ineffective and insecure—if there were no publicly available remedy that could eliminate it. The remedy is thus the product of a public process that acknowledges the validity of the right by making its infringement the ground for the judicial decision. By awarding the remedy that requires the defendant to undo the injury to what is rightfully the plaintiff's, the court publicly attests both to the nature of the right and to the kind of event that is inconsistent with it.

The fundamental feature of the reason conception of remedies is that the remedy matches the infringed right. The structural consideration that underlies this matching is that both the right and the remedy directly link the parties to each other. The reason that the remedy operates on the relationship between the parties rather than on either of them separately is that the remedy corrects an injustice that has a relational character. Just as the causative event involves the defendant's having or having done something that is inconsistent with the plaintiff's right, so the removal of this inconsistency embraces both parties. Thus, under the reason conception, the remedy both reflects and confirms the relational nature of the injustice. In contrast, a remedy that is justified by its application to one or the other of the parties without dealing with them relationally fails to treat the injustice as a reason for the remedy. In the case of such a remedy, the causative event is merely a condition, not a reason.

III THE CONDITION CONCEPTION OF REMEDIES

I now turn to the condition conception of remedies. As was mentioned at the outset, I want to focus on a conspicuous if rather unusual example, the indemnified injunction. Under an indemnified injunction, the plaintiff is entitled to an injunction provided that the defendant is compensated for the damage that the injunction causes. This remedy was not known to exist until 1972. In that year, it was coincidentally employed in the nuisance case of *Spur Industries v Del E Webb Development Co*[26] and suggested in a celebrated article by Calabresi and Melamed that has revolutionised academic thinking about remedies in the US.[27]

Because compensating the defendant is manifestly at odds with the supposedly wrongful behavior that occasions the remedy, the indemnified injunction is an extreme example of the condition conception of remedies. When an indemnified injunction is awarded, the causative event has to be understood not as the reason that grounds the remedy as a matter of justice, but as the occasion that triggers the operation of a normatively independent remedial policy. This gap between response and the normative

26 *Spur Industries v Del E Webb Development Co*, 494 P 2d 700 (Arizona SC, 1972).

27 G Calabresi and D Melamed, 'Property Rules, Liability Rules, and Inalienability: One View of the Cathedral' (1972) 85 *Harvard Law Review* 1089.

ground of the causative event means that the remedy obscures the nature of the injustice being remedied. Indeed, a proponent of the reason conception would say that such a remedy works a new injustice to one or the other of the parties by requiring the defendant to do either too much (if the defendant's behavior was not really a wrong) or too little (if it was). In any event, the extreme nature of this instance of the condition conception makes it an apt illustration of what that conception entails.

A *Spur v Del E Webb*

Consider first the nuisance case.[28] The defendant was the operator of a cattle feedlot built in what had long been an agricultural district. The plaintiff was a real estate developer who had purchased land in the neighbourhood of the feedlot in order to develop an urban area. As the development grew, it came closer and closer to the cattle feedlot, until the feedlot's smells caused the developer to encounter sales resistance from prospective purchasers and persistent complaints from past purchasers. The developer sued in nuisance. The court held that the developer was entitled to an injunction. It also held, however, that having brought into the previously agricultural area the population that makes the granting of an injunction necessary, the plaintiff should also indemnify the defendant for the damages it would sustain by having to move or cease operations under the injunction.

The striking feature of this remedy is that it makes it hard to discern the injustice of, or even to identify, the causative event. Indeed, because the remedy has two parts, the injunction for which the defendant is liable and the indemnification that the plaintiff provides in return for the injunction, it is not even easy to single out the party responsible for the causative event. Nor is it easy to identify the victim of the wrong, especially since the court took into account the interests not only of the parties but also of the residents in the development, who purchased their properties from the developer. On the facts of this case, four possibilities suggest themselves: (i) the feedlot operator wronged the developer; (ii) the feedlot operator wronged the residents; (iii) the developer wronged the feedlot operator; (iv) the developer wronged the residents. None of these possibilities, however, is completely satisfactory.

The first possibility, matching the roles of defendant and plaintiff in the case, is that the feedlot operator committed a wrong against the developer. On this possibility, which accords with the classic understanding of nuisance law,[29] the presence of the cattle feedlot prior to the activity of the

28 *Spur Industries*, above n 26.

29 *Sturges v Bridgman* (1879) 11 Ch D 852 (CA); compare *Miller v Jackson* [1977] 3 All ER 338 (CA). See EJ Weinrib, *The Idea of Private Law* (1995) 194–1295.

developer does not exonerate the operator of the feedlot from what was otherwise a nuisance. The defendant cannot restrict the plaintiff from developing its land, and once the land is developed, the plaintiff's rights in the use of that land are protected by the law of nuisance. This protection includes the availability of an injunction to bring to an end the defendant's interference with the plaintiff's rights. But then it is hard to account for requiring the plaintiff to indemnify the defendant for the injunction. It seems odd that the victim of a wrong should have to indemnify the wrongdoer for exercising the remedy that the law grants to bring about the cessation of that very wrong. [30]

The second possibility, that it was the residents rather than the developer who were the victims of a wrong done by the feedlot operator, looks to the fact that the plaintiff can secure freedom from the smells only by purchasing it. One might infer from this that the defendant did not really commit a wrong against the plaintiff in carrying on with its feedlot operations despite the harm that the smells inflicted on the approaching development. The court adopted this approach. It referred to cases of 'coming to the nuisance' under which a use that is prior in time does not constitute a nuisance at all against parties who subsequently enter the neighbourhood with inconsistent uses.[31] Had only the developer been harmed and not also the purchasers of the houses, it would have dismissed the case on this ground.[32] The plaintiff's entitlement to relief was based on the damage 'to the people who have been encouraged to purchase homes' in the development.[33] Although the remedy is placed in the hands of the developer, the wrong was done to the residents. On this reasoning, the court granted an injunction to a party that was not the victim of a wrong on the expectation that the remedy would be pursued for the benefit of the real victims. This means that, contrary to the ruling idea of tort law,[34] the plaintiff was awarded a remedy on the basis of a wrong done to someone else.

The third possibility is that the developer, although entitled to an injunction, actually committed some sort of wrong against the feedlot operator. The court remarks that in bringing the development into proximity with the cattle feedlot the plaintiff is not 'blameless'.[35] The defendant's business was a lawful one, and the plaintiff was the cause of foreseeable detriment to it. The indemnification is appropriate, the court ruled, in a case in which the developer

30 This is the criticism of the court's treatment by the Holohan J, dissenting in the subsequent case *Spur Feeding Company v Superior Court of Maricopa County*, 505 P 2d 1377 (Arizona SC, 1973).

31 *Spur Industries*, above n 26, 707.

32 *Ibid*, 707.

33 *Ibid*, 708.

34 *Palsgraf v Long Island Railroad Co*, 162 NE 99 (NYCA, 1928).

35 *Spur Industries*, above n 26, 707.

> has, with foreseeability, brought into a previously agricultural . . . area the population which makes necessary the granting of an injunction against a lawful business and for which the business has no adequate relief.[36]

It is as if the court was postulating a notional wrong that consists in populating an area in a way that would foreseeably lead to an injunction against a hitherto lawful business. One problem with this is the implausibility of thinking that building on one's own property and then selling what one has built constitutes a wrong. Another problem is that an inherent element in such a wrong would be the entitlement of the supposed wrongdoer to an injunction, the securing of which would simultaneously be the assertion of a right and the commission of a wrong against the same person.

The fourth possibility is that the developer committed a wrong not against the feedlot operator but against the residents who were exposed to the feedlot's smells. As noted in connection with the second possibility, the court regarded the residents as the true victims of the nuisance, and it awarded the developer the injunction only because of the harm that they suffered. Moreover, as noted in connection with the third possibility, the court also regarded the developer rather than the cattle feedlot operator as the true cause of the feedlot's having to move. Putting these two points together, one might surmise that the developer was primarily responsible for the nuisance suffered by the residents. That the court thought so is indicated by subsequent litigation. At the time of the case brought by the developer, another action in nuisance brought by several hundred residents was also pending against the feedlot operators. The feedlot operator filed a third-party complaint against the developer, so as to be able to obtain indemnity from the developer for the damages for which it might be liable to the residents. The court dismissed the developer's contention that the claim between the developer and the feedlot operator, having been definitively settled by the litigation between them, was res judicata. Consequently, the court concluded that

> 'the [feedlot operator] is entitled to have litigated the conduct of [the developer] as to each of the [residents] and to have the question of indemnity litigated as to each of them.[37]

This decision raised the prospect that the developer would have to compensate the feedlot operator whatever remedy that the residents might be awarded. This, too, seems an odd prospect. The entitlement that the residents had against the developer concerning the smells to which they would be exposed in the new homes they had purchased was a matter of

36 *Ibid.*
37 *Spur Feeding Company*, above n 30, 1379.

contract.[38] If they had no such entitlement through their contracts, it seems strange that they could secure one by the indirect route of suing the feedlot owner in nuisance for harms for which the developer would ultimately have to pay.

From the consideration of these four possibilities emerges the difficulty of specifying the normative ground of the causative event to which the indemnified injunction is the response. The wrong is not the reason for the remedy, because no viable wrong can be established that would match so curiously structured a remedy. The court states the circumstances in which this remedy is available—the developer's bringing in of a population that makes the injunction foreseeably necessary—but these circumstances are merely the conditions that trigger the remedy without providing a normatively coherent reason for it.

Because a sophisticated system of private law aspires to make an intelligible connection between the causative event and the response, the following difficulty arises. On the one hand, the events that include the production of smells by the feedlot operator is considered to be a wrong of some sort because otherwise a court would have no occasion to formulate any remedy at all. On the other hand, once the remedy is formulated, no matching wrong can be located. The remedy is occasioned by a wrong about whose nature the remedy provides no testimony. Like a door swinging without the hinges that attach it to anything, the remedy is both conditioned by and normatively independent of the events that give rise to it.

B The Calabresi–Melamed Framework

That the award of an indemnified injunction obscures the injustice of the causative event is also evident from the analysis of Calabresi and Melamed.[39] In suggesting a unified remedial framework that encompasses both property law and tort law, they disclose the economic basis for a new way, corresponding to *Spur*, of addressing the legal issues posed by pollution. Their analysis, however, is indifferent to the normative character of the entitlements involved.

Calabresi and Melamed argue that the indemnified injunction is necessary to complete the set of remedial possibilities applicable to nuisance claims. Take the conflict between a polluter who is claiming an entitlement to pollute and the victim who is claiming an entitlement to be free from pollution. Under the traditional remedial framework the victim's

38 The developer apparently advertised that purchasers would be able to enjoy the outdoor living that the properties afforded; *Spur Industries*, above n 26, 705.

39 Above n 27.

entitlement can be protected in two ways. An injunction protects the entitlement by what Calabresi and Melamed call a 'property rule', so that in order to continue polluting the polluter must purchase the entitlement from the victim at a value to which the victim agrees. An award of damages protects the victim's entitlement by what they call a 'liability rule', so that so that the polluter pays the victim the value of the entitlement as objectively determined by a court.[40] However, if the victim's claim cannot successfully be made, the entitlement to pollute remains in the hands of the polluter. The effect of this is that the polluter's entitlement is protected by a property rule, because then the victim will have to purchase freedom from pollution by buying out the polluter at the polluter's price. Thus, under the traditional framework, the victim's entitlement is protected by both a property rule and a liability rule, whereas the polluter's entitlement is protected by a property rule only. Stating the entitlement-protecting rules in this way shows, they argue, that something is missing: a liability rule to protect the polluter's entitlement.[41] Under such a rule the victim could stop the polluter from polluting but would have to compensate the polluter on the basis of an objectively determined value. The contemporaneously decided *Spur* case illustrates this. There the developer could force the cattle feedlot operator to cease producing the smells only by indemnifying the feedlot operator for the disruption of its activities. In the terminology of Calabresi–Melamed, *Spur* protected the feedlot operator's entitlement with a liability rule.

The purpose of this additional rule—Rule 4, as it has come to be known—is to render the parties' positions completely symmetrical. The defect of the traditional framework is that the victim's entitlement, but not the polluter's, is protected by a liability rule. Under the Calabresi–Melamed framework both the property and the liability rules that apply to the victim have counterparts that apply to the polluter.[42]

40 Epstein gives a clear definition of these rules and the difference between them: 'A property right gives the individual the right to keep the entitlement unless and until he chooses to part with it voluntarily. Property rights are, in this sense, made absolute because the ownership of some asset confers sole and exclusive power on a given individual to determine whether to retain or part with an asset on whatever terms he sees fit. In contrast, a liability rule denies the holder of the asset the power to exclude others or, indeed, to keep the asset for himself. Rather, under the standard definition he is helpless to resist the efforts by some other individual to take the thing on payment of its fair value, as objectively determined by some neutral party.' R Epstein, 'A Clear View of the Cathedral: The Dominance of Property Rules' (1997) 106 *Yale Law Journal* 2091.

41 Above n 27, 1116.

42 Even if one is attracted, as Calabresi and Melamed are, to the elegance of a remedial framework in which every possibility on the victim's side had a counterpart on the polluter's side, it does not follow that a liability rule is missing on the polluter's side. Instead of adding a liability rule that protects the polluter's entitlement, one could also subtract the liability rule that protects the victim's entitlement, leaving the victim with the protection of a property rule only. Something like this is the position in the Commonwealth jurisdictions, where the plaintiff in a successful nuisance suit is entitled to an injunction except in very limited circumstances; *Shelfer*

The achievement of such symmetry is integral to the economic analysis that informs the Calabresi–Melamed framework. Economic analysis illuminates how the law assists the movement of resources to those who value them most. In the absence of transactions costs this movement is achieved through bargaining, which determines the fate of the resource regardless of the party to whom the law initially assigned it.[43] Because the parties bargain against the background of their respective opportunity costs rather than of the one's rights against the other, each is symmetrically the potential cause of the other's deprivation. Legal determinations matter only when transactions costs disrupt the possibility of bargaining. Inasmuch as the point of such determinations is to move the resource to its most valued use—that is, to replicate the result of bargaining in the absence of a process of bargaining—the law has to have available a set of remedies that situates the parties as symmetrically as they would have been as bargainers. Rule 4 accomplishes this symmetry for liability rules, thereby complementing the symmetry of property rules already present in prevailing framework. With Rule 4 in place, the polluter's entitlement is liable to be bought out by the victim, just as the prevailing framework allows the victim's entitlement to be bought out by the polluter. The result is that the remedy, be it a property rule or a liability rule, can be applied against the one party or the other, depending on the nature of the transactions costs.

The symmetry thus achieved deals with effects. It focuses on the point at which the court determines whether the defendant ceases to pollute, pays damages, is absolved from liability or is indemnified for having to cease polluting. The premise is that, whatever kind of effect the law can impose on the polluter for the protection of the victim's entitlement, it should also be able to impose on the victim for the protection of the polluter's. If the law protects the victim's entitlement with a property rule, it should also protect the polluter's entitlement with a property rule, as in fact it does under the traditional framework. If the law protects the victim's entitlement with a liability rule, it should also protect the polluter's entitlement with a liability rule, as it would be able to do under Rule 4.

The oddity of such symmetry of effect is that it operates despite the asymmetry in the normative character of the parties' entitlements. If the victim triumphs, the entitlement protected by the award of an injunction

v City of London Electric Lighting Co [1895] 1 Ch 287 (CA). For a long time this was also the position in US jurisdictions (see *Whalen v Union Bag and Paper Co*, 101 NE 805 (NYCA, 1916), until the change effected by *Boomer v Atlantic Cement Co*, 257 NE 2d 870 (NYCA, 1970). This would prevent the oddity of an 'entitlement' that others could expropriate at will provided they gave the owner its value; see the strong comments of Idington J in *Canada Paper Co v Brown*, 63 SCR 248 (1922).

[43] RH Coase, 'The Problem of Social Cost' (1960) 3 *Journal of Law & Economics* 1.

or of damages is, in Hohfeldian terms, a claim right.[44] In the law of private nuisance, this is a right that the possessor of land has to be free from 'an inconvenience materially interfering with the ordinary comfort physically of human existence'.[45] The recognition of this right in the victim implies a correlative duty of non-interference for the polluter. The injunction or damages are then supposed to restore the victim to the enjoyment (or to its monetary equivalent) of the right with which the polluter was duty-bound not to interfere. In contrast, however, the polluter's success in staving off this suit does not show that the polluter has a claim right against the victim. Nor is the victim under a correlative duty to continue to suffer from the pollution. If, for instance, the victim encased the property exposed to the pollution in a dome, so that the victim could no longer smell the polluting odors, no duty to the polluter would be violated.[46] The polluter's entitlement is merely a liberty,[47] that is, the recognition that no right of the victim's is being infringed and that therefore the polluter is under no correlative duty to the victim. Accordingly, whereas the victim's entitlement is a claim right correlative to which is a duty on the polluter, the polluter's entitlement is to a liberty correlative to which is not a duty on the victim but the absence of a claim right. The term 'entitlement' used by Calabresi and Melamed is therefore misleading. Its application to both the victim and the polluter within a symmetrical framework of protection masks the difference between a claim right and a liberty—and thus also the difference in their correlatives between being and not being under a duty.

By positing that a liability rule is symmetrically applicable to the entitlements of the polluter and the victim, the Calabresi–Melamed framework flattens the normative landscape in two ways. First, the award of damages against the polluter is no longer seen as the response to the violation of a duty correlative to the victim's right. Applying the notion of duty to the polluter's conduct would destroy the symmetry with the victim's payment—clearly not a matter of duty but rather a condition for getting an injunction—under the indemnified injunction. Instead, the damage award is regarded merely as giving the polluter an option to purchase the victim's entitlement at an objectively established price.[48] The polluter's violation of victim's right is thereby treated as an allowable

[44] WN Hohfeld, 'Some Fundamental Legal Conceptions as Applied in Judicial Reasoning' (1913) 23 *Yale Law Journal* 16, 32.

[45] *Walter v Selfe*, 4 DeG & S 315, 322 (1851).

[46] For a similar point, see HE Smith, 'Exclusion and Property Rules in the Law of Nuisance' (2004) 90 *Virginia Law Review* 965, 1012.

[47] In Hohfeld's terminology, a 'privilege'; above n 44, 33.

[48] D Friedmann, 'Rights and Remedies' in N Cohen and E McKendrick (ed), *Comparative Remedies for Breach of Contract* (Oxford, Hart Publishing, 2005), 3, 7. One of the results of the Calabresi–Melamed analysis is the growth of a complex literature treating liability rules as options. See M Morris, 'The Structure of Entitlements' (1992) 78 *Cornell Law Review* 822, 851–6; I Ayres and P Goldbart, 'Optimal Delegation and Decoupling in the Design of Liability Rules' (2001) 100 *Michigan Law Review* 1; I Ayres, *Optional Law* (2005).

choice, rather than as a wrong. Second, in giving the victim a parallel option to purchase the polluter's entitlement in a case like *Spur*, the indemnified injunction distorts the victim's right. Instead of vindicating the victim's right against the polluter's wrongful conduct, the injunction operates only as the prelude for victim's option to purchase the polluter's abstention from polluting. In this way the Calabresi–Melamed framework of symmetrical liability rules substitutes parallel options for the correlative categories of right and duty.

In sum, then, Calabresi and Melamed put forward a remedial framework of symmetrical effects, even though these effects protect entitlements of differing normative characters. From the standpoint of the reason conception of remedies, this makes little sense, because in that conception the point of the remedy is to match the injustice that motivates it. In the Calabresi–Melamed framework, however, the response is based not on the normative character of the causative event, which it ignores and obscures, but on the efficiency gains that result from movement of resources to their most valued uses. As is typical of the condition conception of remedies, the Calabresi–Melamed analysis treats the causative event merely as the preliminary to a response that is independent of the reason for considering the event an injustice.

IV MONISM AND DUALISM

In recent years commentators on the law of remedies have distinguished two approaches to the relationship between the causative event and the response.[49] The 'monist' integrates the right and the remedy, treating the remedy as the mirror image or reflex of the right—in Peter Birks's words, 'the same thing as the right, looked at from the other end'.[50] The 'dualist' separates the right from the remedy, postulating that the court, in determining the remedy, chooses from the basket of all potential remedies the context-specific one that is most appropriate in the circumstances. How does this distinction between monism and dualism relate to the distinction developed here between the reason conception and the condition conception of remedies?

Obviously these two sets of distinctions overlap, with the reason conception being monistic and the condition conception dualistic. The reason conception treats the remedy as merely the continuation of the

[49] G Hammond, 'Rethinking Remedies: The Changing Conception of the Relationship Between Legal and Equitable Remedies' in J Berryman (ed), *Remedies: Issues and Perspectives* (1991), 87, 90–91; M Tilbury, 'Remedies and the Classification of Obligations' in A Robertson (ed), *The Law of Obligations and Boundaries* (2004), 11, 17–24.

[50] P Birks, 'Definition and Division: A Meditation on Institutes 3.13' in P Birks (ed), *The Classification of Obligations* (1997), 1, 24, quoted in Tilbury, *ibid*, 18.

plaintiff's right in circumstances in which the defendant has, or has done, something inconsistent with that right. In this sense, the remedy is, as Birks said, the right 'looked at from the other end'.[51] Conversely, the dualistic approach allows for the possibility, characteristic of the condition conception, that

> the remedy granted in any case may serve purposes unrelated to the reason(s) for the imposition of the liability in the first place.[52]

The principal difference between the two sets of distinctions is that the reason–condition distinction operates closer to the normative basis of liability, being concerned with conceptualising the relationship between right and remedy in terms not of an adherence to or rejection of precedent, history and established categories,[53] but of the reasons for thinking that justice requires that the defendant be held liable to the plaintiff.

Instancing dualism (as well as the condition conception) is the awarding of punitive damages.[54] Punitive damages are geared, not to restoring the plaintiff's rights, but to punishing the defendant for the high-handed manner in which the wrong was committed. In awarding punitive damages, the court's focus is not on the relationship between the defendant's action and the plaintiff's right,[55] but on the defendant's conduct alone. The restoration of what is rightfully the plaintiff's is therefore not a reason for awarding the plaintiff this variety of damages. Indeed, the normative purpose ascribed to punitive damages requires only that money be taken from the defendant, not that it be given to the plaintiff.[56] To be sure, the defendant's conduct has led to the plaintiff's injury, without which the punitive award would not be made. This is merely to say, however, that the plaintiff's injury serves as a condition, rather than as a reason, for the award. Dualism and the condition conception capture the givenness of punitive damages for a particular legal system. The reason conception, in contrast, raises questions about the adequacy of punitive

[51] *Ibid.*

[52] Tilbury, above n 49, at 19.

[53] JD Davies, 'Duties of Confidence and Loyalty' [1990] *Lloyd's Maritime and Commercial Law Quarterly* 4, 5.

[54] Tilbury, above n 49. Tilbury also gives the example, though more tentatively, of the choice between expectation damages and reliance damages for contract breach. This tentativeness is justified, for it may well be the case that reliance damages rest on a different juridical basis than do expectation damages; see P Benson, 'The Unity of Contract Law', in P Benson (ed), *The Theory of Contract Law: New Essays* 118, 177 (2001). For a response to Benson's views, see R Kreitner, 'Multiplicity in Contract Remedies', in Cohen and McKendrick, above n 48, 19, 35–7.

[55] Unlike aggravated damages, punitive damages do not suppose that the defendant's conduct has made the injury to the right any worse.

[56] In recognition of this, some jurisdictions in the US have legislative mechanisms for directing parts of the punitive damage award to the state.

damages as the response to a wrong that relates the defendant's conduct to the plaintiff's right.[57]

In other contexts, however, the reason conception may assist in narrowing, or at least illuminating, the gap between dualism and monism. By presenting the remedy closer to its normative ground within a conceptual framework that is more abstracted from the particularities of precedent, the reason conception may afford a more unobstructed vista of the issues that divide monism and dualism. In particular, the reason conception may point the way to dealing with a tension that exists in both monism and dualism, and thus to reconciling monism and dualism themselves.

Consider two features of dualism. The first feature is the dualist emphasis on the fact that the law brings into play at the remedial stage certain considerations that were absent earlier. This is especially the case with equitable remedies, where the determination of the remedy is leavened by various grounds for exercising discretion. In the dualist view, the introduction of these new considerations at the remedial stage makes it implausible to regard the remedy simply as the right viewed from the other end. The second feature is that the dualist does not posit the complete separation of the right from the remedy. When recommending the availability of *all* possible remedies, the dualist does not have in mind all the ingenious remedies that the fertile human mind can excogitate—for example, the indemnified injunction and its numerous notional relatives[58]—however disconnected they are from the normative ground of the cause of action. Even a dualist recognises the 'unbreakable relationship' between obligation and remedy, thereby acknowledging that

> the nature of the obligation breached is the starting point and generally the most important factor (while not necessarily the only one) determining the appropriate remedy in any particular case.[59]

Thus, the dualist maintains that the remedial stage involves considerations that are both different from and yet unbreakably related to the infringed right. How is the combination of these apparently incompatible features to be understood?

The monist position faces a parallel challenge. The monist wants to underline the second of these two features, the adamantine nature of the connection between right and remedy. Yet the first feature, that the remedy may be determined by considerations not present in the specification of the right and its infringement, seems also undeniable in the law's remedial

57 Above n 25.

58 Saul Levmore lists 16 remedies available within the Calabresi–Melamed framework; see Levmore, above, n 10, 2173.

59 Tilbury, above n 49, 26; cf also D Wright, 'Wrong and Remedy: A Sticky Relationship' [2001] *Singapore Journal of Legal Studies* 300.

practice. If the monist position is to be plausible, it too must find a way to combine these two features despite the apparent tension between them.

So far as the reason conception is concerned, the monist position that the remedy is 'the same thing as the right, looked at from the other end'[60] has to be understood in a particular way. Under the reason conception the identity of right and remedy means that they form a single continuous normative sequence, so that the right both grounds and limits the remedy. The function of the remedy is to remove the inconsistency with the plaintiff's right that is imputable to the defendant. The plaintiff's right, therefore, is the reason both for the defendant's duty to abstain from doing or having something inconsistent with it and for the defendant's duty to eliminate any such inconsistency should it occur. These duties, being correlative to the same right, are conceptually the same duty, though the duty has a different content before and after the injustice. The right and its correlative duty thus persist through the causative event despite the change that the causative event works in the particular thing to which the plaintiff has a right and in the particular action that the defendant has a duty to perform. The identity of right and remedy, in other words, is one not of content but of normative ground. When one gazes at the right from the other end, one looks at the same thing even though what one may see is different.

One kind of circumstance that may manifest a change in the content of the right at the remedial end is trivial. As was noted above in section II, the causative event may have had effects in time or space that render the specific subject matter of the right irretrievable. For example, the plaintiff may have had a right to a specific thing that was destroyed or to contractual performance at a specific time that has passed. Nonetheless, the right, as a marker of the normative relationship between the parties with respect to the specific thing or to the contractual performance at a specific time, remains intact. The court then requires the defendant to give the plaintiff a quantitative or qualitative equivalent. Although not physically or temporally identical with the original content of the right, this equivalent is from the normative standpoint nonetheless 'the same thing as the right, looked at from the other end'.[61]

More germane to the present discussion is another kind of circumstance, in which the law at the remedial stage refers to fresh considerations that pertain not to the physical or temporal landscape but to the normative one. These fresh considerations arise out of the relationship between the plaintiff's right and the entire system of rights. In this connection, three points have to be kept in mind.

60 Birks, above n 50.
61 *Ibid.*

First, rights are necessarily systematic. A right does not merely give a particular right holder an entitlement to a particular thing. Rather, it exists normatively within a comprehensive system of rights. Rights are the juridical manifestations of the freedom of self-determining beings who interact with one another as equals. Accordingly, a person claiming a right necessarily acknowledges that others also have rights with which the claimant's right must systematically coexist.[62] There is no particular right divorced from its situation within in a system of rights.

Secondly, rights have to be enforced by a court, that is, by a disinterested and impartial public authority. Because a claim of right involves the acknowledgment that others also have such claims within the system of rights, the obligations generated by any particular right can be treated as binding only insofar as there exists a public authority that interprets and enforces all the obligations contained in all the rights considered as a totality.[63] This authority does not give effect to the unilateral will of any particular right holder or look at any right in isolation, but impartially and disinterestedly brings out the normative implications of the system of rights and applies them to each right within the system. Accordingly, a claim of right implies a judicial role in interpreting and enforcing the claim. The claim is, therefore, qualified both by the limits of judicial competence and by the exercise of judgement in accordance with public reason. In this way, the court functions as guardian of the system of rights, preserving the rights of all in their juridical relationships with one another.

Thirdly, the special responsibility of the court as the guardian of the system of rights becomes particularly salient at the remedial stage. The remedy is the point at which the coercive enforcement of the plaintiff's right directly impacts the defendant. It is at this point that a court must be particularly sensitive not only to the plaintiff as the claimant of the right, but also to its own institutional role within the system of rights and to the defendant as a participant in that system.

Thus, within the reason conception, the infringed right that is the reason for the remedy has its being within a system of rights whose meaning is determined by a court exercising its judgement within its institutional competence. In being the 'the same thing as the right, looked at from the other end',[64] as the monist claims, the remedy reflects the right considered not in isolation but as a component of the system of rights. This does not change the right at the remedial stage from what it was initially: the particular right always had normative significance—that is, it generated a duty that the defendant had to treat as binding—only because it belonged to the system of rights.

62 Kant, above n 12, 44–5 [6:255–6].
63 *Ibid.*
64 Birks, above n 50.

Seen in this light, the dualist contention that the remedy may 'serve purposes unrelated to the reason(s) for the imposition of liability in the first place'[65] can also be understood in a way that brings it within the reason conception of remedies. If the reason for imposing liability refers to the infringed right taken in isolation, the remedy may appear to be unrelated to it. However, the moral significance of a right precludes taking the right in isolation from the system of rights as a whole. The system of rights, what Kant called

> the sum of the conditions under which the choice of one can be united with the choice of another in accordance with a universal law of freedom[66]

forms an objective normative order of which the right of the plaintiff is a particularised crystallisation.[67] Thus, so long as it is intelligible within the system of rights, the remedy is not unrelated to the reason for imposing liability, even if it embodies considerations that did not figure in the imposition of liability in the first place.

Systemic considerations, in other words, are always implicit in the right even as initially regarded. In the determination of the remedy, however, the court has to exercise its coercive authority so as not to affect the defendant in a manner inconsistent with the system of rights and therefore with the defendant's status in the community of interacting rights holders. The court therefore makes explicit the systemic considerations appropriate to the circumstances at hand. This difference, between the implicit and the explicit, accounts for the appearance of new considerations at the remedial stage, yet in a way that preserves the centrality of the right, as monists and dualists agree.

One example of the role of systemic considerations about rights, drawn again from the law of nuisance, will have to suffice. As is well known, in Commonwealth jurisdictions the successful plaintiff in a private nuisance suit is entitled, with rare exceptions, to an injunction. This injunction follows from the nature of the plaintiff's right. Because the wrong of nuisance is an interference with the plaintiff's use and enjoyment of property, the injunction forbidding the offending activity restores to the plaintiff the very thing of which the plaintiff was wrongfully deprived. Under the reason conception of remedies, the granting of an injunction is straightforward.

65 Tilbury, above n 49.

66 Above n 12, 24 [231].

67 The notion of 'objective normative order' is drawn from German constitutional law (see the Lüth decision, *Decisions of the Bundesverfassungsgericht—Federal Constitutional Court—Federal Republic of Germany, Volume 2/Part I: Freedom of Speech* (1998), 1) where the same issue arises of the relationship between a particular right and the system of rights. For treatment of this issue from the constitutional perspective, see LE Weinrib, 'The Postwar Paradigm and American Exceptionalism' in S Choudhry (ed), *The Migration of Constitutional Ideas* (2006). I am grateful to Lorraine Weinrib for discussion of this aspect.

But what about the rare exceptions where the plaintiff can get no more than damages for a continuing nuisance? The case of *Shelfer v City of London Electric Lighting Co*[68] provides the classic formulation of the circumstances in which a court may, at its discretion, substitute damages for an injunction. According to the judgment, four factors must all be present: a small injury to the plaintiff's rights, an injury capable of being estimated in money, adequate compensation by a small monetary payment and the oppressiveness to the defendant of an injunction. Under these circumstances the plaintiff is not restored to the use and enjoyment of the property, which is the plaintiff's right, but must instead accept the monetary equivalent of the wrongful injury. To that extent, as the dualist would claim, the remedy does not match the plaintiff's particular right but is rather the product of considerations present only at the remedial stage.

These considerations represent a specific conception of remedial fairness. On the one hand, the plaintiff's injury is small, monetisable and capable of being adequately compensated by a small monetary payment, so that the difference between damages and an injunction is minimal from the plaintiff's perspective. On the other hand, the injunction would be oppressive to the defendant because it would inflict on the defendant a significant hardship from which the plaintiff would derive no substantial benefit. Under these circumstances the only point of seeking an injunction would be to damage the defendant rather than to promote any legitimate interest of the plaintiff. Accordingly, by not awarding an injunction the court prevents the plaintiff from using the judicial process to harm the defendant through a remedy that would not materially benefit the plaintiff. In the language of the civil law, the substitution of damages for an injunction prevents the plaintiff from abusing his or her right.[69]

The notion of abuse of rights is often regarded as introducing into the law considerations of social or moral good that are alien to the idea of rights.[70] A right provides an area of untrammeled freedom for the right holder. The notion of abuse of right seems to contain the contradictory

[68] [1895] 1 Ch 287, 222 (CA).

[69] A similar explanation would apply to the requirement at common law that the plaintiff mitigate his or her damages. It would also apply some of the situations, exemplified by *Patel v Ali* [1984] Ch 283 (CA), in which hardship to the defendant prevents the court from issuing a decree of specific performance of a contract. Similar are situations of laches, in which the prejudice suffered by the defendant as a result of the plaintiff's delay in seeking specific performance is the basis for denying the remedy. These remedial considerations illustrate Tony Weir's observation that 'we are not supposed to have any doctrine of abuse of rights (but it is only the doctrine which is lacking)'. T Weir, 'The Staggering March of Negligence' in P Cane and J Stapleton (eds), *The Law of Obligations: Essays in Celebration of John Fleming* (1998), 99, 124. See also JM Perillo, 'Abuse of Rights: A Pervasive Legal Concept' (1995) 27 *Pacific Law Journal* 37.

[70] S Herman, 'Classical Social Theories and the Doctrine of "Abuse of Rights"' (1977) 37 *Louisiana Law Review* 747; WT Tête, 'Tort Roots and the Ramifications of the Obligations Revision' (1986) 32 *Loyola Law Review* 47, 68–72 (decribing Josserand's conception of abuse of right).

impulses of recognising the right yet limiting the right holder's freedom. Hence the impression arises that the normative basis of the limit is external to the rights perspective.

This impression, however, is mistaken. The idea that the law should not legitimise the infliction on another of gratuitous harm is fully consonant with the normative presuppositions of a system of rights. As observed above in section II, participants in the system of rights are conceived as persons with a self-determining capacity for purposive action. Within this system each person pursues one's self-chosen purposes, subject only to the constraint that one's action be capable of coexisting with the purposiveness of others. This requires that one pursue one's purposes as ends that one is trying to achieve for oneself, not as an obstacle against what someone else is trying to achieve. Actions for the sake of creating mutual obstacles against the actions of others cannot systemically coexist.

As juridical manifestations of self-determining freedom, rights provide the space within which the all right holders may pursue ends of their own. Such ends are consistent with the self-determining freedom of others only if the point of pursuing them is independent of the adverse effect on someone else. When all act to pursue ends of their own in this sense, they all rank equally as persons whose activities can coexist within the system of rights. Conversely, if the freedom to perform an act merely to frustrate the purposes of another were legitimate, rights would be transformed from markers of mutual freedom to instruments of subordination. Accordingly, it would be inconsistent of what is normatively presupposed in the system of rights to allow a right to operate in a way that would harm another without promoting (in the language of the civilians)[71] a 'serious and legitimate interest' of the right holder.

In awarding damages in lieu of an injunction to the victim of a nuisance, the court is acting as guardian of the system of rights, keeping the remedial consequences of the infringement of a particular right aligned with what is normatively presupposed in the system as a whole. The plaintiff is ordinarily entitled to an injunction, as that would restore to the plaintiff the use and enjoyment of the property that make up the content of the plaintiff's right. However, through its determination of the remedy, the court prevents the plaintiff's right from operating in a way that prejudices the defendant without forwarding an interest of the plaintiff. To grant an injunction under the conditions enumerated in *Shelfer* would be inconsistent with the normative grounding of rights in the coexistence of the parties' self-determining freedom. This latter consideration is systemically implicit in all rights, including the particular right infringed by the defendant. Thus, the award of damages rather than an injunction treats

[71] A Gambaro, 'Abuse of Rights in the Civil Law Tradition' in AM Rabello (ed), *Aequitas and Equity: Equity in Civil Law and Mixed Jurisdictions* (1997) 632, 637; A Yiannopoulos, 'Abuse of Right in Louisiana', *ibid*, 690, 700.

the infringed right not as free standing but as situated within the system of rights that is required for the right's normative significance.

Similar observations about the systemic aspect of rights can be made about other circumstances in which new normative considerations are introduced at the remedial stage. Especially in exercising their discretion to grant specific performance, courts often invoke such factors as the difficulty of constant curial supervision, the futility of the remedy, the absence of mutuality, the plaintiff's failure to do equity and the reluctance to enforce a decree of personal service. These factors refer to substantive and institutional aspects normatively presupposed in the system of rights, from the maintenance of the transactional equality of the parties to the avoidance of the court's exceeding its institutional competence. To be sure, the application of these factors to particular circumstances is controversial, as is evidenced, for instance, by the contention that the difficulty of judicial supervision has been overstated.[72] But however such factors ought to figure in particular circumstances, the point for present purposes is that, within the reason conception of remedies, attention to the system of rights rather than merely to a given right in isolation opens up the normative space in which such factors can coherently be considered.

If this is so, the reason conception of remedies may be able to reconcile, at least to some extent, the apparently competing insights of monism and dualism. From the monist perspective, the notion that the remedy is just the right looked at from the other end is maintained, but with the understanding that because a particular right participates in a system of rights, systemic considerations may modulate the remedy. From the dualist perspective, the systemic character of rights may introduce new considerations at the remedial stage while preserving the central importance of the infringed right and the remedy's unbreakable connection with it.

V CONCLUSION

In presenting the two conceptions of remedies, this paper has ultimately been concerned with how remedies might figure within a normatively coherent system of private law. The reason conception maintains this coherence in two ways. First, it integrates the causative event and the response by treating the injustice as an inconsistency with the plaintiff's right that the remedy is supposed to eliminate. The remedy is thus continuous with the right. In contrast, the condition conception fragments private law by making the remedy the locus of considerations that are independent of the injustice of the causative event. Secondly, the reason conception treats rights not as isolated entitlements but as members of a

72 J Berryman, *The Law of Equitable Remedies* (2000), 175.

system of rights, so that the remedy conforms to what is normatively presupposed in the system as a whole. Accordingly, to be continuous with the right, the remedy also has to be continuous with the right's systemic aspects. Only by attending to these two dimensions of juridical coherence can a judge, in determining the remedy, live up to Aristotle's observation that

> to go to a judge means to go to the just, for to be a judge means, as it were, to be the embodiment of what is just.[73]

[73] Above n 2.

2

Rights, Remedies, Wrongs and the Bribe-taking Fiduciary

STRUAN SCOTT*

I INTRODUCTION

THIS PAPER IS about classification of the law. Some attribute a growth in interest in classification to the leadership of Peter Birks.[1] Recent years have seen the development of various classificatory schemes, debates about the usefulness of the schemes so developed (at least some of them) and debates about the usefulness of classifications per se.

This paper considers two complementary classificatory schemes—one proposed by Peter Birks and the other by Rafal Zakrzewski—but its focus is on the second of these schemes. It critiques these schemes in one specific context: the law governing the bribe-taking fiduciary. The emphasis is on New Zealand law and one case in particular, *Attorney General for Hong Kong v Reid*.[2] This is considered in more detail later, but in brief it involved a fiduciary taking a bribe and investing the money in land. The Privy Council held that the fiduciary's principal had a right to trace the bribe into the fiduciary's interest in the land, and treat it as security for repayment.

We all classify, or use classifications; classification is a characteristic human endeavour.[3] '[I]n law', as Lord Steyn observed in *Attorney-General*

* Faculty of Law, University of Otago, New Zealand. I should like to thank Professors Stuart Anderson and Richard Sutton for reviewing drafts of this paper and their valuable suggestions.

1 M Tilbury, 'Remedies and the Classification of Obligations' in A Robertson (ed), *The Law of Obligations: Connections and Boundaries* (Coogee, Cavendish Publishing (Australia) Pty Ltd, 2004), 11.

2 [1994] 1 AC 324 (PC).

3 It has been suggested that 'fundamental to human intelligence is an awareness of patterns and of matches between patterns'. N MacCormack, *Rhetoric and the Rule of Law: a Theory of Legal Reasoning* (Oxford, Oxford University Press, 2005), 207, summarising the views of BS Jackson, *Law, Fact and Narrative Coherence* (Robby, Deborah Charles Publications,1988), ch 2.

v Blake,[4] 'classification is important.' At the very least, we classify to make our legal knowledge manageable. Our classifications enable us to 'orient' ourselves within a legal problem. Moreover, they facilitate the 'communication, stor[ing] . . . and manipula[tion]' of legal knowledge.[5]

But legal classification may have other important purposes. For some, classification is essential for obtaining consistency—treating like cases alike[6]—and, associated with this, certainty and (if it is different) predictability in the law. Indeed, the current interest in legal classification may in part be a response to the debate between the so-called 'monists'[7] and 'dualists'.[8]

Both Birks[9] and Zakrzewski[10] seek this consistency, certainty and predictability in the law. Their respective schemes are important and enlightening, but this paper questions whether they achieve these aims, at least with respect to the bribe-taking fiduciary.

The Birksian scheme is the elder of the two and, as such, perhaps the better known. Birks suggests that rights should be classified according to the causative event from which they arise—from 'manifestations of consent',[11] from 'unjust enrichments', from 'miscellaneous other events'[12]

4 [2001] 1 AC 268, 290.

5 G Samuel, 'Can the Common Law be Mapped?' (2005) 55 *University of Toronto Law Journal* 271, 297. The academic's basic goal of understanding the law—or anything else for that matter—is closely linked to the process of mapping '. . . [T]he process of mapping, or classification, is inseparable from the process of obtaining knowledge': SA Smith, 'A Map of the Common Law?' [2004] *Canadian Business Law Journal* 364, 365

6 P Birks, 'Equity in the Modern Law: an Exercise in Taxonomy' (1996) 26 *University of Western Australia Law Review* 1, 4.

7 Monists argue that there is a close correlation or 'congruence' between a right and the remedy which is granted to support that right. G Hammond, 'Rethinking Remedies: The Changing Conception of the Relationship Between Legal and Equitable Remedies' in J Berryman (ed), *Remedies: Issues and Perspectives* (Scarborough, ON, Thompson Professional Publishing, 1991), 90; DWM Waters, 'Liability and Remedy: An Adjustable Relationship' (2001) 64 *Saskatchewan Law Review* 429, 439.

8 Dualists are said to support 'discretionary remedialism' (P Birks, 'Rights, Wrongs, and Remedies' (2000) 20 *OJLS* 1, 1; P Birks, 'Three Kinds of Objection to Discretionary Remedialism' (2000) 29 *University of Western Australia Law Review* 1). They argue that, in response to an infringement of a right, the courts have (or should have) discretion to select 'the most appropriate [remedy]'. Hammond, *ibid*, 91.

9 Birks, 'Equity', above n 6, 4; Birks, 'Rights', *ibid*, 23.

10 Zakrzewski suggests that his approach contributes to the debate between monists and dualists, as it 'cast[s] a bright light on what is at stake and will assist in the making of and the discussion of the relevant decisions'. R Zakrzewski, *Remedies Reclassified* (Oxford, Oxford University Press, 2005), 223.

11 This subcategory includes contracts, conveyances, wills,and some trusts would also be included; see P Birks, 'Definition and Division: A Mediation on *Institutes* 3.13' in P Birks (ed), *The Classification of Obligations* (Oxford, Clarendon Press, 1997), 32–3.

12 While expressing doubts about this, Birks recognised that this subcategory may include property rights; Birks, 'Rights', above n 8, 28–9. Responding to these doubts, Grantham and Rickett have suggested that property rights should be included within the scheme; see RB Grantham and CEF Rickett, 'Property Rights as a Legally Significant Event' [2003] *CLJ* 717.

(collectively referred to by the term 'not-wrong') or from 'wrongs'.[13] Implicit in this scheme is the assumption that these causative events are distinct, and the distinction can be applied to determine the proper place of any given set of facts and their legal result.

Zakrzewski's scheme is consistent with that of Birks, but it stipulates that the 'right' is bi-fold. Thus, there is the *legal right*, which is given to a party as a result of a causative event, and there is the *remedy*, which is given to enforce that right. In *Remedies Reclassified*,[14] Zakrzewski offers both a new understanding of what constitutes a remedy[15] and a new approach to classifying remedies which is based upon the degree of correlation between the right and the remedy. Employing terms subsequently described by Birks as 'illuminating',[16] Zakrzewski suggests that remedies are either 'replicative' or 'transformative'. A replicative remedy is one where there is a close association between the remedy and the pre-existing right; the remedy is said to be a restatement of the underlying right.[17] In contrast, a transformative remedy arises when a court 'creatively "fashions" a remedy, that is creates rights with new content in and for the particular case'.[18]

Zakrzewski offers little detailed discussion[19] on the content of particular rights and remedies, but he does consider *Reid*, albeit briefly. The imposition of a constructive trust in *Reid* was (and may still be) controversial, but, for reasons considered later, Zakrzewski offers it as an example of a replicative remedy. Just how he gets to the point where he reaches this classification is detailed later. For Birks, the causative event leading to the imposition of the constructive trust in *Reid* was the fiduciary's wrongdoing—Reid's receipt of a bribe.[20] For Zakrzewski, the wrong gives rise to the principal's right to recover the bribe. The tracing remedy given in *Reid* gives effect to that legal right.

Reid and the law's response to fiduciary bribe-takers generally has encouraged me to think more deeply about the schemes offered by Birks

13 P Birks, 'Misnomer', in WR Cornish, R Nolan, J O'Sullivan and G Virgo (eds), *Restitution Past, Present and Future* (Oxford, Hart Publishing, 1998), 8; Birks, 'Definition', above n 11, 19; Birks, 'Rights', above n 8, 37.

14 *Remedies Reclassified*, above n 10. One of the chapters is a development of the author's article 'The Classification of Judicial Remedies' [2003] *Lloyd's Maritime and Commercial Law Quarterly* 477.

15 Zakrzewski defines a remedy as a court order which 'a party obtains to redress a grievance existing before an action is brought ('pre-suit' grievance) and which are available at trial, together with their pre-trial equivalent' (*Remedies Reclassified, ibid*, 44–5, citations omitted). In turn, the association with court orders means that 'remedies are certain jural relationships'; they are 'the rights that arise from a particular class of events, namely, the making of certain judicial commands or statements' (*ibid*, 46–7).

16 P Birks, *Unjust Enrichment* (Oxford, Oxford University Press, 2nd edn, 2005), 166 note 3.

17 *Remedies Reclassified*, above n 10, 166.

18 *Ibid*, 223.

19 *Ibid*, 103.

20 Birks, 'Misnomer', above n 13, 16–17.

and Zakrzewski. In this paper I offer some thoughts on the wrongs/not-wrongs classification and the replicative/transformative classification, focusing on the latter. My thoughts centre around two points.

My first point involves a reservation I have on the day-to-day application of the replicative/transformative classification. Based on the premise that law evolves (consider *Reid*), I suggest that these classifications reflect or record whether or not a remedy applied in a particular case is perceived as applying generally, or, to express this from the perspective of a right, they reflect whether a new right has been recognised or an existing right has been modified.

Thus the classification is historical in that it records the current or orthodox perception of the availability of the remedy. It is not critical; that is to say, it plays only a limited role (if that) in offering new and better ways of classifying the law. The classification is secondary in that it simply records the state of the perception, as opposed to generating it. Accordingly, the classification of the constructive trust in *Reid* as a replicative remedy appears to reflect the current acceptance (at least by some academics) that the remedy in that case was appropriate.

My second point (another reservation) applies to both schemes. This is their ability to explain the variation in results one can find in the case law. Even when the same right appears to be involved, courts have an ability to discern crucial differences between cases, for example by holding that the facts in the case before the court are not 'quite like'[21] those in the precedent cases.[22] I display this with two variations to the facts in *Reid*. It is arguable that the remedy in these situations will differ from those contemplated in *Reid*. Zakrzewski's scheme may be robust enough to handle the existence of remedial variations, but the existence of variations must question the extent to which remedial certainty is achievable.

The two *Reid* variations also question the Birksian assumption that the causative events comprising the categories of not-wrongs and wrongs are distinct. To the contrary, they suggest that there is an overlap between these categories, and that the result in a particular case may be a product of how the court evaluates their competing influences.

21 *Murad v Al-Saraj* [2005] EWCA Civ 959, para [144] per Clarke LJ.

22 A recent illustration of this involving a bribe-taking fiduciary is *Daraydan Holdings Ltd* [2005] 4 All ER 73. There, an agent arranged contracts for the refurbishment of his principal's properties. The agent sought and obtained payment of bribes in excess of £1.8 million from the successful contractor. The court distinguished *Lister & Co v Stubbs* (1890) 24 Ch D 1 on the basis that in that case the price paid by the principal for the goods had not been increased by the amount of the bribe. The court then contrasted this with the position in *Daraydan*, where there was evidence that the contract price had been increased by the amount of the bribe (paras [87]–[91]). Linking the principal's extra payment with the bribe, the court concluded that it could presume that the principal's money (or its proceeds) had been paid to the agent. This was seen as giving the principal a sufficient proprietary interest in the bribe so as to justify the imposition of the trust.

A Structure of this Paper

In section II, I consider Zakrzewski's scheme and discuss briefly the replicative/transformative categories. I go on to discuss briefly the Birksian scheme showing how both taxonomies are consistent with each other

In section III I consider *Reid*. This leads into a discussion of my first reservation with respect to this scheme—the historical quality and secondary nature of the replicative classification.

In the last substantive part—section IV—I consider two variations to the core facts in *Reid*. I suggest that the remedy in these variations may differ from that in *Reid*. Assuming this is so, I consider the implications of this for the schemes advanced by Birks and by Zakrzewski.

II REPLICATIVE AND TRANSFORMATIVE REMEDIES; WRONGS AND NOT-WRONGS

A Replicative remedies

I start with Zakrzewski's classification of remedies as being either replicative or transformative. First, replicative remedies.

In essence, replicative remedies are 'simply restatements of substantive rights existing before'[23] the court order; in other words, the underlying right is 'given direct effect in the order.'[24] To use one of Zakrzewski's examples, a person who confers valuable services upon another may have 'a primary right to the reasonable value' of those services.[25] Zakrzewski does not discuss the circumstances in which this particular primary right arises, but, assuming that it does so, the remedy—a *quantum meruit* award—replicates the right; the point is that the claimant 'receives nothing more nor less than a right to the reasonable value of the services he rendered'.[26]

According to Zakrzewski, a replicative remedy may arise from a 'primary' right or a 'secondary' (or remedial) right. This distinction is derived from Austinian jurisprudence.[27]

A primary right 'is a right which exists independently of a wrong'.[28] The 'contractual right to the payment of an agreed sum and the right to the return of a mistaken payment' are offered by Zakrzewski as

23 *Remedies Reclassified*, above n 10, 78–9, 166.
24 *Ibid*, 79 note 51.
25 *Ibid*, 79.
26 *Ibid*.
27 J Austin, *Lectures on Jurisprudence Vol II*, R Campbell ed, (London, John Murray, 5th edn, 1885), Lecture XLV, 763. See generally *Remedies Reclassified*, above n 10, 13–16.
28 *Remedies Reclassified*, *ibid*, 13.

examples.[29] Infringement of a primary right leads to a 'specific' remedy,[30] which

> usually involves ordering the person who is under the corresponding duty to do what he or she is required to do or to abstain from doing what he or she is required not to do.[31]

So, for example, breach of the contractual right to the payment of an agreed sum leads to an order that the defendant pay that sum.[32] And the remedy for the right to the return of a mistaken payment is said to be '[a]n award for restitution for unjust enrichment'.[33] The remedies in all these examples are said to be replicative, as the underlying right is being 'given direct effect in the order'.[34]

A secondary right is created (though not invariably) where a primary right has been infringed. Rather than conferring a specific remedy, the law sometimes responds to the infringement by creating a 'secondary' right.[35] Secondary rights are said to 'supplant[36] or reinforce[37] infringed primary rights so that the latter may be given at least indirect effect by the courts'.[38] Thus a breach of a contract in respect of which specific performance[39] is not available, typically leads to a secondary 'right to compensation for loss caused by breach of contract',[40] the 'aim' of which 'is to put the claimant into as good a position as if the contract had been performed'.[41]

It should be noted that Zakrzewski does not suggest that there has to be a precise correlation between a secondary right and the primary right it 'substitutes for or reinforces' (as there is in the case of a specific remedy responding to the infringement of a primary right).[42] To the contrary, he

[29] *Ibid.*
[30] *Ibid*, 81.
[31] *Ibid*, 104.
[32] *Ibid*, 106.
[33] *Ibid*, 113. Zakrzewski suggests that this remedy 'encompass[es] all the awards that could have been sought' by the traditional awards of money had and received, money paid to the defendant's use, *quantum meruit* and *quantum valebat.*
[34] *Ibid*, 79 n 51.
[35] *Ibid*, 165. Zakrzewski suggests that the 'need for secondary rights arises because . . . some primary rights are not replicated in court orders or pronouncements, either because (1) replication would be futile (as with rights which cease to exist on breach) or ineffective as it would not undo something which ought not have been done (as with negative rights); or (2) replication would be inefficient or undesirable as a matter of policy (as with some rights to the performance of services).'
[36] This is said to occur when the primary right 'cease to exist on infringement', *ibid*, 165.
[37] This is said to occur when the primary right continues 'to exist but for some reason replication would not adequately effectuate' it, *ibid.*
[38] *Ibid.*
[39] In this context, an order for specific performance replicates or 'gives direct effect to' a 'primary contractual right' to have the contract performed, *ibid*, 138.
[40] *Ibid*, 171.
[41] *Ibid*, 173.
[42] *Ibid*, 166.

suggests that 'the content of the secondary right does not logically follow from the nature of the primary duty breached' and, further, that 'the content of the secondary right, that is, what it entitles the claimant to, is a matter of policy'.[43]

An important point made by Zakrzewski is that secondary rights are rights and not remedies,[44] so it is the breach of the secondary right, not the prior breach of the primary right, that leads to a remedy. For example, breach of the secondary right 'to compensation for loss caused by breach of contract'[45] leads to a court order requiring the payment of a certain sum of money.[46] This remedy replicates the secondary right, which is 'given direct effect in the order'.[47] A remedy which replicates a secondary right is said to be a 'substitutional' remedy[48]; it substitutes for the primary right on which the secondary right is based.

B Transformative Remedies

All the remedies considered so far have been identified as 'replicative'. I now turn to transformative remedies. The key difference between a replicative remedy and a transformative remedy is that the latter is the product of 'the court's order'. As a result, a transformative remedy does not give direct effect to any pre-existing right, whether primary or secondary; rather 'the court's order generates something which is quite different from the rights and duties which already pertain between the parties'[49]; it 'alters . . . the pre-existing rights of the parties'.[50] In other words, the court order 'transform[s] or modif[ies] the legal relations between the . . . [parties] which existed before trial'.[51]

There are two subcategories of transformative remedies: 'immediately enforceable' (or 'coercive') remedies and 'constitutive' remedies. Membership of a particular sub-group depends on whether the transformative

43 *Ibid*, 165–6.
44 *Ibid*, 50–1.
45 *Ibid*, 171.
46 *Ibid*, 50–1: 'The difference between secondary rights to damages existing prior to a court order and rights to damages arising out of such a judicial command is sometimes overlooked as both are indiscriminately called "damages" in practice. The distinction between the two is very fine because the courts give effect to secondary rights by restating them in the court order. But there is also a subtle difference apart from their origin. The former are unliquidated but the latter are usually liquidated. This means that secondary rights to damages are usually rights to compensation, restitution, or punishment in the abstract with the actual amount due being unassessed but rights to damages recast in a court order are usually assessed at a sum certain. The former are substantive rights, not remedies.'
47 *Ibid*, 79 note 51.
48 *Ibid*, 81.
49 *Ibid*, 78–9.
50 *Ibid*, 79 note 52.
51 *Ibid*, 203.

remedy is '[enforceable] without further court proceedings'.[52] If so, it is 'immediately enforceable'.[53] Zakrzewski offers the example of maintenance orders arising in the matrimonial context.[54] If further proceedings are required, then the transformative remedy is said to be 'constitutive'. Zakrzewski gives the following examples of constitutive remedies: adoption orders, marriage dissolution orders and grants of probate.[55]

Putting to one side the question whether a particular remedy is immediately enforceable or is constitutive, it is suggested that care should be taken with some of Zakrzewski's examples. Adoption orders, for example, do change a person's status—they make a person the legal child of a non-biological parent or parents—and in so-doing they create a new status. But these changes occur pursuant to legislative schemes which intend the change in status. Indeed, it can be argued that these schemes (or at least some of them) create a primary right, so, for example, to consider marriage dissolution orders, married couples who bring themselves within the statutory criteria have a right for the dissolution order. Arguably, this is a primary right which the order replicates.

Similar caution must be expressed about other examples. For example, Australian and New Zealand legislators have conferred a wide discretion upon the courts to grant remedies in certain commercial disputes.[56] Zakrzewski suggests that these are further examples of a statutory power to grant a transformative remedy. His point is that there is no substantive right to any particular remedy until the court exercises its statutory 'remedial discretion'.[57] This classification is consistent with Zakrzewski's approach to distinguish between, on the one hand, the existence of a judicial discretion as to the availability of relief in a given situation (for example, the rules on remoteness[58] and whether a bar exists to equitable relief[59]), and on the other hand the existence of a discretion 'to create an entirely new remedy that does not replicate any of the claimant's substantive rights'.[60] The validity of this distinction turns on the assumption that the statutory right to relief does not confer a substantive right to relief. This assumption is questionable, as arguably these statutes

52 *Ibid*, 204.

53 *Ibid*, 204–5.

54 *Ibid*, 217.

55 *Ibid*, 208–9.

56 *Ibid*, 205. His example is s 87 of the Trade Practices Act 1974 (Cth). The New Zealand legislature has conferred extensive jurisdiction upon the courts to grant transformative remedies in what can loosely be described as contractual/commercial disputes, eg the Contractual Remedies Act 1979, s 9; the Contractual Mistakes Act 1977, s 7; the Illegal Contracts Act 1970, s 7.

57 *Ibid*, 206.

58 *Ibid*, 89.

59 *Ibid*, 92–4.

60 *Ibid*, 98.

are conferring a substantive right, not to a particular remedy, but to the remedy the court considers most appropriate.

Putting to one side the statutory examples, and 'some remedies given in relation to estoppel and some mandatory injunctions to undo or prevent a wrong'[61] (the current status of which may be unclear), the so-called remedial constructive trust[62]—the classic example of which is the trust recognised in *Chase Manhattan Bank NA v Israel-British Bank (London) Ltd*[63]—becomes, in Zakrzewski's account, the dominant example of a transformative remedy. This trust is said to be transformative as its 'very existence [depends] on the order of the Court',[64] and it operates to confer 'a proprietary right to someone who, beforehand [i.e. before the court's order], had no proprietary rights.'[65] A critic of *Reid* may attribute similar comments to the result in that case but, as is discussed later, Zakrzewski distinguishes the two cases.

C Correspondence of Right with Remedy

Is a transformative remedy a good or a bad thing? In *Remedies Reclassified* Zakrzewski purports not to answer the question whether judges should 'merely replicate substantive rights as closely as possible' as opposed to 'creatively 'fashion[ing]' a remedy'.[66] He does suggest, however, that his taxonomy 'cast[s] a bright light on what is at stake'.[67] Moreover, it helps identify those cases in which the court 'fashion[ed]'[68] a remedy.

There are two subliminal messages, however, which are at odds with Zakrzewski's supposed neutrality. The first is that replicative remedies are mainstream, by which I mean that in granting a replicative remedy, a judge is 'merely appl[ying] the law',[69] or, in other words, 'restating prior substantive rights'.[70] This is so even if a measure of discretion is involved, because the law has determined the scope of the discretion. The inference from this is that a judge granting a replicative remedy need confirm only that the requisite right(s) exist and, to the extent that the judge is

61 *Ibid*, 216.
62 *Ibid*, 214–15.
63 [1981] Ch 105 (ChD).
64 *Fortex Group Ltd v MacIntosh* [1998] 3 NZLR 171, 172 (CA), discussed in *Remedies Reclassified*, above n 10, 215.
65 *Re Polly Peck (No 2)* [1998] 3 All ER 812, 830 (CA) per Nourse LJ, discussed in *Remedies Reclassified*, *ibid*, 214.
66 *Remedies Reclassified*, *ibid*, 223.
67 *Ibid.*
68 *Ibid.*
69 *Ibid*, 101.
70 *Ibid.*

exercising some discretion, that he or she took into account the relevant factors or standards.[71]

The other linked subliminal message is that there is a stigma with judicially created transformative remedies; that if they are not bad, they are at least suspect or raise further questions. Zakrzewski raises the concern that such remedies 'involve [the courts] making [unconstrained] policy choices in the particular circumstances'.[72] In other words,

> the conditions [for the making of the order are] not judicially expounded with sufficient clarity for one to be able to make the assertion that substantive rights will arise in similar situations due to the availability of the remedies.[73]

But our law is built on individual cases dealing with particular circumstances. From the particular the law develops. It is true the court in *Chase Manhattan*, for example, was resolving a particular dispute, and in the process recognised what was then a novel remedy, and this recognition remains controversial. In so doing, the court was making a policy choice, the full ramifications of which are still being evaluated. However, their Lordships in *Reid* also made a policy decision to recognise a then novel remedy. Apart from the standing of the respective courts, the difference between the two cases may be only a question of degree; one difference is that the policy choice in *Reid* may be more consistent with the current orthodoxy than that in *Chase Manhattan*. For this reason, the degree of 'omniscie[nce] [required] . . . to calculate'[74] the availability and application of the *Reid* constructive trust in our law may be less than that required for the *Chase Manhattan* constructive trust but, as is discussed later, the metes and bounds of *Reid* still need to be determined by subsequent courts.

These considerations led me to re-evaluate the weight that can be put on Zakrzewski's distinctions, if they are to form part of a reliable classificatory scheme. I want now to consider Zakrzewski's approach as it fits within the classificatory scheme proposed by the late Peter Birks.

71 Applying the Dworkin scale of discretions, the discretion here is 'weak'. Either the factors or standard which the court must be considered are known in advance or that factor/standard requires the use of judgment, R Dworkin, *Taking Rights Seriously* (London, Duckworth, 1997), 31. Discussed in *Remedies Reclassified*, above n 10, 87.

72 *Remedies Reclassified*, *ibid*, 100–01.

73 *Ibid*, 217. See also 59.

74 F Nietzsche, *Human, All Too Human*, M Faber and S Lehmann, trans (London, Penguin Classic, 1994), para 106, 'At the waterfall'. Nietzsche's point is that, even though individual acts may appear random, they lead to a predetermined conclusion, so 'if one were omniscient, one would be able to calculate each individual action in advance, each step in the progress of knowledge'. I should like to thank Prof Richard Sutton for drawing my attention to this.

D Wrongs and Not-wrongs

Birks argued that rights should be classified according to the causative event from which they arise. The key division in the Birksian scheme is between 'wrongs' and 'not-wrongs' (that is, 'manifestations of consent', 'unjust enrichments' and 'miscellaneous other events').

This scheme is complementary to that proposed by Zakrzewski and provides a foundation which Zakrzewski develops further. Thus rights (whether primary or secondary) can be seen as arising from one of the causative events. The overlap between the two schemes is revealed when considering Birks's examples of not-wrongs—for example, a contractual obligation (as opposed to breach of contract), a contractual debt, a mistaken payment.[75] In *Remedies Reclassified* Zakrzewski associates these examples of not-wrongs with primary rights, breach of which leads to a specific remedy. The category of 'wrongs' includes acts which are seen as arising independently of any primary right (for example, failure to take reasonable care) and also breaches of not-wrongs. So, for example, a breach of contract[76] is a wrong based on the primary rights of the other party. So too, it is said, is the breach of a fiduciary duty to avoid conflicts of interests,[77] though this appears more complex.[78] In *Remedies Reclassified* Zakrzewski equates these to secondary rights.

Now a key theme in the Birksian scheme is his concerns about discretionary remedialism—the 'nightmare trying to be a noble dream'.[79] Birks's point is that not-wrongs have 'narrow, limited remedial potential'[80] while many wrongs have a 'plurality of remedial strings'.[81] While a plurality of remedy might perhaps indicate a judicial discretion, Birks rejects the claim (that is, that this is an example of discretionary remedialism). The reason, he says, is that either the choice is 'closed down by authority' or it is 'made by the plaintiff'.[82] Zakrzewski restates this message by requiring that the ultimate remedy replicate the secondary right which the plaintiff chooses to enforce.

This ends the overview of Zakrzewski's scheme and its relationship with the Birksian scheme. A key message in Zakrzewski's scheme is the correlation of a remedy with an underlying right. But, as we have seen, the distinction which Zakrzewski advances between replicative and

75 Birks, 'Rights', above n 8, 27–8.
76 *Ibid*, 27.
77 *Ibid*, 31.
78 AK Turner and RJ Sutton, *Spencer Bower, Turner and Sutton, The Law Relating to Actionable Non-Dislosure* (London, Butterworths, 2nd edn, 1990), paras 16.10–16.24; 17.31–17.33; see also below n 140.
79 Birks, 'Rights', above n 8, 23.
80 *Ibid*, 36.
81 *Ibid*, 7.
82 *Ibid*, 33.

transformative remedies can be questioned. This questioning continues in the next section, when the ability of Zakrzewski's scheme to promote remedial certainty is tested in the context of a bribe-taking fiduciary.

III REID AND REPLICATIVE REMEDIES

Reid is an important decision of the Privy Council, and in this section I consider its key facts, its significance and the response it received. This lays the foundation for my reservation about the replicative/transformative and the wrongs/not-wrongs classifications.

The fact that Zakrzewski is able to confidently classify as replicative the remedies in *Reid* and a number of other controversial cases[83] may prove me wrong, but I suggest that his confidence is derived from the degree of acceptance the remedy has received, in particular, whether the remedy is perceived as applying generally. If this is so, then it can be said that a new substantive right has been recognised or an existing substantive right has been modified. The point is that the classification as replicative or transformative depends upon how the remedy is currently perceived. To gauge this, one must look to outside sources, for example the status of the court and subsequent judicial and academic acceptance. As a consequence, the replicative/transformative classification provides little guidance as to whether a new remedy is an evolution of an existing right/remedy or the recognition of a new right. The classification can be said to be historical, by which I mean that it reflects whether the remedy has received acceptance as applicable to all parties in similar situations. Moreover, it is secondary in that it simply records the state of the perception as opposed to advancing a theory or test against which to evaluate the accuracy of the perception.

A Reid's Facts

The facts in *Reid* are straightforward. This is a product of both the interlocutory nature of the case and the nature of the proceedings—determining whether the Crown in Hong Kong (as represented by the Attorney-General) had a caveatable interest in three blocks of land situated in New Zealand.

83 Eg *Attorney General v Blake* [2001] 1 AC 268 (HL)—recognition that an award of restitutionary damages may be available for a breach of contract (discussed in *Remedies Reclassified*, above n 10, 175–6); *Kleinwort Benson v Lincoln City Council* [1999] 2 AC 349 (HL)—recovery for money paid under a mistake of law; and *Woolwich Equitable Building Society v Inland Revenue Commissioners* [1993] AC 70 (HL)—recovery of money paid because of an ultra vires tax demand (both discussed in *Remedies Reclassified*, *ibid*, 57–8).

Reid was a prosecutor who had received bribes from parties seeking to avoid prosecution.[84] In these proceedings it was assumed that he was a fiduciary. Moreover, Reid did not challenge that there was 'an arguable case'[85] that he had acquired the New Zealand properties with bribe money and their Lordships assumed that they had been so purchased.[86] Reid and his wife were the registered proprietors of two of the properties, while Mrs Reid and Reid's solicitor were the registered proprietors of the third. Nevertheless, it was assumed that the land was held in trust for Reid.[87] The Crown claimed that it had an interest in the land which could support a caveat, and in turn the caveat would preclude dealings in the land.

Since *Lister & Co v Stubbs*,[88] the orthodox remedy against a bribe-taking fiduciary has been the imposition of a personal obligation upon the fiduciary to account for the value of the bribe. Applying *Lister*, the New Zealand Court of Appeal in *Reid* held that there was no caveatable interest.[89] The members of that Court considered that, while Reid may have been under a duty to the Crown to account for the unauthorised payments, this did not give rise to a proprietary interest in either the payment or in the land. The Privy Council disagreed.

Their Lordships considered that Reid's obligation to account arose from the time when he first received the bribe. Of course, Reid failed to do so. Utilising the maxim 'equity considers as done that which ought to have been done', their Lordships considered that as an alternative to the obligation to account for the bribe Reid held it (and any traceable products of it) on a constructive trust for the Crown.[90]

B Reid's Acceptance

At the time their Lordships' advice and reasoning were controversial, and for some they remain so.[91] Birks was then a strong defender of *Lister*. In *Introduction*[92] he argued, based on *Lister*, that a proprietary claim could only be brought if there was a sufficient proprietary base. Moreover, in an article which was contemporaneous with *Reid*, he argued that the use of

84 *Reid* [1994] 1 AC 324, 330.
85 *Ibid.*
86 *Ibid.*
87 *Ibid.*
88 (1890) 45 Ch D 1 (CA).
89 *A-G for Hong Kong v Reid* [1992] 2 NZLR 385 (CA).
90 *Reid* [1994] 1 AC 324, 331.
91 Eg Burrows suggests that *Reid* was 'wrongly decided'. He argues that, since the 'gain is not acquired by subtraction from the claimant', there is 'normally no good reason to give proprietary restitution for wrongs.' *The Law of Restitution* (London, LexisNexis, 2nd edn, 2002), 72; see also 499–500.
92 P Birks, *An Introduction to the Law of Restitution* (Oxford, Oxford University Press, paperback edition, 1989), 387–473.

the application of the maxim 'equity regards as done that which ought to be done' to justify the imposition of a constructive trust in these circumstances was conclusory. He observed:

> [the maxim] is less watertight than it may appear. The *Lister* court would probably say that you have to ask more carefully exactly what ought to be done and, if all that ought to be done is to render an account, no appeal to *Walsh v Lonsdale*[93] could confer a property as any specific thing received.[94]

Nevertheless, even then, Birks acknowledged that *Lister* 'had encountered powerful enemies and found rather few friends'.[95]

However, before long Birks had re-evaluated the use of *Walsh v Lonsdale* in these circumstances, and therefore (not necessarily in that order) his opinion of *Reid*. For example, Birks accepted that there could be a proprietary base in *Reid*, observing

> the crucial point may be that [in that case], by an application of *Walsh v Lonsdale*, Lord Templeman did establish the plaintiff's equitable proprietary base, albeit a highly controversial one.[96]

And in his article 'Rights, Wrongs, and Remedies',[97] Birks became more certain, observing that the Crown's equitable proprietary interest in the bribe 'came into existence as the facts happened',[98] as opposed to the exercise of an unconstrained judicial discretion. Then in *Unjust Enrichment* Birks suggested that *Reid* shows that there is 'at least one acquisitive wrong, namely breach of fiduciary duty, which generates property rights'.[99]

Writing in 2004, Zakrzewski may be right to regard the result as (now) non-contentious and, on the basis that the law has recognised that a principal has a secondary proprietary right arising from the fiduciary's breach of duty, to state that the declaration of the constructive trust in these circumstances constitutes a replicative remedy.[100] To the extent that some jurisdictions regard themselves as bound by the approach in *Reid*, or have adopted it,[101] this conclusion appears correct. But this encourages the question 'Why is the remedy in *Reid* replicative?'. This, in turn, encourages

93 (1882) 21 Ch D 9.

94 Birks, 'Property and the Profit of Wrongdoing' (1994) 24 *University of Western Australia Law Review* 8, 12 (citations omitted).

95 *Ibid*, 10–11 (citations omitted).

96 Birks, 'Establishing a Proprietary Base' [1995] *Restitution Law Review* 83, 84.

97 Birks, 'Rights', above n 8.

98 *Ibid*, 18.

99 P Birks, *Unjust Enrichment* (Oxford, Oxford University Press, 2nd edn, 2005), 34.

100 Other may disagree; see, eg *Bowstead and Reynolds on Agency* (London, Sweet & Maxwell, 17th edn, 2001), 6-041, discussing the use of a remedial constructive trust to recover profits acquired in breach of duty to the principal.

101 It has recently received acceptance in the English courts. See *Daraydan Holdings Ltd v Foland International Ltd* [2004] EWHC 622 (Ch), [2005] 4 All ER 73, para [86]. In this case, Lawrence Collins J considered that he was able to distinguish the facts from *Lister* but stated that, had he been unable to do so, he would have applied the reasoning from *Reid*.

the further questions 'How do we know when a remedy is replicative?' and 'Can a transformative remedy evolve into a replicative remedy?'.

C Why is the Remedy in *Reid* Replicative?

This is an important question for, prior to the declaration in *Reid*, a trust had not been recognised in these circumstances. Applying the test of the New Zealand Court of Appeal in *Fortex Group Ltd v MacIntosh*,[102] which Zakrzewski quotes,[103] the trust in *Reid* 'depend[ed] for its very existence on the order of the Court'. This suggests that the trust was a transformative remedy for the purposes of Zakrzewski's scheme. Indeed, the same conclusion can be reached by applying the test formulated by Zakrzewski: 'the court's order [in *Reid*] generate[d] something which [wa]s quite different from the rights and duties which already pertain[ed] between the parties'.[104] Moreover (and this point was not decided in *Reid*), should subsequent courts determine that they have a discretion to determine how the trust operates as against innocent third parties, the trust would be displaying characteristics which Lord Brown-Wilkinson in *Westdeutsche*[105] attributed to the remedial constructive trust.

The answer Zakrzewski gives is that there is a distinction between a new remedy and a transformative remedy. The point is that just because a remedy is new does not mean that it is transformative, though it may be. Zakrzewski draws a distinction between those new remedies which are seen as leading to a new substantive right and those which are not. In the former situation the right is 'the conceptualisation of the availability of a remedy'.[106] The mistake of law case, *Kleinwort Benson Ltd v Lincoln City Council*,[107] is offered as an example. As Zakrzewski observes, in that case their Lordships 'granted [a remedy] in new circumstances and hence [the remedy] . . . did not replicate a prior substantive right'. Nevertheless, the resulting remedy was not transformative. As Zakrzewski explains, the remedy in *Kleinwort Benson* is not transformative because, as a result of

102 [1998] 3 NZLR 171, 172.

103 *Remedies Reclassified*, above n 10, 215.

104 *Ibid*, 78–9.

105 *Westdeutsche Landesbank Girozentrale v Islington LBC* [1996] AC 669, 714–15. HL Lord Brown-Wilkinson observed: 'A remedial constructive trust . . . is a judicial remedy giving rise to an enforceable equitable obligation: the extent to which it operates retrospectively to the prejudice of their parties lies in the discretion of the court.' *Remedies Reclassified*, above n 10, 215 note 75.

106 *Remedies Reclassified*, *ibid*, 58. As Zakrzewski observes in the associated passage: 'Where a remedy is granted in circumstances where it was not previously available and it continues to be or is likely to continue to be granted in such circumstances, the conclusion may be drawn that there is a substantive right in existence that has been generated by the availability of the remedy . . . However, it is assumed that once a substantive right is recognized as existing then it is the substantive right which drives the remedy.' *Ibid*, 57–8.

107 [1999] 2 AC 349.

'this decision . . . it has become meaningful to speak of substantive rights to the return of payments made under mistakes of law'.[108]

This may suggest that a key determinative to the classification of a remedy is whether the remedy is awarded by a jurisdiction's final appellate court, as occurred in *Kleinwort Benson*, in circumstances indicating that the court was intending a change in the law which subsequent courts are to follow. Applying this reasoning to *Reid*, presumably a change in the final appellate court's perception of the underlying right leading to the recognition of a new remedy (as occurred in *Reid*) similarly does not make the remedy a transformative remedy. In the terms of the earlier quoted observation in respect of *Kleinwort Benson*, because of *Reid* 'it has become meaningful to speak of substantive rights' to the imposition of a constructive trust over the proceeds of a bribe,[109] at least for those jurisdictions bound by this decision.

There may be another explanation for classifying the remedy in *Reid* as always having been replicative. Zakrzewski suggests that in some situations—and he gives the example of cases of unjust enrichment—a substantive right may not be able to be precisely defined. As a consequence,

> if the law in this area is uncertain or undeveloped, it is generally the substantive right and the event which brings it into being that are hazy and require further debate and definition, not the remedy. The remedy is only a judicial restatement of the right.[110]

Presumably development of a new remedy in this situation is a by-product of the clarification of the underlying right. Thus, *Reid* can be seen as a development of the underlying right. But, as with the first explanation, this explanation is self-referential; it depends on the conclusion that the court developed the law as opposed to 'fashion[ing] a remedy'[111] so as to achieve a perceived fair result.

The dependence of the classifications on outside sources is further revealed by Zakrzewski's recognition that a transformative remedy can become a replicative remedy.[112] This occurs when, to reuse Zakrzewski's phase, it is 'meaningful to say' that there is now a right to this particular

108 *Remedies Reclassified*, above n 10, 58; *Woolwich Equitable Building Society v Inland Revenue Commissioners* [1993] AC 70 (HL) is given as another example.

109 Interestingly, proponents of corrective justice see *Reid* as consistent with their theory. See EJ Weinrib, 'Restitution and Unjust Enrichment; Restitutionary Damages as Corrective Justice' (2000) 1 *Theoretical Inquiries in Law* 1, 33–4.

110 *Remedies Reclassified*, above n 10, 113.

111 *Ibid*, 223.

112 *Ibid*, 217. (The 'status [of a remedy] may change. Due to the development of the law surrounding it, its availability may in time come to be seen as giving rise to substantive rights in which case it will move to the replicative category'.)

remedy, with the result that, by definition, the remedy can be reclassified as replicative.

Presumably this can apply to a prime example of a transformative remedy—the remedial constructive trust arising in response to a mistaken payment—so as to 'transform' it into a replicative remedy. In this context presumably the constructive trust is said to be transformative because it creates new rights and it is difficult to predict when it will be imposed.[113] But should the law develop such that, for example, the recipient's knowledge of their receipt of a mistaken payment is regarded as giving rise to an obligation (a secondary right) to hold the payment on trust for the payee,[114] then arguably the declaration of a constructive trust in these circumstances would be reclassified as a replicative remedy.[115]

Applying this reasoning to *Reid*, it can be argued that its constructive trust became a replicative remedy sometime after their Lordships gave their advice; presumably when the remedy gained sufficient approval to become mainstream, for example when influential commentators such as Birks overcame their objections to it and modified their respective theories to both accommodate and reflect it.

D The Classification is Historical

Irrespective of whether the remedy in *Reid* was always replicative of a new (or modified) right or became so, this review of *Reid* suggests that the classification of a remedy as replicative or transformative depends on whether or not the remedy in a particular case is perceived as applying generally, so that it can be said that a new right has been recognised or an existing right has been modified. As a result, the classification is historical in that it records the current or orthodox perception of the appropriateness of that remedy, not what might be, nor what was an earlier perception. Indeed, the fact that a particular remedy is currently classified as replicative does not mean it may have once been 'creatively "fashion[ed]"'.[116]

An analogy suggested to me is the evolution of dwarf stars, such as our sun.[117] Starting from a cloud of gas and dust, in the fullness of time a

[113] *Ibid*, 214–15.

[114] *Commerzbank Aktiengesellschaft v IMB Morgan plc* [204] EWHC 2771 (Ch): [2005] 2 All ER (Comm C) 564, para 36, applying *Chase Manhattan* [1979] 3 All ER 1025 as explained in *Westdeutsche* [1996] 2 All ER 961, 996–7 (HL). But see P Millett, 'Proprietary Restitution' in S Degeling and J Edelman (eds), *Equity in Commercial Law* (Sydney, Lawbook Co, 2005), 318, suggesting that *Chase Manhattan* was 'wrongly decided'.

[115] Zakrzewski acknowledges that a transformative remedy may evolve into a replicative remedy. This occurs when 'the availability [of the remedy] . . . come[s] to be seen as giving rise to substantive rights'. *Remedies Reclassified*, above n 10, 217.

[116] *Ibid*, 223.

[117] I should like to thank Prof Stuart Anderson for this analogy.

dwarf star will become a red giant,[118] then a white dwarf[119] and finally a black dwarf.[120] As a result of scientific observation of current stars we have obtained a degree of omniscience[121] in that we can predict the stages a star will go through. So just because a star is now a red giant does not mean that it was once created, then became a dwarf star and, in the fullness of time, will become a white dwarf. Similarly a replicative remedy may have once been a transformative remedy. The replicative/transformative classification simply records the current state of a remedy's acceptance.

IV REMEDIAL CERTAINTY, WRONGS AND NOT-WRONGS

A Overview

So far we have this: replicative remedies cause few problems for the law and the legal classifier, and will generally tend to be favoured by those legal theorists who have been described as 'monists'. Transformative remedies, on the other hand, cause problems for the law and the classifier because their path is uncertain and difficult to predict, and they do not fit into any clear classificatory scheme. They will be opposed by the monists. But, according to Zakrzewski, whether a remedy is replicative or transformative does not necessarily depend on whether it corresponds to the original 'primary right', of which it is the result. It depends instead on whether there is interposed, between the primary right and the remedy, some 'secondary right' which corresponds closely with the remedy (though it need not correspond at all closely with the primary right). And, as we have seen, whether that secondary right exists is not a matter of theory or critique; it is primarily a matter of history.

This picture, though more ungainly than one in which every remedy is closely related to a primary right, is still supportable, if not by monists then at least by those whose primary concern is to seek certainty and consistency in the law. As long as we can identify a general secondary right to which an otherwise wayward remedy is responsive, then the need for certainty and clarity is met. Unfortunately, however, Zakrzewski's scheme does not provide even this degree of assurance. If the recognition that a secondary right exists is historically conditioned, then so too is the extent

118 This occurs when the hydrogen at the core is almost depleted, decreasing the outward pressure from the nuclear reactions. This enables the gravitational field to increase, causing the star to collapse, which temporarily generates more pressure, resulting in the star temporarily increasing in size.

119 In this state, the star is shedding its outer layers, contracting and cooling.

120 With its remaining hydrogen and heat depleted, the star is now a cold, dark mass.

121 Nietzsche, *Human, All Too Human*, above n 74, para 106. See accompanying text.

of that right. Suppose the secondary right, as recognised, is not narrow but general, and not simple but complex, with much room for variation. Then, for any given situation, the remedy may be 'transformative'. And this, I propose to show, is the case with tracing remedies against fiduciaries who take bribes.

This section revolves around two variations—the 'agent to sell' and the 'entrepreneur'—to the core facts in *Reid*. It is arguable that the remedy in these situations will be different from that in *Reid*. These variations do not directly challenge Zakrzewski's taxonomy for, through recognising that new rights can arise and incorporating an element of discretion within the replicative classification,[122] the taxonomy is probably robust enough to survive. But these variations do raise questions about the extent to which remedial certainty is achievable.

Perhaps more significantly, these variations also have implications for the Birksian taxonomy, whereby rights are classified according to the causative event from which they arise. Birks acknowledges that drawing the 'line between wrongs and not-wrongs . . . is an enormously difficult subject'[123] and that in some cases 'this line is very sensitive',[124] but implicit in this taxonomy is the view that these causative events are distinct (albeit that on occasions '[t]wo causative events may lurk in one set of facts'—the so-called alternative analysis[125]).

Birks classifies Reid as a wrongdoer; the constructive trust in *Reid* was 'generated by a wrong'—a breach of fiduciary duty—and 'operat[es] as the remedy for the wrong'.[126] But, interestingly for the utility of his scheme, not all agree with this classification. Burrows, for example, regards the causative event underlying *Reid* as unjust enrichment[127]—a not-wrong. Peter Millett agrees that the causative event is not a wrong.[128] This is a major disagreement.

Another challenge to the Birksian scheme is the attack on what is called (to use Peter Millett's phrase) Birks's 'convoluted analysis',[129] whereby different causative events are said to explain the initial imposition of the trust as opposed to its extension to traceable gains. In some writings Birks suggests that either a wrong or unjust enrichment may be the causative event giving rise to this extension;[130] in other writings he has emphasised

122 See text accompanying nn 110–15 above.
123 Birks, 'Rights', above n 8, 31.
124 *Ibid.*
125 Birks, 'Misnomer', above n 13, 17.
126 Birks, 'Rights', above n 8, 18.
127 Burrows, *Restitution*, above n 91, 66–7 note 19.
128 Millett, 'Proprietary Restitution', above n 114, 310.
129 *Ibid*, 313.
130 P Birks, 'Unjust Enrichment and Wrongful Enrichment' (2001) 79 *Texas Law Review* 1767, 1775 note 29.

that unjust enrichment is the causative event.[131] Implicit in this appears to be the assumption that, post-*Reid*, the courts apply (or should apply) a two-stage analysis: first, to consider whether the bribe is held on trust, and secondly, to consider whether the trust extends to subsequent gains. Applying the Birksian analysis, in the first stage the courts are responding to the fiduciary's wrong (as opposed to a not-wrong, such as unjust enrichment), while in the second stage they are responding to an unjust enrichment. Can this be right?[132] Is it a sensible way of looking at things?

In one of his articles, Birks refers to the 'logic of technicality'; he suggests that this logic 'collapses as soon as the invitation is accepted to look beyond the technicality and consider factual reality instead'.[133] As Millett observes, Birks's analysis 'is not based on anything in any reported case'.[134] Andrew Tettenborn may be more in tune with factual reality than Birks when he suggests that, when considering whether to grant restitution for a wrong, courts use 'unjust enrichment spectacles'.[135] This perception will be extended when I come to discuss the 'agent to sell' and 'entrepreneur' variations; they suggest that (at least sometimes) elements of one or more of these causative events may be present and, to the extent that the court gives preference to one over another, will influence the final result.

Despite these questionable aspects of the Birksian scheme, underlying it is a recognition that the imposition of a trust with respect to the initial bribe (assuming a trust is imposed) does not necessarily mean that the trust will extend to subsequent gains. This is important for Zakrzewski's scheme. As we will see in the 'theme' which follows, the constructive trust is not the only remedy available against a bribe-taking fiduciary; the principal may have a range of remedies.

Following the 'theme' section, I consider my 'agent for sale' and 'entrepreneur' variations to the core facts in *Reid*. I suggest that the remedies in these variations may be different from that suggested by the preceding discussion. This is because a court may see these variations as being more complex than the situation in *Reid* and I consider the implications of this for the Birksian scheme.

After considering both variations, I offer some final comments on both their significance for Zakrzewski's taxonomy and certainty in the law.

131 P Birks, 'Property and Unjust Enrichment: Categorical Truths' [1997] *New Zealand Law Review* 623, 661; P Birks (ed), *English Private Law*, Vol II (Oxford, Oxford University Press, 2000), para 15.191; Birks, 'Wrongful Enrichment', *ibid*, 1785.

132 Millett, for one, thinks not. He suggests that in both situations the causative event is property, in particular trust law, which in turn has been influenced by equity's 'concern to reverse unjust enrichments', Millett, 'Proprietary Restitution', above n 114, 313. The relationship between rights of 'property' and the Birks's scheme of 'obligations' is much too complex to be explored here.

133 Birks, 'Categorical Truths', above n 131, 654.

134 Millett, 'Proprietary Restitution', above n 114, 313.

135 A Tettenborn, 'Misnomer: A Response', in Cornish et al, *Restitution Past, Present and Future*, above n 13, 34.

B Theme: Fiduciary Bribe-taking Generally

(i) The Simple Version

Prior to *Reid* there were two distinct remedies available against the fiduciary:[136]

(i) to seek an order that the fiduciary reimburse the principal for actual losses caused by the fiduciary's fraud;[137] and
(ii) to seek an order that the fiduciary account to the principal for the value of the bribe (the remedy at equity)[138] or to bring an action against the fiduciary for money had and received, so as to recover the value of the bribe (the equivalent remedy at common law). [139]

Applying Zakrzewski's taxonomy. we can say that the principal's primary right is for the fiduciary to perform their obligations faithfully[140] (or, to express the underlying idea in a different way, to 'account for their stewardship'[141]). Breach of this right can be seen as leading to two secondary rights:

—a right to be reimbursed for loss[142] (right A); and
—a right to receive the value of the bribe[143](right B).

These then lead into the specific replicative remedies.

Reid can be seen as adding a third secondary right—Zakrzewski suggests this is a right to obtain a declaration that the bribe is held on a constructive trust for the principal.[144]

136 Additionally there are remedies against the briber. So, if the bribe resulted in a contract between the principal and the briber, rescission may be available. Alternatively the briber may be required to account for the bribe or face liability for any actual loss. *Daraydan Holdings Ltd v Solland International Ltd* [2004] EWHC 622 (Ch), [2005] 4 All ER 73, paras [53]–[54]. *Fyffes Group Ltd v Templeman* [2000] 2 Lloyd's Rep 643 (QBD) is a recent example of a principal seeking relief against the bribe-maker.

137 See *Mahesan S/O Thambiah v Malaysia Government Officers' Co-operative Housing Society Limited* [1979] AC 374 (PC), 381, 383.

138 *Fawcett v Whitehouse* (1829) 1 Russ & M 132. See *Mahesan S/O Thambiah*, *ibid*, 380.

139 *Boston Deep Sea Fishing and Ice Co v Ansell* (1888) 39 ChD 339 (CA). See *Mahesan S/O Thambiah*, *ibid*, 380.

140 *Remedies Reclassified*, above n 10, 145 (discussing the primary right of trust beneficiaries).

141 Millett, 'Proprietary Restitution', above n 114, 310. *Remedies Reclassified*, *ibid*, 146.

142 The fiduciary has an obligation to 'make good any loss arising from their stewardship' and this obligation is implemented through the principal 'falsifying' the fiduciary's accounts. See Millett, 'Proprietary Restitution', *ibid*, 310.

143 From the fiduciary's perspective, this is an obligation to pay over the value of the bribe, 'to account . . . for what they would have received [for the principal] if they had acted with due diligence or proper skill and care' or properly. *Ibid.*

144 *Remedies Reclassified*, above n 10, 202.

(ii) The Elaborate Version

(a) Auxiliary Rights So far, so good. But, as I show in this section, the structure of the principal's rights is more complex then it initially appears to be on Zakrzewski's analysis. Indeed, even prior to *Reid* an additional layer of auxiliary rights could be discerned. These 'auxiliary' rights operate to modify the application of the otherwise bottom-layer rights. So, for example, the right to be reimbursed for loss (right A) is augmented by two auxiliary rights. These are: a right precluding the fiduciary from denying that he or she was acting in breach[145] (auxiliary right A(a)); and a right precluding the fiduciary from denying that the principal suffered any injury[146] (auxiliary right A(b)). The right to receive the value of the bribe (right B) is also augmented by two auxiliary rights. These are a right precluding the fiduciary from denying that he or she was acting in the interests of the principal[147] (auxiliary right B(a)) and a right precluding the fiduciary from denying that the principal could not have obtained that benefit personally (auxiliary right B(b)).[148]

Reid develops these auxiliary rights. For the moment it suffices to note that *Reid* recognises a new auxiliary right. This is a right to require the fiduciary to concede that the principal has rights of property in the bribe. This right is auxiliary to right B (auxiliary right B(c)).

(b) Another Secondary Right (and Associated Auxiliary Rights) As we have seen, *Reid* can be seen as adding a third secondary right. Some may argue, however, that, rather than adding another secondary right, *Reid* effectively replaces the principal's right to receive the value of the bribe (right B) with a right to obtain a declaration that the bribe is held on a constructive trust for the principal. This is because the constructive trust offers the prospect of both greater recovery (the profits derived from the bribe)[149] and preferential recovery. This view of *Reid* is also consistent with the 'simple' version. This argument, however, overlooks implicit changes which *Reid* made to the extent of the fiduciary's obligation to account. The effect of these changes is to make the structure of the principal's rights more complex.

As a result of *Reid*, the fiduciary's obligation is no longer restricted to the initial value of the bribe but may extend to subsequent gains arising

145 *Fawcett v Whitehouse* (1829) 1 Russ & M 132, 39 ER 51; discussed in Millett, 'Proprietary Restitution', above n 114, 310.

146 *Parker v McKenna* (1874) 10 Ch App 96, 124–5; discussed P Millett, 'Bribes and Secret Commissions' [1993] *Restitution Law Review* 7, 15.

147 *Re Biss* [1903] 2 Ch 40, 60; discussed by Millett, 'Bribes', *ibid*, 20.

148 *Regal (Hastings) Ltd v Gulliver* (1942) [1967] 2 AC 134n (HL).

149 In *Reid* their Lordships noted that there was no evidence as to the current value of the three properties: *Reid* [1994] 1 AC 324, 330.

from the fiduciary's use of the bribe.[150] Support for this is provided by Lord Templeman's observation that

> the false fiduciary will receive a benefit from his breach of duty unless he is accountable not only for the original amount or value of the bribe but also for the increased value of the property representing the bribe.[151]

Moreover, Lord Templeman recognised that this extended duty to account may apply where the constructive trust is unable to provide relief:

> If the property representing the bribe decreases in value the fiduciary must pay the difference between that value and the initial amount of the bribe.[152]

This example assumes that the property representing the bribe remains (and has depreciated) but the extended duty to account for the gains arising from the bribe should still apply when no property remains. Assume the fiduciary uses the bribe to acquire property which appreciates greatly in value. The fiduciary then sells that property and uses the proceeds to acquire a cliff-top mansion. Following an unprecedented storm, the mansion falls into the sea. Arguable the fiduciary is personally liable to account for the value of the pre-storm mansion.

The key development brought about by *Reid* is to expand the extent of the fiduciary's obligation to account. True, their Lordships also recognised the availability of proprietary relief, but this should be seen as an auxiliary right. The result is that the new secondary right introduced by *Reid* should be seen as a right to receive the value of the bribe and any gains arising therefrom (right C). We can assume that this right also has similar auxiliary rights as apply to right B. Thus, there is a right precluding the fiduciary from denying that he or she was acting in the interests of the

150 The capture of second generation profits was one of the concerns mentioned in *Lister* in support of the court's recognition of a personal remedy only: *Lister*, above n 88, 15. Prior to *Reid*, this aspect of *Lister* was being questioned. For example, Birks had argued that the obligation to account could be extended beyond merely repaying the value of the initial bribe to repaying the value of any profits. This would make the 'recipient . . . accountable and as such personally liable for the profits made through the bribe even though the victim–principal can claim no property in specific assets purchased with it [the bribe]'. P Birks, 'Obligations and Property in Equity: *Lister v Stubbs* in the Limelight' [1993] *Lloyd's Maritime and Commercial Law Quarterly* 30, 30. Moreover, as a result of a blurring of the distinction between property and obligation in cases such as *Boardman v Phipps* [1967] 2 AC 318 (HL) in at least some secret profit cases, the obligation to account had been extended to include subsequent profits. See also *Hospital Products Ltd v United States Surgical Corporation* (1984) 156 CLR 41 (HCA); *Warman International Limited v Dwyer* (1995) 182 CLR 544 (HCA). *Boardman* can be seen as reviving the association of personal equities or personal obligation with the recognition of 'what are in effect property rights'. In so doing, it questions the *Lister* distinction between obligation and property. So, in *Introduction* (above n 92), for example, Birks seeks to make *Boardman* consistent with his support for *Lister* and his argument for the need for a proprietary base to successfully claim a property right. He notes that 'it would be necessary, on facts such as in *Boardman*, to say that acquisitions in breach of the duty to avoid conflicts is an event which confers ownership on the victim of the breach'. *Introduction*, at 388.

151 *Reid* [1990] 1 AC 324, 331.

152 *Ibid*, 331–2.

principal (auxiliary right C(a)) and a right precluding the fiduciary from denying that the principal could not have obtained that benefit personally (auxiliary right C(b)). *Reid* also advances a third auxiliary right: a right to require the fiduciary to concede that the principal has rights of property in the subsequent gains from the bribe (auxiliary right C(c)). The end result is to confirm that *Reid* does add another 'secondary' right as Zakrzewski suggests, but the right itself and its application is more complex than he suggests.

(c) The Tertiary Nature of the 'Secondary' Rights There is a third way in which the structure of the principal's rights against the bribe-taking fiduciary may be more complex than that suggested earlier: there may be yet another layer of rights.

It is arguable that the suggested primary right is hiding a layer of rights. Recall that the primary right is for the fiduciary to perform their obligations faithfully. This right can be breached in a number of ways, of which the receipt of a bribe is just one. So the principal's right, that the fiduciary will not receive a bribe, becomes a secondary right. If so, the (now) three secondary rights (A, B and C) noted above can be seen as 'tertiary' rights. In turn, the content of these rights is moulded by the operation of the auxiliary rights. The end result is the specific remedy given in a particular case.

(d) Summary A diagram may assist one to better appreciate the 'elaborate' version of the principal's rights against a bribe-taking fiduciary. The hierarchy of rights in the elaborate version is presented diagrammatically in Box 1.

The result is that the range of remedies available to the principal has expanded. So, for example, the principal may seek:

—an order that the fiduciary reimburse the principal for any losses;
—an order that the fiduciary account to the principal for the value of the bribe;
—an order that the fiduciary pay to the principal the value of the bribe, being money had and received on the principal's behalf;
—a declaration that the fiduciary holds the bribe on trust for the principal;
—an order that the fiduciary account to the principal for the value of the bribe and gains arising therefrom;
—a declaration that the fiduciary holds the bribe (and traceable gains therefrom) on trust for the principal.

There may be other remedies, or variations to these. The important point is that while there may still be a correlation between the remedy and the tertiary right, the application of that right is shaped by the auxiliary rights. And, in turn, the application of these auxiliary rights is shaped by the

Box 1: A Primary Right that the Fiduciary Will Perform their Obligations Faithfully/Account for their Stewardship

A secondary right that the fiduciary will not receive a bribe
- —A tertiary right to be reimbursed for any actual loss caused by the fiduciary's receipt of the bribe (right A).
  - —An auxiliary right precluding the fiduciary from denying that he or she was acting in breach (auxiliary right A(a)); and
  - —An auxiliary right precluding the fiduciary from denying that the principal suffered any injury (auxiliary right A(b)).
- —A tertiary right to receive the value of the bribe (right B).
  - —An auxiliary right precluding the fiduciary from denying that he or she was acting in the interests of the principal (auxiliary right B(a));
  - —An auxiliary right precluding the fiduciary from denying that the principal could not have obtained that benefit personally (auxiliary right B(b)); and
  - —An auxiliary right requiring the fiduciary to concede that the principal has rights of property in the bribe (auxiliary right B(c)).
- —A tertiary right to receive the value of the bribe and any gains arising therefrom (right C).
  - —An auxiliary right precluding the fiduciary from denying that he or she was acting in the interests of the principal (auxiliary right C(a));
  - —An auxiliary right precluding the fiduciary from denying that the principal could not have obtained the additional gains personally (auxiliary right C(b)); and
  - —An auxiliary right requiring the fiduciary to concede that the principal has rights of property in any gains arising from the bribe (auxiliary right C(c)).

court's analysis of the underlying fiduciary relationship. This point is developed further in the agent for sale variation.

C Variation I: Agent for Sale

I start with an everyday transaction. Assume that an owner of a motor vehicle and would-be seller ('Seller') employs a used car dealer ('Agent') to be their agent for the purposes of selling their car. Agent is entitled to retain a 10% commission of the sale price. Seller's car has a market value of somewhere between $9,000 and $10,000. Agent tells 'P' about Seller's car. P offers Agent a $1,000 'gift' if Agent 'sells' him the car for $5,000. The deal is done. After deducting the $500 commission, Agent forwards $4,500 to Seller, keeping the $1,000 'gift'. Learning the full facts, Seller becomes interested in the 'gift', for Agent used it to buy a painting, which fortuitously has turned out to be a masterpiece with a true value of $10,000.

Reid suggests that Seller's proprietary claim to the painting (or a claim for its value) will succeed. *Bowstead and Reynolds on Agency*,[153] a leading text on the subject, agrees. It may be that, as a matter of public policy, the courts will also agree—presumably on the ground that bribery of all fiduciaries, not just fiduciary prosecutors, is an evil practice which must be discouraged. And if we see the underlying causative event here as being a wrong, such a result is consistent with Birks's assertion that the law has a licence to mistreat a wrongdoer.[154] If so, a fiduciary will either always hold a bribe (and its product) on a constructive trust for the principal or be required to account for the highest value of the bribe (and its product).

But this is to overlook the warning in *Re Coomber*[155] that '[f]iduciary relationships are of many different types'. Building on this, in the New Zealand Netherlands Society case Lord Wilberforce reminded us that '[t]he precise scope of [the fiduciary obligation] must be moulded according to the nature of the relationship'.[156] Such warnings are pertinent when considering agents for sale. Consider, for example, their obligations with respect to the proceeds of sales. These can vary; for example, the agent may be required to hold the proceeds (either net or gross) on trust. Alternatively, the agent may be entitled to receive the payment as his or her own money and have a corresponding obligation to pay their principal an equivalent sum. A third possibility is that the agent initially receives the payment on trust for the principal but has authority to mix the payment with the agent's own personal funds and thereafter to become a debtor for that sum.[157] As a consequence, depending on the nature of the obligation between the agent and principal, the agent may be a trustee of the proceeds of the sale[158] or merely a debtor.[159] The point is that the under-

153 Above n 100, 6-082.

154 Birks, 'Misnomer', above n 13, 8; Birks, 'Rights', above n 8, 33. Birks's point is that there is 'no logically necessary response to a wrong' and that what the law does 'is a question ultimately of what is useful and acceptable' Birks, 'Wrongful Enrichment', above n 130, 1788. So cutting off a contract breaker's ears for their wrong of breaching the contract could be available 'if extrinsic considerations of utility, proportionality, and humanity did not dissuade'. Birks, 'Misnomer', above n 13, 8. These comments seem odd from someone advocating certainty in the law.

155 [1911] 1 Ch 723, 728–9.

156 *New Zealand Netherlands Society 'Oranje' Inc v Kuys* [1973] 1 WLR 1126, 1130. See also *Birtchnell v Equity Trustees, Executor and Agency Co Ltd* (1929) 42 CLR 384, 408.

157 *Westpac Banking Corporation v Ancell* (1993) 4 NZBLC 103,259, 103,262 (CA), explaining the result in *Thomson v Clydesdale Bank Ltd* [1893] AC 282 (HL).

158 *Burdick v Garrick* (1870) LR 5 Ch App 233.

159 *Kirkham v Peel* (1880) 43 LT 171 AFFD (1880) 44 LT 195.

lying contract between the parties is shaping the agent's fiduciary obligations.

The issue raised by the agent for sale variation is whether proprietary relief for the traceable proceeds of the bribe (here the $10,000 painting)—the approach in *Reid*—or a personal remedy for the value of the painting (an alternative remedy recognised in *Reid*) is available. The significance of this issue is apparent if we assume that the relationship between the agent and the principal was such that the agent was to be merely a debtor for the net proceeds from the sale. Does this distinguish *Reid*?

There is an argument that it does not, for in *Reid* the fiduciary also was not an express trustee, in the sense of having control over a trust fund. Rather, the trust was imposed on the basis of an obligation to repay the principal an amount equivalent to the bribe (and its proceeds).

However, there may be a crucial difference. In the agent for sale variation the agent has the principal's authority to handle the money arising from the sale for his or her personal benefit. Arguably the position was different in *Reid*, for neither the Crown nor Reid contemplated that as a part of his duties he would receive payments from third parties and then have to account for them.[160] Considering the agent for sale variation in more depth, not only do the parties expect that the agent will receive funds, but they may have displaced the rule as stated in *Foley v Hill*[161] (either expressly or impliedly[162]) so that the agent's obligation is to repay the principal an amount equivalent to the proceeds or deemed proceeds. Significantly, the agent may be free to do with the actual proceeds whatever he or she wishes.[163]

Arguably in this situation the maxim so influential in *Reid*—that equity considers as done that which have ought to have been done—should result in requiring the agent to pay their debt—here the bribe. Since the agent is merely the principal's debtor, there is no liability for any identifiable gains, nor is proprietary relief (for the initial bribe) available. If so, the principal's remedy is different from both that of the Crown in *Reid* and their Lordship's suggestion that the personal obligation to account extends to subsequent gains. The remedy returns to an obligation to account for the value of the initial bribe—that is, similar to the quantum in *Lister*. Should proprietary relief be available, typically this should take the form of an equitable lien so as to limit the quantum of recovery.[164]

160 Millett, 'Bribes', above n 146, 28; Millett, 'Proprietary Restitution', above n 114, 324.

161 (1848) 2 HL Cas 28.

162 *Westpac Banking Corp v Savin* [1985] 2 NZLR 41 (CA); *Westpac Banking Corporation v Ancell* (1993) 4 NZBLC 103,259 (CA).

163 A counter-argument is to distinguish the agent's authority to receive as their own money the proceeds of sale from any authority to receive a bribe.

164 Developing an analogy with tracing cases such as *In re Oatway; Herslet v Oatway* [1903] 2 Ch 356, it may be that, in appropriate cases, the lien should be for the total amount the

Whatever the result, this variation shows that two causative events—those of consents (here the contract) and wrongs—are overlapping and the end result is dependent on the court's evaluation of the significance of each event. Observations of the New Zealand Court of Appeal in *Westpac Banking Corporation v Ancell*[165] illustrate how notions of consent and wrong may interact.

Ancell is a knowing receipt case. Wall was a sharebroker. In 1987 there was a collapse of the New Zealand share market. This adversely affected Wall, who, following the default of some clients, was required personally to settle the purchase of shares at their former high price. The Bank assisted Wall in this by extending his overdraft limit on his sole trading account to $1,200,000. Within a few months the Bank had cancelled the overdraft and Wall became bankrupt. But in the meantime, Wall continued to buy and sell shares on his clients' behalf, and to receive funds on their behalf, for example, in the case of Ancell, from deposits withdrawn from other financial institutions. These funds had been paid into the overdrawn trading account and the Bank claimed them.

The Court concluded that the contractual arrangements between the parties had not displaced the trust relationship—so Wall received the proceeds on trust—and that the bank had sufficient knowledge of this. For current purposes, *Ancell* is particularly interesting for illustrating that the Court did not view the argument as being of an 'either/or' type, by which I mean that the relationship was either one of trust or one of debtor–creditor. Rather, even if the relationship was primarily debtor–creditor, the Court suggested that Wall still retained some fiduciary obligations, breach of which could reinstate the trust relationship. This is displayed in the following passage from the judgment in which the Court is reflecting on the significance of a client's authority to pay the proceeds into a mixed (and even temporarily overdrawn) bank account:

> [A] fiduciary must not without the informed consent of the client stand to receive any benefit other than the fiduciary's professional remuneration from the transaction which the fiduciary is retain to carry through, Even if a client impliedly consents to payment into an account which may be temporarily overdrawn in the ordinary course of business it does not follow that the authorisation extends to situations where the broker is in a precarious financial state and the payment is in partial discharge of his personal indebtedness to the bank.[166]

fiduciary is required to account for rather than for the amount of the bribe used in the purchase of a particular asset. Applying this to the agent for sale variation, assume that the agent used only $300 of the $500 'gift' to acquire the painting and the remaining $200 is dissipated. Arguably the principal may have a lien over the painting for $500.

165 (1993) 4 NZBLC 103,259 (CA).

166 *Ibid*, 103,264.

D Variation II: The Entrepreneur

This is an amalgam of the core facts in *Reid* with a *Boardman*[167] twist. Assume that a prosecutor receives a bribe in circumstances which, applying *Reid*, would result in him or her holding it on trust. But rather than using the bribe to buy land (as occurred in *Reid*), the fiduciary uses it with some of his or her own money to buy a controlling interest in company 'A'. Through personal skill, the fiduciary turns the fortunes of company 'A' around, resulting in a significant increase in its share value. The fiduciary then sells these shares and reinvests the full proceeds in another company—company 'B'. As occurred with the earlier company, through the fiduciary's skills the fortunes of this company are improved. The issue is whether the fiduciary can keep any of the gains from his or her involvement in these companies.

This issue brings into sharp relief the different judicial concerns in *Lister* and in *Reid*. In *Lister* Lord Lindley LJ was concerned that a proprietary remedy would catch 'all the profits which he [ie the fiduciary] might have made by embarking in trade with it [ie the unauthorised payment]'.[168] The position in *Reid* is different. Indeed, in *Reid* there were two concerns: to respond to 'an evil practice . . . threaten[ing] the foundations of civilised society'—the 'bribery of policemen and prosecutors'[169]; and to ensure that the proceeds of bribes could not be 'whisked away to some Shangri-La which hides bribes'.[170] Moreover, in *Reid* the concern in *Lister* was not as prominent as there was no evidence of any increase in the land's value,[171] let alone that it was due to the activities of Reid. Acquisition of the land in that case can be analogised with a passive investment. The entrepreneur variation re-raises (and expands) the *Lister* concern; as Burrows observes:

> Constructive trust terminology prima facie indicates that there is no cut-off point: the fiduciary is liable for any profit made from the initial gain.[172]

Resolution of this concern raises difficult issues. For present purposes the important point is that, unless one focuses solely on the fiduciary's initial wrongdoing[173] and concludes that in these circumstances the principal has an auxiliary right precluding the fiduciary from denying that he or she was acting solely in the interests of the principal, there may be no one answer.

167 *Boardman v Phipps*, above n 150.
168 *Lister*, above n 88, 15.
169 *Reid* [1994] 1 AC 324, 330–331.
170 *Ibid*, at 339.
171 *Ibid*, at 330.
172 Burrows, *Restitution*, above n 91, 500.
173 Millett, 'Proprietary Restitution', above n 114, 316.

As noted earlier, Birks anticipates this variation in result. He recognises that the imposition of the constructive trust over the bribe does not necessarily mean that the trust will extend to subsequent gains. Questions about his solution—that in initially imposing the trust the court is responding to a different causative event than it does when it determines whether the trust extends to subsequent gains—does not downplay this recognition.

To some extent this solution is a development of the solution Birks advanced in *Introduction*. There, Birks appears to assume that the fiduciary's wrongdoing would also taint the subsequent gains, thereby making the fiduciary liable for them. Nevertheless, he suggests that the gains may be attributable to a number of sources and that the fiduciary may be able to keep gains attributable to their skill and personal labour.[174] In any event, he offered a remoteness test in the form of 'the first non-subtractive receipt'.[175] Applying this test to the entrepreneurial variation, recovery would be limited to the gains attributable to the company 'A' shares. Interestingly, Birks argues that the result in *Boardman* is consistent with this approach,[176] so presumably this remoteness test is seen as satisfying the concerns with valuing the fiduciary's skill.

In his latter writings, Birks suggests that unjust enrichment is the causative event which the court responds to in determining whether the constructive trust imposed over the bribe extends to the subsequent gains. According to Birks, the fiduciary is unjustly enriched if they used the 'acquisitive opportunities inherent in property' for their personal gain, as these belong to the property's owner.[177] In the Birksian scheme this change in causative event (from wrong to unjust enrichment) is significant as there is no longer a licence to mistreat the fiduciary. Moreover, it more easily allows the court to separate the relevant contributions of the principal (the bribe) and those of the fiduciary.

A prime example of joint contributions is when the fiduciary mixes the bribe with their own money in the acquisition of the appreciating asset. Presumably, the principal is unjustly enriched if he or she attempts to claim gains acquired through the use of the fiduciary's property. The result is to share the gains proportionately. *Foskett v McKeown*[178] is consistent with this. In holding that the fiduciary was entitled to a proportionate share of the asset[179] *Foskett* does change the law,[180] but in so doing it confirms the

174 Birks, *Introduction*, above n 92, 352.
175 *Ibid.*
176 *Ibid*, 353.
177 Birks, *English Private Law*, Vol II, above n 131, para 15.191; Birks, 'Wrongful Enrichment', above n 130, 1785.
178 [2001] 1 AC 102, 131.
179 *Ibid*, 127; 129 per Lord Millett; 110 per Lord Browne-Wilkinson; and 115 per Lord Hoffmann.
180 *Re Hallett's Estate: Knatchville v Hallett* (1880) 13 Ch D 696, 709.

orthodox understanding[181] that the principal is not entitled to claim ownership of all the appreciating asset.[182]

Moving from use of the fiduciary's property as the contributing factor to the fiduciary's skill, in appropriate cases it may be argued that the fiduciary's skill should also be regarded as a contribution, at least when the fiduciary is not precluded from denying that he or she is to dedicate his or her skill solely for the principal's benefit.[183]

In any event, a post-*Lister* development has been the judicial recognition that in appropriate situations a defaulting fiduciary is entitled to an allowance for their skill and effort.[184] Some may explain the awarding of an allowance on the grounds that it is 'an inherent part of the calculation of the profits made by the errant fiduciary',[185] or that the nature of the asset acquired by the fiduciary may require an allowance.[186] It may be that the fiduciary has an independent right to the allowance based on the principal's unjust enrichment—an example of counter-restitution?[187] Then, as in the agent for sale variation, the scope of the fiduciary relationship (which is determined by express or implied consent) may be an important factor.

But the award of an allowance to a defaulting fiduciary is controversial.[188] Indeed, an allowance seems inconsistent with the licence to mistreat wrongdoers identified by Birks.[189] Yet Birks also classifies *Boardman* as an example of a wrong.[190] Perhaps Weinrib[191] is correct that there is a difference between an innocent wrongdoing improver and a wilful wrongdoing improver.

For Weinrib the innocent wrongdoer is entitled to an allowance because his or her acts show a recognition that another has rights which are to be respected. The wrongdoing has arisen because of an incorrect assumption that those rights are not being interfered with. In contrast, the wilful wrongdoer is denying another's rights; as a result, any claim to expenses associated with any improvement 'is normatively incoherent'.[192] While Weinrib's comments were directed at trespassers, he recognised that they

181 *Ibid.*

182 This does not necessarily mean that, in those circumstances where the obligations of the fiduciary require, the fiduciary does not have to account for their share of the profit..

183 *Warman International Ltd v Dwyer* (1995) 182 CLR 544 (HCA).

184 *Phipps v Boardman* [1964] 2 All ER 187, 208 per Wilberforce J; approved in *Boardman v Phipps* [1967] 2 AC 46 (HL).

185 J Palmer, 'The Availability of Allowances in Equity: Rewarding the Bad Guy' (2004) 21 *New Zealand Universities Law Review* 146, 159.

186 *Warman International Ltd v Dwyer* (1995) 182 CLR 544 (HCA).

187 Birks, 'Restitution without Counter Restitution, *Guiness Plc v Saunders*' [1989] *Lloyd's Maritime and Commercial Law Quarterly* 330.

188 See, eg Palmer, above n 185.

189 Birks, 'Rights', above n 8, 33.

190 *Ibid*, 31.

191 Weinrib, above n 109, 29.

192 *Ibid.*

also applied to a fiduciary's claim for an allowance.[193] It may be argued that Boardman was an innocent wrongdoer[194] while Ward in *Guinness Plc v Saunders*—despite the assumptions in that case—was not,[195] but against this Boardman's actions, for example over the inadequacy of his disclosure to the beneficiaries when seeking their consent, did not escape criticism from Wilberforce J.[196]

The controversies over the awarding of an allowance remain, but it seems that commentators and courts are looking beyond the fiduciary's wrong and in so doing they are being influenced by another factor(s) to grant the allowance.

E Significance for the Right–Remedy Correlation

I return to the replicative/transformative classifications. The preceding discussion has assumed that the constructive trust in *Reid* is replicative; it also assumes that the remedies in the two variations are also replicative. But the prospect of different remedies would appear to raise a conundrum as to how to explain the differences. There appears to be two choices.

One choice is conclude that different rights are involved. So, instead of creating an additional right/remedy in favour of the principal for use against the fiduciary, the reasoning in *Reid* may lead to a range of rights/remedies. Despite an expansion in the number of rights, this would preserve a close correlation between right and remedy. Thus, infringement of right 'A' will lead to remedy 'A'; infringement of right 'B' will lead to remedy 'B'; and so on.

The other choice is to conclude that the right is the same in all these situations but accept that it is expressed at a relatively high level of generality—that is, that a fiduciary is not to receive a bribe—and that, responding to the auxiliary rights, the courts have a discretion in shaping the final remedy to fit the facts. This may mean a return to the pre-*Reid* position in that the principal has an 'either/or' choice of remedy against the fiduciary—to seek recovery of the gain (which may include second-generation profits) or to seek reimbursement for any loss.

Either response is consistent with the replicative/transformative classifications for, as we have seen, by definition the replicative classification is consistent with the creation of new remedies. It is also consistent with a

193 *Ibid*, 29 note 42.

194 Both Weinrib and Birks suggest that Boardman was an innocent wrongdoer. Weinrib, above n 109, 29 note 42; Birks, 'Rights', above n 8, 31.

195 In *Guinness Plc v Saunders* [1990] 2 AC 663 (HL) their Lordships declined to grant an allowance, Lord Goff distinguishing *Boardman* on the ground that an allowance is not available where it would encourage a fiduciary to breach their trust.

196 *Phipps v Boardman*, above n 184, 205.

'degree of [weak] discretion'[197] exercised 'according to well-settled, although fairly broadly expressed rules'.[198] But these variations also suggest that the relationship between right and remedy is more complex than the replicative/transformative dichotomy suggests. Moreover, it suggests that the certainty provided by associating remedies with rights is to some degree illusory.

Uncertainty in the application of the law is readily apparent if the court has a discretion (even a weak one). This is because the application of the right per se is more fluid and initially the law seems less clear. Arguments centre upon application of the underlying principle, rather than whether the facts fit within one category or another.

However, uncertainty exists even if there is a growth in the recognition of rights with associated remedies. Here the uncertainty (or room for argument and judicial manoeuvring) arises over whether it was right A which was infringed or right B. Moreover, a court is free to recognise a new right. The result is that the law becomes a range of rights (and remedies) dependent on fine distinctions (and resulting classifications). If so, the law may appear certain. This is because the uncertainty arises in the choice of right.

In addition, whether there is one general right (with associated discretion) or a choice between rights, uncertainty further arises in whether that right (or those rights) have been infringed. Consider *Reid*. The result in that case is dependent upon Reid being a fiduciary. While not discussed in *Reid*, the question whether a public prosecutor is a fiduciary is problematic. Reinforcing an earlier point about the evolution of rights and remedies, the result in *Reid* owes a lot to the expansion in the recognition of fiduciary relationships in cases such as *Reading v A-G*.[199] The point is that such preliminary choices confer significant discretion upon the courts in determining the final result.

V CONCLUSION

Few would disagree that like cases should be treated alike.[200] The problem is determining which cases are alike. While focusing on the solution

197 *Remedies Reclassified*, above n 10, 88.

198 *Ibid*, 91. This quote was made with respect to equitable remedies, eg to grant or to refuse a remedy but it seems to be of universal application. For example, Zakrzewski offers as an example of a weak discretion at common law, the discretion to determine whether a 'broad standan[d] such as reasonable care or reasonable foreseeability' has been met: *ibid*, 89. The contrast is with the so-called 'remedial discretion' exercised in transformative remedies: *ibid*, 97. Here there is 'a choice as to whether to create the remedy and what content it should have, that is, what it should confer on the claimant and, correlatively, what it should require of the defendant'.

199 [1951] AC 507.

200 Birks, 'Equity', above n 6, 4.

proposed by Zakrzewski in *Remedies Reclassified*, this paper has also considered the Birksian solution. Both suggest that the answer lies in good taxonomy.[201] To a degree, their respective schemes are directed at slightly different aspects of this problem. For Zakrzewski, one concern is when a court 'fashion[s] a remedy' for a 'particular case'.[202] But this is the extreme. The more day-to-day concern is that remedies replicate (give direct effect to)[203] the underlying right. For Birks, a particular concern is a growth in remedies for not-wrongs leading to discretionary remedialism. But both Zakrzewski and Birks are similar in seeking a correlation between the remedy and the causative event or the right. The difference is in the level of abstraction they are dealing with—a causative event is a higher level of abstraction than a right.

Both solutions are important and add to our understanding; however, I suggest that they do not capture a dynamism that is present in our judge-made law. This is the perception of individual courts. Few would disagree that the courts 'must act within the defines of the doctrine of precedent',[204] but this doctrine gives considerable scope for courts to determine the final result, including the creation of new remedies (or the extension of particular remedies to new situations, which may be much the same). And this is not necessarily a bad state of affairs; indeed, depending on one's perspective, it may even be good.

As is displayed by the two variations to *Reid*, the dynamism in the law arises because, in a given case, a number of influences (or, to use Birksian terminology, 'causative events') may be present that jostle between themselves to obtain priority over the others for the court's attention.

As a result, 'the discussion of remedies can be a slippery business'.[205] Like Paul Gewirtz (who made the preceding observation), Zakrzewski has sought to lessen this slipperiness[206] by focusing on the right[207] and advancing the replicative/transformative categories. As we have seen, an

201 Of course, some may respond that classifications merely gives us much needed reassurance of consistency. RA Hillman, 'The Many Dimensions of Private Law' (2004) 40 *Canadian Business Law Journal* 384, 390: 'At least in part we want to believe that the law is clear and predictable, and we categorise the law to prove it and to bury the uncomfortable reality that the law is neither of those things.'

202 *Remedies Reclassified*, above n 10, 223.

203 *Ibid*, 79 note 51.

204 *Kleinwort Benson*, above n 83, 378 per Lord Goff.

205 P Gewirtz, 'Remedies and Resistance'(1983) 92 *Yale Law Journal* 585, 592–3. In this article, Gewirtz reflects on the decision of the US Supreme Court in *Brown v Board of Education* 349 US 294 (1955) and the process by which the law 'mediates between the ideal and the real': *ibid*, 587. In *Brown* the Court required the desegregation of schools to proceed with 'all deliberate speed' (at 301). In analysing this order, Gewirtz contrasts 'rights maximising' with 'interest balancing' as alternative approaches by which a court can determine the appropriate remedy.

206 Gewirtz attributes this slipperiness to vague and evolving rights (*ibid*, 592–3).

207 *Ibid*, 592. Gewirtz suggests that in determining a remedy a court 'proceed[s] within boundaries set by basic remedial goals' which, in turn, 'are limited by a definition of the right'.

immediate challenge these categories face is that remedies (and rights) evolve. Moreover, our law is built on individual cases dealing with particular circumstances. From the particular the law develops. A particular remedy's classification as either replicative or transformative can tell us its current state of acceptance (or lack thereof) as representing mainstream or black-letter law. It does not, however, tell us whether the law is undergoing a fundamental change, so what is currently accepted as a transformative remedy may become replicative. Moreover, this classification is dependent on outside sources for evidence of this acceptance.

But the slipperiness in remedies is more elusive and transcends rights. So, for example, as the *Reid* variations illustrate, seeking greater correlation between the right and the remedy, through greater precision in the description of the right, will just open up a new source of slipperiness—the choice of the right. And seeking greater precision is a never-ending task.

Nevertheless, this is a task humans embark upon. The material considered here in conjunction with *Reid* suggests that we should seek guidance ('intellectually satisfying justification for legal results'[208]) in the causative events (and their progeny—rights), but in so doing we should recognise two limitations: first, that the choice of which causative category a particular case fits in influences the way we view that case;[209] and secondly, that causative events do not necessarily operate in isolation to each other.

208 S Wadhams, '"Response" to Stephen A. Smith "A Map of the Common Law"' (2004) 40 *Canadian Business Law Journal* 396, 398.

209 As Professor Samuel has noted, classification affects our appreciation of facts. See Samuel, above n 5, 275: 'There are no such things as purely objective facts; facts only make sense when viewed through particular pre-existing categories or structure models of apparently descriptive contexts.'

3

'Discretion and Remedies'

THE HON P DE JERSEY AC, CHIEF JUSTICE

THE JUDICIAL OATH obliges the judge to render justice according to law, and that is designed to avoid what Brennan J termed 'judicial idiosyncrasy'.[1] Curiously proximately to the achievement of the fusion of law and equity in England, the then Lord Chief Justice, Sir Alexander Cockburn, observed in 1878 that a Judge 'cannot set himself above the law which he has to administer, or make or *mould it to suit the exigencies of a particular occasion*'.[2] It suits my present purpose to quote the form of expression employed by Cockburn CJ, and I overlook for now the circumstance that he was refused a peerage by Queen Victoria 'upon the ground of the notoriously bad moral character of the Chief Justice'.[3]

Many would contend that courts of ultimate authority not infrequently 'mould' remedies to suit the exigencies of particular cases, and especially so if the remedy be equitable; though not perhaps with the boldness of Lord Denning who admonished judges to 'develop the law . . . so that the litigants . . . can have their differences decided by the law *as it should be and is*, and not by the law of the past'.[4]

A propensity to 'mould' cannot, however, be allowed to erode the touchstone of certainty.

Some recent cases in this country, concerning equitable remedies, have provoked the query whether certainty is being maintained. The decision which has aroused probably the most intense critical comment is *Bridgewater v Leahy*,[5] which I raise with circumspection because I was the trial judge who regrettably got it wrong. I raise it because it provides the most interesting fairly recent illustration I can offer of the theme of this paper.

1 *Gollan v Nugent* (1988) 166 CLR 18, 35.
2 *Martin v Mackonochie* 3 QBD 730, 775.
3 *Oxford Dictionary of National Biography*, vol 12 (Oxford, Oxford University Press, 2004), 329.
4 *Ibid.*
5 (1998) 194 CLR 457.

I will return to more detail of the case. For the moment, I mention the view held by a number of commentators that its circumstances lay 'at the very boundary of what constitutes unconscionable conduct' (cf eg *Dr Joachim Dietrich*[6]); and as to the extraordinary width of the discretionary exercise remitted to the Supreme Court for the readjustment of the parties' interests.

It is inevitable subjective notions of fairness strongly influence such determinations. Gibbs CJ in *Amadio*[7] described an unconscientious transaction as one where the party seeking to enforce it has taken 'unfair' advantage of the other. So did Mason J[8] and Deane J.[9] As long ago as seven decades past, Dixon J in *Thompson v Palmer*[10] identified the object of estoppel *in pais* as preventing an 'unjust' departure from an assumption adopted by another, which the court picked up in *Legione v Hateley*.[11] Views on what is 'fair', what is 'just', will certainly differ, whether the source be lay or judicial.

Courts have therefore struggled to establish frameworks which guide these determinations. Hence claims such as in *Muschinski v Dodds*[12]:

> the view that the court can disregard legal and equitable rights and simply do what is fair . . . is contrary to established doctrine in Australia;[13]

and

> the flexible remedy of the constructive trust is not so formless as to place proprietary rights in the discretionary disposition of a court acting according to vague notions of what is fair.[14]

Yet, as Deane J was constrained to acknowledge in that case, 'general notions of fairness and justice . . . remain relevant to the traditional equitable notion of unconscionable conduct . . . '.[15] Relevant, one may ask, even predominant?

In August 1622 at Gray's Inn, Robert Callis Esq, sergeant at law, delivered his famous reading 'on the Statute of Sewers, 23 Hen 8, c5', in which he identified various degrees of discretion. The second and third are apposite:

> (b) *Legalis discretio* is that which Sir E. Coke meaneth and setteth forth in *Rooke's* and *Keighley's Cases* [. . . and this is merely to administer justice

6 (1999) 73 ALJ 112.
7 *Commercial Bank of Australia v Amadio* (1983) 151 CLR 447, 460.
8 *Ibid*, 467.
9 *Ibid*, 474.
10 (1933) 49 CLR 507, 547.
11 (1982–3) 152 CLR 406, 430–1.
12 (1985) 160 CLR 583.
13 *Ibid*, 594–5, per Gibbs CJ,
14 *Ibid*.
15 *Ibid*, 616.

according to the prescribed rules of law];

(c) the third discretion is where the laws have given no certain rule . . . and herein discretion is the absolute judge of the cause, and gives the rule'.[16]

The goal of the courts must be, and is, the establishment of a framework from which the rights of parties may reliably be discerned. The fear being expressed is that we may be veering into Callis's third category, where there is 'no certain rule' and discretion is the 'absolute judge of the cause'.

It is moot, however, whether this is a legitimate concern, or one which simply betrays a rather naive misunderstanding of the reasonable and progressive basis of equity. The opening sentence of the current (4th) edition of *Meagher, Gummow and Lehane's Equity—Doctrines and Remedies*[17] cautions that 'equity can be described but not defined'. Flexibility is the virtue of discretionary equitable remedies, moulded to suit 'ever-varying circumstances'.[18] It is interesting to note that it is this state—the first Australian colony to fuse law and equity, through the Queensland Parliament's *Judicature Act* of 1876—which has thrown up the case (*Bridgewater v Leahy*) topically prompting the question whether the equitable discretion may have become unhelpfully flaccid.

Uncertainties emerging from the general law may impact on statutory regimes as well. An example is section 51AC of the Trade Practices Act, inserted in 1998. That provision outlaws 'unconscionable conduct' by a corporation in the supply of goods or services. It is not a statutorily defined term, but the statute lists circumstances to which a court may refer in determining whether conduct has been unconscionable. The list includes some cast in very broad terms, such as whether 'any unfair tactics' were used against the consumer, and the extent to which the parties 'acted in good faith'.

Driven to explain the statutory concept of unconscionability, the Federal Court has said it is conduct 'irreconcilable with what is right or reasonable'[19]; something morally wrong, 'serious misconduct or something clearly unfair or unreasonable'.[20]

The legislation leaves it to the courts to elucidate these elusive concepts, and to the extent that this has been possible, the scope for subjective interpretation looms large. I empathise with my federal colleagues, but is the client left clearly enlightened about what may or may not occur?

Some of the issues which could arise in a commercial context are of serious complexion, highly relevant to day-to-day operations. For example, would good faith oblige a mortgagee bank, in possession of a

16 Callis 112, 113, *Stroud's Judicial Dictionary* (London, Sweet & Maxwell, 4th edn), 792.

17 RP Meagher, JD Heydon and MJ Leeming (Butterworths, 2002), 3.

18 *Ibid*, 91.

19 *Hurley v McDonalds Australia Ltd* (2000) ATPR 41-741.

20 *ACCC v Simply no Knead (Franchising) Pty Ltd* (2000) 104 FCR 253.

valuation at a figure substantially lower than a customer purchaser is intending to pay for a property, to disclose that valuation to the customer? Could threatening to exercise a legally accrued right in order to encourage the other party to renegotiate a transaction ever fall into the bad faith category? A rigorous insistence on legal rights may be considered tough, but could it ever evidence a lack of bona fides?

What is 'fair' and what is 'just' in the abstract sense is informed by well-established community values. Some will argue that, if these are to be identified, who better than a judge to do so? But while I am obviously not suggesting courts are not in touch with their communities, the fact remains that judges are not necessarily well equipped to determine prevailing community values and social attitudes.

In *Dietrich v R*,[21] Brennan J identified the 'contemporary values' which should relevantly inform the judicial process as not

> the transient notions which emerge in reaction to a particular event or which are inspired by a publicity campaign conducted by an interest group. They are the relatively permanent values of the Australian community.

Lord Steyn has spoken in the House of Lords of the fashioning of rights by reference to what a Judge 'reasonably believes the ordinary citizen would regard as right'.[22]

The question remaining is how those relevant values are to be gauged.

The significance of my present focus, *Bridgewater v Leahy*, falls to be assessed in the context of preceding decisions of the High Court, especially *Amadio* and *Garcia v National Australia Bank Ltd*.[23] While seen as dramatic in their day, those cases nevertheless reflected a reasonably certain and predicable development in the law, with the obligations of lenders helpfully mapped out. Significantly for the present, unconscionability under this body of law was not—in my respectful view—left to be determined by reference to only generalized notions of unfairness.[24]

Amadio concerned contracting parties subject to a special disability, of which the lender was aware, enlivening the lender's obligation to ensure the transaction was properly explained. *Garcia* concerned a wife giving a guarantee of her husband's borrowings, from which she gained no financial benefit. That lender was obliged to ensure she understood the transaction, an instance of what was for a time colourfully termed 'sexually transmitted debt'.

21 (1992) 177 CLR 292, 319.
22 *Macfarlane v Tayside Health Board* [2000] 2 AC 59, 82.
23 (1998) 194 CLR 395.
24 Cf J Pascoe, 'Women's Guarantees and All-moneys Clause', (2004) 4(2) *Queensland University of Technology Law and Justice Journal* 245, 246.

Those decisions were modern expressions of long-standing authority: in the former case, *Blomley v Ryan*,[25] and for the latter, *Yerkey v Jones*.[26] They exemplified the incremental development of the common law. *Amadio* has attracted the commendation of Lord Peter Millett, in the course of his criticism of *Barclays Bank plc v O'Brien*,[27] because it 'substituted an inappropriate bright line rule for a proper investigation of the facts' and 'failed the vulnerable in the process'. His Lordship preferred the alternative *Amadio* approach of relieving against unconscionable bargains.[28]

Those cases bring me to *Bridgewater v Leahy*. The facts in brief were these. Bill York sold grazing land to his nephew Neil, and Neil's wife, for almost $700,000, and by deed forgave the payment of all but $150,000 of that price. Neil had suggested he purchase the property for $150,000. The Yorks had four daughters and no sons. Neil had worked on Bill's land for many years. Bill was anxious the land not be broken up after his death, and was deeply committed to Neil. When he entered into the sale transaction, Bill, although 84 years old, was medically certified as capable of making decisions about his personal affairs. His will predated the sale by three years. He was then of full testamentary capacity. He died a year after the sale. In his will, Bill gave Neil the option to purchase certain properties for $200,000. That property included the land sold under the later transaction. Neil exercised the option. The residuary estate was left to the daughters. Bill's widow and his daughters made a family provision application, but it was dismissed for want of prosecution. On the face of things, Bill acted with rational determination to achieve what he wanted, and without connivance Neil accepted the role of beneficiary. The regrettable 'victims' were Bill's widow and daughters, whom he had chosen, in his testamentary role, to leave in a disadvantaged position.

The majority of the Justices held it was unconscientious for Neil and his wife to retain the full benefit of the deed of forgiveness. The relevant 'special disadvantage' identified by the majority was not within the traditional category. That includes poverty, sickness, infirmity of body or mind, drunkenness, illiteracy.[29] Here it was essentially Bill's emotional dependence on Neil: 'he had an "enormous affection" for Neil (and) "fully trusted him"'.[30]

> The relationship between Bill and Neil meant that, when Neil raised the question of using the proceeds of sale of the Injune land (which yielded the $150,000 Neil offered for the transferred land), they were meeting on unequal

25 (1956) 99 CLR 362.
26 (1939) 63 CLR 649.
27 [1994] 1 AC 180.
28 P Millett, 'Equity's Place in the Law of Commerce' (1998) 114 *LQR* 214, 200.
29 See *Blomley v Ryan*, above n 25, 405.
30 *Ibid*, 492.

> terms. Neil took advantage of this position to obtain a benefit through a grossly improvident transaction on the part of his uncle.[31]

The circumstances founding the conclusion of unconscionability in this case have caused commentators to question whether the court pushed the doctrine too far. Dr Dietrich[32] asked 'was the unconscionability finding driven by the substantively and objectively unequal outcome, as opposed to any obvious procedural unfairness?' Another commentator, Anne Finlay,[33] suggests a 'weakening' of the test for special disability. She argues that:

> reduced to its simplest, in *Bridgewater v Leahy* it seems we had an elderly man, though not one lacking in critical faculties, with a long-term close business and personal relationship with a nephew. Because the nephew suggested a course of behaviour, a sale at undervalue, which ultimately benefited the nephew and because there was no independent advice, but evidence that it would not have made any difference, the majority found unconscionable conduct. Yet the transaction achieved exactly what the man wanted: his farming property to stay in family hands without being broken up and undervalue alone has never been the basis for equitable intervention. Additionally the nephew had sold his own land, something which his uncle had asked him to do. With respect, the majority decision emphasises the fact of the relationship rather than clear evidence of an abuse of that relationship. It is tempting to suggest that the majority disapproved of the transaction because the man's immediate family did not benefit as much as they might have done had the gift not apparently put some of the property beyond a challenge to the will under the family provision legislation.[34]

There is risk that, as with a view endorsed by the High Court in *ABC v Lenah Game Meats Pty Ltd*,[35] 'too broadly defined [unconscionability] may become, in the words of Professor Julius Stone, a "category of meaningless reference"'. One is reminded of Sir Anthony Mason's observation in 1994 that

> the quest for a precise definition which identifies the characteristics of the fiduciary relationship, and other relationships which attract equitable relief, continues without evident sign of success.[36]

31 *Ibid*, 493.

32 Above n 6, 116.

33 A Finlay, 'Can We See the Chancellor's Footprint?: *Bridgewater v Leahy*' (1999) 14 *Journal of Contract Law* 265.

34 See also T Cockburn, 'The Boundaries of Unconscionability and Equitable Intervention: *Bridgewater v Leahy* in the High Court' (2000) 8 *Australian Property Law Journal* 143; P Wilson, 'Unconscionability and Fairness in Australian Equitable Jurisprudence' (2004) 11 *Australian Property Law Journal* 1; and P Vines, 'Challenging the Testator's Mind by Challenging Lifetime Transactions: *Bridgewater v Leahy* as Backdoor Probate Law?' (2003) 10 *Australian Property Law Journal* 53.

35 (2001) 208 CLR 199, 245.

36 A Mason, 'The Place of Equity and Equitable Remedies in the Contemporary Common Law World' (1994) 110 *LQR* 238.

The uncertainty thrown up by *Bridgewater v Leahy* is from one viewpoint unsurprising, in that, of the nine judges involved from trial to High Court appeal, four found unconscionability, whereas five did not.

Another aspect of *Bridgewater v Leahy* that is of possibly greater fascination is what flowed from the finding of unconscionability. The court remitted the proceeding to the Supreme Court of Queensland for it to determine, effectively, how much more than $150,000 in the overall context Neil should have paid for the land, while allowing for Bill's legitimate wish to benefit Neil by his will, in context of the reasonable claims of the widow and daughters on the estate. The majority Justices specifically invited the Supreme Court[37] to give consideration to the question what provision could have been made for Bill's widow and daughters under Part 4 of the Succession Act 1981 (notwithstanding that the application had been dismissed for want of prosecution),[38] hearing further evidence as necessary.[39] The court made a complementary declaration that the deed of forgiveness had 'no effect as to the forgiveness of the amount' to be found by the Supreme Court upon the remission.

The majority's approach assumed the capacity of the court to secure 'practical justice' through readjustment of the parties' positions. Interestingly, this form of relief was not the subject of submissions from the parties. The dissenting Justices' view was[40] that:

> There would be no practical justice as between the estate of the late Bill York, on the one hand, and Neil and Beryl York on the other, in severing the 1988 transaction and simply setting aside the forgiveness of debts. That would produce practical, and substantial, injustice.

The difficulty of the complex exercise remitted to the Supreme Court is confirmed by the subsequent history of the claim. The judge to whom the case was committed (not this writer) convened a number of directions hearings with counsel for the parties. They did not produce any consensus as to what was the real issue, or the detail of any practicable means for its examination, and the parties eventually settled the claim out of court.

Yet it must be acknowledged that the relief envisaged by the majority of the Justices in the High Court was premised on well-established authority: no less than the House of Lords in *Erlanger v New Sombrero Phosphate Company*,[41] where Lord Blackburn said[42] that 'the practice has always been for a court of equity to give relief which is "practically just"'.

37 *Bridgewater v Leahy*, above n 5, 496.
38 *Ibid*, 497.
39 *Ibid*, 494.
40 *Ibid*, 473.
41 (1878) 3 App Cas 1218.
42 *Ibid*, 1278.

The lacuna is any reasonably precise delineation of how the court is to proceed, and one can readily accept Lord Blackburn's ultimate and rather discouraging conclusion,[43] that:

> from the nature of the inquiry, it must always be a question of more or less, depending on the degree of diligence which might reasonably be required, and the degree of change which has occurred, whether the balance of justice or injustice is in favour of granting the remedy or withholding it. The determination of such a question must largely depend on the turn of mind of those who have to decide, and must therefore be subject to uncertainty; but that, I think, is inherent in the nature of the inquiry.

The High Court had confronted this approach earlier than *Bridgewater v Leahy*, in *Vadasz v Pioneer Concrete (SA) Pty Ltd* (1995) 184 CLR 102, quoting with apparent approbation an observation in Story's *Commentaries on Equity Jurisprudence* that the 'interference of a court of equity is a matter of mere discretion . . .': in this context, some would say, a substantial understatement.

There are, of course, limits to what a court of equity may accomplish in these areas, and they are covered, without the need for any embellishment from me, in Meagher et al.[44] But I imagine what in the end may confound a practitioner seeking reasonable certainty when advising in the office is exemplified by the very complexity of the exercise committed to the Supreme Court upon the High Court's remission in *Bridgewater v Leahy*.[45]

The wrinkles wrought by that case aside, it must be acknowledged the High Court has resisted attempts to engraft equitable doctrines inappropriately onto other, well-established, common law landscapes.

In *Tanwar Enterprises Pty Ltd v Cauchi*,[46] the High Court rejected a contention that a vendor of real property was acting unconscionably when exercising a right to terminate a contract upon the purchaser's default in completing in accordance with an essential time stipulation (where, by the time of termination, the purchase could have completed).

The question re-emerged in *Romanos v Pentagold Investments Pty Limited*,[47] where the High Court observed

> equity does not intervene in such a case to reshape contractual relations in a form the court thinks more reasonable or fair where subsequent events have rendered the situation of one side more favourable than that of the other side.

[43] *Ibid*, 1279–80.
[44] Above n 17, 92.
[45] Cf Cook, 'Setting Aside Pre-death Dispositions: a New Approach in Probate Law' (April 1999) LIJ, 72.
[46] (2003) 217 CLR 315.
[47] (2003) 217 CLR 367, 375.

In *ACCC v Berbatis Holdings Pty Ltd*,[48] Gleeson CJ emphasized[49] that, absent exploitation of a specially disadvantaged party, the other will not behave unconscionably by robustly asserting his or her superior bargaining position. The Chief Justice said this:

> A person is not in a position of relevant disadvantage, constitutional, situational, or otherwise, simply because of inequality of bargaining power. Many, perhaps even most, contracts are made between parties of unequal bargaining power, and good conscience does not require parties to contractual negotiations to forfeit their advantages, or neglect their own interests . . . Unconscientious exploitation of another's inability, or diminished ability, to conserve his or her own interests is not to be confused with taking advantage of a superior bargaining position . . .

He spoke uncritically in this context of parties to commercial negotiations using their bargaining power to 'extract concessions from other parties', observing 'that is the stuff of ordinary commercial dealing'. On one view it is odd the arguable reach of equity has meant such confirmations are necessary.

The quest for certainty is exemplified in the UK by *Royal Bank of Scotland plc v Etridge*,[50] where the British courts' 'concern for future certainty . . . (drove) them to the incredibly precise and detailed requirements of Lord Nicholls' speech . . . '.[51] Their Lordships thereby revised the position they had considered responsible only eight years earlier in *Barclays Bank plc v O'Brien*. Time will tell whether the consequences of any uncertainty in Australian law warrant further, even drastic revision by the High Court of the positions presently established in our relevant jurisprudence.

The late Peter Birks, remembered with respect by many attending this conference, quoted a view expressed by Bagnell J in 'Equity in the Modern Law: an Exercise in Taxonomy'.[52] Bagnell J was a Judge of the Family Division in England for six years until his death in 1976. As a matter of presently irrelevant history, I note that, like Cockburn CJ, from whom I quoted at the outset of this paper, Bagnell J died in office.

The complete passage in the judgment of Sir William Bagnell from which Professor Birks quoted reads as follows:

> In any individual case the application of these propositions may produce a result which appears unfair. So be it; in my view, that is not an injustice. I am convinced that in determining rights, particularly property rights, the only justice that can be attained by mortals, who are fallible and are not omniscient, is justice according to law; the justice which flows from the application of sure

48 (2003) 214 CLR 51.
49 *Ibid*, 64–5.
50 [2002] 2 AC 773.
51 Wilson, above n 34, 8.
52 (1996) 26 WALR 1, 23 (cf *Cowcher v Cowcher* (1972) 1 WLR 425, 430).

> and settled principles to proved or admitted facts. So in the field of equity the length of the Chancellor's foot has been measured or is capable of measurement. This does not mean that equity is past childbearing; simply that its progeny must be legitimate—by precedent out of principle. It is well that this should be so; otherwise, no lawyer could safely advise on his client's title and every quarrel would lead to a law suit.

I respectfully adopt that as an appealingly expressed yardstick.

4

The Role of Policy in the Law of Obligations

THE HON JUSTICE SUSAN KIEFEL

JUSTICE CARDOZO, IN his famous series of lectures on the judicial process, stated that 'the final cause of law is the welfare of society.[1] The term 'social welfare', he explained, includes what is commonly spoken of as public policy, the good of the collective body. In this paper I observe the important role that the doctrine of public policy has played in the development of the common law and enquire into its present status in the eyes of judges. Recent medical negligence cases in England and Australia involving claims by parents for the cost of raising and maintaining an unplanned child (*Macfarlane v Tayside Health Board*[2] and *Cattanach v Melchior*[3]) and by a disabled child against the doctor advising her mother (*Harriton v Stephens*[4]) bring into sharp focus issues about its place in law today.

The use, conscious or unconscious, of public policy by the courts was regarded by Professor Winfield[5] as pervading the whole legal system at a time when law had to be made and there was neither much statute nor case law to assist. Long before equity was a separate system, judges had regard to what was to the benefit of the public, although no one talked about public policy. By the fifteenth and sixteenth centuries chancellors were drawing upon it, but their conceptions of public policy were more conscious. Coke, in his writings on Littleton, may be taken to say that the law prefers the public good to the private good and elsewhere implies that public policy is concerned with wrongful acts which are 'repugnant

1 BN Cardozo, *The Nature of the Judicial Process* (New Haven, CT, Yale University Press, 1921), 66, 72.

2 [2000] 2 AC 59.

3 (2003) 215 CLR 1.

4 [2006] HCA 15.

5 PH Winfield, 'Public Policy in the English Common Law' (1928) 24 *Harvard Law Review* 76.

to the state',[6] a phrase which Professor Winfield observes was later equated by Lord Chief Baron Pollock, in *Egerton v Brownlow*,[7] with the phrase 'against the public good'.[8] In the seventeenth and eighteenth centuries, he says, the courts were advancing by somewhat uncertain steps to a narrower application of public policy, although not to a more definite conception of it.[9] In the eighteenth and nineteenth centuries it came to be applied to deny contractual or tortious remedies that were 'repugnant to the interests of the State', 'injurious to the interests of the public' or 'against the public benefit'.[10] *Mitchell v Reynolds*[11], in 1711, was a landmark case in which it was applied to a contract in restraint of trade.[12]

In the early nineteenth century doubts were expressed about the soundness of the use of public policy. Professor Winfield explains:[13]

> In the old days the idea was so transparent, that, although it was all pervasive, it obscured no one's vision. But when it had condensed to something much less nebulous and much more visible, the judges began to wonder where it was going to lead them.

Ideas were fermenting about public policy and lawyers were beginning to see that it needed some sort of 'technical shape'.[14] In 1824 Mr Justice Burrough let loose the historic expression about policy being an 'unruly horse'.[15] Not previously under serious attack, by 1853 public policy had to 'fight for its life'[16] and was saved by the House of Lords in *Egerton v Brownlow*, the 'great case'[17] concerning the importuning of advisers of the Crown to secure the bestowal of honours by the Crown. In that case even the judges who were opposed to its use recognised its existence. The statement which prevailed in the House was that of Lord Chief Baron Pollock, holding that to discard public welfare from consideration was an abdication of office. It was part of the common law that in a new and unprecedented case the public good should prevail.[18]

6 *Ibid*, 82.
7 (1853) 4 HL Cas 1.
8 Above n 5, 83.
9 *Ibid*, 84, referring to WSM Knight, 'Public Policy in English Law' (1922) 38 *LQR* 207, 208–10.
10 *Ibid*, 210.
11 (1711) 1 P Wms 181.
12 Winfield, above n 5, 85.
13 *Ibid*, 86.
14 *Ibid*, 87.
15 Which Winfield notes is said to have been borrowed from Chief Justice Hobart (*ibid*, 87).
16 *Ibid*, 88.
17 As described by McHugh and Gummow JJ in *Cattanach v Melchior* (2003) 215 CLR 1, [62].
18 Above n 7, 148–51.

Mr Knight, in his article on public policy, says that all but one of the judges in *Egerton v Brownlow* treated the term 'public policy' as synonymous with 'policy of the law'.[19] The House of Lords held that the expressions had different meanings and that of public policy was much more extensive. Professor Winfield appears to approve the distinction, but doubts that the reported cases bear it out. He accepts the whole topic of public policy is elusive. He described it as 'a principle of judicial legislation or interpretation founded upon the needs of the community'.[20] In the view of Justice Holmes, every important legal principle is traceable to views of public policy.[21]

The influence of public policy upon the law was analysed by Lord Haldane in *Rodriguez v Speyer Bros*[22] and summarised by Professor Winfield.[23] It takes three shapes. There are rules originally based on public policy which have become so crystallised that only a statute can alter them, instancing the rule against perpetuities. There are cases in which it has not crystallised and depends on no legal principle, but is accepted as a matter of fact. Its application here depends upon the circumstances of each case, for example, cases concerning the legality of wagers. The third type of case is that in which public policy has partially precipitated itself into legal rule but has remained subject to its moulding influence. Here Winfield refers to covenants in restraint of trade, where the principle is that trade must not be fettered, but what was a fetter 150 years ago may not be so now.

Public policy, in whatever form it takes, is necessarily variable. As Winfield observes, it has altered with respect to restraint of trade, to accommodate changed economic theories and religious toleration (although he notes it has narrowed regarding political morality). Its variability, he accepts, has been criticised, but he sees it as a 'stone in the edifice' of the doctrine and not 'a missile to be flung at it'.[24] He then turns to what is perhaps the most difficult question: how is public policy evidenced? He asks: if it is so variable, if it depends upon the welfare of the community at any given time, how are the courts to ascertain it? The answer can be no more than that it may be difficult, but that does not absolve the courts from what the common law regards as a duty.[25]

I do not think it could be doubted that a certain amount of secrecy has attended the application of public policy. Justice Holmes described it as 'the secret root from which the law draws all the juices of life' and acknowledged that it involved 'considerations which judges most rarely

19 Above n 9, 216.
20 Above n 5, 92.
21 OW Holmes, *The Common Law* (Boston, MA Little, Brown & Company, 1881), 35–6.
22 [1919] AC 59, 77–81.
23 Above n 5, 96.
24 *Ibid*, 95.
25 *Ibid*, 96–7.

mention, and always with an apology'.[26] Lord Radcliffe, speaking extrajudicially in 1967, may have approved such an approach. His Lordship said that, whilst there could be no argument about the creative nature of the judicial role[27], '[p]ersonally, I think that judges will serve the public interest better if they keep quiet about their legislative function'. He also said:

> The Judge who shows his hand, who advertises what he is about, may indeed show that he is a strong spirit, unfettered by the past; but I doubt very much whether he is not doing more harm to general confidence in the law as a constant, safe in the hands of the judges, than he is doing good to the law's credit as a set of rules nicely attuned to the sentiments of the day.

Professor Atiyah sees in these remarks a gentle rebuke to Lord Denning[28] and cites similar views expressed by other judges. Whether or not judges generally have shared these views, it may be doubted that the reasoning towards a decision as to what is in the public benefit has not always been exposed.

The cases speak of public benefit, but there is no positive standard applied to which matters affecting public policy are relevant. The application of public policy is negative, usually to deny an interest or a remedy if it is seen as injurious to the public. The assumption upon which it proceeds is that judges will be able to discern the potential for injury to the public good, or a value or standard held by most people in society which may be affected or contradicted by the courts' recognition of an action or a right to relief. Whilst it might also be assumed that judges are not likely to be radical in their views, they may not always accord with those held generally by society or those views may not be identifiable. Justice Kirby, in *Cattanach v Melchior*,[29] instances the opinion expressed by Lord Denning, in a divorce case,[30] that a vasectomy was irresponsible and injurious to the public interest. The other members of the court were quick to distance themselves from these remarks.

Considerations relevant to public policy may include the necessary and proper relationship between citizen and government or concern the authority of the court. In *Wilkinson v Osborne*,[31] Justice Isaacs held void a contract with members of parliament to put pressure on the government to purchase land. In such cases judges may be expected to feel less hesitancy in identifying the relevant values. Other considerations which may be seen to operate in the cases may be explained as based in economics. The

26 Above n 21.
27 CJ Radcliffe, *Not in Feather Beds: Some Collected Papers* (London, Hamish Hamilton, 1968), 265.
28 PS Atiyah, 'Judges and Policy' (1980) 15 *Israel Law Review* 346, 357.
29 Above n 3, [103].
30 *Bravery v Bravery* [1954] 1 WLR 1169.
31 (1915) 21 CLR 89.

approach of the law to some aspects of illegality of contract and equity's refusal to provide a remedy, where advantage is taken of a person in a position of relative disadvantage, have a moral underpinning.

Public policy in contract law has developed largely to a set of rules and principles, and it inheres in equity. In tort law, which remains more fluid, its application is more obvious. In cases involving pure economic loss, the courts have sought the means by which recovery could be limited. The need to do so, based upon concerns of the community bearing indeterminate liability for indeterminate amounts, is itself a policy decision. The means utilised to achieve it, such as the requirement of proximity of relationships have been said to be influenced by the courts' assessment of community standards and demands.[32]

Chief Justice Spigelman, in his judgment in the New South Wales Court of Appeal in *Harriton v Stephens*,[33] was in no doubt that the foundations of the law of negligence were ethical and that a duty of care must reflect values generally, or at least widely, held in the community. The ethical foundations of the neighbour principle may be found in alternative sources—for the religious-minded in the New Testament and for the secular-minded in Immanuel Kant's categorical imperative. The delineation of legal duties has never been derived from an exclusively legal analysis, he said.

Lord Steyn, in *Macfarlane v Tayside Health Board*,[34] accepted that to explain decisions denying a remedy by saying there is no foreseeable loss, no causative loss or no reasonable restitution was to 'resort to unrealistic and formalistic propositions which mask the real reasons for the decision'. He saw no difficulty with the use by judges of their sense of a moral answer to a question. Such an approach, he considered, has been a great shaping force of the common law. However, what may count in a situation of difficulty and uncertainty is not the subjective view of the judge, but what the judge reasonably believes that the ordinary citizen would regard as right. His Lordship posed the question before the House, to hypothetical commuters on the Underground, as: 'Should the parents of an unwanted but healthy child be able to sue the doctor or hospital for compensation or equivalent to the cost of bringing up the child for the years of his or her minority . . .?' He thought they would say 'No' and that the reason for their response would be 'an inarticulate premise as to what is morally acceptable'.[35] Lord Millett, for his part, accepted that moral considerations may play a part in both legal policy and public policy, which he saw as different. Legal policy had regard to a search for justice,

32 *Bryan v Maloney* (1995) 182 CLR 609, 618.
33 (2004) 59 NSWLR 694, [17].
34 Above n 2, 82.
35 *Ibid.*

what was fair and reasonable and necessary to maintain the coherence of the law.[36]

No member of the House of Lords approached the case by reference to public policy, not even Lord Steyn. Indeed, its use was expressly disavowed. Lord Steyn preferred to base his decision upon notions of distributive justice and, with Lord Slynn of Hadley and Lord Hope, held that the claim for costs of caring for a healthy normal child was not fair, just or reasonable. Lord Clyde held that it went beyond reasonable restitution and Lord Millett concluded that the law regarded the birth as a blessing and not a detriment, and the benefits should be regarded as outweighing any loss. Each of the decisions was said to be arrived at by reference to legal policy.

A few years later, in *Cattanach v Melchior*, the High Court of Australia, by a narrow majority,[37] permitted recovery of the costs of raising an unplanned child. It is not without significance that the concessions made about the existence of a duty, its breach and some damage was regarded by the majority as limiting the enquiry to the financial consequences of the birth. The judges in the minority,[38] however, insisted that the damages in question were based upon or involved the parent–child relationship and an assessment of the value of the life of the child or its expense. Justice Hayne alone attributed his approach to considerations of public policy in the sense earlier discussed, the values held by society and the public good. Whilst the judgments contain references to policy, it is of a legal kind. The values spoken of, some of which may be thought to reflect those of society, are those recognised by, or in some way connected to, the law.

Justice Hayne identified two characteristics in the arguments against allowing damages for the cost of bringing up the child. In addition to expanding the field for debate beyond the economic consequences of pregnancy and childbirth, they involve values which it is said are society's values. Those values relate to the worth to be ascribed to the life of an individual and the worth associated with the parent–child relationship.[39] In his Honour's view, public policy forecloses an inquiry into the value of the child; it affirms the desirable relationship of parent and child; and it prevents the parent from harming the child by asserting that burdens outweigh the benefits.[40]

The values identified by Justice Heydon were similar to those referred to by Justice Hayne, but they were said to be embedded in the law and the policy to which they related was the policy of the law. It was the law's

36 *Ibid.*
37 McHugh, Gummow, Kirby and Callinan JJ.
38 Gleeson CJ, Hayne and Heydon JJ.
39 Above n 3, [243].
40 Above n 3, [248], [255]–[259].

policy that the birth of a child is not to be discounted or devalued, for the reason that it is life. The reasons for that policy were that a new life in a family is incapable of estimation in monetary terms; an award of damages would have the result, alien to the goals of a legal system, of encouraging parents to exaggerate matters relating to the child (an 'odious spectacle', said his Honour); the necessary process of valuation smacks of 'commodification of the child'[41]; and it is wrong to place a value on human life or the expense of a human life.[42] The policy of the law, of which his Honour spoke, was said not to depend upon religious values. In his Honour's view, it underpinned much of the common law. There were assumptions made by the law about children; the duties of parents and family life, what his Honour called 'key values'.

The other judge in the minority, the Chief Justice, saw the question as a purely legal one, although it had an ethical dimension. The answer to it was provided by reasons of legal policy relating to indeterminate and imprecise claims.[43] The reason the Chief Justice gave for the insurmountable difficulty in the assessment of damages was the same as the other minority judges: a human relationship is involved and it is neither reasonable nor possible to assign an economic value to it.[44] His Honour rejected an approach which treated the loss as merely consequential, for the reason that this would mean treating human reproduction as a kind of personal injury.[45] Although no mention was made of public policy, the Chief Justice acknowledged that the case raised the question whether the law should treat the creation of the relationship of parent and child as actionable damage. His Honour did not think that either the parties to it or the community would regard it as purely financial. It was a human relationship regarded as fundamental to society. This could be seen by reference to domestic law and international treaties.[46]

Justices McHugh and Gummow, in the majority, were concerned to distinguish between the 'policy of the law' and 'public policy', but did not accept as accurate the distinction drawn by Lord Steyn in *Macfarlane v Tayside Health Board* between 'legal policy' and 'public policy'.[47] The term 'policy of the law', used by Mr Justice Creswell in *Egerton v Brownlow*, was to be preferred. In the passage quoted, his Honour refers to some aspects of illegality of contracts being attributed to public policy, whereas they violated policies which could be seen to be part of the common law. Their Honours disapproved of public policy where it was

41 A term used by Hale LJ in *Parkinson v St James Seacroft University Hospital NHS Trust* [2002] QB 266, 293.
42 Above n 3, [353].
43 *Ibid*, [4]–[6].
44 *Ibid*, [38].
45 *Ibid*, [97].
46 *Ibid*, [38].
47 *Ibid*, [73].

'inherently fluid, adjusted to the expediency of the day, the proper subject of the minister or the member of the legislature', as Lord Radcliffe had described it.[48] His Lordship would expect the law to be indifferent to such considerations, referring to a 'system of values . . . less mutable than this'. Their Honours approved the approach of Justice Isaacs in *Wilkinson v Osborne*.[49] There his Honour had said:[50]

> In my opinion the 'public policy' which a court is entitled to apply as a test of validity to a contract is in relation to some definite and governing principle which the community as a whole has already adopted either formally by law or tacitly by its general course of corporate life, and which the Courts of the country can therefore recognise and enforce. The court is not a legislator: it cannot initiate the principle; it can only state or formulate it if it already exists.

Justice Isaacs went on to say that a bargain contrary to a 'social governing principle' is regarded as prejudicial to the State and contrary to 'public policy'. It is sometimes called 'policy of the law'.

Their Honours posed two questions by reference to *Wilkinson v Osborne*. The first was whether the underlying values respecting the importance of human life, the stability of the family unit and the nurture of infant children are an essential aspect of the corporate welfare of the community. This was answered in the affirmative. The second was whether there was a general recognition in the community that those values demand that there be no award of damages for the cost to the parent of rearing and maintaining a child, who would not have been born but for the negligent failure of the gynaecologist in giving advice after performing a sterilisation procedure. They said the courts could perceive no such general recognition.[51]

The other members of the majority would deny the operation of public policy considerations. Justice Callinan said that almost all of the arguments made against awarding the damages involved emotional or moral values and perceptions about what public policy is or should be. One such argument, identified by his Honour, was that it was repugnant to society to treat the birth of a child as an occasion for an award of damages and said that a judge's personal distaste for the task was insufficient reason for failing to undertake it.[52] There was no 'identifiable universal principle of public policy' that dictated a result different from that obtained by the application of legal principle, his Honour said.[53]

48 *Ibid*, [75], referring to CJ Radcliffe, *The Law and Its Compass* (London, Faber & Faber, 1961), 43–4.
49 Above n 31.
50 *Ibid*, 97.
51 Above n 3, [77].
52 *Ibid*, [292], [296].
53 *Ibid*, [299].

Justice Kirby thought that previous denials of recovery had their foundation in religious, political or social views and specific attitudes to the dignity of the human person, instancing the 'commodification' of the child argument. The 'child as a blessing' argument was another.[54] In his Honour's view, the law has no business in intruding by giving legal effect to assertions about blessings and family relationships, key values and family life.[55] The courts' concern is not with the resultant economic consequences of its decisions. His Honour regarded the judges in *Macfarlane v Tayside Health Board* to have in truth applied public policy, which he likened to 'quicksand'.[56]

The more recent case of *Harriton v Stephens* saw a claim for damages brought by a child born disabled, against the doctor who had failed to diagnose her mother as having rubella. The claim depended upon the mother, properly advised, making a decision to terminate her pregnancy. Unlike *Cattanach v Melchior*, it required the courts to decide whether a duty of care should be recognised. It might be thought to have been novel.

Chief Justice Spigelman considered the claim raised moral or ethical issues which were 'highly contestable' and 'strenuously contested'.[57] The action put in issue the value of the child's life and raised considerations relating to the sanctity of life. Since there was no widely accepted ethical principle, the Chief Justice did not consider that the law should recognise a legal duty to the child.

This approach did not commend itself to the High Court. In the leading judgment of the majority, that of Justice Crennan, it was held that a cause of action could not be made out because the damage claimed was not amenable to being determined by the Court by the application of legal method. A duty of care could not be articulated where the appellant could not prove the actual damage claimed.[58] The comparison necessary to found damages was simply impossible, independent of arguments about the value of life or the repugnance evoked by a claim that a life with disabilities was actionable.[59] The comparison was as between life with disability and non-existence.[60] Justice Callinan also preferred logic to policy.

Whilst not determinative of the matter, Justice Crennan's judgment did consider the value of life argument. In her Honour's view, it was 'odious and repugnant to devalue the life of a disabled person by suggesting that such a person would have been better off not to have been born into a life

54 *Ibid*, [141].
55 *Ibid*, [151].
56 *Ibid*, [158].
57 Above n 33, [24].
58 Above n 4, [225].
59 *Ibid*, [254].
60 *Ibid*, [252].

with disabilities'.[61] It may be recalled that a similar expression of abhorrence had been used by Justice Heydon in *Cattanach v Melchior.* Like Justice Heydon, her Honour said that it expressed not a societal value, but rather one which was embedded in the common law, which saw all humans as valuable.

The correctness of an approach which applies legal principle cannot be doubted. This assumes that something approaching the standard of principle is available. It is, however, as well to bear in mind the observations of Chief Justice Spigelman in *Harriton v Stephens*[62] that judges have become so accustomed to finding legal 'duties' by the application of principles expressed in legal analysis that the determination of duty has come to have the appearance of a purely legal decision. There has been created a false appearance of intellectual autonomy.

Three judges in *Cattanach v Melchior* considered that public policy had informed earlier decisions but had not been acknowledged. Justice Callinan said that he could not help observing 'that the repeated disavowal in the cases of recourse to public policy is not always convincing'.[63] Justice Hayne said that, despite the express disavowal of reliance upon public policy in *McFarlane v Tayside Health Board*, the decision must be seen as affected by considerations of what would best reflect society's needs and society's wishes.[64] Whilst increasing attention had been given to public policy in the law of torts, the courts have frequently failed to articulate policy reasons. Either the effect of a determination, such as deterrence or loss-spreading, has been elevated to a reason for refusal, or the true reasons have been observed behind expressions such as 'fair just and reasonable'.[65] Justice Kirby was even prepared to attribute a motive. In his Honour's view, judges had attempted to 'objectify' the foundation for their arguments to avoid the appearance of an expression of their personal opinion.[66] Judges have no authority to depart from basic doctrine, his Honour said, and certainly could not do so

> on the footing of their personal religious beliefs or 'moral' assessments concealed in an inarticulate premise dressed up, and described, as legal principle or legal policy.[67]

His Honour's criticisms would not appear to be confined to members of other courts.

An approach which hesitates to apply public policy considerations and seeks a solution derived only from the law cannot be criticised. One would

61 *Ibid*, [258].
62 Above n 33, [19].
63 Above n 3, [291].
64 *Ibid*, [217], [219].
65 *Ibid*, [238].
66 *Ibid*, [135].
67 *Ibid*, [137].

not, however, expect the law to be able to provide a direct answer with respect to claims not previously considered. Novel cases have been regarded as the province of public policy. There is no recognition in the judgments that the claims were novel. That may be because the courts were able to find something already recognised by the law which helped to provide the answer, albeit not having the status of principle.

The approaches which deny the application of public policy in the judgments in *Cattanach v Melchior* may be seen to fall into three categories. The first ignores public policy as necessary or relevant to the decision, but at the same time invokes values which might be thought to be those of society and reflecting a moral standpoint. Their invocation is not without relevance. They are used to answer the question posed, which may be seen to shift from whether the law can recognise a claim to whether it should. They are explained as values embedded in the law, underlying the common law or recognised by it. The attribution of a legal characteristic to values is continued in *Harriton v Stephens*. This approach raises the question whether what is involved is entirely the application of legal principle. The use of public policy is not canvassed, so this approach leaves unanswered the question as to the circumstances in which it might be operative.

The second category is perhaps more problematic for the future of public policy. It recognises some form of it, but would prefer to associate it with a view of the law. It would appear to reshape it and constrain its role. The court's legislative role, about which Professor Winfield spoke, is to be limited to some established social principle. Inferentially that is not current public opinion, but that was never said to be relevant to public policy. It is perhaps some standard which is definite and interchangeable and already in operation within the community. There can be no argument that standards or values derived from the larger part of society have been relevant to public policy considerations. It may be that 'social principle' does not include a moral standpoint. The term does not suggest it. The examples given of it in the case are to subjects, expressed in general terms, that are unlikely to produce the response that a moral viewpoint might.

The third category contains two approaches which reason from an opposition to moral viewpoints. The more extreme would appear to deny the relevance of any moral standpoint to the purposes of the law, even those which might be said to be held generally within society. It would appear to deny a judge the role of identifying them. This approach may amount to a negation of public policy in the law. The other approach would apply it to values only universally held and does not recognise any such values. The absence of an agreed standard might provide the basis for the law's refusal, as Chief Justice Spigelman suggested, albeit in connection with the recognition of a duty of care. The emphasis in that approach is upon a legal entitlement to damages which follows upon concessions made on the appeal.

It may be that if the appeal in *Cattanach v Melchior* had taken a different shape, and if some of the arguments against allowing the claim were less emotionally charged, there may have been more frank discussion about the use the courts will or will not make of public policy. As it is, the cases may raise more questions than they answer. Even if there is no suggestion of assessments of the public good as relevant, there remain expressions of what may be repugnant to society, expressions of values or of moral or ethical standards, although given a legal character. Many social values have a role with respect to some of the more difficult questions which may arise, in an age where humanity itself is the subject of exploitation. Will they be narrowed to a social principle already in use, or will a lack of such a principle result in the law declining an extension of liability? It may, however, be discerned that the courts are striving for purely legally derived solutions and this may leave little room for the application of traditional notions of public policy. There may be a number of reasons for this shift in approach, not least being a desire to avoid a legislative role, which is of course inherent in public policy, and which has drawn severe criticism of the courts in more recent times. It may be that if public policy was fighting for its life in *Egerton v Brownlow*, it is now on life support.

Part II

Performance

5

Substitutionary Damages

STEPHEN A SMITH*

IN A TYPICAL private law action the claimant alleges that she has suffered a loss at the defendant's hands. This loss can be described in two ways. First, the loss may be described as the loss of the very 'thing' that was damaged, destroyed, lost, taken or not provided as a result of the defendant's breach—for example, a particular piece of property or a service. Thus a claimant whose car was destroyed by the defendant is likely to complain that she has 'lost' her car. Alternatively (or in addition), the loss may be described as the loss of the abstract value of the thing that was damaged, destroyed, lost, taken or not provided as a result of the defendant's breach. Thus a claimant whose car was destroyed may complain that she has lost the pleasure she would have enjoyed by using the car or the income she would have made by reselling it.

At first blush, these two ways of describing loss appear to fit neatly with the basic distinction in the law of remedies between specific relief and damages. Specific relief, such as an order of specific performance or an injunction, appears designed to ensure that the claimant obtains (or does not lose) the very thing that she lost (or will lose in future) as a result of the defendant's breach. An order that a vendor specifically perform his obligation to deliver goods ensures that the claimant obtains the very goods promised under the contract. By contrast, an order to pay damages appears designed to ensure that the plaintiff obtains the abstract value of the thing that was lost. The claimant does not receive the thing she owned or was promised, but is instead awarded money—an abstract mark of value. Thus, where goods are delivered late, the claimant will be awarded a monetary sum calculated to equal the value, to the claimant, of timely delivery.

But on closer inspection the picture is more complicated. In particular, many damage awards appear to be set not at the value of the claimant's loss, but at the cost of repairing, replacing or obtaining a substitute for

* Faculty of Law, McGill University. I would like to thank Ruth Sefton-Green and Lionel Smith for their comments on an earlier version of this essay.

whatever was damaged, destroyed, lost, taken or not provided (hereafter 'lost').[1] In a tort action for damage to goods, for example, the claimant is typically awarded a sum equal to the cost of repairing or replacing the goods. Similarly, in a contractual action for non-delivery of goods, the buyer is typically awarded a sum equal to the cost of purchasing similar goods elsewhere. Of course, in many cases the cost of repair, etc can be regarded as a measure of the value of the thing that was lost. Most of the things we own or contract to buy are used to realise benefits that we value more highly than whatever sums of money are required to purchase these things. That is why we buy them. But, since similar benefits could be realised by using substitutes, the abstract value of the things we own is usually equal to the cost of purchasing such substitutes. A claimant who is awarded the cost of cure obtains a sum of money sufficient to purchase something that has the same value as whatever was lost. But in some cases, the cost of cure is greater than the value of the loss. It may cost hundreds of thousands of dollars to repair a trivial defect in a newly constructed building.[2] Similarly, the cost of replacing a damaged chattel may far outweigh whatever value the owner placed on the chattel.

This distinction in the law of damages between what may be labelled the 'value of loss' and 'cost of cure'[3] methods of assessment is well known; however, the orthodox understanding is that these are two methods of achieving the same objective—ensuring that the defendant compensates the claimant for her loss.[4] Unlike 'adjectival' damages (punitive damages, nominal damages, restitutionary damages, etc), both the value of loss and cost of cure methods are found in textbooks on damages as part of the discussion of ordinary damages. Both methods are assumed to be subject to the same general conditions, such as the remoteness and mitigation principles. The orthodox view thus supports the idea that the distinction between specific relief and damages reflects the distinction between the loss of a specific thing and the loss of the value of a thing.

The argument of this paper is that the orthodox view is wrong; more specifically, the argument is that the orthodox view that cost of cure

1 Burrows, *Remedies for Torts and Breach of Contract* (2004, 3rd edn), 209–24, 232–46; Waddams, *The Law of Damages* (2003, 4th edn), 3–82, 105–18, 133–5, 144–6; *McGregor on Damages* (2003, 17th edn), 685–7, 772–4, 857–9, 884–9, 1059–62; *Benjamin's Sale of Goods* (4th edn), 833–4; *Hudson's Building and Engineering Contracts* (1994, 11th edn), 1036–7.

2 See the cases cited below in n 11.

3 'Cost of cure' is sometimes understood to refer only to awards calculated at the cost of repairing a defective contractual performance. The meaning adopted in this essay is intentionally broader.

4 See, eg McGregor, above n 1, 12: 'The object of an award of damages is to give the claimant compensation for the loss or injury he has suffered'. The conventional view was affirmed by Lord Mustill in *Ruxley Electronics and Construction Ltd v Forsyth* [1995] 3 WLR 118, 127, when he said, in reference to cost of cure and value of loss awards, 'There are not two alternative measures of damages, at opposite poles, but only one; namely the loss truly suffered by the promisee'.

awards are ordinary damage awards is wrong.[5] A value of loss award can reasonably be described as a 'compensatory award': it is an order that the defendant compensate the claimant for the loss caused by the defendant's breach. Cost of cure awards are different: their aim is to undo or avoid (so far as this can be done) the tangible change in the claimant's world that will be, or has already been, brought about by the defendant's breach. Cost of cure awards aim to put claimants in the actual (not metaphorical) position they would have been had the breach not happened; they do not compensate for losses, but instead eliminate or prevent them (at least, as much as they can be eliminated or prevented). Though not identical to specific relief, the aim of cost of cure awards is closer to that of specific relief than the aim of ordinary (value of loss) damage awards. Cost of cure awards are a close substitute for what the defendant should have done (that is, perform his primary duty); as such, they may be called 'substitutionary specific relief damages' or, more simply, 'substitutionary damages'.

The paper is divided into two parts. The first part explains why the traditional view that cost of cure and value of loss awards share the same objective cannot be sustained. In the second part the idea of substitutionary damages is introduced, situated within the broader framework of private law duties, and used to explain the basic rules governing cost of cure awards as well as certain features of the law governing specific relief. The relationship between substitutionary damages and the mitigation principle is also addressed in the second part. Throughout, the discussion is limited to cases involving the loss of property or services.[6]

[5] Versions of this argument have been made before, notably by Coote, 'Contract Damages, *Ruxley* and the Performance Interest' [1997] *CLaw Journal* 537; McKendrick, 'The Common Law at Work: The Saga of *Alfred McAlpine Construction Ltd v Panatown Ltd* (2003) 3 *Oxford University Commonwealth Law Journal* 145; Eisenberg, 'Actual and Virtual Specific Performance, The Theory of Efficient Breach, and the Indifference Principle in Contract Law' (2005) 93 *California LR* 975; and Webb, 'Performance and Compensation: An Analysis of Contract Damages and Contractual Obligation' (2006) 26 *OJLS* 41. The arguments advanced by each of these authors differ in important respects from that advanced in this essay, most notably in focusing exclusively on damages for breach of contract. The latter point applies also to a version of this argument that I advanced in *Contract Theory* (2004), 420–5. The treatment in Waddams, above n 1, of what the author calls damages for 'loss of property' and damages for 'loss of use of property' anticipates many of the arguments in this essay. The view of damages defended in this essay also draws heavily on civilian approaches to classifying damage awards; see, eg ss 249–51 of the *BGB* (the German Civil Code).

[6] The implications of this essay's argument for damage awards in other cases, in particular personal injury cases, are discussed briefly in the conclusion.

I THE ORTHODOX VIEW: COST OF CURE AS EQUIVALENT TO VALUE OF LOSS

As already noted, the orthodox view regards both cost of cure awards and value of loss awards as ordinary damage awards. They are presented as two ways of achieving the same end. Given the obvious differences in how cost of cure and value of loss awards are actually calculated, this view needs to be defended. There appear to be three justifications that have been or could be offered for the traditional view. Each assumes that the general aim of damages is to ensure that defendants compensate claimants for their losses, and each then interprets cost of cure awards as compensatory awards. The second of these assumptions is the focus of my remarks below.[7]

A Cost Awards as Indirect 'Specific' Compensation

Perhaps the simplest possible justification for the orthodox view supposes that the natural way to achieve the compensatory aim of damages is to order that the defendant actually replace (or repair, etc) the thing that was lost as result of her breach. Cost of cure awards do not, of course, achieve this result directly, but they are explained, on this view, as an indirect method of ensuring the claimant is able to obtain a 'compensatory' replacement for whatever was lost. Value of loss awards are thus explained as a second-best form of 'monetary' compensation, awarded only where 'specific' compensation is not possible or desired.

The difficulty with this first suggestion is that the loss that a cost of cure award is meant, in this view, to be compensation for will not exist if the award actually achieves its end. The term 'compensation' does not have a settled meaning in law or ordinary language. But whatever meaning is given to the term, it is clear that compensation must be compensation for a loss (or a harm, an injury, an infringement of a right, etc). Yet a cost of cure award, according to the explanation now being considered, is designed to ensure that the plaintiff obtains a replacement (or repair, etc) for the very thing (property, service, etc) that was lost. If the award achieves its purpose, the relevant loss will be eliminated (or prevented). The effect of the award (assuming it is used for the purpose for which, in this explanation, it is intended) is therefore that there is no loss for

[7] A fourth possible justification, suggested by Ernest Weinrib's contribution to this book, is that all damages, including value of loss damages, are a form of substitute specific relief. This argument requires more attention than can be given here, but it is suggested that, like the second and third justifications examined above, it cannot explain why the cost of cure measure is sometimes greater than the value of loss measure. If the two measures have the same rationale and are applied to the same breach, how can they lead to different sums?

which the award could then be regarded as a compensation for.[8] This does not mean that relief of this kind is inappropriate (the conclusion of this paper is exactly the opposite); the point is merely that such an order cannot plausibly be described as 'compensatory'—or, at least, it cannot be so described without adopting a radically different understanding of 'compensatory' from that normally adopted in the law and elsewhere. If ensuring that the claimant gets the property or service to which she has a right is compensation, then ordinary specific relief is also compensation.

B Cost Awards as Proxy Value Awards

A second possible justification for the orthodox view is that cost of cure awards are disguised value of loss awards. In this view, all damage awards are ultimately value of loss awards. What is distinctive about cost of cure awards is merely that they are calculated using an indirect method for assessing the value of a loss.

The process by which courts quantify losses cannot be reduced to a simple formula. But in broad terms, and confining our attention to cases where the loss is property or a service, the process may be described as one of determining what sum of money would leave the claimant indifferent between being given that sum and not suffering the loss.[9] In theory, this is a straightforward question; in practice, the difficulty is that different people value identical things differently. Claimants therefore have an incentive to exaggerate the value of their loss. The courts can, and do, ask for evidence to support the claimant's valuation, but in many cases the necessary evidence resides in the claimant's head, especially if the property or service was to be used for non-commercial purposes. Further, even in cases where in theory the valuation can be established on objective grounds (as in most commercial cases), the required evidence is often complex and contestable. The value of a property or service to a commercial party resides in the stream of future revenues or reductions in costs that it will provide.

Against this background, the cost of curing a breach (where cure is possible) is sometimes interpreted as an indirect, but practically simple, way of estimating the claimant's valuation of the relevant loss. In a competitive market, the cost of cure will usually approximate the price the

[8] The 'cure' will, of course, leave untouched whatever loss is suffered as a result of not having the use of the property or service in the period between breach and cure. Such losses are properly redressed by loss of value awards.

[9] In practice, few claimants are indifferent between damages and performance, even from a purely financial perspective, because of the time and expense involved in going to court to obtain a damage award. Note also that the approach described above assumes that the mitigation and remoteness principles are applied when identifying the loss that a value of loss award is meant to compensate for.

claimant paid or agreed to pay for the property or service (or portion thereof), adjusted for inflation. The market price thus provides a rough estimation of the claimant's valuation since it is reasonable to assume that the claimant values the property or service at least as much as she was willing to pay for it. A claimant who agrees to pay $1,000 for a chattel presumably places a monetary valuation on the chattel of at least $1,000. The claimant might have been willing to pay more than the market price for the property or service had it been necessary to do so, but this would not justify awarding over the market price since the claimant can always take her cost of cure award and use it to purchase a similar property or service in the market, thereby obtaining whatever value, etc, the original property or service would have been able to provide. The indifference point cannot be higher than the market price since the claimant would always prefer such an amount to not suffering the relevant wrong.

The cost of cure is thus often a good proxy of the value of loss. However, there is a difficulty with explaining cost of cure awards generally on this basis in that there are many cases where the cost of cure is greater than the value of loss. For example, if the claimant purchased the property or service at below the market price or under a mistaken assumption about her need for the property or service, or if her needs changed since the purchase was made, then the cost of cure may exceed the value of the loss. The 'proxy' explanation suggests that in cases of this kind the courts should refuse cost of cure awards—but courts do not do this. On the contrary, courts routinely[10] order cost of cure awards in cases where they have good evidence that the value of the loss is less than the cost of cure.[11] For example, in *Radford v De Froberville*[12] the claimant was awarded the not insubstantial cost of building a contracted-for wall between his property and an adjoining property even though the court determined that the value of the wall to the landlord was almost nil. In sale of goods cases the purchaser is routinely awarded cost of cure regardless of the value to him of the object. As Lord Moulton stated in *Williams v Agius*:[13]

> It is immaterial what the buyer is intending to do with the purchased goods. He is entitled to recover the expense of putting himself into the position of having those goods.[14]

10 The exceptions, which do not affect the point made here, are discussed below.

11 Seem eg *Radford v De Froberville* [1977] 1 WLR 1262; *Williams v Agius* [1914] AC 510; *Rodoconachi, Sons & Co v Milburn Bros* (1866) 18 QBD 67; *Mouat v Betts Motors Ltd* [1959] AC 71; *Jones v Stroud District Council* [1986] 1 WLR 1141; *Joyner v Weeks* [1891] 2 QB 31; *Mertens v Home Freeholds Co* [1921] 2 KB 526.

12 *Ibid.*

13 Above n 11, 530–31.

14 The granting of cost of cure awards in such cases cannot be explained on the basis that the two measures are equal once the non-pecuniary losses that common law courts traditionally ignore when computing value of loss are taken into account. The limits on recovery for non-pecuniary losses, which have little force today (see, eg *Farley v Skinner* [2002] AC 732)

C Cost of Cure as a Consequential Loss

A third possible justification for the orthodox view is that the cost of cure represents an ordinary consequential loss. In this view, the cost of cure is not a separate measure of damages, but rather one aspect of the loss that a value of loss award is meant to compensate for.[15] The underlying idea is that a normal consequence of the defendant's breach in cases in which it is possible to cure the loss is that the defendant will do just this—and thereby incur a loss in the form of the purchase price. For example, if a vendor fails to deliver a chattel, the buyer will normally still need the chattel and so will purchase it from someone else. The cost of cure therefore represents an actual or anticipated expense incurred as a consequence of the breach. This explanation fits neatly with the rule (discussed in more detail below) that cost of cure awards are unavailable where the claimant has not purchased an alternative and has no intention of doing so.[16] If the claimant has no intention of paying for a cure, then the cost of doing so cannot be regarded as a consequence of breach.

Again, however, this justification cannot explain why courts are willing to make cost of cure awards where the cost exceeds the value of the loss. To be sure, if the claimant has paid, or will pay, for a cure, then she has or will suffer a loss equal to the cost of purchasing that cure. But to award compensation for losses of this kind contradicts the principle that claimants may not recover for losses that they could have reasonably avoided. Choosing to purchase a substitute that costs more than it is worth is a clear example of unreasonably increasing the value of one's losses. The cost of cure in such cases may therefore be a consequence of the breach, but it is the kind of consequence that courts normally ignore when assessing loss.

were traditionally applied only to contract claims and so cannot explain cost of cure awards in tort cases. Further, many of the contract cases in which cost of cure is awarded despite exceeding the value of the loss involve commercial parties whose interests in performance are presumably entirely pecuniary. In *Radford*, above n 11, for example, the claimant was a commercial landlord who did not live on the property. Finally, in *Ruxley Electronics*, above n 11, the House of Lords, while refusing cost of cure on the facts of the case, made it clear that such awards could be made where the cost is greater than the value of the property or service, including its non-pecuniary value.

15 'If the plaintiff establishes that the contractual work has been done or will be done, then in all normal circumstances, it seems to me that he has shown that the cost of doing it is, or is part of, his loss and is recoverable as damages': *Tito v Waddell (No 2)* [1977] Ch 106, Megarry V-C at 333. See also the decisions of Lords Jauncey and Lloyd in *Ruxley Electronics*, above n 4; and Burrows, above n 1, 211.

16 *Tito v Waddell, ibid; Dodd Properties v Canterbury City Council* [1980] 1 WLR 433; *The Maersk Colombo* [2001] EWCA Civ 717; *Wigsell v School for the Indigent Blind* (1982) 8 QBD 357; *James v Hutton* [195] 1 KB 9; *Radford v De Froberville*, above n 11; *Ruxley Electronics*, above n 4.

II COST OF CURE AS SUBSTITUTIONARY DAMAGES

If the arguments of the previous section are correct, cost of cure awards cannot be explained as variants of value of loss awards. In particular, they are not compensatory awards, even if compensation is understood very broadly. In this section it will be argued that the purpose of cost of cure awards is exactly what it appears to be: to ensure that the defendant does what is necessary to place the claimant, so far as possible, in the actual (not metaphorical) position that she would have been in had the defendant performed his primary duty. Cost of cure awards are 'substitutionary specific relief damages' or, more simply, 'substitutionary damages'. Ordinary specific relief ensures that the claimant is put in the actual position she would have been had the defendant performed his primary duty by ordering that the defendant do just that—perform her primary duty. Cost of cure awards are a substitute for ordinary specific relief in cases where ordinary specific relief is not possible or desirable. They ensure that the claimant ends up in the same position she would have been in had it been possible to order ordinary specific relief, but they do this indirectly, by means of a substitute award.[17] Understood in this way, a cost of cure award is a distinct species of damages, similar in this regard to punitive or nominal damages.

The argument proceeds in two parts. The first part explains why it makes sense, from the perspective of ordinary moral understandings, to suppose that courts might order substitutionary damages. The second part argues that regarding cost of cure awards as substitutionary damages is consistent, in broad terms, with what courts actually do.

A Substitutionary Damages Give Effect to an Ordinary Moral Duty

Understood as substitutionary damages, cost of cure awards do nothing more than give legal force to an ordinary and well-recognised moral duty. Suppose that I accidentally destroy my neighbour's bicycle by carelessly running over it with my car. No one would dispute, I hope, that I have a duty to replace the bicycle. If my neighbour were away, I might fulfil this duty by purchasing a replacement myself, but in the ordinary case, I would fulfil the duty by giving my neighbour the purchase price of a replacement. If my neighbour suffered a loss because she was without a bicycle for a

[17] Although judges generally share the conventional view that cost of cure awards are a form of ordinary damages, when they actually make such awards they often affirm the view described in the text above. Thus, in a Manitoba case where cost of cure was awarded in respect of a building contract, Trueman JA stated: 'The owner of the building is, therefore, entitled to recover such damages . . . as will put him in a position to have just the building he contracted for': *Pearson-Burleigh Ltd v Pioneer Grain Co Ltd* [1933] 1 WWR 179.

period of time, I would also feel bound (I hope) to offer something in the way of compensation, but the purchase price would not be compensation for the loss suffered as a result of my actions.[18] It would be completely unacceptable to offer a lower sum on the ground that a less expensive bicycle would satisfy my neighbour's needs—and so compensate for her loss—just as well; nor would it be acceptable for my neighbour to accept my money and then use it for something else. The payment of the purchase price (though not payment by way of compensation for other losses) is made on the understanding that it will be used to replace the bicycle.

The situation is no different where the loss arises from the non-performance of a promise or agreement. Suppose that I rent my neighbour's bicycle for the summer for a price of $10. If I accidentally destroy the bicycle it is again indisputable that I have a duty to replace it (either personally or by paying for a replacement) and, again, it would be unacceptable to offer something less on the ground that my neighbour does not value her bicycle as much as the cost of a replacement. It should also be clear that my duty to obtain or pay for a replacement bicycle is different from my promissory duty. My promissory duty is to return my neighbour's actual bike in the condition I received it. It is impossible for me to fulfil this duty. My duty to pay for a replacement arises as a substitute for this duty.[19]

Of course, actual breach of contract cases are often different from the example just given in that it remains possible for the defendant to perform his primary duty, albeit at a later date than originally agreed. A vendor who fails to deliver goods on the contractually specified date can normally deliver the same goods at a later date. In such cases, a duty to pay for a reimbursement does not arise: as long as the primary duty to perform is in force, the loss that the substitute duty would cure is only a potential loss. The defendant cannot be under a duty both to perform the contract and to pay for substitute performance.

At the same time, the fact that the actions specified in a contract are physically capable of being performed does not mean that the defendant is still able to perform his primary contractual duty. For the delivery of goods or the construction of a building to count as performance of a contractual

18 This distinction between compensation and cure is reflected in situations involving true neighbours by the different norms associated with compensation and cure. It is generally not considered good manners to offer a neighbour money if your aim is to 'compensate' for a loss (flowers or a bottle of wine or something similar is more appropriate), but money is perfectly acceptable, indeed the norm, when the aim is enable the neighbour to purchase a cure, eg to replace damaged property.

19 These examples make clear that the duty to pay for a cost of cure should not be (and in practice is not) limited to contract cases. This is one reason for rejecting Webb's view that cost of cure awards in contract cases are a form of actual specific performance (which Webb defends on the ground that the duty to pay is either an implied term of the contract or is otherwise close enough to the defendant's primary contractual duty to qualify as identical): see Webb, above n 5. This explanation fails to explain why cost of cure is regularly awarded in non-contract cases.

duty, the duty itself must still be in force. Aside from cases in which the relevant actions are no longer physically possible, this can happen in two ways. The first, and most common, is where the defendant's breach gives the claimant the right to terminate the contract and the claimant acts on this right. Where this happens the defendant is by definition no longer able to perform his primary duty because that duty no longer exists.[20] But, just as in a case of physical impossibility, a duty arises on termination to pay for a replacement. The duty is the same duty as that which arises in the simple case of property damage described a moment ago. Suppose I agree to the purchase of a certain brand of bicycle, to be delivered next Friday, and make payment in advance. Delivery is not made on Friday, nor is it made at any time during the next three months, despite my repeated requests. Eventually, I call the vendor and tell him that I am terminating the contract. I then obtain the same bicycle from another vendor and send the first vendor the bill. As a matter of ordinary morality, it is uncontroversial that the first vendor is responsible for the second vendor's bill. It would be no defence to say that I suffered no loss, say because I did not really need a bicycle or did not need such an expensive one. Where courts award cost of cure in cases involving terminated contracts, it is this duty that they are enforcing.

The other way that a contractual duty which is physically capable of being performed may cease to exist as a legal duty is where the court, rather than the claimant, extinguishes the duty. In breach of contract cases this will typically happen by the court declining to make an order of specific performance in a case where performance is still possible and the contract is not otherwise terminated. In such a case the court's decision not to order specific relief has the effect in law of extinguishing the defendant's duty to perform. We know this because if the defendant subsequently performs his primary duty this will not satisfy his court-ordered duty to pay damages.[21] Once the court order to pay damages has been made, the defendant's only duty is to comply with that order. Where (as is typical) damages are calculated as the cost of cure, this duty can be explained, as in the previous cases, on the ground that a duty to pay for a cure arises in any case in which, although the primary duty can no longer be performed, substitute performance remains possible.

There is nothing mysterious, therefore, about the concept of substitutionary damages: individuals who have wrongfully harmed or injured others should, so far as possible, do whatever is necessary to undo that wrong. The normal way of doing this is to pay for the cost of curing the breach. Payment is the closest substitute possible for doing what the

20 Thus specific performance cannot be ordered where the contact has been terminated: *Johnson v Agnew* [1980] AC 367, 392.

21 *Rysak v Rysak and Bugajaski* [1966] 2 All ER 1036.

defendant should have done in the first place. Specifically, the preceding discussion suggests that a duty to pay for a cost of cure is appropriate where four conditions are satisfied: (i) the defendant has breached his primary duty; (ii) the breach cannot be cured by subsequent performance of the primary duty (because performance is impossible or the duty no longer exists); (iii) the breach (or parts of it) can be cured by paying a third party to repair, replace or provide the relevant property or service; and (iv) the claimant has paid, or will pay, for such a cure. This account is broadly consistent with the cases in which cost of cure is awarded by common law courts. In any case in tort or contract where cure is possible and where specific relief is impossible, not desired or refused by the court, the court will normally make a cost of cure award.

B The Intention Requirement

The rule that cost of cure will be awarded where a cure is possible is not applied in cases where the claimant has not paid for a cure and has no intention of doing so.[22] This qualification fits neatly with the idea that cost of cure awards are substitutionary damages. A cost of cure award is intended to allow the claimant to cure the breach: if the claimant has no intention of doing this, the rationale for the award disappears. Admittedly, the courts refuse to claw back cost of cure awards if the claimant does not carry through with her intention to pay for a cure.[23] In theory, the money in such cases should be returned if it has been given as substitutionary damages.[24] The courts' refusal to claw back cost of cure awards may therefore be one consequence of the traditional failure to distinguish the different aims of cost of cure and value of loss awards.[25] However, this refusal is also explicable on other grounds. In most cases where cost of cure awards are made the actual sum awarded can be justified (as we have seen) either as substitutionary damages or as value of loss damages. Thus, unless (and until) courts explicitly distinguish substitutionary damages from value of loss damages it would be improper to make all cost of cure awards conditional. The current practice undoubtedly also reflects a concern for finality of litigation. A particular problem in this regard is that if a cost of cure award were clawed back the court would normally have to make a new value of loss award. The existence and amount of any claim for a value

22 See the cases cited above in n 16.

23 *Ruxley Electronics*, above n 4 at 126.

24 Note that clawing back of cost of cures is in principle appropriate even if the justification for awarding cost of cure were that the cost of paying for a cure is an ordinary consequence of breach. possible. If the claimant does not pay for the cost of cure, then she is overcompensated.

25 Thus Lord Jauncey's refusal in *Ruxley Electronics*, above n 4, 126, to consider attaching conditions to any award seemed to be based in part on his view that the same rule must apply to both cost of cure and value of loss awards.

of loss award turns in part on whether a cost of cure award is given. If cost of cure is not given (or clawed back), the claimant's loss is normally larger than it would be otherwise. A rule that allowed both cost of cure awards and loss of value awards to be re-litigated, and in the same case, has obvious practical drawbacks.

C Cost of Cure must be 'Reasonable'

A second, less commonly applied exception to the normal rule is that cost of cure will not be awarded where the claimant's decision or intention to obtain a cure is 'unreasonable'.[26] The precise meaning of 'unreasonable' is open to debate, though it is clear an award is not unreasonable merely because it is more than the value of loss. Something more is required. In *Ruxley Electronics Ltd v Forsyth*,[27] where the cost of curing a defect in a swimming pool was apparently refused on the basis that the award would be unreasonable,[28] the cost of cure was described by Lord Mustill as 'wholly disproportionate'[29] to the value of the loss and by Lord Lloyd as 'out of all proportion'.[30]

The concept of substitutionary damages does not itself explain the 'reasonableness' qualification. Our primary duties to perform contracts, not trespass, etc for which substitutionary damages are substitutes are not qualified by a reasonableness standard. Admittedly, a concept of reasonableness often plays a role in determining if a primary duty exists in the first place, but if the duty exists (as must be assumed if the court has found a breach), it is no defence that the cost of performing the duty is, for example, wholly disproportionate to its value. But the concept of substitutionary damages suggests where we should look for an explanation of the reasonableness requirement. The obvious analogue to the rule that cost of cure will not be awarded where the cost is unreasonable in relation to its value is the rule that ordinary specific relief will not be ordered where this would cause undue hardship to the defendant. In some cases the hardship is non-pecuniary in nature, such as where the defendant has a special connection to property that she was contractually obliged to deliver

26 This rule is applied to both tort and contract claims: see, eg *Dodd Properties (Kent) Ltd v Canterbury City Council* [1980] WLR 433, 456–7; *The Alecos M* [1991] 1 Lloyd's Rep 120 (CA); *East Ham Corporation v Bernard Sunley & Sons Ltd* [1966] Act 406, 4324–35; *Ruxley Electronics*, above n 4.

27 Above n 4.

28 This may not have been the only or even the primary reason for refusing cost or cure in this case. Although the court's assessment of the value of the loss (£2,500) was much lower than the cost of cure (£21,560), the decision to refuse the cost of cure may have been based on the court's view that claimant lacked a genuine intent to do the work; see, eg Lord Lloyd, *ibid*, 138.

29 *Ibid*, 127.

30 *Ibid*, 136.

to the claimant.[31] In many cases, though, the hardship is straightforwardly financial: the cost of performance far exceeds its value to the claimant.[32] The precise justification for this rule need not concern us; it is sufficient to observe that whatever justification is given should apply equally to cases where the claimant is seeking substitutionary damages. If it is thought permissible to deny ordinary specific relief on the basis that the cost of performance is grossly disproportionate to the value of performance, it should be equally permissible to deny substitutionary damages where its cost is grossly disproportionate to its value. By contrast, if a cost of cure award is an ordinary damage award, as the orthodox view supposes, then the reasonableness rule is highly anomalous. It has never been supposed that an order of ordinary damages may be refused on the ground that the amount sought, though proved as damages, is unreasonable or would cause hardship to the defendant. If a loss has been proven, the claimant has a right to damages equal to the value of that loss.

D Substitutionary Damages and the Availability of Ordinary Specific Relief

Cost of cure awards, understood as substitutionary damage awards, are closely related, though not identical, to orders of specific relief. It should not be surprising, therefore, to find that the idea of substitutionary damages helps in understanding the law governing the availability specific relief.

Perhaps the most fundamental principle in the law governing specific relief is that such relief is only available where damages are 'inadequate'. But if by 'damages' is meant ordinary value of loss ('compensatory') damages, this principle is deeply puzzling. The principle does not seem to fit the standard cases in which specific relief is ordered. Three examples will suffice. By far the most common order of specific relief (though it is not usually described in these terms) is an order to pay a sum owing under a contract, that is to say, a debt. A defendant who has failed to pay a sum due under a contract will be ordered to do just that—to pay the sum.[33] Yet courts never ask whether damages would be adequate in such cases. There is a historical explanation—an order to pay a debt was available from the Courts of Law—but this does not explain why even today courts do not ask whether damages would be adequate in such cases. Moreover, if the point of damages is to compensate for loss, then an order to pay damages would seem in principle an entirely adequate response to a failure to pay a

31 Eg *Patel v Ali* [1984] Ch 283.

32 See, eg *Tito v Waddell*, above n 15, 326; *Morris v Redland Bricks Ltd* [1970] AC 652.

33 Burrows, above n 1, 433–40.

debt: the loss is easy to assess and a monetary loss is by definition fully compensable by monetary damages.

A second group of cases where specific relief is routinely awarded is where the defendant is involved in an ongoing breach of duty, as, for example, an ongoing trespass, nuisance or breach of a restrictive covenant. In many of these cases the claimant's damages are admittedly difficult to quantify, but in other cases there is little difficulty in assessing loss, or at least no more difficulty than in an ordinary trespass, nuisance or breach of contract case, each of which may require the court to predict future contingencies.[34] In some cases where the loss is certain, the court has suggested that damages are inadequate because the injury will be significant.[35] In others, they have said that damages are inadequate because the injury will be trivial.[36] Neither makes sense from the perspective of compensation. Courts routinely award compensatory damages for both very small and very large injuries, and do so without apparent difficulties.

Yet a third group of cases in which specific relief is routinely ordered is where the claim is for breach of a contract to sell land[37] or a unique chattel.[38] The judgments in these cases rarely explain why damages are inadequate. It is sometimes said that damages are inadequate because a substitute cannot be purchased, but, as has already been observed, this consideration is irrelevant from the perspective of compensation. If the aim of damages is to compensate for a loss, then it goes without saying that the nature of the compensation will not be the same as the loss. Some commentators have suggested that damages are inadequate because of the difficulty of assessing the value, to the claimant, of a unique chattel or piece of land.[39] But if this is the problem, it is a strange use of language to say that damages are inadequate: why not just say damages are uncertain? A more concrete objection is that courts award specific relief for failure to deliver a unique chattel or land even where the value of the chattel or land is easily assessed, as, for example, where the buyer was purchasing for resale or long-term investment.[40] Further, courts have explicitly stated that difficulty of assessing loss is not in itself sufficient reason to award specific relief.[41] Finally, this explanation exaggerates the difficulty of assessing loss or at least exaggerates the significance of such difficulties. In cases where

[34] Eg *Woolerton and Wilson Ltd v Richard Costain Ltd* [1970] 1 WLR 411.

[35] Eg *Shelfer v City of London Electric Lighting Co* [1895] 1 Ch 287.

[36] '[T]he very fact that no harm is done is a reason for rather than against the granting of an injunction': *Woolerton and Wilson*, above n 34 at 411.

[37] Eg *Sudbrook Trading Estate Ltd v Eggleton* [1983] 1 AC 444.

[38] Eg *Falcke v Gray* (1859) 4 Drew 651.

[39] Kronman, 'Specific Performance' (1978) *University of Chicago Law Review* 351.

[40] Brenner, 'Specific Performance of Contracts for the Sale of Land Purchased for Resale or Investment' (1978) 24 *McGill Law Journal* 513; Burrows, above n 1, 460; *Falcke*, above n 38.

[41] *Fothergill v Rowland* (1873) LR Eq 132; Burrows, above n 1, 466.

specific performance is no longer possible (say, because the property is lost or validly transferred to a third party), the courts do not appear to find assessing the loss a particularly difficult task. In addition, any uncertainty about the amount of damages to be awarded could be solved by erring on the side of the claimant.

It is thus difficult to see in what sense damages are inadequate in the kinds of cases in which specific relief is most commonly ordered—at least, if by 'damages' is meant an award intended to compensate the claimant for the value of her loss. Further, even if it could be shown that a damage award would provide inadequate compensation, it is not clear why this should matter. Why should the enforceability of the claimant's primary right (to performance) turn on whether the court can satisfactorily enforce an entirely different right (to compensation for injury)? These rights are causally related in that the right to compensation arises from an infringement of the primary right, but their normative or justificatory grounds are entirely different. The right to performance of a contract arises because the defendant entered a contract; the right to compensatory damages arises from the commission of a wrong.

The principle which is said to determine the basic availability of specific relief is therefore almost completely inexplicable if the conventional view of damage awards is accepted. However, the principle is explicable if some damage awards are substitutionary damage awards. If 'adequacy of damages' means 'adequacy of substitutionary damages', then damages will be inadequate wherever an award of substitutionary damages is not possible or feasible. Damages are inadequate in such cases because they will not enable the claimant to cure the breach. This is an appropriate consideration when deciding whether to grant specific relief: the case for denying specific relief is obviously much stronger if the court has the option of awarding the claimant the near-equivalent of specific relief. Admittedly, if the court's only concern were to protect the claimant's primary right, then specific relief would be ordered every time it was possible and desired. But there are well-known practical and moral problems associated with specific relief.[42] In particular, every court order to do or not do something raises, to varying degrees, concerns about supervision[43] and servitude.[44] These concerns must be weighed against the benefits of specific relief, and these benefits, in turn, depend in part on whether a close equivalent to specific relief is possible.

42 Burrows, above n 1, 472–3, 569–73.

43 *Ryan v Mutual Tontine Westminister Chambers Association* [1893] 1 Ch 116. See also Lord Hoffmann in *Co-operative Insurance Society Ltd v Argyll Stores (Holdings) Ltd* [1998] AC 1, 12.

44 See, eg *De Fransesco v Barnum* (1890) 45 Ch D 430, 438, where Fry LJ expressed a concern over turning 'contracts of service into contracts of slavery'.

Most of the cases in which specific relief is ordered—or refused—are explicable on this basis.[45] In cases where the primarily obligation is itself monetary, such as a contractual debt, the supervision and servitude concerns are minimal, and are in any event equivalent to those raised by cost of cure and value of loss awards. In such cases none of the possible reasons for refusing specific relief apply and thus there is no reason to even ask whether 'damages' are adequate.[46] At the other extreme, where the primary obligation is highly personal, as, for example, in most contracts of employment, the supervision and servitude issues are of sufficient weight to rule out specific relief entirely, regardless of the availability of substitute performance. It is no surprise, therefore, that courts refuse specific relief in such cases without even considering if damages are adequate.

Most cases fall between these extremes in that, while servitude and supervision concerns arise, these concerns are insufficiently weighty to rule out specific relief categorically. In these cases the availability of substitutionary damages is an important consideration. For example, the specific enforcement of a vendor's obligation to deliver goods under an ordinary contract of sale raises only minor supervision and servitude concerns. However, substitute performance is also readily and straightforwardly available in such cases, so on balance the argument for specific relief is not compelling. By contrast, where the object of the sale contract is unique, the argument for specific relief is strong because a substitutionary damage award is not possible.[47] The typical cases in which negative injunctions are awarded are similar. An order *not* to do something normally raises relatively few supervision and servitude issues in comparison to orders *to do* something (though there are obvious exceptions, which are recognised by the courts[48]). Equally important, substitutionary damages are not a viable alternative in such cases: in general, only the defendant can ensure that he does not cause a nuisance, trespass, breach a covenant, etc.

Courts typically will not order specific performance of building contracts. This is not surprising, given that such contracts raise reasonably significant supervision and servitude issues (though these can be exaggerated) and substitute performance is nearly always available. Specific performance of building contracts is ordered, though, in cases

[45] 'The most important factor in determining whether damages are adequate is whether money can buy a substitute for the promised performance': Burrows, above n 1, 459.

[46] Thus one explanation for the result in *Beswick v Beswick* [1968] AC 58 is that the defendant's obligation was monetary and therefore the usual reasons for refusing specific relief did not apply.

[47] The award of specific performance in *Sky Petroleum Ltd v VIP Petroleum Ltd* [1974] 1 WLR 576 is consistent with this explanation because, while the goods (petroleum) were not literally unique, the court found that substitutes were difficult to obtain during the oil crisis occurring at that time.

[48] As, for example, where the effect of a negative injunction would be to force the defendant to comply with a positive contractual obligation: *Warner Bros Pictures Inc v Nelson* [1937] 1 KB 209.

where the work is to be done on the defendant's property, as, for example, where land is purchased subject to an agreement to build a road or wall on the land.[49] From the perspective of supervision, servitude and any other concerns about specific relief, the obligations in these contracts are indistinguishable from obligations in other building contracts. In contrast, from the perspective of whether an order of damages will allow the claimant to obtain substitute performance, there is an obvious difference: the claimant cannot obtain substitute performance because the work must be done on the defendant's land.

It seems evident that in these and other cases the principle that specific relief is available only where damages are inadequate makes sense only if it is accepted that damages refers here to substitutionary damages. This is not to suggest that the courts' decisions in this area of the law are beyond reproach: a strong case can be made that courts sometimes give excessive weight to the supervision and servitude concerns, especially where the defendants are corporations. The concept of substitutionary damages helps to make the law intelligible, but it does not render it immune from criticism.

E Mitigation and Dates of Assessment

The mitigation principle is generally understood to provide that a defendant is not liable for losses that, while causally related to the breach, could have been avoided had the claimant acted reasonably.[50] In the usual description, the term 'loss' is not qualified; in particular, no distinction is drawn between the loss of a 'thing' and the loss of the value of that thing. The thesis defended in this essay suggests, however, that the principle should apply differently depending on whether the damage award is intended to give the claimant the very thing she lost (that is, a cost of cure award) or intended to compensate her for the value of her loss (that is, a value of loss award).

In respect of both kinds of awards, it is, of course, first necessary to identify which thing or things that the claimant has lost may be attributed to the defendant's breach. Thus the mitigation principle is sometimes invoked to explain why a claimant cannot obtain a remedy—of any kind—in respect of property that was damaged through a chain of events

[49] Eg *Wolverhampton Corp v Emmons* [1901] 1 KB 515; *Wolverhampton & Walsall R Co v London & North-Western R Co* (1873) LR 16 Eq 433.

[50] 'The fundamental basis [of damage assessment] is thus compensation for pecuniary loss naturally flowing from the breach; but this first principle imposes on a plaintiff the duty of taking all reasonable steps to mitigate the loss consequent on the breach and debars him from claiming any part of the damage which is due to his neglect to take such steps': Lord Haldone in *British Westinghouse Electric v Underground Electric Rlys Co of London Ltd* [1912] AC 673, 689.

causally related to the defendant's breach but where the damage could have been avoided had the claimant taken reasonable steps. Beyond such determinations, which are in any event arguably better explained using notions of contributory negligence or causation, the mitigation principle should be inapplicable to cost of cure awards. As in an ordinary claim for specific relief, a claimant seeking substitutionary damages is asking to be placed in the actual position she would have been in had the breach not occurred. Once the court has identified the thing or things that the claimant has lost as a consequence of the defendant's breach, the only task remaining is to determine the cost of replacement. The possibility that awarding the claimant a lessor sum of money might give the claimant equal satisfaction or 'value' is irrelevant. Of course, the sum specified in a cost of cure award must be 'reasonable' both in the sense (discussed earlier) that it cannot be 'wholly disproportionate' to the value of the loss and in the sense that the claimant cannot ask to be reimbursed for a cure that is unreasonably expensive. The court should not award the costs of obtaining a substitute good from halfway around the world if the same good is available at a lower price next door. But 'reasonableness' in these senses is not equivalent to mitigation. By contrast, the mitigation principle is relevant in a further sense when assessing value of loss claims. A claimant should not be awarded compensation for lost benefits (whether in the form of income, pleasure, etc) where those benefits would not have been lost had the claimant acted reasonably.

As already mentioned, the usual description of the mitigation principle draws no distinction between the different notions of loss reflected in cost of cure and value of loss awards, but what courts actually do is broadly consistent with this distinction. The mitigation principle is, of course, applied to the assessment of the value of a loss. A claimant who seeks damages for lost profits resulting from a breach of contract will not recover for profits that he could have obtained had he acted reasonably following the breach. With rare exceptions,[51] though, the mitigation principle is not applied when calculating cost of cure awards. On the contrary, the basic rules governing the availability of cost of cure awards flatly contradict the mitigation principle. If the mitigation principle were applied to the assessment of cost of cure awards, then cost of cure would be refused wherever the cost was greater than the value of the cure. From the perspective of a concern for mitigation, any difference between the cost of cure and its value is a 'loss' that could be avoided. By choosing to pay for substitute performance, the claimant is increasing her losses. Yet we have seen that courts are willing to award the cost of cure where it is

[51] Eg *Asamera Oil Corp Ltd v Sea Oil & General Corp* [1979] 1 SCR 633. It is undeniable that the traditional failure to clearly distinguish cost of cure awards from value of loss awards has influenced what judges actually do.

greater than the value of cure.[52] Thus, while the courts do not say that mitigation is inapplicable to cost of cure awards, the basic rule for determining the availability of such awards precludes the operation of the mitigation principle.

It might be thought that even if the mitigation principle is not generally applied to cost of cure awards it is applied in one specific respect: the rule that determines the date for assessing the cost of obtaining a cure is sometimes explained using the mitigation principle. The traditional rule, which is confirmed for claims involving the sale of goods by section 51 of the Sale of Goods Act, 1979, is that the cost of obtaining a cure is prima facie assessed as of the date of breach. It is not uncommon for the courts to apply a later date, particularly (though not exclusively) where the claimant had a bona fide expectation that performance might be achieved either by the defendant's voluntary decision or as a result of a court order,[53] but the traditional rule remains the default position. This rule is sometimes explained on the ground that the mitigation principle requires the claimant to seek a substitute immediately in order to minimise the losses arising from the breach.[54]

The main difficulty with this suggestion, as others have noted,[55] is that, even assuming the mitigation principle requires claimants to seek a substitute in every case, it is often reasonable for a claimant to wait before doing this. Aside from cases where the claimant reasonably expects the defendant to perform (where the traditional rule is in any event rarely applied), there are cases where the claimant reasonably requires time to locate and finance an alternative purchase. More generally, if, as is normal, there is no reason to think the market price will rise, then it is not unreasonable, from the perspective of mitigation, to wait before purchasing a substitute. This is doubly true where the market price is expected to fall.

Admittedly, the date of breach rule is also difficult to explain using the idea of substitutionary damages. In principle, courts should distinguish three situations when determining the date of assessment for substitutionary damages. The first is where the claimant had been seeking ordinary specific relief up to the trial, such that the duty to pay for a cure only came into effect at the moment the court refused specific relief. In these cases the appropriate date for determining the cost of cure is the date of trial or even the date of judgment. The second situation is where the claimant seeks reimbursement for the price of a cure that she has already

52 See cases in n 11 and accompanying text.

53 See, eg *Wroth v Tyler* [1974] Ch 30; *Johnson v Agnew*, above n 20; *Wilson v London Globe Finance Corp Ltd* (1897) 143 TLR 15; *Mertens v Home Freeholds Co* [1921] 2 KB 526 (CA); *Radford*, above n 11; *East Ham Corporation*, above n 26.

54 'In contracts for the sale of goods, for instance, where there is an available market, the date of non-delivery is generally the appropriate date because it is open to the plaintiff to mitigate by going into the market immediately': Oliver J in *Radford*, above n 11, 1285.

55 Bridge, *The Sale of Goods* (1997), 552; Waddams, above n 1, 29, 593.

paid for. Here the appropriate date for assessing the cost of cure is prima facie the date on which the payment was made. The third situation is where the claimant seeks payment on the basis that, while she has not yet purchased a cure, she intends to do so. In these cases the appropriate date is again prima facie the date on which the defendant actually makes the payment.

The courts' approach to the first group of cases fits easily with the idea of substitutionary damages because it is in precisely these kinds of cases that an exception to the date of breach rule is routinely made.[56] The second and third categories of cases, where the date of breach rule is usually applied, are not easy to explain from the perspective of substitutionary damages. The most plausible explanation, if not justification, for the date of breach rule in these cases is that it operates as a crude form of anti-speculation rule.[57] In these cases, the date at which the duty to pay crystallises should in principle be set by the claimant, as it is the claimant who decides if and when she will purchase a cure. However, there is an obvious risk that the claimant could abuse this choice by speculating at the defendant's expense. If the claimant can set the date of assessment unilaterally, then, in cases where the defendant failed to provide property or services under a contract, the claimant will have an incentive to wait and see if the market price goes up or down. If the price goes up, it will be advantageous to ask for cost of cure; if the price goes down, it will be advantageous to keep the contract purchase price (or get it back if it is already paid) and then purchase a cheaper substitute. In cases involving property damage, there is less danger of speculation, though there remains the problem (if the choice of date is left to the claimant) that the claimant has no incentive to obtain a good price. A claimant whose property was damaged could move slowly in a rising market knowing that the defendant will have to pay the higher price.

One way to prevent speculation and, more generally, to ensure that the claimant acts reasonably in deciding if and when to obtain a cure is to impose a duty to act in good faith. For better or worse, the common law has traditionally shown little interest in imposing duties of this kind, preferring instead to impose easily administered 'bright-line' rules. The date of breach rule seems best explained on this basis. It is a clear and easily administered rule that guards against certain kinds of unreasonable behaviour, in particular speculation at the defendant's expense. The date of breach rule is, however, a crude way of preventing speculation. It should not be surprising, therefore, to find that courts are increasingly willing to create exceptions. In cases where the date of assessment makes a difference

56 *Johnson*, above n 20; *Suleman v Shahasavari* [1988] 1 WLR 1181.
57 Bridge, above n 54 at 561.

(which are rare), the current practice is to replace the date of breach rule with something approaching a reasonableness rule.[58]

A final observation is that mitigation and other principles for assessing loss are often relevant for other reasons in cases where substitutionary damages are awarded. A claimant who obtains an order of substitutionary damages will normally have a valid claim for value of loss damages for losses arising from not having the use of the relevant property or service in the period between the breach and the cure. This claim is no different from a claim for value of loss damages that is added to a request for ordinary specific relief—an everyday occurrence. Thus a disappointed buyer claiming the cost of purchasing goods from a third party will normally have suffered 'non-curable' losses as a result of not obtaining the goods on the promised date. The same is true where an exact substitute is not available, so that the claimant is instead awarded the cost of obtaining a near substitute. The loss of value arising from the difference between the original and the substitute is another non-curable loss. Such losses are properly the subject of an ordinary damages claim, and their assessment is properly limited by principles such as mitigation. In many cases where cost of cure is awarded, the courts therefore properly apply the mitigation principle to the value of loss part of the award. The current practice of not distinguishing clearly between cost of cure and value of loss can obscure this distinction.

III CONCLUSION

In this essay I have argued that interpreting cost of cure awards as substitutionary damages fits both what the courts do and what they should do. The essay does not, however, provide more than an initial exploration of each of these issues. From the perspective of understanding what courts do, perhaps the most obvious unanswered question is how the idea of substitutionary damages fits with awards in personal injury cases. On the one hand, it seems odd to suppose that a monetary award might be thought capable of putting a claimant in the actual position she would have been in had she not suffered her injury. You can buy a new car, identical to the car that you lost, but you cannot buy a new leg. On the other hand, there is a straightforward sense in which many awards in personal injury cases are designed precisely to pay for the cost of cure (at least, where medical expenses are paid for privately). The cost of an operation to mend a broken leg is literally the 'cost of cure'. The operation may not restore the leg to the identical condition it was in prior to the injury, but there seems no reason to suppose a perfect cure is necessary for an award to qualify as

58 See cases cited above in n 52.

substitutionary damages. Substitutionary damages are closely related to specific relief, but they are not the same thing.

From a normative perspective, the idea of substitutionary damages appears to support the traditional view that the purpose of remedial orders is to vindicate individual rights. The opposing view, according to which remedies are designed primary to give individuals incentives to behave properly (for example, efficiently) in future, fits uneasily with substitutionary damages.[59] The argument that damage awards are intended to give individuals incentives to perform their legal obligations when, but only when, the cost of doing so is less than the value of that performance is plausible insofar as damages are set equal to the value of the claimant's loss. But this argument is much harder to make if damages are understood to have a substitutionary as well as compensatory aim. At the same time, the idea of substitutionary damages raises new questions for the traditional rights-based view. The idea, common to rights-based theorists, that damages reflect a notion of corrective justice fits neatly with the idea of substitutionary damages. There is a straightforward sense in which substitutionary damages are designed to correct the injustice arising from the defendant's wrongful action. Like specific relief, substitutionary damages are intended to undo, in a literal sense, the effects of breach. The question then raised is whether an alternative non-corrective-justice explanation must be given for value of loss awards.

These are questions for the future. The basic argument of this essay is that the understanding of damage orders in the common law needs to be fundamentally overhauled. Specifically, the traditional assumption that cost of cure and value of loss awards have the same underlying aim is mistaken. While value of loss awards can plausibly be described as sharing the compensatory aim that is widely assumed to be the aim of damages generally, cost of cure awards are different. Cost of cure awards are more closely related to specific relief than to value of loss awards. Like specific relief, their aim is not to compensate the claimant for a loss but instead to ensure that the claimant ends up, so far as possible, in the actual position she would have been in had the breach not occurred.

[59] I discuss each of these views in more detail in Smith, above n 5, 387–413.

6

The Inadequacy of Damages as a Remedy for Breach of Contract

RALPH M CUNNINGTON*

I INTRODUCTION

In *AG v Blake* Lord Nicholls declared:

> It is . . . well established that an award of damages, assessed by reference to financial loss, is not always 'adequate' as a remedy for a breach of contract.[1]

The concept of inadequacy has played a significant role in the development of contract remedies over the past two decades. This paper examines the meaning of inadequacy in this context with the aim of furthering our understanding of the principles and policies that underlie the law of remedies.

The following section of the paper identifies the circumstances in which compensatory damages are deemed to be inadequate. Section III examines why damages are deemed to be inadequate. Section IV considers the significance of inadequacy and what we can learn from this about the nature of contractual obligations and the law's response to breach of contract. The final section considers how the problem of remedial inadequacy has been addressed by the development of new remedies for breach of contract.

II WHEN ARE DAMAGES INADEQUATE?

The concept of the inadequacy of damages has been used as a reason to justify a number of alternative remedies for breach of contract. In this section, four such remedies will be considered and the circumstances in

* Lecturer in Law, University of Birmingham. I am very grateful for all the comments I received when I presented an earlier version of this paper at the Obligations III conference at the University of Queensland on 14 July 2006. I would also like to thank the British Academy for their financial support of this research.

[1] [2001] 1 AC 268, 283.

which damages are said to be inadequate will be identified. This discussion will lay the foundation for the subsequent analysis of the reasons why damages are inadequate.

A Specific Relief

In *Wilson v Northampton and Banbury Junction Rly Co*, Lord Selbourne famously declared that,

> the court gives specific performance instead of damages, only when it can by that means do more and complete justice.[2]

Specific performance is only available when compensatory damages are inadequate to do justice between the parties. This adequacy-of-damages test is both long established and controversial. Professor Dawson once described it as 'an unnecessary and irksome restriction of specific performance', which is applied in an 'arbitrary and irrational' way.[3] There may be some truth in this, but the test is generally considered to perform an invaluable role in restraining the use of contempt-backed remedies. Over the years, the courts have established a number of well-recognised situations in which damages are deemed to be inadequate. In such situations, the court has jurisdiction to order specific performance but may, of course, refuse to make such an order on discretionary grounds.[4]

(i) No Market Substitute

If no market substitute for performance is available, damages are deemed to be inadequate. This is the reason why contracts concerning land are specifically enforceable. The courts assume that land is unique and that no market substitute is available.[5] On this basis, specific performance is available in respect of contracts for the sale of land (even if the land is bought for resale[6]), for the grant of an interest in land and even for the grant of a license to occupy land.[7]

2 (1874) 9 Ch App 279, 284.

3 J Dawson, 'Specific Performance in France and Germany' (1959) 57 *Michigan Law Review* 495, 532.

4 These discretionary considerations are discussed in greater depth at pp 139–41.

5 *Adderley v Dixon* (1824) 1 Sim & St 607, 610 per Leach VC; *Sudbrook Trading Estate Ltd v Eggleton* [1983] 1 AC 444, 478 per Lord Diplock. This assumption may be outdated in an age where houses can be made to order on large residential estates.

6 See *Pianta v National Finance and Trustee Ltd* (1964) 38 ALJR 232, 233 per Barwick CJ (HCA). But contrast *Heron Bay Investments Ltd v Peel-Elder Developments Ltd* (1976) 2 CPC 338 (Ont HC). For discussion see J Berryman, 'Specific Performance, Uniqueness and Investment Contracts' [1984] *The Conveyancer* 130.

7 *Verall v Great Yarmouth Borough Council* [1981] QB 202. This is surprising, given that a contractual licence does not create an interest in the land capable of binding successors in title to the licensor: *Ashburn Anstalt v Arnold* [1989] Ch 1.

A different approach is taken in respect of contracts for the sale of stock or goods. This is not because of their personal nature; it is clear that the court 'applies the same general equity to all contracts'.[8] Rather, it is because, in the words of Sir John Leach,

> damages at law, calculated upon the market price of the stock or goods, are as complete a remedy to the purchaser as the delivery of the stock or goods contracted for; inasmuch as, with the damages, he may purchase the same quantity of the like of stock or goods.[9]

In more recent years, the courts have started to recognise that there are many circumstances in which damages will not provide an adequate remedy to the purchaser of stock or goods because of the lack of availability of substitutes on the market. For example, in *Duncuft v Albrecht* the court granted specific performance of a contract for the sale of shares in a railway company, on the ground that 'railway shares are limited in number' and 'are not always to be had in the market'.[10] A distinction is drawn between contracts for the sale of private shares, where specific performance is generally available, and contracts for the sale of public shares, where it is not.[11] This is because public shares are dealt in on the market, and therefore damages provide an adequate remedy since they can be used to purchase substitute performance.[12]

There are two further instances where specific performance may be ordered of contracts for the sale of personal property. First, specific performance will be ordered where the subject matter of the contract is unique on the ground that a market substitute cannot be acquired.[13] Secondly, specific performance may be ordered of contracts for the sale of non-unique goods if circumstances exist that mean that substitutes are *practically* unavailable.[14]

(ii) Damages would be Difficult to Quantify

The second situation in which damages are deemed to be inadequate will sometimes arise as a corollary of the first. If supply of alternative performance is restricted, it may be extremely difficult for the court to quantify compensatory damages because it is unclear how much it will cost the plaintiff to obtain alternative performance. In such circumstances

8 *New Brunswick and Canada Ry and Land Co v Muggeridge* (1859) 4 Drew 686, 698 per Kindersley VC.

9 *Adderley v Dixon*, above n 5, 610. See also *Falcke v Gray* (1859) 4 Drew 651, 657–8 per Kindersley VC.

10 (1841) 12 Sim 189, 199 per Shadwell VC.

11 *Oughtred v IRC* [1960] AC 206; *Neville v Wilson* [1997] Ch 144.

12 *Re Schwabacher* (1908) 98 LT 127, 128 per Parker J.

13 *Falcke v Gray*, above n 9.

14 *Sky Petroleum Ltd v VIP Petroleum* [1974] 1 WLR 576.

damages will be found to be inadequate and specific performance will be ordered.[15]

For similar reasons, specific performance has been ordered of contracts to sell or pay annuities because the value of the rights is difficult to ascertain,[16] and of contracts to execute a mortgage for money already lent because the value of having security for the loan is impossible to quantify.[17] Likewise, contracts to indemnify have been specifically enforced on the ground that the,

> computation of damages in such a cause must depend upon examination of long and intricate accounts . . . which cannot be made upon a trial at law.[18]

The courts have also enforced contracts for the sale of debts on the ground that damages in such cases can only be calculated by conjecture.[19]

(iii) Insolvency of the Defendant

Some commentators contend that damages will be inadequate if the defendant is unable to pay them. In other words, damages will be inadequate if they are proved to be ineffective. Spry adopts this position, claiming that:

> A significant risk that a legal remedy such as damages will be ineffective on the ground of the inadequate resources of the defendant or otherwise, may of itself justify the conclusion that it is inadequate.[20]

This conclusion is rather doubtful. There is a sparsity of authority on the point.[21] As Spry notes, the Court of Appeal did order an injunction in *The Oakworth* on the ground that the defendants had no assets to satisfy a damages claim.[22] However, the other cases cited by Spry concern either an interlocutory injunction for which protection of the claimant's interests is

15 See *Adderley v Dixon*, above n 5, 611 per Leach VC; *Buxton v Lister* (1746) 3 Atk 383; *Evans Marshall & Co Ltd v Bertola SA* [1973] 1 WLR 349, 380 per Sachs LJ.

16 *Adderley v Dixon*, *ibid*; *Clifford v Turrell* (1841) 1 Y & C Ch Cas 138; *Beswick v Beswick* [1968] AC 58.

17 *Ashton v Corrigan* (1871) LR 13 Eq 76; *Swiss Bank Corpn v Lloyds Bank Ltd* [1982] AC 584.

18 *Ranelaugh Earl v Hayes* (1683) 1 Vern 189 at 190. See also *Sporle v Whayman* (1855) 20 Beav 607. Cf *McIntosh v Dalwood* (No. 4) (1930) 30 SR (NSW) 415.

19 *Adderley v Dixon*, above n 5, 611 per Leach VC.

20 I Spry, *The Principles of Equitable Remedies* (London, Sweet & Maxwell, 5th edn, 1997), 68. See also *Doloret v Rothschild* (1824) 1 Sim & St 590, 598 per Leach VC. See also the argument in favour of the relevance of insolvency in: HL McClintock, 'Adequacy of Ineffective Remedy at Law' (1932) 16 *Minnesota Law Review* 233.

21 In *Doloret v Rothschild*, *ibid*, 598, Leach VC suggested that insolvency does provide a basis for specific performance. However, the judgment seems to go too far when it suggests that damages will never be an adequate remedy because the benefit of such a remedy 'must depend upon the personal responsibility of the party'.

22 *Associated Portland Cement Manufacturers Ltd v Teigland Shipping A/s (the 'Oakworth')* [1975] 1 Lloyd's Rep 581, 583 per Lord Denning MR.

of the essence[23] or an injunction against trespass, where different considerations apply.[24]

If the solvency of the defendant really is of relevance, then special considerations will need to apply to ensure that other creditors are not prejudiced. This will inevitably mean that the insolvency of the defendant will not of itself constitute grounds for finding damages to be inadequate. Insolvency will need to be accompanied by some other basis, such as difficulty in quantifying damages,[25] otherwise specific performance would be available for every creditor of the defendant. It is clear that this is not the current state of the law.[26] If insolvency is to be of relevance to the issue of inadequacy, it can only be of secondary and parasitic relevance in support of other bases for inadequacy.

(iv) Only Nominal Damages Available

The final and most significant situation in which damages may be held to be inadequate is where damages are merely nominal because the claimant has suffered no pecuniary loss. In *Beswick v Beswick*,[27] Mr Beswick made a contract with his nephew whereby the nephew promised to make payments to Mr Beswick's widow during his lifetime in return for Mr Beswick's promise to transfer his business to the nephew. When Mr Beswick died, the nephew refused to pay and Mrs Beswick brought an action for breach of contract in her capacity as Mr Beswick's personal representative. The nephew argued that, since Mr Beswick had died, his estate had suffered no loss as a result of the breach of contract, and thus nominal damages were adequate. The House of Lords rejected this argument, claiming that it 'wholly misunderstood' the adequacy test. 'Equity will grant specific performance when damages are inadequate to meet the justice of the case', Lord Upjohn asserted.[28] Far from being a reason to deny specific performance, the fact that only nominal damages could be recovered was the main reason why specific performance should be ordered according to the House of Lords.[29]

23 *Evans Marshall v Bertola*, above n 15, 380–1 per Sachs LJ.

24 *Hodgson v Duce* (1856) 2 Jur NS 1014. See discussion of insolvency and injunctions in: R Sharpe, *Injunctions and Specific Performance* (Aurora, Ontario, Canada Law Book Ltd, 1983), 283–4.

25 Which it was in *Evans Marshall v Bertola*, above n 15.

26 E Fry, *Specific Performance of Contracts* (London, Stevens, 6th edn, 1921), 30.

27 [1968] AC 58.

28 *Ibid*, 102 per Lord Upjohn.

29 *Ibid*, 81 per Lord Hodson, 77–8 per Lord Reid, 90–1 per Lord Pearce, 102 per Lord Upjohn. The decision in *Beswick v Beswick* was followed in *Sudbrook Trading Estate Ltd v Eggleton* [1983] 1 AC 444, where the House of Lords ordered specific performance of a number of option agreements to purchase freehold reversions at a price to be agreed upon by valuers.

B Loss of Amenity Damages

Over the years, a number of exceptions have developed to the traditional rule that a claimant cannot recover damages for loss of amenity.[30] For example, damages for loss of amenity can now be recovered where the object of the contract is to afford pleasure, eg a contract for the supply of wedding photographs or for the supply of a family holiday.[31] In recent years this exception has been extended so that it is no longer necessary to show that the 'object of the contract' was the provision of pleasure or peace of mind. Instead, it is sufficient to demonstrate that the object of 'the term' broken was to provide pleasure or freedom from distress, and that the term was an important one within the context of the contract as a whole.[32] Although the inadequacy of alternative remedies is not treated as a pre-requisite for an award of loss of amenity damages, it is clear that remedial inadequacy does play an important role in the courts' decision-making process. This can be illustrated by reference to two of the leading cases in the area.

In *Ruxley Electronics & Construction Ltd v Forsyth*,[33] Forsyth agreed to build a swimming pool in Ruxley's garden. The contract specified that the pool would have a diving area seven feet, six inches deep. When constructed, the diving area was only six feet deep. This was still a safe depth for diving and one which did not affect the value of the pool. Forsyth was not happy, however, and he brought an action for breach of contract claiming the cost of having the pool demolished and rebuilt, a sum of £21,500. At first instance the judge rejected the claim for 'cost of cure' damages on the ground that it was an unreasonable claim in the circumstances, but awarded Forsyth £2,500 for loss of amenity. This award was reversed by the Court of Appeal but restored by the House of Lords.

Lord Mustill was unimpressed by counsel's argument that Forsyth should recover nothing at all unless he could prove that the defect had depreciated the market value of the property. Such a conclusion 'would be unacceptable to the average householder, and it is unacceptable to me', urged Lord Mustill.[34] For his Lordship, there would be something wrong with the law if Forsyth was left with no more than nominal damages; such damages would be inadequate. Loss of amenity damages were required to recognise Forsyth's loss of 'consumer surplus'.[35]

30 The rule has its origins in *Addis v Gramophone* [1909] AC 488.

31 *Jarvis v Swan Tours* [1973] QB 233; *Jackson v Horizon Holidays* [1975] 3 All ER 92.

32 *Farley v Skinner* [2002] 2 AC 732, 749–50 per Lord Steyn. See D Capper, 'Damages for Distress and Disappointment—The Limits of Watts v Morrow' (2000) 116 *LQR* 553, 556.

33 [1996] AC 344.

34 *Ibid*, 360.

35 *Ibid*, 360–1. The term 'consumer surplus' was originally used by D Harris, A Ogus and J Phillips, 'Contract Remedies and the Consumer Surplus' (1979) 95 *LQR* 581.

Lord Lloyd agreed, but he was of the view that loss of amenity damages were available on the more traditional ground that the contract was one 'for the provision of a pleasurable amenity'.[36] With respect, this conclusion is rather doubtful given that Ruxley did not promise either explicitly or implicitly to confer a pleasurable amenity on Forsyth. Nevertheless, it seems that Lord Lloyd would have reached the same result by a different route had he not been able to adapt the traditional exception to fit the facts. His Lordship recognised that the approach he had adopted would not have been available in most cases and continued:

> What is then to be the position where, in the case of a new house, the building does not conform in some minor respect to the contract, as, for example, where there is a difference in level between two rooms, necessitating a step. Suppose there is no measurable difference in value of the complete house, and the cost of reinstatement would be prohibitive. Is there any reason why the court should not award by way of damages for breach of contract some modest sum, not based on difference in value, but solely to compensate the buyer for his disappointed expectations? Is the law of damages so inflexible . . . that it cannot find some middle ground in such a case?[37]

A similar conclusion was reached on the facts of *Farley v Skinner*.[38] Mr Farley employed Mr Skinner to survey a house that he was contemplating purchasing as a country residence. The house was close to Gatwick airport, so Farley asked Skinner to investigate, in addition to the usual matters, whether the property would be affected by aircraft noise, telling him that he did not want to be on a flight path. Skinner reported that he thought it unlikely that the property would suffer greatly from aircraft noise. After moving in, Farley discovered that the house was close to a navigation beacon which is used by aircraft waiting to land at Gatwick and, as a result, the property was substantially affected by noise. Farley brought an action for damages, alleging that Skinner had been negligent in carrying out his obligations under the contract. At first instance, the judge held that Farley was not entitled to recover damages on a diminution of value basis because the price paid coincided with the market value of the property taking the aircraft noise into account. Instead, he awarded Farley damages of £10,000 for the distress and inconvenience caused to him by the aircraft noise. This award was upheld by the House of Lords.

Again, it seems that the inadequacy of nominal damages measured on the diminution of value basis was of particular significance to their Lordships. Lord Scott observed:

> Ruxley's case establishes, in my opinion, that if a party's contractual performance has failed to provide to the other contracting party something to which

36 *Ibid*, 374.
37 *Ibid*.
38 [2002] 2 AC 732.

that other was, under the contract, entitled, and which, if provided, would have been of value to that party, then, if there is no other way of compensating the injured party, the injured party should be compensated in damages to the extent of that value.[39]

For Lord Scott, damages measured on the diminution of value basis were inadequate because they were nominal and did not compensate the claimant for the full extent of his loss.

C Gain-based Damages

Gain-based damages for breach of contract were recognised for the first time in English law in *AG v Blake*.[40] Lord Nicholls, who delivered the leading speech in the case, insisted that gain-based damages should only be available in exceptional cases where damages and other contract remedies are shown to be inadequate.[41] This is unsurprising, given that gain-based damages have grown out of the court's equitable jurisdiction to award damages in lieu of specific relief under Lord Cairns' Act.[42] In his speech in *Blake*, Lord Nicholls presented a summary of the existing law on gain-based damages.[43] Many of the cases relied upon by his Lordship concerned an award of damages under Lord Cairns' Act,[44] and the case held out as the 'solitary beacon' for gain-based damages in contract was itself an equitable damages case.[45] Equitable damages are only available when the court has jurisdiction to entertain an application for specific performance or an injunction.[46] Such jurisdiction is only present when damages are shown to be inadequate. The logical consequence of this is that equitable damages (and by implication, gain-based damages) are only

39 *Ibid*, 766.

40 [2001] 1 AC 268. One should not be deflected by Chadwick LJ's recent suggestion that *Blake* damages are 'a flexible response to the need to compensate the claimant for the wrong which has been done to him' (*WWF – World Wide Fund for Nature v World Wrestling Federation Entertainment Inc* [2007] EWCA Civ 286, [59]). Account of profits is incontrovertibly a gain-based remedy: see R Cunnington, 'The Measure and Availability of Gain-Based Damages for Breach of Contract' in D Saidov and R Cunnington, *Contract Damages: Domestic and International Perspectives* (Oxford, Hart Publishing, 2008).

41 *Ibid*, 285.

42 Lord Cairns' Act was repealed by the Statute Law Revision Act 1883, but s 5 of that Act preserved its general effect (*Leeds Industrial Co-operative Society Ltd v Slack* [1924] AC 851). Today, all of its provisions are enacted in s 50 of the Supreme Court Act 1981. For a fuller discussion of the relationship between equitable damages and gain-based damages for breach of contract, see R Cunnington, 'Equitable Damages: A Model for Restitutionary Damages' (2001) 17 *Journal of Contract Law* 212, 217–23.

43 Above n 1, 278–86.

44 See, eg *Bracewell v Appleby* [1975] Ch 408; *Surrey County Council v Bredero Homes* [1993] 1 WLR 1361; *Jaggard v Sawyer* [1995] 1 WLR 269. The speech even contains a heading titled 'Damages under Lord Cairns' Act': [2001] 1 AC 268, 281.

45 *Wrotham Park v Parkside Homes* [1974] 1 WLR 798.

46 See s 50 Supreme Court Act 1981.

available when damages are deemed to be inadequate. So when are damages inadequate for the purpose of an award of gain-based damages?

(i) No Market Substitute

The court will hold that damages are inadequate if there is no market substitute for performance. This is often the case where the breach is a breach of a negative covenant, as seen on the facts of *Blake* itself. Blake was a former member of the Secret Intelligence Service who in 1944 signed an agreement not to divulge any official information gained as a result of his employment. Blake broke this agreement in 1966 when he fled to Moscow and wrote an autobiography outlining details of his work with the Secret Intelligence Service. The Crown sued Blake for breach of contract.

Had the Crown been awarded compensatory damages (which it was not),[47] it would have been impossible for those damages to have been used to purchase substitute performance. It was too late; Blake had already divulged the official information and there was no way that this act could be undone. To that extent, there was no market substitute for performance and damages were inadequate. This explains why Lord Nicholls emphasised the significance of the obligation breached:

> The present case is exceptional. The context is employment as a member of the security and intelligence services. Secret information is the lifeblood of these services.[48]

There was no substitute for Blake's performance. Damages could not be used to right Blake's wrong. Therefore compensatory damages were inadequate.

By way of contrast, gain-based damages were refused on the facts of *AB Corporation v CD Company*,[49] because a market substitute for performance was available. The case concerned the wrongful withdrawal of a vessel from a charter after the market had risen. An Arbitration Tribunal, chaired by Sir Christopher Staughton, refused to award gain-based damages on the ground that,

> there should not be an award of wrongful profits where both parties are dealing with a marketable commodity—the services of a ship in this case—for which a substitute can be found in the market place.[50]

In other words, damages were adequate on the facts of the case because the award could be used to purchase a market substitute.[51]

47 Because the Crown had suffered no pecuniary loss. See below at p 125.
48 Above n 1, 286.
49 [2002] 1 Lloyd's Rep 805.
50 *Ibid*, [10].
51 See Mance LJ's comments on the case in *Experience Hendrix v PPX* [2003] EWCA Civ 323, [2003] EMLR 25, [33].

(ii) Damages are difficult to quantify

Compensatory damages will also be inadequate where they are difficult to quantify. *Esso Petroleum v Niad*[52] was the first reported decision to apply the ruling in *Blake*. It concerned the operation of a petroleum marketing scheme called 'Pricewatch'. Petrol dealers agreed to report competitors' prices and to abide by prices set daily by Esso, which were intended to match the competition. Dealers received financial support by Esso to assist them to do this. Niad broke the agreement by failing to maintain prices as agreed on four occasions. Morritt VC awarded Esso an account of the profits received by Niad. In his view, compensatory damages were inadequate because it would be 'almost impossible to attribute lost sales to a breach by one out of several hundred dealers who operate Pricewatch'.[53] In order to formulate a claim for expectation damages, Esso would have been required,

> to establish that it has lost sales of motor fuels by reason of the failure of Niad to charge at or below the Pricewatch recommended price. This may not be easy.[54]

So damages were found to be inadequate on the ground that they were difficult, if not impossible, to quantify.

Damages were also held to be inadequate for the same reason in *Experience Hendrix v PPX*.[55] PPX exploited various master recordings of Jimi Hendrix in breach of a settlement agreement. In holding that Experience Hendrix was entitled to gain-based damages, Mance LJ noted that compensatory damages would have been inadequate,

> because of the practical impossibility in each case of demonstrating the effect of a defendant's undoubted breaches on the appellant's general programme of promoting their product.[56]

Peter Gibson LJ agreed, stating that the claimant's difficulty in establishing financial loss was crucial to making an award of gain-based damages.[57]

(iii) Only nominal damages available

Again, the most common reason for holding that compensatory damages are inadequate in the law of gain-based damages is the fact that damages would be nominal because the claimant has suffered no pecuniary loss.

52 [2001] EWHC Ch 458.
53 *Ibid*, [63].
54 *Ibid*, [56].
55 Above n 51.
56 *Ibid*, [38].
57 *Ibid*, [58].

Damages were held to be inadequate for this reason on the facts of *Blake*. Lord Nicholls noted that,

> an award of damages, assessed by reference to financial loss, is not always 'adequate' as a remedy for breach of contract.[58]

On the facts, damages assessed by reference to financial loss were inadequate because the Crown had suffered no pecuniary loss as a result of Blake's breach.

The same reason was given for the inadequacy of damages in *Wrotham Park v Parkside Homes*,[59] the case held out by Lord Nicholls as the solitary beacon for gain-based damages in contract. The defendant, Parkside Homes, erected homes on their land in breach of covenant. A mandatory injunction was refused on the ground that it would have constituted an unpardonable waste of much needed houses.[60] Instead, Brightman J awarded damages. Compensatory damages, measured by reference to diminution of value, would have been nominal because the value of the plaintiff's land had been unaffected by the construction of the new houses. Brightman J considered that this result was unsatisfactory—'justice would manifestly not have been done'[61]—and for that reason he awarded gain-based damages calculated at 5% of Parkside's anticipated profit.[62]

This approach was followed recently in *O'Brien Homes v Lane*.[63] The facts were very similar: the defendant had breached a restrictive covenant but the value of the claimant's land had been unaffected. David Clarke J awarded gain-based damages,[64] noting that an award of nominal damages was,

58 Above n 1, 282.
59 Above n 45.
60 *Ibid*, 811.
61 *Ibid*, 815.
62 Some jurists contend that the damages awarded in *Wrotham Park* were compensatory: see *WWF—World Wide Fund for Nature v World Wrestling Federation Entertainment Inc* [2007] EWCA Civ 286, [59] per Chadwick LJ; P-W Lee, 'Responses to a Breach of Contract' [2003] *Lloyd's Maritime and Commercial Law Quarterly* 301, 302; M Graham, 'Restitutionary Damages: The Anvil Struck' (2004) 120 *LQR* 26, 27–8; M McInnes, 'Gain, Loss and the User Principle' (2006) 14 *Restitution Law Review* 76, 84–6; A Tettenborn, 'Gain, Loss and Damages for Breach of Contract: What's in an Acronym?' (2006) 14 *Restitution Law Review* 112, 113. However, there are convincing reasons why the damages awarded in *Wrotham Park* were gain-based, although assessed on a different basis to the damages awarded in *Blake*: see Cunnington, above n 40; J Edelman, *Gain-Based Damages* (Oxford, Hart Publishing, 2002), ch 3.
63 [2004] EWHC 303.
64 The judge considered that the damages awarded were compensatory. However, this was based on a misunderstanding of the nature of the damages awarded in *Wrotham Park*. See P Birks, 'Profits of Breach of Contract' (1993) 109 *LQR* 518; J Edelman, 'The Compensation Straight-Jacket and the Lost Opportunity to Bargain [2001] *Restitution Law Review* 104; A Burrows, *The Law of Restitution* (London, Butterworths, 2003), 477; R Cunnington, 'A Lost Opportunity to Clarify' (2007) 122 *LQR* 47.

not a result which would appeal to the court, any more than such an argument appealed to Brightman J in the *Wrotham Park* case.[65]

It has been shown that there exist a number of situations in which compensatory damages are inadequate for the purpose of an award of gain-based damages. These circumstances roughly correspond to those in the law of specific performance, which is unsurprising, given the history of gain-based damages in English law.

D Punitive Damages

Finally, it is necessary to briefly consider the law relating to punitive damages.[66] Such damages are currently unavailable for breach of contract in England and Australia but are available in Canada, where the crucial prerequisite for an award is the inadequacy of compensatory damages.[67] The cases offer little by way of guidance as to when compensatory damages will be inadequate, but the issue of deterrence appears to be crucial.[68]

In *Royal Bank of Canada v W Got & Associate Electric Ltd*,[69] the claimant bank ordered the defendant, Got, to repay a loan without giving reasonable notice. The bank then applied to the court for a motion to appoint a receiver. The master granted the order in reliance on a misleading affidavit tendered by the bank which created a 'false air of urgency'. The bank was held liable for breach of contract and Got was awarded compensatory damages. In addition to this compensatory sum, Got received punitive damages due to the manner in which the breach of contract was committed. In the opinion of the court, the bank's conduct was so sharp and such an affront to 'the administration of justice' that the small award of compensatory damages was *insufficient to deter* the bank, and others, from repeating the conduct.[70]

[65] Above n 63, [11].

[66] The label punitive is adopted in this paper rather than exemplary because it more aptly describes the purpose of the damages embracing punishment, example, vindication and deterrence.

[67] *Whiten v Pilot Insurance Company* (2002) 209 DLR (4th) 257, 295 and 303 per Binnie J, 160 per LeBel J; *Royal Bank of Canada v W Got & Associate Electric Ltd* (2000) 178 DLR (4th) 385, 395 per McLachlin and Bastarache JJ delivering the unanimous judgment of the court. The inadequacy of damages test also applies in English law in regard to punitive damages in tort: *Rookes v Barnard* [1964] AC 1129, 1228 per Lord Devlin; *Kuddus v Chief Constable of Leicestershire Constabulary* [2002] 2 AC 122, 144 per Lord Nicholls, 161 per Lord Scott.

[68] For a robust defence of the deterrence rationale for punitive damages, see J Edelman, 'In Defence of Exemplary Damages' in this volume.

[69] Above n 67, 385.

[70] *Ibid*, 395 (emphasis added).

Damages were held to be inadequate on similar grounds in *Whiten v Pilot Insurance Company*.[71] The defendant insurers refused to pay out on Mrs Whiten's insurance policy following a fire at her home. The insurer claimed that Mrs Whiten had burned down the house and persisted in this allegation in a hostile and confrontational manner for over two years despite the fact that three experts confirmed that there was no evidence of arson. Pilot's action required Mrs Whiten to spend $320,000 in legal costs to collect the $345,000 that was owed to her. At trial, the jury awarded both compensatory damages and punitive damages. The punitive award was upheld by the Supreme Court, which confirmed that the correct test to apply was the,

> 'if but only if' test, i.e., punitive damages should be awarded 'if but only if' the compensatory award is insufficient.[72]

On the facts of the case compensatory damages were held to be inadequate because they were manifestly insufficient to deter the defendant and others from repeating the same outrageous, opportunistic and exploitative conduct.[73] It clearly weighed heavily upon the court that the insurer had made use of its dominant bargaining position in an attempt to force Mrs Whiten into a disadvantageous settlement. The decision in *Whiten* should be contrasted with that in *Sylvan Lake Golf and Tennis Club Ltd v Performance Industries Ltd*[74](decided on the same day), where the Supreme Court declined to award punitive damages. The case concerned a written agreement to purchase a golf course, which, by virtue of the defendant's fraud, did not reflect the earlier oral agreement for the purchase. In holding that compensatory damages plus costs were an adequate remedy, it was significant to the court that the contract was between businessmen who were equals.[75] Nothing more was needed to achieve the objectives of retribution, deterrence and denunciation.

III WHY DAMAGES ARE INADEQUATE

Having considered the circumstances in which damages are deemed to be inadequate it is now necessary to consider the reasons why damages are inadequate in those situations.

71 Above n 67.
72 *Ibid*, 305.
73 *Ibid*, 305–6.
74 (2002) 209 DLR (4th) 318.
75 *Ibid*, [88].

A No Market Substitute

Why are damages deemed to be inadequate when no market substitute is available? According to Lord Redesdale, it is because damages,

> would not give the party the compensation to which he is entitled; that is, would not put him in a situation as beneficial to him *as if the agreement were specifically performed*.[76]

A contracting party is entitled to be put in a position as beneficial to him as if the agreement had been performed. In other words, he is entitled to have his interest in performance protected. An award of damages will fail to do this unless the damages can be used to purchase substitute performance. For this reason, whenever substitute performance is unavailable, damages are deemed to be an insufficient 'remedy and satisfaction for the loss of the performance of the contract'.[77]

It is clear that a party to a contract is entitled to performance itself and not merely to the economic value of performance. *Pacta sunt servanda*—agreements must be kept. Of course, it is not necessary for the promisor himself to perform, but if he fails to provide the bargained-for performance he must provide the promisee with the means of obtaining performance from an alternative source. Damages will provide such means if market substitutes are available. However, where the subject matter of the contract is unique,[78] or where supply is restricted[79] or only available from the promisor himself,[80] damages will be inadequate for this purpose. The award will provide insufficient protection to the bargained-for interest in performance of the contract.

The fact that damages are deemed to be inadequate where a market substitute is unavailable demonstrates that the law is committed to protecting the performance interest of contracts. Parties will be required either to perform or to provide a remedy that constitutes a satisfactory substitute for performance. Damages will not be such a remedy if no market substitute is available.

B Damages are Difficult to Quantify

An award of damages is inadequate where those damages are difficult to quantify because the innocent party will be left with something less than

76 *Harnett v Yielding* (1805) 2 Sch & Lef 549, 553 per Lord Redesdale (emphasis added).
77 *Falcke v Gray*, above n 9, 657 per Kindersley VC.
78 *Falcke v Gray*, *ibid*.
79 *Sky Petroleum Ltd v VIP Petroleum*, above n 14.
80 *AG v Blake*, above n 1.

the performance he had bargained for. In *Adderley v Dixon*, a case concerning a contract for the sale of a debt, Leach VC said,

> to compel the Plaintiff in such a case to take damages would be to compel him to sell the annual provision during his life for which he had contracted at a conjectural price.[81]

Damages are inadequate because they fail to protect the innocent party's bargained-for interest in performance. As Spry notes, 'adequacy . . . of damages must be considered from a practical and not a theoretical point of view'.[82] If damages are likely, in practice, to leave the claimant in a worse position than performance of the contract, then damages will be deemed to be inadequate.[83] Remedial inadequacy will inevitably arise where damages are merely a rough estimate of the loss sustained by the claimant.

The case of *Esso v Niad* illustrates the point. The claimant had undoubtedly suffered a pecuniary loss (in the form of lost sales) as a result of the defendant's failure to charge at or below the Pricewatch recommended price. The problem was that the loss could not be accurately quantified. If Esso had been left with damages calculated by mere conjecture, then the court would have failed to protect Esso's bargained-for interest in performance. Such a decision would have given Niad and the other participants in the Pricewatch scheme every incentive to break the agreement again, knowing that the damages they would be required to pay would be significantly less than the value of the performance they had agreed to render. Such a failure to protect Esso's contractual rights would have undermined the Pricewatch scheme altogether. As Salmon LJ noted in *Decro-Wall v Practitioners*, damages calculated by conjecture are 'a positive encouragement to contract-breakers'.[84] For this reason, damages are inadequate if they are difficult to quantify.

C Insolvency of the Defendant

Insolvency of the defendant is a controversial basis for finding damages to be inadequate, as noted above. However, assuming that insolvency is a valid ground for inadequacy, this is because adequacy is to be assessed 'from a practical and not a theoretical point of view'.[85] In *Evans Marshall v Bertola*, Sachs LJ said that the court will ask: 'Is it just, in all the circum-

81 Above n 5, 611.
82 Spry, above n 20, 66.
83 *Evans Marshall v Bertola*, above n 15, 380 per Sachs LJ.
84 *Decro-Wall International SA v Practitioners in Marketing Ltd* [1971] 1 WLR 361, 372.
85 Spry, above n 20, 66.

stances that a plaintiff should be confined to his remedy in damages?'[86] This question should be answered both by reference to the adequacy of damages as a substitute for performance and the likelihood that the damages will be paid. The court must ask: 'Are the defendants good for the money?'[87] If not, then the award of damages will be worthless. Instead of receiving the bargained-for performance agreed to in the contract, the claimant will receive an unenforceable money judgment. This will fail to protect the claimant's bargained-for interest in performance and, for this reason, it will be inadequate.

D Only Nominal Damages are Available

This is undoubtedly the most significant basis for finding compensatory damages to be inadequate. It has been used to justify awards of loss of amenity damages, gain-based damages and orders of specific performance. But why are damages deemed to be inadequate in such circumstances?

At the outset it is important to note that this ground is proven unworkable when taken to its extreme. This is what Campbell and Wylie show in their critique of *Hendrix* in the *Cambridge Law Journal*.[88] They give the following hypothetical cases by way of contrast:

> The defendant agrees to deliver generic goods to the claimant for a price of £1 m. Part of the factory in which he intended to make the goods is then destroyed by fire, and, were he to try to perform his obligations by rescheduling his production in order to still make the goods himself, it would cost him £1.5 m to do so. These goods are available on the market for £1.1 m. The rational thing to do is to breach. On 'traditional' damages rules, the defendant will be liable for £100,000 market damages, that sum representing, of course, the excess of the claimant's payment to a third party seller over the contract price, and it is rational for the defendant to breach because this is smaller than the £500,000 extra expense which actual performance would cause him . . .
>
> But let us imagine that the goods were available on the market for £1 m. The defendant will *a fortiori* wish to breach, but things are very different from the restitutionary perspective. The claimant now has no loss on compensatory rules, and it is difficult to see why this will not generate a restitutionary claim . . . It is, we submit, impossible to distinguish these two cases on the ground that in one of them compensatory damages are nominal; the logic of disgorgement of wrongful profits must apply to both (and if it applied to merely one it would still be completely unacceptable).[89]

86 Above n 15, 379 per Sachs LJ.
87 *Ibid*, 380.
88 D Campbell and P Wylie, 'Ain't No Telling (Which Circumstances are Exceptional)' (2003) 62 *CLJ* 605.
89 *Ibid*, 615–16. See also D Harris, D Campbell and R Halson, *Remedies in Contract and Tort* (London, Butterworths, 2nd edn, 2002), 267.

Campbell and Wylie construct a 'straw man' in order to condemn the availability of gain-based damages for breach of contract. The second hypothetical situation that they present is an extreme and unlikely example. The claimant has suffered no loss as a consequence of the breach;[90] he is able to obtain substitute performance from an alternative source at no extra cost. In this unlikely scenario it is indisputable that damages would be adequate since they would put the claimant 'in a situation as beneficial to him as if the agreement were specifically performed'.[91] Thus damages would provide sufficient protection to the claimant's bargained-for interest in performance since the only interest he has is in the economic value of performance. In such cases the parties understand their obligations as disjunctive, requiring them either to perform or to pay damages. No court has ever decided that nominal damages are inadequate in such a case.

These scenarios are nonetheless rare. More common is the situation in which the claimant has a non-pecuniary interest in performance which would be left unprotected by an award of nominal damages. These non-pecuniary interests take many different forms. In *Beswick*,[92] the promisee had an interest in performance for the benefit of a third party, his wife. In *Ruxley*,[93] the claimant had a subjective non-pecuniary interest in obtaining a swimming pool seven feet, six inches deep regardless of whether that depth increased the value of his property. In *Farley*,[94] the claimant had a bargained-for interest in obtaining a house free from aircraft noise. In *Blake*,[95] the Crown had an interest in preventing its employees from disclosing information obtained in the course of their employment. In *Wrotham Park*,[96] the claimant had an interest in limiting the number of houses built on its land. In each case, compensatory damages assessed by reference to financial loss were inadequate because they failed to take into account these bargained-for non-pecuniary interests.

People in society frequently enter into contracts for non-financial reasons. Consumers do so as seen in *Ruxley* and *Farley*; family members do so as seen in *Beswick*; governments do so as seen in *Blake*. The law of contract is committed to facilitating these transactions and does so by protecting performance, not merely the economic value of performance. Because of this, nominal damages assessed by reference to pecuniary loss

90 Campbell and Wylie concede that it could be argued that damages are adequate because the claimant has suffered no loss. However, they reply that this may be difficult to prove if the claimant contends, influenced by *Hendrix*, that he has suffered a loss which is difficult to quantify. *Ibid*, 616.

91 *Harnett v Yielding*, above n 76, 553 per Lord Redesdale.

92 Above n 27.

93 Above n 33.

94 Above n 38.

95 Above n 1.

96 Above n 45.

will be deemed to be inadequate where the innocent party's objectives can only be achieved by performance of the contract. In such cases damages will fail to give the claimant 'clear and full compensation'.[97] They will, in the words of Lord Upjohn, be 'inadequate to meet the justice of the case'.[98]

In summary, nominal damages will not always be inadequate. If the parties only bargained for the economic value of performance, then nominal damages will meet the justice of the case so long as no pecuniary loss was sustained as a result of the breach. Campbell and Wylie's second case fits into this category. However, where the bargained-for interest in performance consists of some non-pecuniary benefit, nominal damages will be inadequate because the award will fail to adequately protect the claimant's bargained-for interest in performance.

E Insufficient Deterrence

Damages are deemed to be inadequate where they are insufficient to 'accomplish the objectives of retribution, deterrence and denunciation'.[99] There is an important assumption behind this basis of inadequacy: breach of contract should be denounced and deterred by the court. The reason for this is the commercial desirability of preserving the security of transactions. This will be considered in greater detail in the following section.[100] Compensatory damages are usually adequate to effect deterrence and denunciation,[101] but where a defendant has exploited his superior bargaining position to deny the claimant his bargained-for interest in performance, compensatory damages might be inadequate to effect deterrence and denunciation. This occurred on the facts of both *Whiten* and *Got*. The defendants were in a position of superior bargaining power, which they exploited in an attempt to deter the claimant from enforcing his rights. An award of compensatory damages would have been inadequate to accomplish the goal of deterrence since it would have merely compelled the defendant to do what it had already promised to do. Such an award would have given the defendant and others every incentive to repeat the breach since, at worst, they would be required to pay the promisee damages equivalent to the bargained-for performance; at best they would escape liability altogether, because the promisee would be deterred from taking action to enforce his rights.

97 J Story, *Equity Jurisprudence* (Boston, MA, Little & Brown, 1st edn, 1836), 34.
98 Above n 27, 102 per Lord Upjohn.
99 *Whiten v Pilot Insurance Company*, above n 67, 303 per Binnie J.
100 See below at pp. 137–8.
101 *Royal Bank of Canada v Got*, above n 67, 394 per McLachlin and Bastarache JJ.

Because the law of contract is committed to preserving the security of transactions it is committed to deterring breaches of contract. Usually compensatory damages will be adequate for this purpose, but if the contract breaker abuses his bargaining position in order to avoid compensation this constitutes a serious 'affront to the administration of justice'[102] and requires an alternative remedy.

IV THE SIGNIFICANCE OF THE INADEQUACY OF DAMAGES

The discussion in sections II and III has shown that there are numerous situations in which damages are inadequate because they fail to put the promisee 'in a situation as beneficial to him as if the agreement were specifically performed'.[103] In other words, damages are found to be inadequate because they fail to protect the promisee's bargained-for interest in performance. What are the implications of this conclusion?

A Recognition of the Obligation to Perform

First, the recognition that an award of damages is frequently an inadequate remedy for breach of contract necessitates the rejection of Oliver Wendell Holmes's claim that contractual promises entail no obligation to perform. Holmes famously purported to wash idealistic theories of the law in 'cynical acid' by banishing words of moral significance from the law.[104] In doing so, he claimed that the 'only universal consequence of a legally binding promise, is that the law makes the promisor pay damages if the promised event does not come to pass'. Thus, each party is 'free from interference until the time for fulfilment has gone by, and therefore free to break his contract if he chooses'.[105] Holmes insisted that contracts are nothing more than disjunctive obligations:

> The duty to keep a contract at common law means a prediction that you must pay damages if you do not keep it—and nothing else. If you commit a tort, you are liable to pay a compensatory sum. If you commit a contract, you are liable to pay a compensatory sum unless the promised event comes to pass, and that is all the difference.[106]

102 *Ibid*, 395 per McLachlin and Bastarache JJ.
103 *Harnett v Yielding*, above n 76, 553 per Lord Redesdale.
104 OW Holmes, 'The Path of the Law' in *Collected Legal Papers* (New York, Harcourt Brace, 1920), 179.
105 OW Holmes, *The Common Law*, M de Wolfe Howe, ed (London, Macmillan, 1968), 236.
106 Holmes, above n 104, 175.

The problems with Holmes's theory have been well documented,[107] yet it continues to exert considerable influence.[108] The theory cannot be sustained, however, in light of the law's insistence that compensatory damages are frequently an inadequate response to a breach of contract. If the obligation created by a contract really is just a disjunctive obligation either to perform or to pay damages, then an award of damages will necessarily be an adequate response to a breach of contract. The fact that damages are frequently found not to be adequate demonstrates that there is more to a contract than merely a disjunctive obligation.

In *The Hansa Nord*, Roskill LJ famously asserted that 'contracts are made to be performed and not to be avoided'.[109] In a similar vein, Oliver LJ insisted that 'the purpose of a contract is performance and not the grant of an option to pay damages'.[110] Unquestionably this corresponds to what the parties intend. Buckland reminded us: 'One does not buy a right to damages, one buys a horse'.[111] Performance is usually the one and only ground for formation of a contract. In most situations, a person enters into a contract because he desires to receive that which the other party is offering and because he places a higher value on the other party's performance than on the cost he will incur to obtain it.[112] Contracts are formed because the parties wish to acquire an interest in the promised performance. This interest has been labelled the 'performance interest'. Professor Coote explains it as follows:

> What distinguishes an effective contractual promise from any other is that it is intended to, and does in fact, confer on the promisee an enforceable legal right to have the promise performed.[113]

107 F Pollock, *Contracts* (London, Stevens, 1911), 192; F Pollock, *Pollock–Holmes Letters*, M de Wolfe Howe, ed (Cambrige, Cambridge University Press,1942), vol 1, 3, 78–80, vol II, 234–5; P Atiyah, *Essays on Contract* (Oxford, Clarendon Press, 1986), 58–66; D Friedmann, 'The Efficient Breach Fallacy' (1989) 18 *Journal of Legal Studies* 1; R Cunnington, 'Should Punitive Damages be Part of the Judicial Arsenal in Contract Cases?' (2006) 26 *Legal Studies* 369, 385–9.

108 Holmes's theory undoubtedly influenced the emphasis upon damages in LL Fuller and WR Perdue, 'The Reliance Interest in Contract Damages' (1936) 46 *Yale Law Journal* 52 and G Gilmore, *Death of Contract* (Columbus, OH, Ohio State University Press, 1974). The theory still exerts considerable influence today: D Campbell and D Harris, 'In Defence of Breach: a Critique of Restitution and the Performance Interest' (2002) 22 *Legal Studies* 208, 218; S Waddams, *The Law of Damages* (Aurora, Ontario, Canada Law Book Ltd, 4th edn, 2003), para 11.250; A Farnsworth, 'Legal Remedies for Breach of Contract' (1970) 70 *Columbia Law Review* 1145, 1216.

109 *Cehave NV v Bremer Handelsgesellschaft mbH* [1976] QB 44, 71.

110 *George Mitchell v Finney Lock (Seeds) Ltd* [1983] QB 284, 304.

111 F Buckland, 'The Nature of Contractual Obligation' (1944) 8 *CLJ* 247, 249–51.

112 D Friedmann, 'The Performance Interest in Contract Damages (1995) 111 *LQR* 628, 629.

113 B Coote, 'The Performance Interest, *Panatown*, and the Problem of Loss' (2001) 117 *LQR* 81. See also B Coote, 'Contract Damages, *Ruxley*, and the Performance Interest' [1997] *CLJ* 537, 540–3.

B The Wrongfulness of Breach

A contract confers on the promisee an enforceable legal right to have the promise performed. This explains why breach of contract is a civil wrong in English law.[114] Several commentators have doubted this proposition. Notably, Professors Campbell and Harris have claimed that breach of contract should only be treated as a wrong if it is committed in bad faith.[115] However, this misunderstands the nature of a wrong. Whilst in colloquial usage the language of wrongdoing invokes notions of blameworthiness and fault, this does not correspond to the legal usage of wrongdoing. As Professor Birks has shown: 'A legal wrong is a breach of a duty recognised by law'.[116] It is nothing more. Hence a person who sells a car belonging to another commits the wrong of conversion, even though he carefully attempted to verify the title of the person who sold it to him.[117] Likewise, a fiduciary such as Mr Boardman is accountable for the profits he makes from his breach of fiduciary duty even though he acted 'with complete honesty throughout' and in 'an open and honourable manner'.[118] A wrong is a breach of a duty recognised by law. Fault and harm are commonly observable in the breach but they are not necessary and they are not sufficient.[119]

Breach of contract is a civil wrong because it is a breach of the promisee's legal right to have the promise performed. The crucial implication of this analysis is that there is no fixed measure of response to a breach of contract. This point requires emphasis because of the common assumption that compensatory damages are the one and only response to a breach of contract.[120] This is incorrect because, as Professor Birks has contended,

> the content of the remedial or secondary obligation triggered by a wrong is for the law to decide as a matter of policy constrained only by extrinsic considerations.[121]

114 See, eg *AG v Blake*, above n 1, 278 per Lord Nicholls.
115 Campbell and Harris, above n 108, 220.
116 P Birks, 'The Concept of a Civil Wrong' in D Owen (ed), *Philosophical Foundations of Tort Law* (Oxford, Clarendon Press, 1995), 51.
117 *Hollins v Fowler* (1872) LR 7 QB 616; *Marfani & Co Ltd v Midland Bank Ltd* [1968] 1 WLR 956, 971 per Diplock LJ.
118 *Boardman v Phipps* [1967] 2 AC 46, 104 per Lord Cohen, 105 per Lord Hodson.
119 P Birks, 'Rights, Wrongs and Remedies' (2000) 20 *OJLS* 1, 31.
120 Proponents of this view usually rely upon Baron Parke's statement in *Robinson v Harman* (1848) 1 Ex 850, 855; 154 ER 363, 365. See, eg *British Westinghouse Electric and Manufacturing Co Ltd v Underground Electric Railways Co of London Ltd* [1912] AC 673, 689 per Viscount Haldane LC; *Stoke-on-Trent City Council v W & J Wass Ltd* [1988] 1 WLR 1406, 1410 per Nourse LJ; *Ruxley Electronics*, above n 33, 355 per Lord Jauncey, 365–6 per Lord Lloyd; *Alfred McAlpine Constructions v Panatown Ltd* [2001] 1 AC 518, 533–4 per Lord Clyde.
121 Birks, above n 116, 51.

It is necessary to note a crucial distinction here between the position adopted in this paper and the position assumed by Holmes. Holmes argued, to use the terminology of John Austin,[122] that the primary obligation of a contract is disjunctive: the promisor is required either to perform the contract or to pay damages. On this analysis, contractual breach is not a violation of a primary right. Rather, it is an election to perform the alternative primary obligation; an election to pay damages instead of performing. Understood this way, breach of contract is not a wrong; it is a 'not-wrong'. This has important implications when it comes to the law's response to a breach of contract. The crucial distinction between a wrong and a not-wrong is that the label 'wrong' operates as a licence to the law to mistreat the wrongdoer.[123] The law has a wide choice as to response to a wrong. By contrast, not-wrongs leave very little room for choice. Because the defendant has not breached a legal duty the law has no general licence to mistreat the defendant. In the context of a claim for breach of contract this means that the only remedy available to the court is an award of compensatory damages. Obviously, this conclusion is impossible to reconcile with the cases in which compensatory damages have been held to be inadequate. If the primary right of the contract is a right to receive damages, then it is nonsense to speak of damages being inadequate.[124]

English law deems damages to be inadequate because the primary right created by a contract is the right to receive the bargained-for performance. By entering into a contract, the parties declare, 'I am bound to do what I have promised to do'.[125] When one of the parties fails to perform his contractual obligations he violates the other party's primary right to receive performance. This constitutes a wrong and creates remedial or secondary rights. Whilst the content of the rights triggered by a not-wrong must mirror the content of the primary right, the content of the remedial rights triggered by a wrong is, in principle, a mere matter of policy. In the words of Professor Birks:

> The law has a free choice of what it shall be, subject only to extrinsic considerations such as values of proportionality, determinacy, humanity, and so on.[126]

122 J Austin, *Lectures in Jurisprudence*, R Campbell, ed (London, John Murray, 3rd edn, 1869), Lecture XLV.

123 Birks, above n 119, 33.

124 A similar argument is made by C Webb, 'Performance and Compensation: An Analysis of Contract Damages and Contractual Obligation' (2006) 26 *OJLS* 41, 49.

125 C Fried, *Contract as Promise* (Cambridge, MA, Harvard University Press, 1981), 19.

126 Birks, above n 116, 47.

C The Need for Protection of Performance

We can only discern the rules relating to the availability of remedies for breach of contract if we understand the policies and values underlying the recognition of the primary duty to perform a contract. Professor Stephen Smith has shown that performed contracts achieve two different things and that, as a result, breaches of contract harm victims of the breach in two different ways.[127] First, performed contracts achieve a tangible result by shifting resources (broadly construed) between the contracting parties. Secondly, performed contracts achieve an intangible result by helping to create bonds of trust between contracting parties.

The second intangible result of performed contracts roughly corresponds to Fried's account of the nature of promising in *Contract as Promise*. Fried contends that promising provides an essential institution by which a person may bind himself to another so that the other may rely on his future performance to the benefit of both parties.[128] The law of contract defines and regulates the practice of promising and provides a device by which a person can create expectations in another. By virtue of the Kantian principles of trust and respect,[129] it is wrong, Fried claims, to breach this convention by dishonouring the promise. As a result, there is a moral obligation to perform.

The problem with Fried's theory is that it adopts an unduly individualistic conception of the law of contract by insisting that all promises should be binding regardless of their social context. Professor Raz has provided a compelling critique of Fried's theory showing that the underlying purpose of contract law is the protection of 'both the practice of undertaking voluntary obligations and the individuals who rely on that practice'.[130] Raz reaches this position by applying Mill's harm principle[131] to institutional harm.[132] He contends that the law plays an essential supportive role in making contracts outside of the framework of ongoing relations much more common by making them more reliable. Without this supportive institution, voluntary undertakings would frequently be compromised, and harm would be caused to the commercial world and society in general because of a lack of certainty.[133] Raz concludes that the enforcement of voluntary obligations is not, in itself, a proper goal of contract law.

127 S Smith, 'Performance, Punishment and Contractual Obligations' (1997) 60 *MLR* 360, 367.

128 Fried, above n 125, 16.

129 I Kant, *The Metaphysical Elements of Justice*, J Ladd, trans (Indianapolis, IN Bobbs-Merrill, 1965), 54–5.

130 J Raz ,'Promises in Morality and Law' (1981–1982) 95 *Harvard Law Review* 916, 933.

131 JS Mill, *On Liberty* (Cambridge, Cambridge University Press, 1989).

132 Raz, above n 130, 937. See also J Feinberg, *Social Philosophy* (Englewood Cliffs, NJ, Prentice Hall,1973), 33–5.

133 The need for such institutional protection has been developed by others: see I Jackman 'Restitution for Wrongs' [1989] CLJ 302; Friedmann, above n 107, 7–8.

However, the enforcement of contracts can be justified as a means to an end, in preventing the debasement of the practice of undertaking voluntary obligations.

The policy underlying the law's recognition of the primary duty to perform a contract is a commitment to the protection of both the individuals concerned and the practice of undertaking voluntary obligations. When a court declares compensatory damages to be inadequate it is really declaring compensatory damages to be inadequate to fulfil this purpose. This rightly concerns the law because, unless the parties are confident that their bargained-for interests will be protected, they will be reluctant to contract at all, and the benefits of coordination and constructive action will be frustrated.[134] To prevent this happening, the courts have developed an armoury of specific and substitutionary remedies to vindicate the claimant's bargained-for interest in performance.[135] To this we now turn in the final section of the paper.

V ADDRESSING THE PROBLEM OF INADEQUACY

In section III a number of circumstances were identified in which damages are said to be inadequate. In section IV we saw that the reason why an award of damages is inadequate in such cases is because it fails to protect the parties' bargained-for interest in performance. English law is committed to maintaining society's confidence in the facilitative institution of contracting. To ensure that confidence is maintained, the courts will award an alternative remedy whenever compensatory damages are inadequate to protect the claimant's interest in performance. The courts have a broad array of remedies at their disposal to address remedial inadequacy.

A Loss of Amenity Damages

In many cases an expanded conception of loss will provide the solution. Instead of assessing damages by reference to the market value of perform-

134 J Finnis, *Natural Law and Natural Rights* (Oxford, Clarendon Press, 1980), 325; P Jaffey, 'Efficiency, Disgorgement and Reliance in Contract: a Comment on Campbell and Harris' (2002) 22 *Legal Studies* 570, 573; J Danforth, 'Tortious Interference with Contract: A Reassertion of Society's Interest in Commercial Stability and Contractual Integrity' (1981) 81 *Colorado Law Review* 1491, 1509 and 1511–14.

135 For an excellent taxonomy of remedies that divides replicative remedies into specific remedies (replicating primary rights) and substitutionary remedies (replicating secondary rights), see R Zakrzewski, 'The Classification of Judicial Remedies' [2003] *Lloyd's Maritime and Commercial Law Quarterly* 477; R Zakrzewski, *Remedies Reclassified* (Oxford, Oxford University Press, 2005), 103–202.

ance, the courts have shown an increased willingness to take into account the personal preferences of the claimant. In *Ruxley*, Lord Mustill said that,

> the law must cater for those occasions where the value of the promise to the promisee exceeds the financial enhancement of his position which full performance will secure.[136]

His Lordship adopted the terminology of Harris, Ogus and Phillips[137] and labelled this excess as the 'consumer surplus'. He insisted that, where such a surplus exists, 'the law should recognise it and compensate the promisee if the misperformance takes it away'.[138] Following *Ruxley*, it appears that loss of amenity damages are available whenever,

> a party's contractual performance has failed to provide to the other contracting party something to which that other was, under the contract, entitled, and which, if provided, would have been of value to that party.[139]

It has even been suggested that the defendant's failure to perform is itself a loss for which the claimant can be compensated,[140] although this view has been subjected to some criticism.[141] An expanded conception of loss will undoubtedly go a long way towards dealing with remedial inadequacy, but there will continue to be situations in which damages are inadequate to protect the claimant's bargained-for interest in performance. In such situations an alternative remedy will be required.

B Specific Relief

The primary remedy adopted to address the problem of inadequacy (and thus the secondary remedy for breach of contract) is specific relief.[142] Specific relief can be ordered whenever damages are inadequate to do justice between the parties. It clearly provides optimal protection to the claimant's bargained-for interest in performance since it replicates the claimant's primary right to have the contract performed.[143] In practice,

136 Above n 33, 360.
137 Harris et al, above n 35.
138 Above n 33, 361.
139 *Farley v Skinner*, above n 32, 766 per Lord Scott.
140 This seems to be the sense in which Lord Nicholls used the term 'loss' in *AG v Blake*, above n 81, 282. Lords Goff and Millett both believed that the respondent had a compensatory claim for lost performance (even though no financial loss had been suffered) on the facts of *Alfred McAlpine Construction Ltd v Panatown Ltd* [2001] 1 AC 518, 547–54 per Lord Goff, 585–92 per Lord Millett. See also *St Martins Property Corporation Ltd v Robert McAlpine Ltd* [1994] 1 AC 85, 96–7 per Lord Griffiths.
141 *McAlpine v Panatown*, *ibid*, 533–4 per Lord Clyde. See also Webb, above n 124, 54.
142 In the form of either specific performance or an injunction.
143 Although specific performance replicates the claimant's primary right, it is still recognising a secondary right since it is a response to the wrong of breach. Specific performance will only be ordered if the defendant has already breached the contract or if it is anticipated that he will

however, the courts are often reluctant to order specific relief. This may be for a number of reasons. Specific relief may be impossible because the date for performance has already passed.[144] It may be undesired because the claimant wishes to have nothing further to do with the promisor. It may be unavailable because the contract is for the provision of personal service.[145] Alternatively, relief might be denied because it is difficult for the court to supervise.[146] Or specific relief might be rejected for discretionary reasons, eg hardship to the defendant,[147] the conduct of the plaintiff,[148] lack of mutuality,[149] delay[150] or reasons of public policy.[151]

None of these reasons are due to unwillingness on the part of the court to protect the claimant's bargained-for interest in performance. Rather, they relate to the peculiar nature of specific relief as a contempt-backed equitable remedy. Specific performance of a contract for personal service is denied because it is considered to be undesirable for the courts to use the coercive machinery of contempt proceedings to compel the continuance of a 'personal relationship' between unwilling parties.[152] Specific performance of a contract to continue to run a business is refused because of the impracticability of requiring the court to give an 'indefinite series of rulings to ensure the execution of the order'.[153] The discretionary considerations, such as delay, hardship, the conduct of the claimant and the mutuality requirement, all relate to the equitable nature of specific relief. Finally, because performance is often only of value if rendered within a specific time frame, specific relief will be unavailable if the time for performance has passed. Whenever specific relief is denied for one of these reasons it is because specific relief is impossible, impractical or undesirable.

commit a breach: see A Burrows, *Remedies for Torts and Breach of Contract* (London, LexisNexis, 2004), 456. Cf Birks, 'Rights, Wrongs', above n 119, 27; Webb, above n 124, 50.

144 *AG v Blake*, above n 1; *Esso Petroleum v Niad*, above n 52.

145 *Johnson v Shrewsbury & Birmingham Rly* (1853) 3 DM & G 914; *Brett v East India Shipping Co* (1864) 2 H & C 404; *Chappell v The Times Newspaper* [1975] 1 WLR 482; *De Francesco v Barnum* (1890) 45 Ch D 430.

146 *Co-op Insurance v Argyll Stores (Holdings) Ltd* [1998] AC 1; *Ryan v Mutual Tontine Westminster Chambers Association* [1893] 1 Ch 116; *JC Williamson Ltd v Lukey and Mulholland* (1931) 45 CLR 282.

147 *Shell UK v Lostock Garage Ltd* [1976] 1 WLR 1187; *Patel v Ali* [1984] Ch 283, 288 per Goulding J.

148 *Mountford v Scott* [1975] Ch 258; *Walters v Morgan* (1861) 3 DF & J 718; *Quadrant Visual Communications Ltd v Hutchinson Telephone (UK) Ltd* [1993] BCLC 442.

149 *Price v Stange* [1978] Ch 337, 367–8 per Buckley LJ; *Blackett v Bates* (1865) LR 1 Ch App 117; *Flight v Bolland* (1828) 4 Russ 298; *Lumley v Ravenscroft* [1895] 1 QB 683.

150 *Lazard Bros & Co Ltd v Fairfield Property Co (Mayfair) Ltd* (1977) 121 SJ 793; *Amec Developments Ltd v Jury's Hotel Management (UK) Ltd* (2001) 82 P & CR 22; *Harris v Williams-Wynne* [2005] EWHC 151.

151 *Ewing v Osbaldiston* (1837) 2 My & Cr 53; *Sutton v Sutton* [1984] Ch 184; *Wroth v Tyler* [1974] Ch 30.

152 See Smith, above n 127, 368–9; A Kronman, 'Paternalism and the Law of Contracts' (1983) 92 *Yale Law Journal* 763.

153 *Co-Op Insurance v Argyll Stores (Holdings) Ltd* [1998] AC 1, 12 per Lord Hoffmann.

It is not because the court is any less committed to protecting the claimant's bargained-for interest in performance. The problem of inadequacy remains and the court must consider alternative remedies.

C Gain-based Damages

The main alternative to specific relief (and thus the tertiary remedy for breach of contract) is gain-based damages. In *AG v Blake* Lord Nicholls said:[154]

> In practice . . . specific remedies go a long way towards providing suitable protection for innocent parties who will suffer loss from breaches of contract which are not adequately remediable by an award of damages. But these remedies are not always available . . . Then the breach is irreversible . . . In the same way as a plaintiff's interest in performance of a contract may render it just and equitable for the court to make an order for specific performance or grant an injunction, so the plaintiff's interest in performance may make it just and equitable that the defendant should retain no benefit from his breach of contract.

Gain-based damages are available when damages are inadequate and specific relief is unavailable. In such circumstances, 'the breach is irreversible', and gain-based damages are awarded as an alternative to specific relief.[155]

Professor Beatson has spoken of gain-based damages as being 'in reality a monetised form of specific performance'.[156] This seems to be correct for two reasons. First, the 'deterrent' reason: if a person knows that he will be stripped of his profits, he will be deterred from breaking the contract in the first place. Thus, while specific relief compels the defendant to perform the contract through the threat of coercive sanctions, gain-based damages perform the same function by removing any incentive to breach. The second reason is what I refer to as the 'value' reason: gain-based damages require the defendant to return the value of his breach. The sum awarded is equivalent to the value of specific performance; or, conversely, it is equivalent to the value of non-performance to the defendant.

154 [2001] 1 AC 268, 282 and 285 per Lord Nicholls. See also *WWF—World Wide Fund for Nature v World Wrestling Federation Entertainment* [2006] EWHC 184 (Ch), [137] per Peter Smith J.

155 Elsewhere I argue that equitable damages (and, by implication, gain-based damages) are best viewed as an 'alternative' rather than a 'substitute' for specific relief because they are available even when full equitable relief has been refused: Cunnington, above n 42, 234–5. See *Jaggard v Sawyer* [1995] 1 WLR 269.

156 J Beatson, *The Use and Abuse of Unjust Enrichment* (Oxford, Oxford University Press, 1991), 17. See also P Maddaugh and J McCamus, *The Law of Restitution* (Aurora, Ontario, Canada Law Book Ltd, 1990), 432–8; *Adras Building Material Ltd v Harlow and Jones Gmbh* [1995] RLR 235, 241 per S Levin J, 272 per Barak J. Elsewhere in this volume Professor Stephen Smith argues that 'cost of cure' damages are a form of 'substitute specific relief'; see Smith, 'Substitutionary Damages'.

At this juncture, it is important to note a crucial distinction between two different measures of gain-based damages. These were identified by Mance LJ in *Experience Hendrix v PPX*. His Lordship distinguished between the *Blake* measure, which requires the defendant to 'give up' a gain, and the *Wrotham Park* measure, which requires the defendant to 'give back' a gain.[157] In *Blake*, the defendant was required to give up all his profits regardless of whether it could be shown that the profits had been derived directly from the Crown. Indeed, it seems that the Attorney General would still have been entitled to claim gain-based damages even if Blake had been able to show that all of his profits had been generated by his own work and skill.[158] The *Blake* measure was a real assessment of the actual profits received by the defendant as a consequence of his breach.

By contrast, the *Wrotham Park* measure was a judicial assessment of the objective value received by the defendant as a consequence of his breach. Dr Edelman has described the damages in *Wrotham Park* as,

> a monetary award which reverses a transfer of value. It is an award which gives back value transferred from a claimant to a defendant as a result of a defendant's wrong and is almost always measured by the objective gain received by the defendant.[159]

The *Wrotham Park* measure is a judicially determined value placed on the objective benefit transferred from the claimant to the defendant. It is not tied to the actual profit made by the defendant and, indeed, can exceed the *Blake* measure, where the defendant, by his own incompetence, has failed to make any profit.[160]

These two measures of damages are both gain-based, but they perform very different functions. As has already been noted, an award of gain-based damages approximates to a monetised form of specific relief because it removes the incentive to breach and compels the defendant to give up the value of his non-performance. On a closer examination it can be seen that the *Wrotham Park* measure fulfils the latter function (but rarely the former) whilst the *Blake* measure fulfils the former function (and sometimes the latter).

Wrotham Park damages literally require the defendant to pay a just price for the value of non-performance. Brightman J described the award as,

157 For a more detailed analysis of this distinction, see Edelman, *Gain-Based Damages*, above n 62, ch 3; J Edelman, '*Attorney-General v Blake* Revisited' [2003] *Restitution Law Review* 101, 105; Cunnington, above n 40. See also *WWF*, above n 155, [119] per Peter Smith J.

158 For examples of this, see *Boardman* v *Phipps*, above n 119; *Regal (Hastings) Ltd v Gulliver* [1967] 2 AC 134n.

159 Edelman, *Gain-Based Damages*, above n 62, ch 3, 66.

160 Above n 51, [26]. See also *Sempra Metals Ltd (formerly Metallgesellschaft Ltd) v Inland Revenue Commissioners* [2007] UKHL 34; [2007] 3 WLR 354 (HL) at [230] per Lord Mance.

> such sum as might reasonably have been demanded by the plaintiffs from Parkside as a *quid pro quo* for relaxing the covenant.[161]

In other words, the sum was the objective value of release from Parkside's contractual obligations.[162] Such damages require the defendant to give back the value of non-performance but they do not constitute an absolute deterrent to breach because the defendant may still retain some of the profit made from his breach.[163] For this reason, such damages are a monetised form of specific performance only in a very weak sense, in that the award requires the defendant to give back the value of his breach. *Blake* damages, on the other hand, are a monetised form of specific performance in a stronger sense. An award of *Blake* damages constitutes an absolute deterrent to breach since it compels the defendant to disgorge all of his profit. The award may not, however, compel the defendant to give up the value of his non-performance since it is measured on a subjective basis. To illustrate the point, consider the facts of *Wrotham Park* itself: had Parkside Homes (through its own incompetence) been unable to make any profit from the construction of the additional homes, damages assessed on the *Blake* basis would have been nil. This sum would have constituted an absolute deterrent to breach (since it would have removed any incentive for Parkside to breach), but it would not have compelled Parkside to pay for the objective value of non-performance.

A crucial distinction exists between *Wrotham Park* damages and *Blake* damages. The former do not amount to an absolute deterrent to breach and therefore fall short of a monetised form of specific performance. Their purpose is to provide an alternative remedy in situations where compensatory damages are inadequate and specific relief is unavailable. The reasons given by the courts as to why specific relief is unavailable fall into two categories: (i) reasons why the court 'will not' order specific relief such as delay, hardship and public policy; and (ii) reasons why the court 'cannot' order specific relief such as impossibility or the need for constant supervision. As a general rule, the court will award *Wrotham Park* damages if the reason falls within the first category because protection of the performance interest does not require specific relief/full disgorgement. If the reason falls within the second category the court will award *Blake*[164] damages because protection of the performance interest requires absolute deterrence of breach. In most situations one of these two remedies will be

161 Above n 45, 815.

162 This has led some to argue that the damages awarded in *Wrotham Park* were assessed on compensatory principles by reference to a 'lost opportunity to bargain'. See above p 125.

163 Although, if the objective value of the benefit transferred to the defendant is the same as (or more than) the defendant's profit, then *Wrotham Park* damages will also constitute an absolute deterrent to breach.

164 Or *Wrotham Park* damages, as an alternative, if the defendant has failed to make a profit.

sufficient to protect the claimant's bargained-for interest in performance. In exceptional cases, however, an alternative remedy may be required.

D Punitive Damages

Punitive damages have been recognised as the quaternary remedy for breach of contract in Canadian law. It seems that punitive damages will be awarded where the contract-breaker has attempted to avoid not just the primary obligation of performance, but also the secondary obligation to pay damages. This is what happened on the facts of *Whiten.*[165] Pilot Insurance refused to pay out on Mrs Whiten's insurance claim in the hope that she would be deterred from pursuing the claim due to the prohibitive cost of litigation. Binnie J noted that the need for denunciation was aggravated because the conduct was,

> persisted in over a lengthy period of time (two years to trial) without any rational justification, and despite the defendant's awareness of the hardship it knew it was inflicting (indeed, the respondent anticipated that the greater the hardship to the appellant, the lower the settlement she would ultimately be forced to accept).[166]

Pilot was attempting not only to avoid performance but also to avoid paying damages. It knew that,

> the more devastating the loss, the more the insured may be at the financial mercy of the insurer, and the more difficult it may be to challenge a wrongful refusal to pay the claim.[167]

Pilot abused its position of power[168] in an attempt to avoid both its primary and secondary obligations. The same occurred on the facts of *Got.*[169] The Royal Bank of Canada abused its position in an attempt to deprive Got of both his right to performance and his right to receive compensation. It seems that a distinction exists between a contract breaker who is prepared to compensate and a contract breaker who attempts to avoid compensation. The additional deterrence of punitive damages is required to protect the facilitative institution of contract in the latter situation.[170]

It is unclear, as yet, whether punitive damages have a role to play in any other situations. In principle, there seems to be no reason why they should

165 Above n 67.
166 *Ibid*, 299.
167 *Ibid*, 306 per Binnie J.
168 *Ibid*, 305 per Binnie J.
169 Above n 67.
170 B Chapman and M Trebilock, 'Punitive Damages: Divergence in Search of Rationale' (1989) 40 *Alabama Law Review* 741, 783. See also Smith, above n 127, 374–6.

not be available. Indeed, it might be argued[171] that they have an invaluable role to play in those exceptional cases where equitable relief is refused and gain-based damages are unavailable because the defendant has failed to make a profit from the breach.[172] It is to be expected that the quaternary remedy has a broader role to play than has presently been recognised.

VI CONCLUSION

This paper has shown that there are numerous situations in which an award of compensatory damages may be deemed to be an inadequate remedy for breach of contract. This is often because the award fails to put the promisee 'in a situation as beneficial to him as if the agreement were specifically performed'. A number of conclusions can be drawn. First, it follows that the obligation created by a contract is not disjunctive i.e. to perform or to pay damages. If the obligation were disjunctive, damages would never be an inadequate remedy for breach. Secondly, the obligation created by a contract is an obligation to perform. Breach of this obligation is a wrong giving rise to remedial rights. The purpose of these remedial rights is the protection of the promisee's interest in performance, which is important both for the promisee himself and for the institution of contracting. Thirdly, an award of compensatory damages will usually be adequate for this purpose (and it is thus the primary remedy for breach) because it enables the promisee to purchase substitute performance from an alternative source. In some situations, however, substitute performance will be unavailable or will be insufficient to protect the promisee's bargained-for interest in performance. In such cases the courts will turn to specific relief or gain-based damages as alternative remedies. The purpose of these remedies, and indeed the purpose of all contract remedies, is the protection of the promisee's bargained-for interest in performance. This purpose has been influential in the history of contract remedies and is sure to influence its future.

171 See Cunnington, above n 107, 389–93.

172 The residual value of punitive damages in such situations was recognised by Peter Smith J in the context of a claim for breach of statutory duty in *Design Progression Ltd v Thurloe Properties Ltd* [2005] 1 WLR 1, 29. On the facts of the case, there was no claim for gain-based damages because the defendant had failed to succeed in his profit making purpose.

Part III

Compensation

7

A Good Faith Perspective on Liquidated Damages†

JW CARTER* AND ELISABETH PEDEN**

I INTRODUCTION

A General

EXCEPT TO THE extent that they have provided for a different result, the parties to a legally binding contract are taken to have agreed to pay such damages as the law requires on any breach of the agreement. The ability to provide for a different result includes an ability to agree in advance what damages are payable in the event of breach. An 'agreed damages clause' is such an agreement. Such clauses are more common in some contracts than others, but the commercial purpose in all cases is to provide certainty and to save the expense of proving loss.[1] Unlike an exclusion of liability, an agreed damages clause is, potentially at least, for the benefit of both parties.[2]

Agreed damages clauses are also in the public interest because they reduce the incidence of litigation. However, to permit unbridled freedom in relation to the sum[3] payable under an agreed damages clause would be inconsistent with the legal policy, which insists on compensatory rather

† The paper on which this chapter is based has not been revised since the conference.

* Professor of Commercial Law, University of Sydney; General Editor, *Journal of Contract Law*; Consultant, Freehills.

** Associate Professor of Law, University of Sydney; Book Review Editor, *Journal of Contract Law*; Consultant, Freehills.

1 For a recent statement, see *Philips Hong Kong Ltd v Attorney General of Hong Kong* (1993) 61 BLR 41.

2 See *Cellulose Acetate Silk Co Ltd v Widnes Foundry (1925) Ltd* [1933] AC 20; *Suisse Atlantique Société d'Armement Maritime SA v NV Rotterdamsche Kolen Centrale* [1967] 1 AC 361.

3 Generally we restrict our analysis to stipulations for the payment of money. See further below, text at n 61.

than punitive damages.[4] Accordingly, the law recognises a distinction between an agreed damages clause which is a genuine liquidation of damages and a penalty clause. The former, but not the latter, may be enforced by action. Although the sum agreed upon may turn out to be equal to the amount which a court would award as damages, to require equality as a condition precedent to validity would largely destroy the utility of the facility. Thus, the law does not require the amount stipulated to be equal to what a court would award, and an agreed damages clause is not invalid merely because it is proved to provide for a level of damages which exceeds the promisee's actual loss. Indeed, in most cases, the promisee's actual loss is (or ought to be) largely irrelevant to the validity of the provision.

How the distinction between liquidated damages and penalties is drawn and how the law gives effect to the distinction are complex questions. Given the history of contract law, in principle two approaches might be taken to the distinction. One approach would be to regard a penalty provision as void and ineffective, with the result that the promisee is relegated to a claim for unliquidated damages in relation to any breach to which the penalty applies. Alternatively, the law could permit the promisee to enforce the agreed damages provision to the extent to which it validly liquidates damages, ignoring the penal aspect. In effect, the law would relieve against the penal component of the clause.

In historical terms, while the first solution is a common law approach, the second is an equitable one. The choice between the two would logically give rise to different tests. The former emphasises the idea that damages should not be punitive or coercive. The latter emphasises that it would be unconscionable to enforce the entire payment.

It seems fair to say that the modern law contains elements of each approach. That is one reason for certain complexities and apparent inconsistencies in the law. However, today it would be pointless to try to analyse the distinction between liquidated damages and penalties in terms of 'law' and 'equity'. In any event, although it is important to devote some attention to the legal basis for the distinction,[5] we are not concerned in this paper to determine whether there is any separate 'equitable jurisdiction' in relation to penalties.

Our principal concern, as the title to the paper indicates, is to examine the role of good faith in relation to the distinction between liquidated damages and penalties, and the process of characterisation that the distinction requires. To some extent the paper is prompted by the recent decision of the High Court of Australia in *Ringrow Pty Ltd v BP Australia*

[4] We do not attempt to consider whether agreed damages clauses may be drafted to permit the recovery of a profit made by the promisor which is not a loss to the promisee. Cf K Mason and JW Carter, *Restitution Law in Australia* (Sydney, Butterworths, 1995), §1824.

[5] See below, text at n 15.

Pty Ltd,[6] which is discussed below. Most of the cases on agreed damages clauses which have come before the courts in the past 40 years have involved chattel leases and hire-purchase agreements.[7] Those decisions have tended to push the law of penalties in a particular direction, and led to suggestions that the law requires substantial accuracy between the estimated sum and the amount likely to be awarded in a common law claim. The importance of *Ringrow* is that it has arrested that development. Thus, the High Court approved and applied[8] a statement of principle by Mason and Wilson JJ in *AMEV-UDC Finance Ltd v Austin*,[9] to the effect that an agreed sum is 'only characterized as a penalty if it is out of all proportion to damage likely to be suffered as a result of breach'.

The High Court in *Ringrow* saw this approval and application as a necessary reassertion of the approach to liquidated damages enshrined in the classic decision of the House of Lords in *Dunlop Pneumatic Tyre Co Ltd v New Garage and Motor Co Ltd*,[10] emphasising the role of freedom of contract. Nevertheless the idea that an agreed damages clause will be characterised as a penalty 'only' if it is 'out of all proportion' should not be taken at face value. There are, of necessity, limitations on the 'out of all proportion test'. The view which we wish to put forward is that a good faith perspective assists in explaining not only why the High Court was correct in *Ringrow* to reassert the out of all proportion test, but also the limits on that test.

B Thesis

Good faith refers to 'honesty'. With due respect to those who think otherwise, good faith is not an independent rule or requirement of contract law to be found in an implied term of the contract. It is simply incorrect to assert that all contracts include an implied term requiring parties to act in good faith because good faith is inherent in the institution underlying contract law as a whole.

In relation to contract law as a whole, the task of ensuring good faith in negotiation and performance is achieved by specific doctrines and rules. Although the work of good faith is sometimes achieved by the implication of terms, and notwithstanding that good faith operates in relation to the rules regulating the implication of terms, except in specific contexts or

[6] (2005) 222 ALR 306, [2005] HCA 71.

[7] Leading cases include *Bridge v Campbell Discount Co Ltd* [1962] AC 600; *O'Dea v Allstates Leasing System (WA) Pty Ltd* (1983) 152 CLR 359, 45 ALR 632; *AMEV-UDC Finance Ltd v Austin* (1986) 162 CLR 170, 68 ALR 185; *Esanda Finance Corp Ltd v Plessnig* (1989) 166 CLR 131; 84 ALR 99. A notable exception is *Philips Hong Kong*, above n 1.

[8] Above n 6, (2005) 222 ALR 306, 314 (para [31]).

[9] Above n 7, (1986) 162 CLR 170, 190.

[10] [1915] AC 79.

circumstances good faith is not implied as a term of the contract.[11] In other words, as we have explained elsewhere,[12] because it is inherent in the institution which we call contract, good faith informs the processes of rule formulation and rule application.

In our view, ultimately, agreed damages clauses are characterised as provisions for liquidated damages rather than penalties because the amount designated has been determined in good faith. However, we do not put forward the view that good faith should be applied in place of the applicable legal rules. The basis for the modern law are the principles stated in the *Dunlop* case.[13] To seek to replace those principles with 'good faith' would misconceive the role of good faith in contract law. The specific rules which have been developed to assist in the characterisation of an agreed damages clause as either liquidated damages or a penalty are of necessity informed by—and give effect to—good faith in contract negotiation and enforcement. Good faith is not, and is not designed to be, an onerous standard. It cannot therefore be equated with 'reasonableness'.[14] Instead, it sets a minimum standard to which all rules of contract law must conform, either in the sense of requiring good faith or in the sense of promoting good faith. As we explain below, the penalty rules do not merely promote good faith, they *require* it.

Our thesis is therefore that the rules which make up the law of penalties have been formulated to ensure that only honest pre-estimations of damage are effective to liquidate damages. The relevance of *Ringrow* to this thesis is that the out of all proportion test is of general application because a determination which is 'out of all proportion' does not conform to the legal rules and therefore cannot have been made in good faith. However, because in some contexts an agreed damages clause which may appear to satisfy the out of all proportion test will nevertheless fail under those rules, the test cannot explain all the cases in which clauses have been held to be penal. Nor was that the High Court's intention. The case is an important affirmation of the principle of freedom of contract, but it does not dispense with the requirement of genuineness, which is the hallmark of a liquidated damages provision. Therefore, it does not decide that, where the parties agree upon a sum which is not accurate, or is clearly wrong, the clause will be upheld so long as the inaccuracy or error does not result in an amount which is 'out of all proportion'. The rules applied to determine whether an agreed damages clause is an invalid penalty are in our view more discerning

11 Those circumstances include statute. See, eg Insurance Contracts Act 1984 (Cth), s 13 (implied term of utmost good faith).

12 See JW Carter and E Peden, 'Good Faith in Australian Contract Law' (2003) 19 *Journal of Contract Law* 155.

13 See below, text at n 29.

14 Cf *Restatement (Second) Contracts* 1979, §356(1) (amount must not be 'unreasonably large'). See also E Peden, 'When Common Law Trumps Equity: the Rise of Good Faith and Reasonableness and the Demise of Unconscionability' (2005) 21 *Journal of Contract Law* 226.

than that. But their application will in all cases ensure that an amount which is a genuine (honest) pre-estimation of loss is enforceable.

C Basis of the Law of Penalties

Contract doctrine as a whole and most specific contract rules are concerned to promote good faith rather than to require it. Therefore, notwithstanding that they give effect to good faith, parties are usually free to contract out of the rules of contract law. But that is not true of the rules in relation to the law of penalties. Although we do not propose to consider in detail the jurisdictional basis for not enforcing an agreed damages clause which is a penalty, it is necessary to explain why freedom of contract does not include freedom to agree to a penalty.

The concern of the law of penalties is to strike a satisfactory balance between freedom of contract and the ideas—based on policy and good faith—that promisees should not be permitted to recover punitive sums and that promisors should not be coerced by the threat of penal imposition on breach. The law having struck that balance, the parties must adhere to it. If they do not, their agreed damages clause will be characterised as an unenforceable penalty. The cases seem now to accept that, under the modern law, the basis for the restriction on freedom of contract is a matter of public policy.[15]

The law of penalties is therefore one of a handful of doctrines under which the inherent validity of a clause may be questioned on a common law basis even though there is no illegality. In that respect, the law of penalties is analogous in effect to the doctrine of restraint of trade.[16] Accordingly, an agreement which includes a penalty is not an illegal agreement. Therefore, where the promise has been executed although the promisor may have restitutionary rights in relation to the penal sum, this is not because it is illegal for a promisor to pay a penalty. It would seem to follow from this approach that the jurisdiction formerly applied in equity is no longer applicable. For example, in *AMEV-UDC Finance Ltd* Mason and Wilson JJ recorded[17] that the 'equitable jurisdiction to relieve against penalties withered on the vine'.

[15] See *Robophone Facilities Ltd v Blank* [1966] 1 WLR 1428, [1966] 3 All ER 128. See also *Restatement (Second) Contracts* 1979, §356(1).

[16] And, as in that context, it is unclear whether a penalty is a void or unenforceable provision. See *Financings Ltd v Baldock* [1963] 2 QB 104, 120; *Citicorp Australia Ltd v Hendry* (1985) 4 NSWLR 1, 39–40. Cf *Pigram v Attorney-General (NSW)* (1975) 132 CLR 216, 221, 6 ALR 15. Either way, the clause is 'in practice a dead letter' (*Jobson v Johnson* [1989] 1 WLR 1026, 1039 per Nicholls LJ).

[17] Above n 7, (1986) 162 CLR 170, 191. Cf *Yarra Capital Group Pty Ltd v Sklash Pty Ltd* [2006] VSCA 109, paras [19]–[20], where Chernov JA (with whom Warren CJ agreed, Ashley JA not deciding) suggested that 'unconscionability' is an additional basis on which to have a penalty struck down.

That a court will not enforce an executory promise to pay a penalty reflects the rule (of public policy) that punitive damages are not awarded for breach of contract.[18] It is therefore tempting to see the law of penalties as simply giving effect to the compensation principle of damages, that is, the basic idea that damages for breach of contract should do no more than compensate the plaintiff. Indeed, in *Legione v Hateley*[19] Mason and Deane JJ defined a penalty in the following terms:[20]

> A penalty, as its name suggests, is in the nature of a punishment for non-observance of a contractual stipulation; it consists of the imposition of an additional or different liability upon breach of the contractual stipulation.

However, for three reasons it is an inadequate explanation of the modern jurisdiction in relation to penalties to say that it gives effect to the compensation principle of damages. First, it is clear that the law is more concerned to ensure that there is no punitive element than to ensure that overcompensation never occurs. It cannot be doubted that in some cases plaintiffs have recovered greater sums under liquidated damages clauses than would otherwise have been awarded as damages.[21] There is, nevertheless, a degree of tension between the compensation principle and the enforcement of an agreed damages clause which provides for the payment of a sum of money in excess of the amount to which the promisee would be entitled if put to proof.[22]

Secondly, it follows that literal application of the compensation principle, or Mason and Deane JJ's concept of an 'additional or different liability', would lead to any clause which stipulated for a greater amount than a promisee's actual loss necessarily being a penalty. Clearly, as the out of all proportion test emphasises, that is not the position.

Thirdly, the law of penalties may pursue other goals, or the application of the rules may have beneficial effects other than preventing over-compensation.[23] For example, in *AMEV-UDC Finance Ltd* Mason and Wilson JJ suggested:[24]

> The doctrine of penalties answers, in situations of the present kind, an important aspect of the criticism often levelled against unqualified freedom of contract, namely the possible inequality of bargaining power. In this way the courts strike a balance between the competing interests of freedom of contract and protection of weak contracting parties . . .

18 See JW Carter, *Carter on Contract* (Sydney, LexisNexis Butterworths), §41-020.

19 (1983) 152 CLR 406; 46 ALR 1.

20 (1983) 152 CLR 406, 445, 46 ALR 1. Cf *Workers Trust & Merchant Bank Ltd v Dojap Investments Ltd* [1993] AC 573, 578.

21 See eg *Philips Hong Kong*, above n 1.

22 See further below, text at n 46.

23 Cf C J Goetz and R E Scott, 'Enforcing Promises: An Examination of the Basis of Contract' (1980) 89 *Yale LJ* 1261.

24 Above n 7, (1986) 162 CLR 170, 194.

This does not mean that proof of inequality of bargaining power is necessary.[25] Indeed, it is doubtful whether inequality of bargaining power can be seen as a constituent element of the rules used to characterise agreed damages clauses.[26] A few cases have suggested in passing that inequality of bargaining power is a basis on which to strike down an agreed damages clause, yet there is no conclusive statement to that effect at the appellate level.[27] Under statute or as part of the application of vitiating factors, such as unconscionability, inequality of bargaining power can be used to strike down a contract as a whole, rather than one particular term that seems to operate unfairly for one party. In the penalty context, inequality of bargaining power may explain why the amount chosen is excessive. Thus, in our view, it is the fact that good faith underlies those rules that they may sometimes operate to prevent exploitation of a superior bargaining position. But that is quite different from saying that consideration of inequality of bargaining power is an integral part of the penalty rules.

II GOOD FAITH AND THE DUNLOP PRINCIPLES

A Introduction

We do not put forward the view that good faith should be applied in place of Lord Dunedin's analysis in the *Dunlop* case. That analysis remains the authoritative doctrinal basis for deciding whether the amount in question has been determined in good faith. In other words, consistently with the proper role of good faith in contract law, the analysis expresses the legal rules which require good faith. Those rules police good faith and deny validity to a clause which does not conform to the legal rules.

However, it is appropriate at this stage to consider the general propositions and specific tests which comprise Lord Dunedin's analysis and the relevance of that analysis to our good faith thesis.

[25] Cf *A Schroeder Music Publishing Co Ltd v Macaulay* [1974] 3 All ER 616, 623, [1974] 1 WLR 1308, 1315.

[26] Nevertheless, even in recent cases reference has been made to 'unconscionability' and 'unconscionable conduct' as considerations directly relevant to whether the provision at issue is properly characterised as being penal. See below, text at n 38.

[27] See eg *Philips Hong Kong*, above n 1, where the Privy Council suggested that 'situations where one of the parties to the contract is able to dominate the other as a choice of terms of a contract' would be an exception to the normal operation of the penalty principles. See also *State of Tasmania v Leighton Contractors Pty Ltd* [2005] TASSC 133, para [31]: 'The question was whether, given the nature of the contract, its complexity, value and the bargaining strength of the parties the amount of $8000 was, in all the circumstances, a penalty as of the date of the agreement.'

B Propositions and Tests

It will be recalled that Lord Dunedin began his analysis with three general propositions of law:[28]

> 1. Though the parties to a contract who use the words 'penalty' or 'liquidated damages' may prima facie be supposed to mean what they say, yet the expression used is not conclusive. The Court must find out whether the payment stipulated is in truth a penalty or liquidated damages. This doctrine may be said to be found passim in nearly every case.
>
> 2. The essence of a penalty is a payment of money stipulated as in terrorem of the offending party; the essence of liquidated damages is a genuine covenanted pre-estimate of damage (*Clydebank [Engineering and Shipbuilding Co v Don Jose Ramos Yzquierdo y Castaneda* [1905] AC 6]).
>
> 3. The question whether a sum stipulated is penalty or liquidated damages is a question of construction to be decided upon the terms and inherent circumstances of each particular contract, judged of as at the time of the making of the contract, not as at the time of the breach (*Public Works Commissioner v Hills* [1906] AC 368 and *Webster v Bosanquet* [1912] AC 394).

Lord Dunedin went on to explain that there are various tests which may be applied to give effect to the general propositions of law. He said:[29]

> 4. To assist this task of construction various tests have been suggested, which if applicable to the case under consideration may prove helpful, or even conclusive. Such are:
>
> (a) It will be held to be penalty if the sum stipulated for is extravagant and unconscionable in amount in comparison with the greatest loss that could conceivably be proved to have followed from the breach. (Illustration given by Lord Halsbury in *Clydebank case* [1905] AC 6.)
>
> (b) It will be held to be a penalty if the breach consists only in not paying a sum of money, and the sum stipulated is a sum greater than the sum which ought to have been paid (*Kemble v Farren* (1829) 6 Bing 141; 130 ER 1234). This though one of the most ancient instances is truly a corollary to the last test. Whether it had its historical origin in the doctrine of the common law that when A promised to pay B a sum of money on a certain day and did not do so, B could only recover the sum with, in certain cases, interest, but could never recover further damages for non-timeous payment, or whether it was a survival of the time when equity reformed unconscionable bargains merely because they were unconscionable,—a subject which much exercised Jessel MR in *Wallis v Smith* (1882) 21 Ch D 243—is probably more interesting than material.
>
> (c) There is a presumption (but no more) that it is penalty when 'a single lump sum is made payable by way of compensation, on the occurrence of one or

28 Above n 10, 86–7.
29 *Ibid*, 87–8.

more or all of several events, some of which may occasion serious and others but trifling damage' (Lord Watson in *Lord Elphinstone v Monkland Iron and Coal Co* (1886) 11 App Cas 332 [at 342]).

On the other hand:

(d) It is no obstacle to the sum stipulated being a genuine pre-estimate of damage, that the consequences of the breach are such as to make precise pre-estimation almost an impossibility. On the contrary, that is just the situation when it is probable that pre-estimated damage was the true bargain between the parties (*Clydebank Case* [per] Lord Halsbury [1905] AC 6 at 11; *Webster v Bosanquet* [1912] AC 394 at 398 [per] Lord Mersey).

C Time and Basis for Classification

The first and third of Lord Dunedin's general propositions concern the 'construction' of the agreement. The first expresses a familiar idea in construction law: that the use of a term which has a technical legal meaning may attract a presumption that it is accurately used.[30] However, the presumption may be rebutted.[31] Lord Dunedin's reference to the position 'in truth' is a reference to the legal effect of the clause, that is, its construction as a matter of law, not fact. The court cannot ignore the parties' expressed intention, but it is entitled to go behind it. This ability to go behind the parties' expressed intention is an aspect of good faith, and part of the more general concern of commercial construction, namely, that labels are not conclusive where the legal effect of a contract is at issue.[32] That explains the first proposition and assists in the explanation of the third.

The use of the word 'construction' in the third proposition is misleading. The issue is not an orthodox issue of construction; it is one of substance and legal operation, rather than form and intention.[33] Therefore, the classification of an agreed damages clause as liquidated damages or a penalty cannot be based solely on the intention of the parties as determined under orthodox construction principles. Rather, the clause must be 'construed' on the basis of the operation of the contract and in

30 Cf *L Schuler AG v Wickman Machine Tool Sales Ltd* [1974] AC 235 ('condition').

31 See eg *Clydebank Engineering and Shipbuilding Co Ltd v Don Jose Ramos Yzquierdo y Castaneda* [1905] AC 6 ('penalty' for late delivery construed as a provision for the payment of liquidated damages); *Bridge v Campbell Discount Co Ltd* [1962] AC 600 (stipulation for payment of 'agreed compensation' was construed as a penalty).

32 A common illustration is an agreement that occupancy of land is pursuant to a 'licence', rather than a 'lease'. See, eg *Street v Mountford* [1985] AC 809; *KJRR Pty Ltd v Commissioner of State Revenue* [1999] 2 VR 174, 177, 183; *Bruton v London & Quadrant Housing Trust* [2000] 1 AC 406.

33 See *O'Dea*, above n 7, 152 CLR 359, 400. Cf *Lordsvale Finance Plc v Bank of Zambia* [1996] QB 752, 762–3.

light of considerations of public policy. The injunction that the clause must be construed at the time of contract formation, although consistent with general principles of contract construction,[34] is more a reflection of good faith than those general principles. In essence, the concern is with good faith pre-estimation, and the fact that the actual loss is less than or greater than the amount stipulated is at most of circumstantial relevance. But the more practical point is that actual loss need not be proved. There is no presumption of invalidity, and the onus of proving that a clause is a penalty rests on the promisor.[35] It follows that, although the promisee may choose to present evidence to support an agreed damages clause, there is no requirement to do so.[36]

The 'in terrorem' idea has not, in terms, figured prominently in modern cases. Nevertheless, Lord Dunedin's second proposition is the cornerstone for the distinction between liquidated damages and penalties, as well as the application of the tests which he propounded. It expresses one aspect of good faith. The reason the 'in terrorem' idea is not directly applied is the same reason that good faith is not directly applied, namely, that the conclusion that the clause is 'in terrorem' is, largely at least, one drawn from the application of Lord Dunedin's propositions and tests. In other words, it is more a matter of legal inference than a matter for proof. Accordingly, the courts have tended to focus more on whether the clause 'is a genuine covenanted pre-estimate of damage'. When they raise the issue of inequality of the parties it may be that courts indirectly raise the idea of 'in terrorem' payments. Yet, as we discussed above, inequality of bargaining power might well lead to the inclusion of a penalty provision, but there is no advantage in adding that inquiry to the *Dunlop* principles.

D Pre-estimation

The four tests stated by Lord Dunedin to 'assist' with the 'task of construction' are necessarily subordinate to his three general propositions of law. However, Lord Dunedin said that the tests may in some cases be 'conclusive'. Thus, some at least of the tests may operate as propositions of law.

The first test establishes both a criterion and a basis for comparison. The criterion is an amount which is 'extravagant and unconscionable'. This is the origin of the out of all proportion test stated in cases such as *AMEV-UDC Finance Ltd* and applied in *Ringrow*. The basis for comparison was stated by Lord Dunedin as being the 'greatest loss that

34 See Carter, *Carter on Contract*, above n 18, §13-100.

35 See *Robophone Facilities*, above n 15, [1966] 1 WLR 1428, 1447; *Multiplex Constructions Pty Ltd v Abgarus Pty Ltd* (1992) 33 NSWLR 504, 527.

36 See further below, text following n 80.

could conceivably be proved to have followed from the breach'. However, this is not the only basis for comparison relied on in the cases. Thus, in *AMEV-UDC Finance Ltd*, Mason and Wilson JJ[37] referred to the 'damage likely to be suffered as a result of breach', and in *Ringrow* the High Court made reference to a 'genuine pre-estimate of damage'. The former is, perhaps, the more common basis for comparison in the recent cases. Although the reference to a sum being 'unconscionable in amount' in Lord Dunedin's first test has sometimes been treated as showing the continued role of equity,[38] that is inconsistent with the comment made in the second test. Thus, the reference to an amount being 'extravagant and unconscionable' is a reference to a sum which is manifestly excessive[39] and has not been determined in good faith.

Lord Dunedin must have taken it as a rule of law for his second test that damages are not available for the late payment of money, because it is otherwise impossible to see how a sum can be 'extravagant and unconscionable in amount' merely because it is 'a sum greater than the sum which ought to have been paid'. It is, moreover, impossible to reconcile with the good faith rationale. Notwithstanding its repetition in recent cases,[40] the second test is best seen as a reflection of the law current at the time of *Dunlop*. It cannot be taken at face value today.[41]

The presumption stated by Lord Dunedin in *Dunlop* in his third test, quoting from *Lord Elphinstone*'s case, also reflects good faith. If the contract stipulates for the payment of a 'single lump sum' in relation to several events the consequences of which are variable, it is obvious that there may not have been a genuine attempt at assessment. Thus, the onus shifts to the promisee to prove that the agreed damages clause is a genuine pre-estimate. However, he explained:[42]

> I think *Elphinstone's* case, or rather the dicta in it, do go this length, that if there are various breaches to which one indiscriminate sum to be paid in breach is applied, then the strength of the chain must be taken at its weakest link. If you can clearly see that the loss on one particular breach could never amount to the stipulated sum, then you may come to the conclusion that the sum is [a] penalty.

37 Above n 7, (1986) 162 CLR 170, 190.

38 See, eg *Multiplex Constructions Pty Ltd v Abgarus Pty Ltd* (1992) 33 NSWLR 504, 509–10; *Yarra Capital Group Pty Ltd v Sklash Pty Ltd* [2006] VSCA 109, paras [19]–[20].

39 See *Photo Production Ltd v Securicor Transport Ltd* [1980] AC 827, 850 per Lord Diplock (a penalty is a clause providing for a payment which is 'manifestly intended to be in excess of the amount which would fully compensate the other party for the loss sustained by him in consequence of the breach'). Cf his analysis in *Robophone Facilities*, above n 15, [1966] 1 WLR 1428, 1447–8, [1966] 3 All ER 128, 142–3.

40 See eg *Ringrow*, above n 6, (2005) 222 ALR 306, 309 (para [11]).

41 See further below, text at n 67.

42 Above n 10, 89.

Thus, if the promisor can show that there is one breach (to which the clause was intended to apply) in respect of which the clause would be extravagant and unconscionable in amount, the clause will be a penalty. In the context of liquidated damages provisions applicable on termination for breach, the Australian courts have in recent years more or less ignored the requirement that the 'strength of the chain must be taken at its weakest link', and treated the loss expected to flow from termination as the applicable criterion.[43]

The good faith basis for the rules is also apparent in Lord Dunedin's fourth test. Where damages are difficult or impossible to assess, the law could take the view that agreed damages provisions should not be used, because it is, or may be, more or less impossible to know whether the sum stipulated is a reliable quantification. But the law takes the opposite view. As Lord Dunedin said:[44] 'that is just the situation when it is probable that pre-estimated damage was the true bargain between the parties'. More than any other rule, it shows that 'genuineness' is linked with honesty rather than accuracy. The parties benefit from the certainty which the agreed amount provides. Having to pay more than a party's actual loss on some occasions is simply the price of that certainty.[45] But it is also, contextually, a situation in which there is no obvious applicable measure of the promisee's loss.

E The Out of All Proportion Test

As noted above, the out of all proportion test is a reformulation of Lord Dunedin's first test, which he expressed in terms of 'extravagant and unconscionable'. As also noted, there is a degree of tension between the compensation principle and the enforcement of an agreed damages clause which provides for the payment of a sum of money in excess of the promisee's actual loss, a tension which surfaces in the preference of recent cases to express the criterion by reference to the loss or damage 'likely' to be suffered, rather than Lord Dunedin's 'greatest loss that could conceivably be proved'. Of more general relevance are decisions which appear, at least superficially, to illustrate a shift away from the traditional conception of a penalty as a provision stipulating for an amount which is not a genuine pre-estimation in favour of a requirement based on a concern for substantial accuracy.

[43] See below, text at nn 62, 74.

[44] Above n 10, 88. See also *Waterside Workers' Federation of Australia v Stewart* (1919) 27 CLR 119.

[45] See *Robophone Facilities*, above n 15, [1966] 1 WLR 1428, [1966] 3 All ER 128 per Diplock LJ.

These tensions were not lost on Mason and Wilson JJ in *AMEV-UDC Finance Ltd*. Referring to the more recent decisions on penalties, they said:[46]

> These decisions are more consistent with an underlying policy of restricting the parties, in case of breach of contract, to the recovery of an amount of damages no greater than that for which the law provides. However, there is much to be said for the view that the courts should return to the *Clydebank* [1905] AC 6 at 10–11, 17 and *Dunlop* [1915] AC 79 at 87 concept, thereby allowing parties to a contract greater latitude in determining what their rights and liabilities will be, so that an agreed sum is only characterized as a penalty if it is out of all proportion to damage likely to be suffered as a result of breach: see *Robophone Facilities Ltd v Blank* [1966] 1 WLR 1428 at 1447–8; [1966] 3 All ER 128 at 142–3; UK [*sic*] Law Commission, *Penalty Clauses and Forfeiture of Monies Paid*, Working Paper No 61, 1975, paras 33, 42–4.

Arguably, their statement that 'there is much to be said for the view that the courts should return' to the approach in the classic cases suggests that, in Mason and Wilson JJ's view, the law had already departed from those cases and moved to a position where substantial accuracy (in the prediction of actual loss) is required.

To some the demise of the equitable approach has also suggested a movement from a requirement of genuineness in pre-estimation to one of substantial accuracy. This is one interpretation of Meagher JA's judgment in *P C Developments Pty Ltd v Revell*.[47] Applying *AMEV-UDC Finance Ltd*, he explained that, in terms of the applicable test, the law has adopted:[48]

> the purely mechanical test whether the provision sought to be impugned does or does not exceed the loss or damage which the innocent party could obtain if he sued for damages for breach of contract.

Unless restricted to the narrow category of case, where the agreed damages clause applies to a single breach the damages for which are easy to assess, this statement does not capture the proper approach. Moreover, even if Meagher JA's reference to the provision providing for an amount which does 'not exceed the loss or damage which the innocent party could obtain if he sued for damages for breach of contract' is read (as it no doubt should be)[49] as referring to an amount which does not substantially exceed the amount to which the innocent party would obtain if put to proof, it cannot

46 Above n 7, (1986) 162 CLR 170, 190.
47 (1991) 22 NSWLR 615.
48 *Ibid*, 650.
49 He cited *Forestry Commission of New South Wales v Stefanetto* (1976) 133 CLR 507, 519; 8 ALR 297 as an illustration of his 'purely mechanical test'. The reference in that case (by Mason J) is to a 'genuine pre-estimate of loss or damage' (*Dunlop*, above n 10, 86).

possibly be of universal application. The same is, in our opinion, true of the out of all proportion test.

III GOOD FAITH AND LIMITATIONS ON THE OUT OF ALL PROPORTION TEST

A Application of the Out of All Proportion Test in *Ringrow*[50]

Recently, the High Court considered the *Dunlop* principles and explained its views on the out of all proportion test in *Ringrow*. The case concerned a contract for the sale by BP Australia of a service station (BP Lansvale) formerly operated by BP Australia and agreement by the purchaser (Ringrow) to operate the service station and sell BP Australia's products as a franchisee. Several contracts were entered into. These included a sale contract, an Option Deed (under which BP Australia could re-purchase the service station) and a BP Branded Privately Owned Sites Agreement (POSA).

The Option Deed provided that the option to re-purchase was exercisable only on termination of the POSA. The Option Deed fixed the price as the market valuation of the service station—as an operational service station—as determined by an independent valuer. Under the sale contract and the POSA, Ringrow would become subject to an obligation to pay liquidated damages if the POSA was terminated. The applicable amount depended on the time of termination, but was fixed by reference to the expected benefit to BP Australia of Ringrow's operation of the service station for the five-year term of the POSA.

Ringrow breached a clause of the POSA when on more than one occasion it bought fuel for resale to the public from a supplier other than BP Australia. This led BP Australia to serve a notice on Ringrow terminating the POSA pursuant to the POSA. It then exercised its right under the Option Deed to buy back the service station. Ringrow's allegation that the Option Deed was void or unenforceable as a penalty was rejected in the Federal Court of Australia,[51] which held that BP Australia's termination of the POSA and exercise of the option were valid and effective.

In Ringrow's unsuccessful appeal it did not claim that the payment of agreed damages was per se a penalty. However, it put forward various arguments designed to show that the obligation to retransfer the service

50 See E Peden and JW Carter, 'Agreed Damages Clauses—Back to the Future?' (2006) 22 *Journal of Contract Law* 189.

51 See (2003) 203 ALR 281, [2003] FCA 1297 (Hely J); (2004) 209 ALR 32, [2004] FCAFC 206 (Full Court).

station meant that the contractual provisions were penal in operation. This included the fact that goodwill was excluded from the resale price. The High Court rejected Ringrow's arguments.

The High Court delivered a single joint judgment. It quoted[52] at length from Lord Dunedin's speech in *Dunlop*[53] and said that the statement continues to represent the law in Australia. The High Court accepted that Lord Dunedin's speech might be applied to the transfer of property, as well as the payment of money. In such a case, the High Court said[54] 'Lord Dunedin's statement requires a different approach from that employed in typical penalty cases', and explained that

> one relevant comparison would be between the price payable by the respondent to the appellant on retransfer of BP Lansvale by the appellant, and the actual value of what is transferred.

However, the court stressed[55] that 'a mere difference in amount is not enough'. The difference must be '"extravagant and unconscionable"'[56] or there must be a '"degree of disproportion" sufficient to point to oppressiveness'.[57]

The only evidence concerning goodwill was provided by an expert, who stated that there was no valuable goodwill at the time of retransfer. Therefore, so the High Court thought, Ringrow could not prove that it would be disadvantaged by the price paid by BP Australia. Moreover, the cumulative imposition of the obligation under the option and the liquidated damages clause was not oppressive, or 'extravagant and unconscionable in comparison with the loss which flowed from the breach of the POSA'.[58] Gleeson CJ, Gummow, Kirby, Hayne, Callinan and Heydon JJ stated:[59]

> The principles of law relating to penalties require only that the money stipulated to be paid on breach or the property stipulated to be transferred on breach will produce for the payee or transferee advantages significantly greater than the advantages which would flow from a genuine pre-estimate of damage.

The High Court repeated the appellation to the concept of freedom of contract. It stated that the law of penalties should be remembered as an exception to the concept of freedom of contract. Therefore, to be a penalty, the amount or benefit must be extravagant and unconscionable in amount.

52 (2005) 222 ALR 306, 308–9 (para [11]).
53 Above n 10, 86–7. See above, text at n 28. The High Court omitted the first principle and test (d) from its quotation.
54 See (2005) 222 ALR 306, 311 (para [21]).
55 *Ibid*, 312 (para [21]).
56 The quotation is from *Dunlop*, above n 10, 87.
57 See (2005) 222 ALR 306, 312 (para [21]).
58 *Ibid*, 312 (para [25])
59 *Ibid*, 313 (para [27]).

The mere fact that it is 'lacking in proportion' would not be enough; it must be 'out of all proportion'.[60]

Even on the assumption that the distinction between liquidated damages and penalties was applicable to the exercise of the option,[61] the reasoning of the High Court is in some respects unorthodox. First, the fact that the events which could lead to termination of the POSA were many and varied might suggest that Lord Dunedin's 'weakest link'[62] analysis was applicable, but it was not considered. One reason for this is perhaps that it was not contended that the agreed damages amount was itself a penalty. Thus, focusing on the price payable, there was in fact a relevant single event, namely, exercise of the option following termination of the contract. On that basis, the decision stands or falls according to whether the price fixed by valuation could be treated as a genuine one when the valuer was instructed to ignore goodwill.

Secondly, it is not clear why the relevant comparison was between the price payable, that is, under the agreed basis for valuation, and the 'actual value' of BP Lansvale, rather than a comparison of the amount determined under the agreed basis for valuation and the least value which might be placed on the service station (determined at the time of entry into the contract). Similarly, to use the criterion (itself somewhat unorthodox) stated in the passage quoted above, it is not clear why the relevant comparison was not between the amount determined under the agreed basis for valuation and a 'genuine pre-estimate' of the value of the land. Generally, any difference between the agreed damages and the actual loss is at best circumstantial evidence of the nature of the clause. Presumably, this aspect of the case is to be explained by the nature of the retransfer obligation.

B Penalties and the Assessment of Damages

One conclusion which might be drawn from *Ringrow* is that the out of all proportion test is applicable in all cases. However, in our view that conclusion is wrong. Because good faith is the underlying concept, and because determination of a sum which is not out of all proportion is not synonymous with a good faith assessment, there must be limitations on the test. The source of these limitations is, of course, the *Dunlop* principles themselves. These, in turn, reflect important aspects of the rules on damages assessment. In our view it is the underlying requirement of good

60 *Ibid*, 314 (para [32])

61 But see *CRA Ltd v NZ Goldfields Investments* [1989] VR 873 (provision in joint venture agreement entitling party to call for assignment of defaulting party's interest at market value less 5% not subject to the distinction).

62 See above, text at n 42.

faith which explains the relevance of some of the more specific aspects of damages assessment.

Relevantly, there are three principal situations in which the out of all proportion test may not be applicable:

1. where the agreed damages clause is activated by a single breach and there is a conventional measure of damages in relation to the obligation which the clause does not reflect;
2. where the law requires the assessment of damages to take a particular circumstance into account but the agreed damages clause does not do so; and
3. in any other case where, in the circumstances, accurate pre-estimation of the loss is straightforward.

Each of these is potentially a qualification to the out of all proportion test. Each depends on conclusions of law about how damages for breach of contract would be assessed and the relevance of those conclusions to the particular clause in issue. It is therefore appropriate to consider briefly the relationship between the characterisation of an agreed damages clause as a penalty or liquidated damages and the damages rules themselves.

The assessment of damages necessarily depends on the facts of each particular case. Because the law relating to the distinction between liquidated damages and penalties requires the parties' pre-estimation to be tested as at the time of contract formation, pre-estimation is necessarily somewhat problematic. The law should not require, and there is no reason to expect, a completely accurate prediction. Equally, however, it must be wrong to assume that the parties are entitled to ignore realities and take fanciful losses into account. Good faith requires the conception of loss which the agreed damages clause addresses to bear some resemblance to the likely position of the parties at the time of breach. In many cases it will also require the agreed assessment to reflect the operation of legal rules regulating and quantifying damages.

Although the assessment of damages is far from being an exact science, the rule in *Hadley v Baxendale*[63] is a unifying feature for remoteness considerations, and in relation to most commercial contracts it is generally possible to determine how the plaintiff's loss is appropriately measured, at least on a prima facie basis. Further limitations on recovery of damages are imposed by causation and principles of mitigation of loss, as well as specific rules in relation to what losses are recoverable as a matter of law. All these features are potentially relevant to whether the parties have arrived at a genuine pre-estimate of loss. However, the *Dunlop* principles do not require the amount chosen to be a mirror image of their operation, and an amount may be determined in good faith even though it does not

[63] (1854) 9 Ex 341, 354; 156 ER 145, 151.

conform to all aspects of the common law of damages. There are four important points.

First, a party who might be unable to claim in respect of a particular loss because it falls under the second limb of the rule in *Hadley v Baxendale* may nevertheless liquidate that loss in an agreed damages clause. Second limb losses may therefore be taken into account in determining an agreed damages amount.[64] Whether or not the communication of an amount, but not the loss, is deemed satisfaction of the legal requirements for the application of the second limb of the rule in *Hadley v Baxendale* does not need to be considered. Thus, a liquidated damages clause need only specify an amount that is a genuine pre-estimate of an anticipated loss because of 'special circumstances', and the agreement by the other party to pay that amount will be binding, even though this loss may not be recoverable at common law. Indeed, the out of all proportion test ensures that the clause is enforceable even if the anticipated loss does not occur, providing the loss was included in good faith.

Secondly, in relation to mitigation, the law takes the view that if the amount determined under an agreed damages clause is a genuine pre-estimate it is not subject to the mitigation rules. For example, if an agreement with a consultant provides that on wrongful termination of the consultant's employment the employer will pay an amount equal to two months' salary by way of liquidated damages, the fact that the consultant takes up another position one week after wrongful termination does not impact on the liquidated damages clause. On the other hand, in some situations, if it is clear that some distinct benefit will be obtained on breach of the agreement, a clause which ignores the element of mitigation may be a penalty.

Thirdly, in many situations a breach to which the agreed damages clause applies will be the subject of a conventional measure of damages. For example, on a breach of warranty the conventional measure of the plaintiff's loss is the difference between the value of the subject matter as warranted and the actual value of the subject matter. In the commercial context, where a conventional measure of damages is applicable it will in most cases be appropriate for this measure to be taken into account when considering an agreed damages clause relating to the breach. Accordingly, absent special circumstances, if the agreed damages clause bears no relation to the conventional measure it must at the very least arouse suspicion.

Fourthly, although not all the specific rules which may affect a party's common law damages need to be taken into account when fixing a figure, the cases illustrate that, particularly where a formula is chosen as the basis

64 See *Robophone Facilities*, above n 15, [1966] 1 WLR 1428, 1447–8 per Diplock LJ, [1966] 3 All ER 128. See also *Philips Hong Kong*, above n 1.

for the assessment of damages under the agreed damages clause in accordance with a conventional measure, any discrepancies between the formula and the common law basis for assessment (under the conventional measure) must be considered. While not every error is fatal, the impact and reason for the error must be investigated.

C Single Breach with Conventional Measure

In order to be a genuine pre-estimate of loss, an agreed damages clause must bear some relation to what the law regards as recoverable losses. Lord Dunedin's reference to the 'greatest loss that could conceivably be proved to have followed from the breach'[65] assumes that the promisee might have suffered and recovered that loss. But if damages recoverable under the second limb of *Hadley v Baxendale* are put to one side, in the commercial context pecuniary losses are assessed according to conventional measures, such as those enshrined in the damages provisions of the sale of goods legislation.[66]

It follows that if an agreed damages clause relates to a single breach, and the breach is of a kind to which a conventional measure applies, the clause may be a penalty if it purports to liquidate damages on a different basis. That is not so much because the amount is out of all proportion—although that may be the case anyway—but because the clause is vitiated by error. The classic example was given by Lord Dunedin in *Dunlop*, namely, a promise to pay money. In the second of his three 'tests' in *Dunlop*, Lord Dunedin said a clause will be penal

> if the breach consists only in not paying a sum of money, and the sum stipulated is a sum greater than the sum which ought to have been paid.[67]

Two aspects of the modern cases are relevant here. First, as discussed below, the Australian cases have avoided the application of the money sum rule in cases where a contract is terminated by focusing on the fact of termination rather than the fact that the breach which led to termination may be 'not paying a sum of money'.

Secondly, the law approaches 'not paying a sum of money' more generously than at the time of *Dunlop*. In his second test in *Dunlop*, Lord Dunedin took his uncompromising stance on obligations relating to the payment of money because at that time the law did not permit the recovery of damages for the late payment of money. Notwithstanding that

[65] Above text at n 29.
[66] See eg Sale of Goods Act 1923 (NSW), ss 53 (non-delivery), 54 (breach of warranty).
[67] See also *Workers Trust & Merchant Bank Ltd v Dojap Investments Ltd* [1993] AC 573, 578 per the Privy Council ('general rule that a term which requires one party in the event of breach to pay . . . a sum of money to the other party is unlawful as being a penalty').

the High Court in *Ringrow* quoted the second test as an ingredient of the modern penalty rules, it is difficult to see how it can be reconciled with the advances made, particularly in Australia, in relation to damages for the late payment of money. Indeed, the High Court has all but abandoned the rule that damages cannot be recovered for the late payment of money.[68] An agreed damages clause in the form of interest may therefore be upheld, and there is no reason why the out of all proportion test should not be applicable. In this way, developments in the law of damages must influence the question of what should be regarded as a genuine pre-estimate of loss. Nevertheless, in the case of loans, increases in the rate of interest payable are closely scrutinised. For example, in *Lordsvale Finance Plc v Bank of Zambia*[69] Colman J considered that a small increase in the interest payable under a loan may be justified. In respect of other contracts, the law should logically simply require the choice of an appropriate rate of interest.

More generally, where accurate pre-estimation of the promisee's loss is reasonably straightforward because there is an obvious (applicable) measure of loss, it is appropriate for courts to consider how faithful the parties have been to the measure. Genuineness, because it reflects good faith, assumes or includes an element of appropriateness in the basis for assessment. While the mere fact of error is not conclusive, where the error is made by a person who is well aware of the loss likely to be recoverable, any deviation from that measure must be justified. However, there is no reason to treat the mere possibility of over-compensation[70] or the fact of minor errors in the agreed formula as fatal. Thus, we would question the application of the penalty rules in *Lombard North Central Plc v Butterworth*.[71] In the context of the hire of computer equipment, the contract deemed every breach by the hirer to be a breach of condition and repudiation of the contract. Since the hirer was liable to pay loss of bargain damages on termination, the agreed damages clause was not a crucial consideration. However, the English Court of Appeal appears to have considered that the difference between the amount recoverable as loss of bargain damages (£6,869.97 plus interest) and the amount payable under the contract as agreed damages (£7,042.82) made the agreed damages clause a penalty.

[68] See *Hungerfords v Walker* (1989) 171 CLR 125, 84 ALR 119.

[69] [1996] QB 752, 763, 767. Cf *Yarra Capital Group Pty Ltd v Sklash Pty Ltd* [2006] VSCA 109.

[70] See also *Esanda Finance Corp Ltd v Plessnig* (1989) 166 CLR 131; 84 ALR 99, where the fact that a surplus would occur if the amount recovered on resale, when added to the amount actually paid by the hirer, exceeded the owner's loss was ignored as too unlikely an occurrence.

[71] [1987] QB 527. See K Nicholson (1988) 1 *Journal of Contract Law* 64; H Beale (1988) 104 *LQR* 355.

D Requirement to take Particular Circumstance into Account

It was noted earlier that one feature of the history of agreed damages clauses in the second half of the twentieth century is that the rules were most frequently discussed in the context of chattel leases and hire-purchase contracts. That led to a degree of distortion, by an apparent concern with accuracy rather then whether the amount chosen was in fact out of all proportion to the loss likely to be suffered. Clauses were regularly struck down as penalties for two reasons.

First, the clauses were often easy targets because they employed formulas which included—from the perspective of damages assessment—clear errors. A common example is the fact of accelerated recovery of a money sum. Thus, in *O'Dea v Allstates Leasing System (WA) Pty Ltd*[72] clause 12 in a 36 month lease of a 'Mercedes Benz' prime mover provided that all money due for 'unexpired terms' should 'become immediately due and payable' by the lessee, plus 'reasonable costs of repossession', on termination for breach by the hirer. The sum which the lessor sought was in the nature of a penalty in that it could not be regarded as a genuine pre-estimate of the loss likely to be suffered by the lessor on termination of the lease. Similarly, in *AMEV-UDC Finance Ltd* a contract for the lease of certain printing equipment stated that on default in the payment of rent the lessor could terminate and recover the whole unpaid balance of the total rent. On the authority of *O'Dea*, this was a penalty.[73] It was not a genuine pre-estimate of loss. In each case, whether or not the lessor would recover an amount which (in money terms) was out of all proportion with its loss, the clauses in question could not be regarded as genuine pre-estimates of loss because they took no account of benefit to the lessor of acceleration of payment.

The second reason clauses were struck down is that courts have been unwilling to take losses flowing from termination into account when evaluating the clause. In cases where the agreement does not make every breach a fundamental breach or repudiation, the breach may or may not be a serious matter. That fact alone has led the English cases to hold agreed damages clauses quantifying loss of bargain damages to be penalties.[74] That is inevitable if the clause must be tested at the 'weakest link'. For English courts, applying the 'weakest link' approach of *Elphinstone*'s case (as approved in *Dunlop*), the fact that the contract in question might be terminated for a minor breach—indeed, one involving

[72] (1983) 152 CLR 359, 45 ALR 632.

[73] See also *AMEV Finance Ltd v Artes Studios Thoroughbreds Pty Ltd* (1989) 15 NSWLR 564.

[74] H McGregor, *McGregor on Damages* (London, Sweet & Maxwell, 17th edn, 2003), §13-056.

the non-payment of money—is a sufficient basis for striking down an agreed damages clause expressed in terms of loss of bargain damages.

The Australian cases have avoided the problem by taking the loss caused by termination into account. The Australian courts, by focusing on termination as the event on which damages are payable, have been able to avoid the 'weakest link' approach. Having decided that a provision requiring payment of the balance of the rental is necessarily a penalty, the High Court indicated in *AMEV-UDC Finance Ltd* that a clause which genuinely liquidated loss of bargain damages would be enforceable. This was acted on in *Esanda Finance Corp Ltd v Plessnig*.[75] An agreed damages clause applicable on termination of a hire-purchase contract relating to a prime mover was held to be valid where it provided for recovery of rent payable and storage, maintenance and resale expenses less the total rent paid by the hirer, the best wholesale price reasonably obtainable for the goods and a rebate of terms charges. The clause was upheld because it was a genuine pre-estimation of loss of bargain damages. This approach is applied whether or not the breach which leads to termination is a serious one.

Another relevant feature of these cases is that they deal with contexts in which the parties have chosen a formula rather than a money amount. The focus tends to shift from whether the amount in question—determined by applying the formula—is out of all proportion to whether the formula is appropriate. Rather than applying an out of all proportion test, because the parties have clearly adopted a loss of bargain approach, the question is whether the formula is substantially correct. Thus, in *Plessnig* some concern was expressed over what must have been, in money terms, a minor matter, namely, giving credit for resale of the goods on a wholesale basis rather than on a retail sale.[76] However, the approach was explicable on the basis that the owner was a financier and the error did not vitiate the clause. In our view, this is consistent with the good faith requirement.

Whether *Ringrow* is consistent with this approach is perhaps a matter of conjecture. Although the High Court applied the out of all proportion test, the agreed damages provision was expressed as a formula. Like the chattel lease cases, the clause became applicable on termination of the contract. Although the formula was not an estimate of loss of bargain damages, the question was whether application of the formula would produce a figure which was out of all proportion to the loss or damage likely to be suffered. In other words, in *Ringrow* the question, logically, was whether the formula would produce a figure which was substantially less than the actual value of the land. On that basis, the crucial question was whether the express omission of goodwill from the formula made the

[75] (1989) 166 CLR 131, 84 ALR 99.
[76] See further below, text at n 78.

clause a penalty. If Ringrow was entitled to payment for goodwill,[77] the fact that the formula expressly omitted goodwill from the calculation of the price would suggest that there was no genuine pre-estimation unless it could be predicted, at the time when the contract was agreed, that omission of goodwill from the formula would not produce a result which was 'out of all proportion' with a valuation which included goodwill.

D Pre-estimation of the Loss is Straightforward

It would, to say the least, be strange—from a good faith perspective—if the law took no notice of the fact that in some contexts accurate pre-estimation of the loss is straightforward. Indeed, Lord Dunedin's analysis requires that to occur. The discussion above illustrates one aspect of this. If there is an applicable conventional measure of loss, accurate pre-estimation of the loss is straightforward because there is an established measure or formula. The law provides clear guidance on how (common law) damages should be assessed. Unless the circumstances are unusual, as where the clause liquidates a loss recoverable (if at all) on the basis of the second limb of the rule in *Hadley v Baxendale*, the parties must generally take this into account.

A more general perspective on the cases on chattel leases and hire-purchase contracts (and also the decision in *Ringrow*) is that if the parties are in a position to make an accurate pre-estimation they may not get the benefit of the out of all proportion test. Where a finance company enters into a chattel lease, it well knows the value of the property and the income which it can produce. Application of the requirement of genuineness inevitably attracts a concern for a higher degree of accuracy than in other cases. Accurate pre-estimation of the loss is straightforward. Indeed, that is the business of the finance company. In an operating lease the calculation is (in broad terms) incidental costs plus the difference between the rent which the lessee agreed to pay and the market rent. Some discount must be made to reflect the time value of money.[78] And if the lease is a finance lease, account must be taken of the residual value of the goods. Where the agreed damages clause does not conform, it may be held to be a penalty. For example, in *Beneficial Finance Corp Ltd v Sharker*[79]

[77] It appears that the reason for omitting reference to goodwill was that BP Australia was not interested in acquiring the goodwill built up by Ringrow. In that respect the reference to 'an operational service station' may have been to a service station capable of being operated on acquisition. See the analysis by Hely J (2003) 203 ALR 281, 306–7, [2003] FCA 1297, paras [113]–[117].

[78] Cf *Bridge v Campbell Discount Co Ltd* [1962] AC 600 ('agreed compensation for depreciation' clause a penalty because the amount described as 'depreciation' would become progressively less the longer the vehicle was used). See GHL Fridman (1963) 26 *MLR* 198.

[79] (1993) 32 NSWLR 161, 172.

Wood J held such a clause to be a penalty where no rebate was given for the increased value of the chattels on termination of an equipment rental agreement. Although he described the amount as 'out of proportion, extravagant or unconscionable', that seems more reflective of the fact of error than of a significant pecuniary divergence.

IV SOME PRACTICAL CONSIDERATIONS AND IMPLICATIONS

If it is correct to say that good faith underlies the rules which are applied to determine whether an agreed damages clause is a penalty or liquidated damages, one question which arises is whether the promisee should attempt to provide evidence that the amount stipulated was determined on a bona fide basis. Although the fact that the onus of proving that an agreed damages clause is a penalty rests on the promisor suggests that the promisee does not need to justify the clause, in practice the promisee will need to be prepared to defend the clause. Thus, the cases acknowledge that in many situations a mere reading of the clause will raise a suspicion or inference that it is a penalty. Moreover, where a single sum is agreed to fall 'on the occurrence of one or more or all of several events, some of which may occasion serious and others but trifling damage',[80] a presumption of penalty may arise.

The law should encourage good faith pre-estimates. That implies that it should respect an assessment of agreed damages which is based on a genuine attempt to calculate actual loss. If such calculations have been made, the better view is that evidence of such calculations is admissible.[81] In some contexts such evidence would be of considerable probative value. For example, where the contract is a government procurement contract under which commercial profit is not the motive for entry into the contract, the conventional measures of damage used in the commercial context, although otherwise applicable, may not reflect the actual loss. A liquidated damages clause is appropriate for three reasons. First, although the conventional measure is not reflective of the loss which the government may suffer, it will nevertheless be presumed to apply. Secondly, the government's likely loss may fall into the second limb of the rule in *Hadley v Baxendale*.[82] As already noted, second limb losses may be included in an agreed damages clause even if the likelihood of such losses being suffered has not otherwise been communicated. Thirdly, proof of loss is likely to be

80 See *Lord Elphinstone v Monkland Iron and Coal Co* (1886) 11 App Cas 332, 342 per Lord Watson (see above, text following n 29).

81 See *Multiplex Constructions Pty Ltd v Abgarus Pty Ltd* (1992) 33 NSWLR 504.

82 (1854) 9 Ex 341, 354, 156 ER 145, 151.

more time consuming and expensive than in a purely commercial context.[83]

The case in which evidence of pre-contract calculations is most likely to be indicative of good faith is where the calculations have been communicated. However, there is no reason why communication of the pre-contract calculations should be a condition precedent to their admissibility. There may be good commercial reasons for not communicating the information which the calculations embody. And in the context of a government procurement contract the information may be very sensitive.

V CONCLUSION

As we have explained, our objective in this paper has been to explain that good faith provides an appropriate perspective for the law on liquidated damages. The role of good faith lies in explaining and justifying the penalty rules. Although we have not sought to replace those rules with a single concept of good faith, we have endeavoured to show that the concept can play a role in evaluating the legal principles and the decisions in which those principles have been applied. In particular, the application of the 'out of all proportion' test is informed by good faith both at the general level of validating the test and, at a more specific level, in determining the scope of its application. Several points have emerged, but we would emphasise two particular points.

First, from the perspective of good faith, the discussion above indicates that, once it is established that the parties have adopted a particular formula or basis for damages assessment in their agreed damages clause, the validity of the formula or basis will be tested under the penalty rules with due regard to the current rules on damages assessment. If the formula or basis reflects a generally accepted formula or basis for assessment, good faith dictates that the parties must generally take into account those circumstances which the law regards as applicable to the formula or basis. Lack of good faith is shown more by error than a lack of proportion. For example, in *Ringrow* application of the out of all proportion test would have been more easily justified if the elements of the formula chosen by the parties were appropriate, that is, the formula was itself a genuine one. That, in turn, depended on whether it was necessary for the option clause to take goodwill into account. Otherwise, it embodied an error which in particular circumstances could have led to payment of an amount substantially less than the fair value of the land. Of course, the clause was held by

[83] See, eg *Philips Hong Kong*, above n 1 (government included liquidated damages clause in highway construction contract upheld, as loss would be 'virtually impossible to calculate precisely in advance. In the case of a governmental body the nature of the loss it will suffer as the result of the delay in implementing its new road programme is especially difficult to evaluate').

the High Court to be valid even though it expressly failed to take account of goodwill.

Secondly, the approach in the Australian cases where the agreed damages clause is activated by termination for breach is applicable whether or not the breach which leads to termination is a serious one. Although the cases also insist that particular circumstances be taken into account, it would clearly be wrong to say that the amount stated in an agreed damages clause must take account of all the particular rules relating to damages. If it is clear that they have been ignored, a court will carefully consider the impact. Thus, the decisions in *O'Dea* and *AMEV-UDC Finance Ltd* reflect the rule of damages that where a money sum payable in the future is recovered as damages, the agreed damages must make some allowance for the time value of money. They also illustrate that, in cases where the parties have adopted a formula for calculating agreed damages in preference to a money sum, it is generally inappropriate to look simply at a comparison between the actual loss and the amount determined under the formula and to conclude that the sum arrived at by applying the formula is or is not a penalty by reference to whether the difference is small or great.

In *Socony Mobil Oil Co Inc v West of England Ship Owners Mutual Insurance Association Ltd (The Padre Island) (No 2)*,[84] Bingham LJ pointed out that the principles stated in *Dunlop*[85] 'have been the subject of remarkably little judicial development'. In one sense that reflects the longstanding importance of good faith. Considering those principles through the looking glass of good faith today helps explain their operation over the last 90 years. The content of good faith in the modern law is different from its content in 1915, which helps to explain why, although the tests may have remained the same, their application has not.

[84] [1989] 1 Lloyd's Rep 239, 254 (reversed without reference to the point [1991] 2 AC 1).
[85] Above n 10, 86–8 (see above, text at n 28).

8

Economic Loss and the Duty of Care: a Study in the Exercise of Legal Justification

KIT BARKER*

"Save us from this fog and give us a clear sky, so that we can use our eyes"

(Homer, *The Iliad*, Rieu, trans (Harmondsworth, Penguin, 1956), 333, cited by Kirby J in *Barclays Oyster Pty Limited and Another v Ryan* [2002] HCA 54, [211].

I INTRODUCTION

FEW TOPICS ARE as vexed in private law as the question of when one party owes a duty of care to avoid harming another's pure economic interests. The problem is not simply one of identifying the exact boundaries of liability per se, but in divining the best overall method via which the issue should be approached. In England, at least three nominally distinct approaches are currently taken, all of which bear the authority of the House of Lords—an 'incremental' method of reasoning by analogy with existing categories of case;[1] a strategy based on the twin concepts of 'assumption of responsibility' by a defendant and 'reasonable reliance' by a claimant;[2] and a three-stage approach based on the

* Associate Professor, University of Queensland. I am greatly indebted to Jenny Steele and Mark Lunney for their helpful insights on an earlier draft. All views and defects remain entirely my own.

[1] *Caparo Industries v Dickman* (HL) [1990] 2 AC 605.

[2] This approach was affirmed most recently in *Commissioners of Customs and Excise v Barclays Bank plc* [2006] UKHL 28, but has been formulated in a number of very different ways historically. Two models now dominate: a 'narrow' one ('relationship equivalent to contract' entailing direct communication or dealing between the parties), as presented in *Hedley Byrne & Co Ltd v Heller & Partners Ltd* [1964] AC 465 529, per Lord Devlin; *Williams v Natural Life Health Foods Ltd* (HL) [1998] 1 WLR 830; and a 'wide' one ('undertaking of a task' in

'foreseeability' of harm, 'proximity' and 'fairness, justice and reasonableness'.[3] The relationship between these approaches is troubled, and some judges have sceptically suggested that it does not really matter which one takes because they all tend to yield the same result, once the facts and policy issues are properly considered.[4] In new types of case, we are now encouraged to apply the second and third in turn (and in that order), with the first acting as a cross-check upon the results, so as to ensure that they remain reasonably consistent with legal precedent.[5]

In Australia, after a period of considerable turmoil,[6] the High Court now seems to have settled (how fleetingly is still unclear) on a single, 'multifactoral' approach.[7] This is intended to be true to the spirit of incrementalism, but eschews both the rigid categorisation of cases and high-level generalisations in favour of lower-level ideas applied across the board, case by case.[8] These ideas include (but are not confined to) the foreseeability of harm, the impact of liability upon a defendant's commercial autonomy, the prospect of indeterminate liability, a claimant's vulnerability and the defendant's knowledge of the risk created by his conduct.[9] In the same way as the English approach has been criticised for being overly abstract and discretionary,[10] the multifactoral or 'salient features' approach has sometimes been said to disclose no general

circumstances in which another is generally reliant on the defendant for protection), according to *Henderson v Merrett Syndicates Ltd* (HL) [1995] 2 AC 145; *White v Jones* [1995] 2 AC 207, 273, per Lord Browne-Wilkinson.

3 *Caparo*, above n 1.

4 *Bank of Credit and Commerce International (Overseas) Ltd (In Liquidation) v Price Waterhouse (No 2)* [1998] PNLR 564, 586, per Sir Brian Neill; *Dean v Allin & Watts* [2001] EWCA Civ 758, [33], [2001] 2 Lloyd's Rep 249, 259, per Lightman J; *Barclays*, above n 2, per Lord Mance. In *Barclays*, both Lords Hoffmann and Mance suggest that the second approach displaces the third in cases involving the negligent provision of advice.

5 *Barclays*, above n 2, [4] per Lord Bingham, [93] per Lord Mance, [2004] EWCA Civ 1555, [23, 40] per Longmore LJ.

6 Various approaches have been tried, including: (i) knowledge or means of knowledge that the plaintiff individually, and not merely as a member of an unascertained class, will suffer loss—*Caltex* (1976) 136 CLR 529, per Gibbs J; (ii) proximity: *Sutherland Shire Council v Heyman* [1985] 157 CLR 549 ('*Heyman*'), per Deane J; *Bryan v Maloney* (1995) 182 CLR 609; and (iii) general reliance: *Heyman* [1985] 157 CLR 549, per Mason J.

7 *Perre v Apand* [1999] HCA 3, per McHugh J; *Woolcock Street Investments Pty Ltd v CDG Pty Ltd* [2004] HCA 16, per McHugh J. This approach has since been deployed in a case involving physical harm and omissions in *Crimmins v Stevedoring Industry Finance Committee* [1999] HCA 59, but recent cases on psychiatric harm revert to the concept of 'reasonable foreseeability' as the determinant of duty in cases of that type: *Annetts v Australian Stations Pty Ltd* (2002) 211 CLR 317; *Gifford v Strang Patrick Stevedoring Pty Ltd* [2003] HCA 33. Note that the multifactoral approach is confined to new cases and is not intended to undermine existing precedents.

8 *Ibid.*

9 *Perre*, above n 7, [105] per Mc Hugh J.

10 *Ibid*, [79–82]; *Sullivan v Moody* [2001] HCA 59, [49] per Gleeson CJ, Gaudron, McHugh, Hayne and Callinan JJ.

approach at all.[11] Both the criticisms of and the contrasts between the English and Australian approaches may actually turn out to have been exaggerated, as I venture to suggest later in this chapter, but it is clear that neither is seen as ideal.

A single answer to the question when a duty of care is owed is not to be expected, but a stable, principled approach to the way in which it is asked really ought to be an attainable ambition.[12] The purpose of this chapter is to reflect more closely upon the reasons why the task has proven so problematic and to provide some methodological suggestions which are sensitive to the difficulties. The problems for legal reasoning turn out to be of two sorts. They relate in part to the individual justifications (reasons) used by judges in economic loss cases, which are difficult to isolate and much contested. They also stem, however, from a number of more general problems which obstruct the integration of these reasons into coherent legal rules and principles. These distinct, but associated, sources of difficulty are considered in sections II and III respectively. Section IV provides some conclusions and critical reflections on method, the thrust of which I hope will be useful to judges in both jurisdictions.

II REASONS: IDENTIFYING RELEVANT JUSTIFICATIONS

A key to understanding the restrictive approach which courts have taken in cases of negligently inflicted pure economic loss is the realisation that their concerns have not historically related to the nature of the loss itself, but rather to a number of contingent issues which tend to arise in instances in which it happens to take this form.[13] From the point of view of corrective justice, such losses are no less deserving of redress in principle than cases of damage to the person or to property. They represent a form of harm which a wrong-doing defendant has a basic moral responsibility to rectify.[14]

[11] C Witting, 'The Three Stage Test Abandoned in Australia—or Not' (2002) 118 *LQR* 214, 218. It is assumed for these purposes that the multifactoral and salient features approaches are the same, which is probably an oversimplification. They are nonetheless generally regarded as consistent.

[12] On the need for a stable analytical method, see *Graham Barclay Oysters Pty Ltd v Ryan and Others* [2002] HCA 54, [211] per Kirby J.

[13] *Murphy v Brentwood* [1991] 1 AC 398, 485, per Lord Oliver; J Gordley, 'The Rule against Recovery in Negligence for Pure Economic Loss: an Historical Accident ?' in M Bussani and VV Palmer (eds), *Pure Economic Loss in Europe* (Cambridge, Cambridge University Press, 2003), ch 2, 25; P Cane, 'The Blight of Economic Loss: Is There Life after *Perre v Apand?*' [2000] *Torts Law Journal* 246. For a seminal analysis of some of these contingent 'policy' issues, see Stapleton, 'Duty of Care and Economic Loss: A Wider Agenda' (1991) 107 *LQR* 249.

[14] *Caltex Oil (Australia) Pty Ltd v The Dredge Willemstad* [1976] 136 CLR 529, 570, per Stephen J (there is no difference in 'morality' or 'justice' between pure and consequential economic loss); *Perre*, above n 7, [123] per McHugh J (the law of negligence protects economic interests 'in its quest for corrective justice'); *Arthur JS Hall & Co v Simons* [2002] 1 AC 615,

Some writers, it is true, have attempted to set up relevant, moral distinctions between pure economic losses and interferences with proprietary or possessory interests,[15] but their attempts generally run into difficulties of one sort or another. The strongest argument—that such interests simply rank lower in the list of human values[16]—has considerable intuitive appeal, but falls short of explaining why they should be unprotected in principle. Whilst it accurately recites the fact that we tend to regard other interests as more important, it does not explain why economic interests are not important enough to merit protection in their own right against behaviour which is culpably careless.[17] The intuition that intangible financial interests are less valuable than property also seems increasingly questionable, given the central part they play as investment vehicles in modern market economies. Whereas, in the past, much of our wealth was tied up in tangible form, this is less so in today's world than ever before. Moreover, whilst property clearly has some personal 'added value' over abstract wealth in many instances,[18] it does not always. Landlords frequently choose to buy houses, for example, simply for investment purposes—as instantiations of wealth pure and simple—not because the property has any real meaning to them, or expresses anything particular about who they are. In a modern, fast-moving, mobile and market-driven world, economic interests can no longer be viewed as a peripheral social phenomenon. They are central to modern life.

From this point of view, Lord Oliver's famous statement in *Murphy v Brentwood*,[19] that causing economic loss does not need to be justified in the same way as damage to property and is not in itself 'wrongful', admittedly looks very odd. If one scrutinises more closely the passage in which

681, per Lord Steyn (an advocate's liability for pure financial loss follows the 'basic premise that there should be a remedy for a wrong'); *Woolcock*, above n 7, [106] per McHugh J (liability of builders for defective premises 'would advance the cause of corrective justice, one of the rationales of the law of negligence').

15 Weir, 'Abstraction in the Law of Torts—Economic Loss' [1974] *City of London Law Review* 15; Witting, 'Distinguishing between Property Damage and Pure Economic Loss in Negligence: a Personality Thesis' [2001] *Legal Studies* 481; Benson, 'The Basis for Excluding Liability for Economic Loss in Tort' in DG Owen (ed), *Philosophical Foundations of Tort Law* (Oxford, Oxford University Press, 1996). Benson's argument (carelessly causing economic loss is legally wrongful only where it violates some prior exclusive right) finds some resonance in the speech of Gaudron J in *Hill v Van Erp* (1997) 188 CLR 159, 198 (who indicates that it is easier to establish liability where there is interference with a claimant's 'precise legal right') but appears, with respect, to beg the question which the law of negligence has to decide. As Witting indicates (at 501), it also runs into difficulties in explaining misstatement cases.

16 Weir, above n 15; Cane, above n 13.

17 Bussani and Palmer, above n 13, 21–3, indicate that arguments about 'relative priorities' work on the basis of a 'silent premise' that legal resources are insufficient to accommodate them all. The argument then effectively dissolves into a pragmatic concern about the effect of liability on judicial resources, akin to that sometimes encountered in the context of arguments about 'indeterminacy,' below.

18 Weir, Witting, above n 15.

19 [1991] 1 AC 398, 487.

the statement appears, however, it is clear that his Lordship's point was not that a *moral* distinction can be drawn between the different types of loss. Rather, it was that the normal approach to the question of *legal duty* had to be 'qualified' when it came to economic harm, such that something more than its mere foreseeability would be required for liability to arise.[20] It is not, therefore, that carelessly causing economic harm *needs no moral justification (is not in itself morally questionable)*, but that, whatever the basic moral position of a careless actor, we may be justified in *restricting* her *legal responsibility* for other reasons. This is certainly the way in which the issue was understood by Lord Denning right from the start,[21] and courts in both England and Australia now tend to take that view. Unravelling the various judicial reasons for discriminating between moral and legal responsibility in economic loss cases is, however, a decidedly more problematic business.

A Absence of Social Loss—Neutral Wealth Transfers

One possible reason provided by McHugh J in *Perre v Apand* [22] is that, whilst economic losses invariably harm a particular person, they sometimes entail no 'social' harm, because the individual loss gets cancelled out by the benefits it yields to third parties. An example would be where the careless interruption of the electricity supply to a defendant's business premises detrimentally affects his production and thereby reduces his market share, which is then simply taken over by an enterprising competitor. Negligence in these circumstances results in wealth transfer, it is said, but no harm is done overall. 'Tis an ill wind that blows nobody any good.

There are two immediate difficulties with this reasoning, even assuming the example to be realistic.[23] For one thing, exactly the same 'wealth transfer' phenomenon occurs where the claimant loses production as a result of damage to his property (for example, his plant) or person (as where he is no longer able to operate his business as a consequence of injury).[24] But at another level entirely, as a system of private rights, tort law is generally unconcerned with aggregate social harm. It focuses on damage done to individual interests and, indeed, exists precisely to protect

20 *Ibid.* His Lordship rejected any moral distinction at 485.

21 *SCM Ltd v W J Whittall* [1971] 1 QB 337, 344; *Spartan Steel & Alloys v Martin* [1973] QB 27, 36.

22 Above n 7, [72]; Feldthusen, 'Pure Economic Loss in the High Court of Australia: Reinventing the Square Wheel?' (2000) 8 *Tort Law Review* 33, 50–1; Feldthusen and Palmer, 'Economic Loss and the Supreme Court of Canada: An Economic Critique of Norsk Steamship and Bird Construction,' (1995) 74 *Canadian Bar Review* 427.

23 The 'zero social loss' hypothesis is questionable. See Rizzo, 'The Economic Loss Problem: A Comment on Bishop' (1982) 2 *OJLS* 197; Witting, above n 15, 495–6.

24 In either case, the loss of production is readily recoverable, as 'parasitic' upon injury to property or person: *Spartan Steel & Alloys v Martin* [1973] QB 27.

them against the potential tyranny of collective calculus. The possibility that a claimant's carelessly inflicted economic 'minus' will be cancelled out by 'pluses' to other market operators fails to provide a convincing reason to rule out a duty of care. If it did, we would live in a very insecure world indeed. Our rights would logically be up for grabs by anyone able to make at least as much profit out of them as we ourselves.

B Stifling Legitimate Competition

A similar, but distinct, concern is that liability for pure economic loss could stifle legitimate competitive behaviour.[25] According to McHugh J in *Perre v Apand*,[26] this argument focuses on the potential impact of liability on the private right of an individual to pursue her commercial interests, not (like the previous one) on broader social effects. It is an argument for the protection of a defendant's personal autonomy.

Whilst the right to compete is clearly an important aspect of individual freedom, there is actually more than one way in which it can be understood. It can thus be construed narrowly, as a right to engage in legitimate competition with others[27] (in which case it is presumably an issue in only a minority of cases where claimant and defendant are active in the same economic sector, or commercial transaction); or, much more broadly, as a right to run one's business free of precautionary costs which are so high as to unreasonably undermine its general competitiveness (economic viability).[28]

The narrow version of the argument describes a good reason for ruling out a duty of care in some cases. If claimant and defendant are economic competitors, their position will be analogous to that of parties engaged in the arm's-length negotiation of a contract who tacitly embrace the value of self-interest. The intrusion of 'neighbourly' obligations of care would represent an unwelcome violation of an accepted commercial norm, the fruits of which are reaped in the same way as its costs are consensually

25 *Heyman* (1985) 157 CLR 424, 503, per Deane J; *Bryan*, above n 6, 618 per Mason CJ, Deane, Gaudron JJ, 632 per Brennan J; *Hill*, above n 15, 175 per Dawson J, 193 per Gaudron J; 211 per McHugh J; *Esanda Finance Corporation Ltd v Peat Marwick Hungerfords* (1997) 188 CLR 241, 254 per Dawson J; *Perre*, above n 7, [32–3] per Gaudron J, [114] per McHugh J, [182] per Gummow J; *Dovuro Pty Ltd v Wilkins and Others* [2000] FCA 1902, [30–1] per Brennan J; *Woolcock*, above n 7, [21] per Gleeson CJ, Gummow, Hayne and Heydon JJ, [78] per McHugh J.

26 *Ibid*. The same interpretation appears to be taken by Gaudron J, [32–3]. See also *Woolcock*, above n 7, [78]; *Dovuro*, *ibid*, [30–1] per Brennan J (rev'd on other grounds [2003] HCA 51).

27 This appears to be Cane's interpretation, above n 13.

28 In *Perre*, above n 7, McHugh J shifts between interpretations, but his reference at [101] to the need to 'avoid unreasonable burdens' on defendants clearly encompasses the broader argument. He affirms this in *Woolcock*, above n 7, [78].

born.[29] By contrast, the broad interpretation of the right to compete (as a right to be commercially competitive) discloses a far weaker basis for eradicating a defendant's responsibility. The potential burden of preventive precautions to a defendant's business may be one consideration in determining whether the risk to which she has exposed a claimant's interests is unreasonable, but it does not seem a good reason to entirely displace her moral responsibility for considering them. Where the prospective risk is one of damage to property or person, for example, potential precautionary costs are weighed and balanced in the scales of the breach inquiry,[30] but they do not rule out the obligation to take care. The moral justification for taking a different approach simply because the prospective harm is economic rather than physical is very hard to see.

An added complication is that, whilst the dominant contemporary interpretation of the competition argument is based on a defendant's personal autonomy, it has also, on occasion, been understood as a broader, instrumentalist concern about the effects which liabilities might have upon the functioning of the market economy as a whole.[31] In this guise, it has more in common with the first argument about 'wealth transfer' than it does with McHugh J's concern about personal autonomy. It abstracts from the particular interests of the parties to the dispute and is speculative in the sense that the effects of tort liabilities on the health of a market-economy are hard to predict and courts have little empirical data upon which to base their conclusions.

It is not insignificant that, whilst the High Court of Australia has often referred to the significance of a claimant's right to compete, in no case to date has it been used as a justification for ruling out a duty of care. A little reflection discloses good reasons for this. Although the narrower version of the autonomy argument is sound, it is rarely in point: there is no sense in which builders and house purchasers,[32] solicitors and beneficiaries,[33] or potato suppliers and growers[34] can realistically be construed as economic competitors. Equally, the broader (and decidedly more suspect) version is largely irrelevant where the defendant is already under an independent

29 Note however that the law already makes incursions into the competitive domain via the 'economic torts'. Parties to contractual negotiations also owe duties of care in respect of information given, both at common law and (commonly now) under statute. The key question is thus what constitutes 'legitimate' competition according to the commercial norm. In *Hill*, above n 15, 198, Gaudron J suggests that the legality of behaviour is key (it is never 'legitimate' pursuit of self interest to interfere with the ('precise') 'legal rights' of others). In *Perre*, above n 7, [116] McHugh J regards legality as relevant but inconclusive, the ultimate question being whether behaviour constitutes 'sharp or ruthless practice' going beyond community tolerance.

30 *Bolton v Stone* (HL) [1951] AC 850.

31 *Bryan*, above n 6, 632, per Brennan J. See also Holmes J, 'The Path of the Law' (1897) 10 *Harvard Law Review* 457, 466 ('the *public good* [my emphasis] is supposed to be best preserved by free competition').

32 *Bryan*, ibid; *Woolcock*, above n 7.

33 *Hill*, above n 15; *White*, above n 2.

34 *Perre*, above n 7.

obligation to incur precautionary costs. Such an obligation will arise whenever a defendant's conduct poses a foreseeable physical risk to the claimant, or consists in the provision of services pursuant to a contract.[35] In these cases, obligations of economic precaution add little extra to the defendant's bill.

C Indeterminate Liability

A third concern, which is most often cited in cases involving negligent advice or 'relational' economic loss, relates to indeterminate liability. This argument is notoriously indeterminate in itself. In fact, Cardozo CJ's infamous statement in *Ultramares Corporation v Touche*[36] has too often been used as a hold-all for a variety of sub-forms of argument, some of which purport to be concerned with the moral implications of economic loss liabilities and some of which do not. These need to be isolated and addressed individually if they are to be the slightest bit meaningful.

The less common forms of the argument relate to: (i) the possibility that actions might be postponed for an indeterminate period of time as a result of financial harm assuming a 'latent' and therefore undiscoverable form[37]; (ii) administrative arguments about the prospects of courts being swamped by vexatious litigation[38]; (iii) the idea that allowing one type of economic loss claim will open the door to others (the 'slippery slope' argument)[39]; and (iv) the moral impropriety of imposing on a defendant high levels of liability disproportionate to his fault.[40] The spectre of large liabilities is

35 *Hill*, above n 15 (contractual duty of care to testator); *Perre*, above n 7 (contractual duty of care to potato purchasers); *Woolcock*, above n 7 (tort duty already owed to purchasers regarding person and property); *Dovuro*, above n 25 (revised on other grounds [2003] HCA 51) (tort duty regarding seed user's property interests); *Johnson Tiles Pty Ltd v Esso Australia Ltd* [2003] VSC 27, [962] (duties owed to third party employees regarding physical safety).

36 (1931) 174 NE 441, 444.

37 *Bryan*, above n 6, 626, per Mason CJ, Deane and Gaudron JJ; *Woolcock*, above n 7, [107] per McHugh J, [166], [180–1] per Kirby J, [219] per Callinan J. The concern is most often voiced in defective premises cases, but was also mentioned by McHugh J in *Hill*, above n 15, 216, on the basis that it may be a long time before a solicitor's advisory errors in respect of a will are discovered.

38 *Esanda*, above n 25, 288, per McHugh J; *Perre*, above n 7, [169] per Gummow J (*obiter*); *Johnson Tiles*, above n 35, [778], [950–955] per Gillard J (*obiter*). *Woolcock*, above n 7, [97] per McHugh J (obiter).

39 *Leigh and Sillivan Shipping v The Aliakmon* (HL) [1986] AC 785, 816–7, per Lord Brandon; *Barclays*, above n 2, per Lord Walker (liability of banks would also entail liability of other non-commercial parties with notice of freezing injunctions).

40 *Caltex*, above n 14, 551 per Gibbs J, 591 per Mason J; *San Sebastian Pty Ltd v Minister Administering the Environmental Planning Act 1979* (1986) 162 CLR 349, 354 per Gibbs, Mason, Wilson, Dawson JJ; *Perre*, above n 7, [169] per Gummow J; *Macfarlane v Tayside Health Board* (HL) [2000] 2 AC 59, 91 per Lord Hope, 106 per Lord Clyde; *Barclays*, above n 2, [111] per Lord Mance; Rabin, 'Tort Recovery for Negligently Inflicted Economic Loss: A Reassessment' (1985) 37 *Stanford Law Review* 1513,1534. For criticism, see Stapleton, 'Duty of Care Factors: A Selection from the Judicial Menus' in Cane and Stapleton (eds), *The Law of Obligations: Essays in Celebration of John Fleming* (Oxford, Clarendon Press, 1998), 59, 65–6.

said to stem either from the ease with which inaccurate financial information can be transmitted to a wide audience, or from the close interdependency of financial interests and the capacity of a single act to send foreseeable 'ripples' down the financial chain. More popular versions relate to (v) the undesirable effects which such high levels of liability might have upon the availability and/or price of services and the economy as a whole[41]; (vi) the potential uncertainty for defendants about the likely 'class' of affected persons,[42] given the 'ripple effect' phenomenon referred to above; and (vii) the potential uncertainty for defendants about the extent or type of their prospective liabilities.[43]

Many of these arguments have legitimately been questioned. Unacceptable time delays logically seem best precluded via the limitation of actions[44] and 'administration of justice' arguments by summary judgment, the striking out of unmeritorious claims or increased judicial resources. The idea that compensation for economic loss ought to be proportionate to moral wrongdoing is also highly dubious[45] and, in any event, ruling out a duty of care where loss is large does not achieve proportionate responsibility, it eradicates it completely. The perverse result of succumbing to this strain of reasoning would be that the more harm one did, the less likely one would be to be held responsible not just for some of it, but for any of it.

Problems of this nature may explain why the High Court of Australia has recently preferred to understand the concept of 'indeterminacy' in terms of the last two arguments identified. It is not immediately obvious, however, how *ex ante* uncertainties about the likely class of potential victims or the type/quantum of economic loss are relevant morally or instrumentally to a defendant's liability, other than by making it more difficult (and therefore more expensive) for her to arrange appropriate

41 This argument is often voiced in cases involving advisory services (eg *Hill*, above n 15, 214, per McHugh J (dissenting), but is not so confined: *Johnson Tiles*, above n 35, [777] per Gillard J. See further Bishop, 'Negligent Misrepresentation through Economists' Eyes' (1980) 96 *LQR* 360.

42 *McMullin and Another v ICI Australia Operations Pty Ltd and Others* [1997] 72 FCR 1, 76 per Wilcox J; *Hill*, above n 15, 180 per Dawson J, 193 per Gaudron J, 215 per McHugh J (dissenting); *Perre*, above n 7, [50], [107–8] per McHugh J; *Dovuro*, above n 25, [29] per Branson J; *Johnson Tiles*, above n 35, [906] per Gillard J; *Goodwill v British Pregnancy Advisory Service* [1996] 1 WLR 1397.

43 *Hill*, above n 15, 180 per Dawson J (damage must not be 'at large'), 193 per Gaudron J, [215–16] per McHugh J (dissenting). *Esanda*, above n 25, 285, per McHugh J; *Perre*, above n 7, [107–8] per McHugh J; *Woolcock*, above n 7, [219] per Callinan J. See contra, *Johnson Tiles*, above n 35, [906], [920] per Gillard J. For an approach focusing on uncertainty about claimant class and type (but not exact amount) of loss, see Beach, 'Indeterminacy: The Uncertainty Principle of Negligence' (2005) 13 *Torts Law Journal* 1.

44 *Woolcock*, above n 7, [180–1] per Kirby J (dissenting); *Johnson Tiles*, above n 35, [906] per Gillard J.

45 It does not apply in cases of property damage. Introducing it here therefore reintroduces the same moral distinction between property interests and economic interests which judges have generally rejected.

levels of liability insurance. The worries are then not about uncertainty itself, but about the indirect effects which it is likely to have on the provision or pricing of services (sub-argument (v) above), or on the most 'efficient' (cheapest, easiest) way of distributing the loss. These concerns are again speculative, in the sense that any assessment of their merits entails detailed knowledge of relevant insurance markets and (even more problematically, perhaps) accurate prediction of the effects which liabilities might have on insurance premiums, market prices and service provision.

An alternative way of understanding the concern about the uncertainties associated with 'ripple effects' is that they are relevant not from the point of view of their indirect social effects on prices, services or loss-distribution, but because of their potential impact upon a defendant's autonomy. The ability to plan one's future is, after all, an important aspect of personal choice, and liabilities which are wholly incalculable might represent a sword of Damacles suspended over defendants' heads, unduly inhibiting their freedom of action. This argument would avoid difficult speculation about the possible social impact which the uninsurability of such losses might have, but the question remains whether the mere incalculability of a foreseeable loss is a good enough moral reason for denying a person's responsibility to pay for it, when it has been carelessly caused. If the potential size of a liability is insufficient reason from the point of view of a defendant's autonomy to relieve him of liability (as McHugh J suggests),[46] it is hard to see how uncertainties about the nature or extent of that liability can be, since the indirect costs of such uncertainties for a defendant's freedom of action are almost certain to be less than the full weight of the liabilities themselves.

In the event, then, not only have arguments relating to indeterminacy until very recently been insufficiently distinguished from one another, but if, as seems to be the current thinking in Australia, they relate to uncertainties about liability for defendants, one still needs to know why such uncertainties are important if one is to formulate anything like a coherent approach to liability. It is hard to see how the incalculability of a prospective liability weighs more heavily upon a defendant's freedom of action than its actual size, so that if it is really the uncertainty rather than the size of liability that is key, it is tempting to conclude that this must be because of its indirect bearing upon the question of which party is in a better position to insure against the loss. Those further from the ripple's epicentre will be closer to its potential effects and therefore in a better position to assess and insure against the harm. The snag with this rationalisation is that the High Court of Australia currently bluntly denies that the respective insurance positions of the parties are relevant to

[46] *Perre*, above n 7, [107–8].

liability,[47] which leaves us at something of a loss. A possible reaction is to regard the denial with circumspection, but that brings significant justificatory difficulties of its own. Perhaps the most one can say at the current point in time is that if the relative insurability of economic losses is relevant, this is something that should be openly admitted, rather than buried within 'indeterminacy' arguments.[48] Accepting this, it is probably best considered as part of the debate about ways in which a claimant might reasonably have protected himself (considered further below), though even then it is questionable whether it should rule out a duty of care, as we shall see.

D Coherence and Conflict

A fourth concern relates to potential conflicts which economic duties of care might yield with other legal systems or norms—to the potential 'emasculation of other bodies of legal doctrine.'[49] This issue typically attends the expansion of any body of law into fields which are already the subject of legal governance or commercial bargaining, of which this is clearly one. As with the indeterminacy argument, it has a number of distinct manifestations, which include: (i) the worry that duties of care might contradict the way in which risks have been consciously allocated by parties to a dispute in the context of a contractual matrix[50]; (ii) the concern that they may undermine an existing domestic or international statutory regime regulating parties' conduct or remedies[51]; (iii) worries that liability might produce ethical conflicts for professionals by extending legal responsibility

47 *Caltex*, above n 14, 580–1 per Stephen J; *Perre*, above n 7, [130] per McHugh J. See, in contrast, *Johnson Tiles*, above n 35, [1093–110] per Gillard J (insurability of a claimant's loss is relevant to the question of whether she had an alternative means of protection).

48 Interestingly, English courts have recently begun to make open reference to arguments of this type at the highest appellate level: see eg *Barclays*, above n 2, per Lord Mance, discussed further below. For the view that the role of insurance has been drastically underplayed by judges and academics alike (albeit in the context of personal injury litigation), see Lewis, 'How Important are Insurers in Compensating Claims for Personal Injury in the UK{?}' (2006) 31 *The Geneva Papers* 323.

49 *Hill*, above n 15, 184, per Dawson J; *Perre*, above n 7, [5] per Gleeson CJ, *Woolcock*, above n 7, [102] per McHugh J. For the same concern expressed outside the economic loss context, see *Sullivan*, above n 10, [50] per Gleeson CJ, Gaudron, McHugh, Hayne and Callinan JJ.

50 Fleming, 'Tort in a Contractual Matrix,' 1995 (3) *Tort Law Review* 12; *Bryan*, above n 6, 622 per Mason CJ, Deane and Gaudron JJ (obiter); *Johnson Tiles*, above n 35, [1144–5]; *Simaan v Pilkington Glass* [1988] QB 758; *Henderson v Merrett Syndicates Ltd* (HL) [1995] 2 AC 145.

51 *The Aliakmon*, above n 39 (Hague Convention giving rise to the Hague Rules); *Caparo*, above n 1 (Companies Act 1985); *Woolcock*, above n 7, [102–105] per McHugh J (Statutes of Limitation); *Barclays*, above n 2 (Civil Procedure Rules and Contempt Proceedings). This concern is most obviously relevant where the defendant is a public body imbued with statutory powers or duties: *Sullivan v Moody* (2001) 207 CLR 562.

beyond their immediate clients[52]; (iv) fears that liability might undercut the immunities normally provided to directors by principles of corporate personality[53]; and (v) concerns that the creation of new negligence liabilities might bring courts into conflict with their own constitutional role, by embroiling them in areas of social policy better suited to reform via the Parliamentary process.[54]

Conflict concerns arise regularly, even where 'indeterminacy' is absent. As tort law gradually expands its protection of economic interests, they will feature ever more prominently, since such interests are so regularly (and rightly) the object of commercial risk-allocation and statutory attention. All versions of the argument require detailed consideration of individual facts to determine whether potential conflict is present. They are not unique to cases involving economic loss, or the law of tort.[55] Moreover, whilst ruling out a duty of care will often be the only way of avoiding conflict, it should be born in mind that more sensitive mechanisms may exist for resolving the tension. It may sometimes be more appropriate, for example, to align the standard of care owed in tort with a contractually specified standard[56] than to reject any tort duty out of hand on the basis that the two obligations might hypothetically clash. Courts should also not be overly ready to assume that statutory remedial regimes are intended to exhaustively define parties' remedies, particularly when the remedies they do offer are ill-adapted to effectively compensating the harm done.

E Alternative Means of Protection

A final, highly topical judicial concern is that a claimant may have an alternative means of protecting himself against economic harm.[57] Whether or not private insurance is regarded as one such means is still a matter of great uncertainty, as intimated above, but a contractual warranty apparently might be,[58] as might a private law remedy,[59] a public law appeal

52 *Clarke v Bruce Lance* [1988] 1 WLR 881.

53 *Williams v Natural Life Health Foods Ltd* (HL) [1998] 1 WLR 830.

54 *D & F Estates v Church Commissioners* (HL) [1989] AC 177, 210 per Lord Bridge; *Murphy*, above n 13, 457 per Lord Mackay, 472 per Lord Keith, 492 per Lord Oliver, 498 per Lord Jauncey; *Bryan*, above n 6, 644 per Brennan J (dissenting).

55 The same constraints operate upon the recent, rapid expansion of the law of restitution, which constitutes another device for the protection of economic interests.

56 *The Aliakmon*, above n 39, [1985] QB 350, 397–8 per Lord Goff (although note that this approach was rejected in the House of Lords [1986] AC 785, because of the complexity of the relevant contractual provisions, which made synthesis of the duties apparently very difficult); *Henderson v Merrett Syndicates Ltd* (HL) [1995] 2 AC 145, 206 per Lord Browne-Wilkinson.

57 *Perre*, above n 7, [120–121] per McHugh J; *Woolcock*, above n 7, [85] per McHugh J.

58 *Ibid.*

59 *White*, above n 2, 262, per Lord Goff (rectification of *inter vivos* transactions). Note, however, that in *Walker v Geo Medlicott* (Eng CA) [1999] 1 WLR 727 Mummery LJ accepted a

mechanism,[60] or the possibility of obtaining independent verification of the reliability of information[61] or building work.[62] The High Court of Australia currently targets this concern via the concept of 'vulnerability'. Whether a claimant is 'vulnerable' to economic harm turns on whether she was unable reasonably to protect herself against it by reason of 'ignorance, or social, political or economic constraints'.[63]

An immediate uncertainty is whether this is a concern about the (un)reasonableness of the individual claimant's own failure to protect herself on the individual facts, or embodies a broader judicial strategy for distributing the burden of precaution between different social groups, such as the builders of defective premises and their purchasers. If the former, then it is common to all negligence cases and in that way wholly uncontroversial, but the justification for regarding it as reason to rule out a duty of care is then unclear. An unreasonable failure to protect oneself is a well-established basis for reducing the damages one can claim on grounds of contributory negligence or failure to mitigate loss. Exceptionally, it might be regarded as founding a conclusion that one caused one's own loss, or that the latter was too remote a consequence of the defendant's negligence to justify holding him legally accountable for it. It is not usual, however, to regard the fact that one has a reasonable responsibility for protecting one's own interests as relieving a defendant in principle of his responsibility to avoid harming them. A claimant's own failings do not make his injurer's actions right. This suggests either that courts are mistaken in regarding the availability of an alternative means of protection as a factor negating a defendant's duty of care (though it has a clear role to play at lower levels in the negligence inquiry in relation to causation, remoteness and the mitigation of damage), or that that the second interpretation of the argument better represents courts' truc concerns.

If the latter is the case, the idea is that whatever an individual claimant's actual circumstances, the fact that claimants in the same class normally have the capacity to protect themselves (for example, by virtue of their economic power or commercial sophistication) is a good enough reason in itself to allocate the responsibility for economic precaution to her, rather than the defendant. The debate about 'vulnerability' and 'alternative

duty as having been correctly conceded (*obiter*) even though rectification might have been available. Its availability was regarded as relevant instead to the mitigation of loss. Note that generally there is no obligation to mitigate by engaging in speculative litigation: *London and SE Building Society v Stone* [1983] 1 WLR 1242.

60 *X (minors) v Bedfordshire County Council* (HL) [1995] 2 AC 633. This is questionable, since such remedies ordinarily provide no compensation for harm done: *Phelps v Hillingdon LBC* (HL) [2001] 2 AC 619, 672, per Lord Clyde. Such remedies may, however, be intended to constitute an 'exclusive regime' in some cases, giving rise to the conflict argument, above.

61 *Esanda*, above n 25.

62 *Woolcock*, above n 7, [32].

63 *Ibid*, [80] per McHugh J.

means of protection' is then pertinent in the sense that it raises the question of which of two social groups ought to bear the onus of precaution, but is overtly distributive in nature. From the point of view of those who think that broad, distributive criteria are irrelevant to the outcome of negligence claims (McHugh J seems to be one),[64] the first interpretation will be preferable, though it will require detailed investigation in each case into the individual circumstances of the particular claimant. The majority in *Woolcock* seem to endorse this type of approach. Callinan J's blanket suggestion, however, that all purchasers of real estate (as a group) have ways of protecting themselves[65] seems closer to the second view, since it makes no apparent attempt to assess whether or not such means were available to an individual claimant on the facts.

If we adopt the former view, as I suggest here that we should, a key question which courts may need to reconsider is the extent to which the availability of private insurance against economic harms is something which individual claimants should now consider as a matter of course. Courts' formal insistence on the irrelevance of such insurance seems inconsistent with the suggestion in *Woolcock* that a claimant may sometimes be expected to protect herself by obtaining a contractual warranty from a vendor, which is, after all, simply another way of insuring herself against the risk. The relevance of insurance to tort liability is supported to some degree by recent comments of Lord Hoffmann[66] (albeit in the context of a debate about liability for property damage under the rule in *Rylands v Fletcher*[67]) and Lord Mance in the House of Lords' most recent economic loss decision, *Commissioners of Customs and Excise v Barclays Bank*.[68] In the latter case, his Lordship clearly thought that the difficulties for a claimant in obtaining first party protection were relevant, though they were ultimately outweighed by the insurance costs which non-commercial defendants might have to bear, if economic duties of care were extended in the manner proposed.[69]

F Summary

The justifications currently used by judges for restricting legal responsibility for pure economic loss are very ill-defined at best and in no sense logically unique to cases involving losses of this type. Two of the justifications I have examined (legitimate competition, indeterminate liability) can be inter-

64 *Perre*, above n 7, [130].
65 *Ibid*, [212], [224].
66 *Transco plc v Stockport Metropolitan Borough Council* [2003] UKHL 61, [46], [49].
67 (1868) LR 3 HL 330.
68 [2006] UKHL 28.
69 *Ibid*, [102].

preted either as autonomy-based arguments focusing on the moral effects of liabilities on defendants, or as broader, instrumentalist arguments about the social or economic repercussions which such liabilities might have. The argument about alternative means of protection can likewise be understood either as a way of refocusing our attention on familiar issues about a claimant's reasonable responsibility for protecting herself which are highly individualised and fact-specific, or as relating to broader issues about the distribution of precautionary costs between different social groups. The most clearly defined justifications relate to conflict and wealth transfer, the former of which seems a perfectly sound and increasingly relevant concern in a system seeking to navigate its way through other systems and norms, but the latter of which is, with respect, incompatible with the idea of tort law as a system for the protection of private rights and should probably be discarded altogether.

III CONCEPTS: INTEGRATING JUSTIFICATIONS INTO LEGAL REASONING: PROBLEMS AND IDEALS

A Problems

The preceding section discloses a number of good explanations for the general incoherence of courts' approach to the duty of care question in economic loss cases. Courts' justifications are almost universally ill-defined and some are normatively suspect. Aside from their individual failings, these justifications also exhibit a number of collective characteristics which make them difficult to integrate coherently into legal principles and rules. These features have implications for the style of approach that should be taken to the duty of care question, which I address shortly.

(i) Positive Principles, Negative Justifications

Firstly, all the justifications are negative, acting as they do as reasons to restrict the scope of liability for harm caused by fault. This makes them difficult to express in terms of positive duty principles without some risk of obscurity and inaccuracy. Positive justifications for liability convert relatively precisely into positive liability criteria. The reasonable foreseeability of harm, for example, features universally as a prerequisite for duty in all common law approaches and is the best—perhaps the only really well—understood duty 'principle'. By contrast, it is hard to express negative concerns such as those relating to indeterminate liability or economic competition in anything other than their own terms. Attempting to address them through positive liability principles such as 'proximity of relationship' 'reliance,' 'assumption of responsibility' 'vulnerability' or 'knowledge of risk' tends to obscure them and can draw judicial aim away from its mark. This may indeed explain why Lord Wilberforce chose in *Anns*[70] to break the duty of care inquiry down into two distinct stages—one (Lord Atkin's neighbour principle) reflecting primarily positive reasons for liability based upon the reasonable contemplation of likely harm, and one consisting simply in 'negativing considerations'. Whatever the difficulties associated with this approach,[71] it had the obvious merit of avoiding difficult translations from negative reason to positive principle and drove the various concerns out into the open, enabling them to be better identified and targeted.

By contrast with Lord Wilberforce, courts in both England and Australia remain hesitant about expressing legal requirements in economic loss cases directly in terms of negativing policy concerns.[72] This is not to say that the latter are regarded as unimportant—they are actually now identified and discussed as central even in England—but simply that their translation into liability principles is thought to be an important component of the process of legal justification. This may be because courts are still uncomfortable being seen as direct arbiters of 'policy', but these days it is actually at least as likely to be that legal rules and principles are simply thought to offer a level of certainty which policies inherently lack.[73] Anyone familiar with the confusion currently attaching to duty of care concepts in both jurisdictions may be forgiven for finding this more than a little ironic, but the theory is sound enough.

(ii) Coherent Principles, Multiple Justifications

Secondly, even if we eradicate some of the more dubious concerns we explored in section II, they are clearly multiple. This makes their distillation into a singular principle of liability extremely difficult. The greater the number of reasons we try to accommodate within a rule, the more difficult it becomes to formulate it in a way which coheres with them all.

There are only a limited number of ways of dealing with this problem. One is to abandon the search for general principles as a will-o'-the wisp and deploy something akin to a structured judicial discretion instead. This

70 *Anns v Merton London Borough Council* [1978] AC 728, 751–2.

71 The main problem stemmed from the idea of 'prima facie duty' arising at stage one, which seems (perhaps mistakenly) to have been interpreted as reversing the onus in new categories of case, thereby leading to an overly expansive approach.

72 See, eg *Caltex* (1976) 136 CLR 529, 567, per Steven J. In *Perre*, above n 7 McHugh J suggests, [95] that the new multifactoral approach actually deploys the relevant policy reasons as legal principles, but whilst the various factors clearly come much closer to expressing judicial reasons, some are still opaque translations of them: 'knowledge of risk' and 'vulnerability' stand out in this regard. Note that the view that the various policy considerations are legal principles is rejected by Kirby J, [284].

73 *Ibid.*

enables a wide variety of reasons to be deployed across a very broad range of cases, but it can markedly reduce the predictability of outcomes. The second option is to break up the case law into a number of smaller, factual categories or 'pockets' in the hope that a narrower range of concerns can be identified with each category.[74] That ought in theory to give the development of coherent liability rules within each category a more realistic chance. The difficulties with this, as Professor Stapleton has explained,[75] are that the various judicial concerns I have identified tend to spill over between categories; that any increase in the coherence of liability principles within the categories can be at the expense of coherence between them; and that it leaves one with no obvious reasoning apparatus to deploy outside categories, in entirely new types of case.

English and Australian courts now grapple with the problem of multiple policy concerns in subtly different ways. England has persisted with general principles, whilst also recognising that the law must respect and develop incrementally from existing categories. By contrast, the Australian multifactoral approach purports to firmly reject both generalisation[76] and categorisation.[77] In some respects, it resembles the operation of a structured discretion, though decision-making is much more tightly constrained than that expression implies, because it entails the use of only those factors recognised in the cases and at a cautious, incremental pace.[78] Also, although the approach formally rejects categorisation (in the sense that the failure of a case to fit within an existing pocket of case law is not regarded as determinative), it is only used when a case falls outside a space in which liability rules are clearly settled.[79] In this respect, the strategy is much closer to that prevailing in England than may at first appear to be the case. Both approaches purport to leave existing rules and categories intact and to work outwards from them. The key difference is that, in deciding new cases, they deal with the wide variety of policy arguments through concepts formulated at rather different levels of abstraction. The English approach works through a superstructure of higher-level principles, whereas the multifactoral approach deploys concepts which are closer to

[74] B Feldthusen, *Economic Negligence* (Toronto, Carswell, 3rd edn, 1994), ch 1; B Feldthusen, 'Pure Economic Loss in the High Court of Australia: Reinventing the Square Wheel?' (2000) *Tort Law Review* 33. This approach has the approval of the Supreme Court of Canada.

[75] Above n 13.

[76] *Perre*, above n 7, [81] per McHugh J.

[77] *Ibid*, [75]. This must be carefully qualified. All that appears to be meant is that the duty issue will not be determined purely by asking whether a case falls within an existing category or can be seen as a viable extension of one. It does not discard categories completely. See further the text, below.

[78] *Ibid*, [404] per Callinan J.

[79] *Ibid*, [94] per McHugh J.

ground level in the sense that they relate more directly and individually to the various normative concerns.

(iii) Legal Principles and Social Justifications

A third feature is that some of the justifications cited by courts relate to the social effects of economic loss liabilities, rather than to concerns which are identifiably particular to the parties on the facts. This is difficult insofar as it opens up the possibility of a gap between the ends of private law and its means, in ways that have deeply troubled Professors Weinrib[80] and Cane.[81] Even if it is impossible (and inappropriate) for judges to ignore all of the effects which liabilities might have when setting the scope of tort rights, private litigation is clearly not the best mechanism for proactively implementing broad social policies such as loss-distribution, because of the informational constraints to which it is subject and the constitutional limits of the judicial role.

This is not necessarily to say that all arguments which are framed in terms of fears about the effects of tort liabilities are inconsistent with private law's constraints and therefore inappropriate.[82] Some arguments which look 'social' in orientation may simply be generalised ways of stating the implications of tort liabilities for individual rights. We have seen, for example, that concerns about the effect which liabilities might have on economic competition can be understood in two ways—one of which centres on the health of the market economy as a whole (which is largely imponderable), and the other of which expresses a legitimate concern for the rights of individual defendants to make their way freely in the world. The same ambiguity exists in relation to arguments about indeterminacy and alternative means of protection, some versions of which are more compatible with private law's bipartite systemic constraints than others. Unless these constraints are to be significantly relaxed, however, their necessary implication is that courts should generally avoid reference to justifications which are based on the achievement of social ends, rather than on the effects which liability rules might have for private rights.

80 For Weinrib, tort law as an instantiation of corrective justice can only coherently sustain arguments based on private, Kantian rights. All instrumentalist justifications are suspect insofar as they fail to respect the correlativity of the parties' legal relationship in private law disputes. For a classic statement, see Weinrib, *The Idea of Private Law* (Harvard, 1995), esp ch 5.

81 Cane, 'Distributive Justice and Tort Law' (2001) 4 *New Zealand Law Reports* 401, 418–19; 'Corrective Justice and Correlativity in Private Law' (1996) 16 *OJLS* 471. Cane's concerns are different to Weinrib's. His objection is not to the use of distributive criteria in defining tort rights per se, but to the use of those which are inconsistent with the structural limitations of private law.

82 In 'The Disintegration of Duty' in MS Madden (ed), *Exploring Tort Law* (2005), 143, 176–86, Weinrib distinguishes between two different types of 'policy' reasoning, only one of which is inconsistent with his view of corrective justice. This is reasoning which refers to 'independently desirable goals' external to the parties' correlative relationship.

(iv) Different Orders of Justification

Finally, the justifications I have identified are of different normative orders, in the sense that they bear in different ways and with differing degrees of force upon a defendant's legal responsibility. Some, such as the concern to avoid undercutting express contractual allocations of risk, statutory policy and the freedoms of commercial competitors, disclose reasons which are strong enough entirely to negate the positive case for a precautionary duty. Others, however, such as the concern that duties of care might lead to 'disproportionate' liability or obligations which are unduly burdensome to individuals in terms of precautionary cost, or that they might detract from a claimant's responsibility for taking reasonable measures to protect himself, seem to describe reasons only for limiting the extent of the precautions which a defendant should be required to take or the amount of liability which ought to be imposed on a case-by case basis.

This mixing of concerns of different orders within the duty inquiry further complicates the search for a principled approach and raises the question whether arguments of the latter sort might not be accommodated better elsewhere within the negligence inquiry, when courts consider issues of breach, causation and remoteness of damage. For example, an alternative response to the 'ripple' phenomenon, which apparently creates such difficulties for the size and determinacy (certainty) of claims, could be to develop distinct remoteness of damage rules in cases of pure economic loss which require something more stringent than simply that the loss be 'foreseeable' in a general way if a defendant is to be liable for it. This is effectively what Lord Denning proposed in *Parsons (Livestock) Ltd v Uttley Ingham & Co Ltd*.[83] The idea was never taken up, but the distinctions beginning to creep into Australian law between 'first line' economic loss claimants and others[84] (or between defendants who are merely negligent and those who are 'reckless' as to risk because they have greater 'knowledge'[85] about its prospective effects) are not far removed from his idea that economic harms should have to be foreseen at higher levels of probability in order to satisfy the remoteness inquiry.[86] Which approach

[83] [1978] QB 791, 802–3.

[84] *Perre*, above n 7, [112] per Mc Hugh J; *Fortuna Seafoods Pty Ltd v The Ship 'The Eternal Wind'* [2005] QSC 4.

[85] *Perre*, above n 7, [10], [13] per Gaudron J, [47], [67], [104], [111], [131–2] per McHugh J, [325] per Hayne J.

[86] Cane, above n 13, identifies the problems of 'indeterminacy' with a similar idea of 'causal remoteness,' but relates this idea to remote claimants, not damage. This appears to be his justification for tackling the issue via the duty of care inquiry. There is clear support for this strategy in psychiatric damage cases (where similar issues arise), but it may be logically questionable. It is losses, not claimants, that are 'caused' by negligent conduct, so that if causal remoteness is the key to cases involving 'ripple effects,' it seems logical to assume that it is the remoteness of the effects themselves, not the remote nature of the relationship with any given claimant that is the key concern.

one takes to the 'indeterminacy' issue (duty of care or remoteness of damage?) turns upon the relative importance accorded to certainty and particular justice respectively. It is generally assumed that certainty requires a response to the problem which rules out a duty of care, on the basis that this promotes more open consideration of the relevant concern and sends a very clear social message about who bears the relevant precautionary burden. The effect of this strategy, however, can be to wield a sledgehammer to crack a nut. The legal response (no duty on the part of the defendant to consider the claimant's interests at all) becomes disproportionate to its underlying normative justification (uncertain or excessive amounts of liability). This, as I indicate further below, is something that should generally be avoided, if the law is to claim to be in touch with its underlying reasons in a sensitive and coherent way.

Accommodating concerns about ripple effects via the remoteness inquiry would ironically do no more than return us to a mode of analysis deployed more than a century and a half ago in *Cattle v Stockton Waterworks*.[87] In a similar vein, there seems to be space to consider the relative burdens of precaution as between claimant and defendant (that is, both the broader version of the personal autonomy argument and the narrower interpretation of the argument about alternative means of protection) through fact-sensitive inquiries into breach, causation, contributory negligence and mitigation.[88]

B Methodological Ideals

Given the nature of these difficulties, how, then, should we approach the task of legal reasoning in economic loss cases? What are the ideals? Without attempting to be exhaustive, I believe there are five.

(i) Sensitivity to the Force of Justification

First, courts should accommodate the various justificatory arguments at a place within the overall negligence inquiry which accurately reflects their normative force. Otherwise, justice is only bluntly done. Whilst blunt justice is often to be found in the early stages of a legal system's development and has the advantage of sending very powerful social messages, a mature, sophisticated system of law should constantly be increasing the sensitivity of its rules to their underlying justifications. This alignment

87 (1874–75) LR 10 QB 453. Note that in many 'liberal' European systems these problems are accommodated via the 'ordinary requirements' of conduct, fault, damage and causation, with particular emphasis on the last of these. See Bussani and Palmer, above n 13, 205–6.

88 On alternative legal remedies and mitigation, see *Walker*, above n 59.

between rules and their reasons is a vital precondition of the law's normative coherence.

The implication of this in the current context is that probably only a small, powerful minority of the justifications we have examined ought to entirely negate a duty to take care of another's economic interests. This minority may still apply in a good number of cases, but its membership should be less. It should comprise the concern that liabilities will yield some direct conflict with other systems via which economic dealings have been structured or regulated; and the analogous concern that tort duties may contradict commercial norms operating between economic competitors.

(ii) Respect Structural Constraints

Secondly, the justifications used by courts must respect the structural and constitutional limits of private litigation.[89] Both forms of constraint raise legitimate question marks against the use of arguments about the distribution of loss between different social groups, as opposed to the claimant and defendants' respective individual responsibility for the harm suffered. For this reason, I have suggested, it may be preferable to understand concerns about the availability of alternative means of protection as individualistic arguments about the reasonableness of particular claimants' behaviour on the facts, rather than as arguments about the way in which loss should be distributed between different interest-groups. Whilst 'commercial' purchasers of defective real estate do generally have ways of protecting themselves which consumers do not, this should not preclude the High Court of Australia from allowing a claim in instances in which such means were in fact lacking, any more than it should necessarily mean that consumers should be entitled to claim in full where such means were readily and reasonably available to them. The informational constraints of private law also suggest that McHugh J is right to cast the concern about legitimate competition primarily in terms of individual autonomy, rather than in broader, utilitarian terms.

(iii) Occam's Razor

Thirdly, courts should avoid unnecessary conceptual multiplication. This is the principle of Occam's razor.[90] In the current context, it means that we should avoid approaching the duty of care question in a host of different ways. The multiplication of conceptual approaches, all of which are aimed at addressing the same issue is likely to yield duplication, inconsistency and

[89] On structural constraints, see Cane, above n 81.

[90] Russell, *History of Western Philosophy* (London, 2nd edn, 1961), 462–3; Barker, 'Wielding Occam's Razor: Pruning Strategies for Economic Loss' (2006) 26 *OJLS* 289.

incoherence as between cases raising similar concerns. This has proven an obvious problem in the past and remains a particular difficulty in England, where several nominally distinct approaches are taken to the duty issue, the interrelationship of which still remains unclear. If it is true that they can all be manipulated to yield the same result,[91] this clearly begs the question as to why we need more than one.

(iv) Optimal Transparency between Reasons and Concepts—The Avoidance of Fiction

Fourthly, courts should aim for optimal transparency in their reasoning, by which I mean that whatever approach is taken, it should leave the justifications for decisions as visible as possible. I have already touched on the difficulty of this, given that the relevant justifications are both negative and multiple, but, assuming the legitimacy of the judicial desire to translate arguments into legal concepts and principles, there is one obvious pitfall which can usefully be avoided. This is the use of fictional analogies between the situations in which duties of care are imposed by courts and relationships of contract or trust. In particular, it is unhelpful to continue to mediate the various negative justifications for restricting economic loss liability in negligence through the question of whether a claimant has 'assumed responsibility' for his conduct.[92] There are, of course, good explanations as to why courts use fictions, which have been explored in depth by Professor Fuller.[93] Such devices help to overcome inevitable gaps in the fabric of legal justification, which judges do not necessarily have the time to fill, as new cases arise.[94] More generally, analogies may actually be an integral part of the way in which we think. Psychologically, we tend to digest new experiences (here, new legal questions) by converting them into terms which are familiar to us.[95]

Both these observations about the attraction of fictions help to explain why a judge faced in 1963 with the unfamiliar question of when duties of care should be owed in respect of economic loss caused by negligent misstatement might choose to answer in terms of relationships 'equivalent to contract'.[96] Such duties were, after all, owed prior to that date in

[91] Above n 4.

[92] Barker, 'Unreliable Assumptions in the Modern Law of Negligence' (1993) 109 *LQR* 461. See, contra, Feldthusen, 'Liability for Pure Economic Loss: Yes, but Why ?' (1999) 28 *University of Western Australia Law Review* 84 (advocating the concept as a 'core justification' in some categories of case). In more recent defences of this concept, judges have claimed that the concept entails no fiction, because it refers only to the voluntary doing of a task. But it is then hard to see how the idea can usefully discriminate between cases of positive misfeasance in which recovery should be allowed and cases in which it shouldn't.

[93] Fuller, *Legal Fictions* (Stanford, CA, Stanford University Press, 1967), esp ch 2.

[94] *Ibid*, 65.

[95] *Ibid*, ch 3.

[96] *Hedley Byrne & Co Ltd v Heller & Partners Ltd* [1964] AC 465, 529 per Lord Devlin.

relationships in which a contract or relationship of trust was present and *Hedley Byrne* was, it is often pointed out, very close to being a contract case. Nonetheless, even Fuller accepts that there comes a stage at which fictions must be allowed to die a dignified death.[97] Like scaffolding, they serve as a valuable temporary instrument in the construction of new structures of thinking, but can messily obstruct the view, once the building is complete.[98] There is a particular danger, he notes, that, having initially used a fiction as a tool for understanding things that are unfamiliar to us, we become so fixated on it that it becomes in our minds not merely a means for better understanding the issue, but the very issue itself.[99]

To my mind, this is what has happened in cases in England, where the 'assumption of responsibility' concept remains current as one determinant of duty,[100] despite several laudable judicial attempts to kill it off.[101] Now that our imposition of economic duties of care has advanced beyond the point at which anything like the contractual analogy holds water, we should, I suggest, dispense with it altogether. It is surprising that the House has declined to do so[102] now that it has another technique to hand (the *Caparo* approach), not least because the chief saviour of the modern assumption of responsibility approach—Lord Goff—has shown himself in the past to be openly hostile to misleading, 'quasi-contractual' analogies.[103] As Gummow J has wisely observed in the current context, [104] the spirit our times is hostile to such fictions. Aside from proving hopelessly indeterminate,[105] the assumption of responsibility concept is yielding damaging anomalies of its own. Most strikingly, it has led to the not uncommon, but clearly mistaken, view that, where an assumption of responsibility is present, a duty of economic care should follow without further inquiry.[106] This was never likely to be the case, since there may be negativing justificatory concerns present on the facts of a case which call for a duty to be rejected, even where an 'assumption of responsibility' is present, as the old cases on

97 Above n 93, 14–23. Whether they live or die is ultimately based on whether they can be usefully redefined or become overly strained (22).

98 *Ibid*, 70, citing Gray, *Nature and Sources of the Law* (2nd edn, 1921), 35.

99 *Ibid*, 118–21.This is the 'original sin' of human reasoning—a failure to drop fictions out of the 'final reckoning' such that they become masters of reasoning, not its servants.

100 Above n 2.

101 *Smith v Eric S Bush, Harris v Wyre Forest District Council* (HL) [1990] 1 AC 831, 862 per Lord Griffiths; *Caparo*, above n 1, 628 per Lord Roskill, 637 per Lord Oliver.

102 See, most recently, *Barclays*, above n 2. The House unanimously affirmed the approach, at least in cases involving the negligent provision of advice, seeking to strengthen and narrow its meaning to its original form.

103 Goff and Jones, *The Law of Restitution* (London, Sweet & Maxwell, 5th edn, 1998), 5–11.

104 *Pyrenees Shire Council v Day* [1998] HCA 3, [163].

105 Barker, above n 92.

106 *Henderson v. Merrett Syndicates Ltd (No 1)* [1995] 2 AC 145, 181 per Lord Goff. See also *Barclays*, above n 2, per Lord Hoffman.

advocates' immunities demonstrate.[107] The analogy has given rise to a significant misconception: a concept the design of which is apparently to accommodate a number of negative justificatory concerns (in particular about indeterminate liability and conflict) is now thought to provide a sufficient positive justification for a duty of care. Fuller's warning has gone unheeded. The fiction of contract, once a means to an end, has become an end in itself with a beguiling, disruptive force of its own.

Interestingly, whilst Australian judges have expressed equal scepticism about the *Caparo* approach,[108] it has not been on the basis that the concepts it uses are 'fictional.'[109] This seems right. On Fuller's view, even the elusive concept of 'proximity' is unlikely to qualify as a fiction, since it expresses no proposition which is obviously counter-factual. It acts more as a shorthand, abstract way of expressing a complex idea about legal relationship.[110] In fact, the real substance of Australia's antipathy to the *Caparo* method, aside from the accurate but slightly bizarre accusation that it engages courts in discussing policy issues,[111] seems to lie in the view that general concepts are unhelpful in determining concrete outcomes in particular cases, because they are too far removed from the facts and too prone to discretionary manipulation.[112] That is a different, difficult, connected matter to which I now turn.

(v) Balance the Particular and the General—Reasons, Dispositive Rules and Abstract Principles

The fifth methodological ideal is that courts strike an appropriate balance between the development of lower-level, dispositive rules governing outcomes in particular categories of economic loss case and higher-level principles. We must focus not on either the general or the particular, but on both, and on creating a constructive and reflexive relationship between them, which affords to courts a degree of both certainty and flexibility.

Australia has rejected the idea of categorisation as determinative and this is clearly right in the sense that the arbitrary factual classification of a case should not dictate its outcome. The multifactoral approach also eschews high-level abstractions (generalisations) in favour of flexible, lower-level ideas spanning the various case-groupings. These ideas are

107 See *Rondel v Worsley* [1969] 1 AC 191 (since overruled in England in *Arthur JS Hall & Co v Simons* [2002] 1 AC 615). Similarly, a lawyer 'undertaking' an advisory task may also owe no duty by virtue of the possibility of a conflict between that duty and his duty to his client: *Clarke v Bruce Lance* [1988] 1 WLR 881.

108 Above n 10.

109 By contrast, this accusation is made about 'general reliance' in *Pyrenees Shire Council v Day* [1998] HCA 3, [163] per Gummow J.

110 Fuller, above n 93, 28–9.

111 *Sullivan*, above n 10, [49] per Gleeson CJ, Gaudron, McHugh, Hayne and Callinan JJ.

112 *Ibid.*

undoubtedly located closer to the operative policy concerns driving judicial decisions, and are much more transparent in the sense discussed in the preceding section. At the same time, however, the approach makes no attempt to express what Lord Atkin would have termed a 'general conception'[113] of the types of relations giving rise to a duty to take care. The list of factors is self-confessedly non-exhaustive, which leaves no broader reasoning strategy available in new cases other than the mandate that courts should proceed analogically, case by case, like ancient mariners hugging an unknown coastline,[114] or that they should address the duty of care question bluntly in its own terms in the light of a case's 'salient features'.

Perhaps this is right. It is unlikely that the method will in itself produce results which are strikingly different to those under the various English approaches. Both approaches are avowedly incremental in outlook, and such (admittedly very significant) differences as exist are more likely to be the product of the different emphasis which judges in England and Australia place upon the various underlying policy concerns than on the precise conceptual vehicle chosen to organise and express them. Nonetheless, the more transparent multifactoral approach tends to disregard the organising and synthesising function of higher-level principles in just the same way that the English approach can be criticised for failing to develop concepts which are sufficiently close to judicial reasons to enable more precise predictions to be made about likely outcomes.

The ideal, in my view, lies somewhere between the two approaches, and if I were rashly to make a prediction, that is where I think we shall all end up, if we are not actually there already. Although factual categories should not prove normatively determinative, the practical likelihood is that lower-level liability criteria will develop within each type of economic loss case. Although factual categories mean nothing in themselves, they are initial filters for our understanding of normative concerns. Even under the Australian approach, they are accorded respect.[115] At the same time, in developing these loose factual categories and in confronting new facts, courts will inevitably reach for higher-level concepts and principles to give structure and expression to the common reasons underpinning existing categories and rules. There are already signs of a reversion to this higher-level approach in the High Court of Australia, where McHugh J, pioneer of the lower-level 'multifactoral' approach, has subsequently located these factors within a broader investigation into the existence of a sufficiently 'close and direct relationship' of 'neighbourhood' between the

113 *Donoghue v Stevenson* [1932] AC 562, 580.

114 *Perre*, above n 7, [93] per McHugh J.

115 This stems from the fact that the multifactoral approach is primarily designed to assist in dealing with new cases, not to undermine existing categories and rules.

parties.[116] With respect, it is hard to see how this differs from the formally disapproved concept of 'proximity' and gives credence to Kirby J's accusation[117] that the law in Australia has now come full circle to something approximating its Atkinian point of departure. Conversely, in England, there are clear signs in *Customs and Excise Commissioners* that their Lordships recognise the perils of overabstraction and the need to supplement abstract principles with detailed discussion of lower, operative concerns. Lord Mance has thus noted that what really matters is how and by reference to what low-level factors the various abstract concepts are interpreted in practice.[118]

The approach hinted at by Lord Mance deploys higher-level principles only as a basis for organising, changing and developing lower-level rules, not as a substitute for them, which has significant advantages for reasons explained by Professor Raz.[119] An approach which relies solely on such principles will necessarily be uncertain, whereas one which conversely relies solely on particular rules in individual cases will run into developmental difficulties when familiar territory is left behind. It will have only a weak dynamic force. An approach which combines lower-level norms with higher-level principles has a reasonable chance—the best chance, I believe—of accommodating the judicial need to keep an eye on both the particular and the general; and of the law to be both stable and reasonably dynamic.

According to this view, abstract principles like foreseeability of harm and proximity of relationship have a continuing and important role to play in synthesising and developing the various different factual categories and precedents—in allowing the justifications in the individual cases to be abstracted upward and then deployed reflectively downward into other cases, both old and new. This method of reasoning (illustrated crudely in Figure 1 below) is not actually much different from the process of analogical reasoning between one type of case and another,[120] except insofar as principles enable the law's collective reasons to be deployed more dynamically—further from existing case law—than analogical reasoning alone might allow. They also provide a common analytical framework for thinking—as Kirby J would say, a means for 'steering the judicial mind through the task at hand,'[121] which is vital if an ordered,

116 *Graham Barclay Oysters Pty Ltd v Ryan* [2002] HCA 54, [99].
117 *Ibid*, [244].
118 *Barclays*, above n 2, [83].
119 Raz, 'Legal Principles and the Limits of Law,' (1972) 81 *Yale Law Journal* 823, 842.
120 Sherwin 'Restitution and Equity: An Analysis of the Principle of Unjust Enrichment' (2001) 79 *Texas Law Review* 2083, 2110. Sherwin expresses a preference for analogical reasoning precisely because it is likely to lead to a slower pace of legal development, but this may be at the expense of guidance in completely new case types, located far from existing precedents.
121 *Perre*, above n 7, [283].

NEGLIGENCE

Duty of Care

Principles	Foreseeability (Reason 1)	Proximity/Legal Relationship (Reason 2, Reason 3, Reason 4)		'Justice/Policy'	
Categories (Facts)	Category 1	Category 2	Category 3	Category 4	upward abstraction to principles
Rules	Rule 1	Rule 2	Rule 3	Rule 4	downward reflection to rules
Reasons	Reason 1 Reason 2	Reason 1	Reason 1 Reason 3	Reason 1 Reason 2 Reason 4	

Fig 1. Abstraction to and Normative Reflection from Higher-level Principles.

consistent approach to the consideration of cases is to prevail across the field.

The use of higher-level abstract principles only really causes problems when we try to set them to ends for which they were not designed. Naturally enough, if we try to use them not as tools to assist in organising, creating or developing rules, but as determinate rules or 'tests' of liability, we will come away with an acute sense of disappointment. Students tend, I find, either to treat the *Caparo* approach as if it were such a test (at which point they become understandably frustrated at its lack of dispositive power) or, at the other extreme, as if it were a fictional sham, somehow designed to pull the wool over our eyes and disguise the policy-based decisions which judges are making. It is, then, as if judges were engaged in some conspiracy to conceal their legislative role. Neither interpretation is true to the way the approach is used. The former misconstrues the purely organisational and developmental function of its abstract concepts, whilst the latter is generally unfair to judges. There is also an obvious tendency to assume that abstract concepts necessarily invite subjective discretions and appeal to open, moral standards.[122] That is again a misconception in the current context, as least as far as the *Caparo* approach goes. This is because the concepts of 'proximity' and 'justice' deployed within its framework look downward to—and derive their meaning from—existing precedents, not upward towards an uncertain, star-filled, discretionary sky.

122 *Ibid*, [82] per McHugh J.

Legal principles, unlike their moral counterparts, have a grounding in the fabric of the law.

IV CONCLUSIONS AND REFLECTIONS

A stable method for approaching the issue of when a duty of care is owed in respect of another's intangible economic interests is a vital precondition to the long-term coherence of the law and it is hoped that, at the very least, this chapter has helped to develop a clearer vision of what it is that makes the task so difficult. Both England and Australia have struggled with the difficulties of defining relevant reasons for constraint in economic loss cases and in working these reasons into positive rules and principles which are sensitive to the normative force of the various individual justifications, the structural constraints of private litigation, the need for transparency in legal reasoning and the need to accommodate the inevitable 'new case' lying awkwardly outside existing categories and precedents.

England and Australia are currently set on their own methodological paths, and it would be an overly simplistic assessment which indicated that one was right and the other wrong. The best hope for a coherent approach seems, in fact, to lie somewhere between them: in the adoption of a single reasoning strategy deploying both legal rules which are sufficiently close to the ground to provide reasonable certainty and predictability in particular cases, and of higher-level abstract principles which enable courts to take a structured overall approach to the inquiry and to synthesise their experience of a wide range of individual cases in developing the law dynamically. Within this strategy, the coherence of courts' approach can also be increased by eliminating as far as possible the use of fictions from the language of legal justification, and by unloading the duty inquiry of some its current justificatory burden.

This lightening of the justificatory load can be achieved, I have suggested, first, by eradicating from courts' consideration some concerns which are simply not appropriate; and secondly, by relocating others to lower levels of the negligence inquiry, where more sensitive weighting can be given to their normative force. Most clearly overdue for eradication is the argument that economic losses are not socially harmful. With respect, this is unlikely to be true and cannot in any case be pertinent in a system of private rights that takes itself at all seriously. Broad arguments about loss-distribution, or the effects of economic duties on the health or the market economy, are probably also suspect, if for no other reason than that they exceed the informational constraints of the private litigation system. By contrast, a number of justifications are up for eviction from the duty of care inquiry and relocation elsewhere. These are: concerns about the possible precautionary burdens to defendants associated with economic duties of care (to be dealt with via breach); concerns about the moral limits of responsibility for losses caused by 'ripple effects' (remoteness); and arguments about delay and latent loss (limitation), fears of floods of claims causing administrative chaos (strike-out, summary judgment, settlement) and arguments about alternative means of protection open to a claimant (causation, remoteness, contributory negligence, mitigation). This strategy of relocation would leave the duty inquiry free to accommodate two of the most powerful arguments—the importance of an individual's freedom to compete (narrowly interpreted) and, connectedly, the importance of ensuring that economic duties do not conflict with other legal mechanisms or norms for dealing with economic interests. Other, equally powerful, concerns may need to be added to the list in particular cases, but this reorganisation of the various justificatory arguments would, in my view, still lead to a more coherent approach to the duty question, as well as, vitally, to the more sensitive dispensation of justice.

No doubt there will be some who strongly object to this 'downgrading' of the majority of the arguments, on the basis that most disputes about pure economic loss will then dissolve into detailed 'factual' inquiries. That, it might be argued, will simply lead to more uncertainty not less, because relevant policy arguments will get buried out of sight instead of being openly aired. It will also reduce the strength of the social message, evident in Lord Oliver's bold statement cited at the outset, that causing pure financial loss is not really 'wrong'. There is no reason, however, to think that any other stage of the negligence inquiry is any less charged with 'policy' issues, or that they cannot openly be discussed as such. Moreover, if one focuses on any of the recent cases on pure economic loss in Australia, it soon becomes evident that the courts' approach to the duty issue is already very particularised, entailing detailed consideration of the circumstances in every case. This in itself says something about the appropriateness of the traditional message about the careless causing of economic loss not being 'wrongful' in today's world. It is not so much, these days, that carelessly doing harm to economic interests fails to ignite our moral interest, but that we need to assume a balanced, coordinated approach to their protection, which takes account both of a claimant's own capacity to protect these interests and of other ways in which economic relationships are (for very good reason) regulated and protected.

9

Compensation for Breach of Trust—The Remoteness Impasse

DARRYN JENSEN*

I BACKGROUND

IN *BRISTOL AND West Building Society v Mothew*[1], the English Court of Appeal recognised that the measure of compensation payable in respect of a breach of a trustee's duty of care and skill is limited by the same rules of 'causation, remoteness of damages and measure of damages' as are to be applied in respect of common law negligence claims.[2] This means that the measure of compensation is limited in two respects. First, the compensable loss is limited to those kinds of harm which are foreseeable consequences of the defendant's negligent act and, secondly, the defendant is deemed not to be responsible for any exacerbation of the harm of which the immediate cause is an unforeseeable intervening event. These rules may be referred to collectively as remoteness rules.[3] In *Mothew*, it was said that these common law rules apply in the context of the equitable relationship of trustee and beneficiary 'by analogy'.[4] To put the matter another way, the common law rules which operate to limit the quantum of recovery should apply in relation to the equitable claim for lack of care and skill insofar as that claim performs the same role in relation to the equitable relationship of trust as the common law negligence claim performs in relation to other relationships.

The *Mothew* decision has been followed in New Zealand.[5] Whether it will be followed in Australia remains to be seen. The Western Australian

* Lecturer, TC Beirne School of Law, The University of Queensland. The author acknowledges the comments and suggestions of Charles Rickett, Ross Grantham, David McLauchlan, Tony Lee, Peter Butler and Russell Hinchy.

1 [1998] Ch 1.

2 *Ibid*, 17 per Millett LJ.

3 Elliot calls them 'remoteness criteria'; see SB Elliot, 'Remoteness Criteria in Equity' (2002) 65 *Modern Law Review* 588.

4 [1998] Ch 1, 17.

5 *Bank of New Zealand v New Zealand Guardian Trust Co Limited* [1999] 1 NZLR 664.

decision of *Permanent Building Society v Wheeler*[6] had done for company directors what *Mothew* did subsequently for trustees, but *obiter* remarks of the High Court of Australia in *Youyang Pty Ltd v Minter Ellison Morris Fletcher*[7] provide a clear signal that the High Court, as presently constituted, does not look favourably upon the *Mothew* line of reasoning. Heydon J was not a member of the bench which decided *Youyang*, but his Honour, writing extrajudicially, has revealed that he is a *Mothew*-sceptic.[8]

The apparent impasse over the issue of whether common law remoteness rules apply to claims against trustees for breach of their duties of care and skill is one aspect of a broader controversy about the nature of the relationship between common law and equity. One side of the controversy supposes that common law and equity are inter-dependent systems which are to be understood and interpreted as a single, coherent body of principle. Protagonists on this side of the debate, such as Burrows, maintain the view that, where common law and equity are doing essentially the same work, they should operate according to the same rules.[9] Protagonists on the other side of the debate are inclined to line up with Hedley in saying that '[t]he whole point of equity is that it is different to the common law'.[10] Getzler has expressed a liking for Macnair's metaphor of 'the wall of the common law overgrown by the ivy of equity' and has added that 'neither stone nor plant can stand without the other, but mineral and vegetable do not combine completely into a new amalgam'.[11] This is not so much a denial of the possibility of doctrinal fusion as it is a warning against doctrinal fusion which is pursued too eagerly without due consideration of how the work performed by equitable principles may differ from that done by their apparent common law analogues. The particular issue raised by *Mothew* so closely represents the principal issue at stake in the broader controversy that it is not surprising that positions on *Mothew* have become deeply entrenched.

If there is a way out of the trenches, it must take the form of an appeal to values which both sides of the debate can recognise to be fundamental to the operation of decent systems of law. It is reasonable to suppose that both sides of the debate are committed to the idea that adjudication of

[6] (1994) 11 WAR 187, 247–8 per Ipp J (Malcolm CJ and Seaman J agreeing).

[7] (2003) 77 ALJR 895, 902.

[8] JD Heydon, 'Are the Duties of Company Directors to Exercise Care and Skill Fiduciary?' in S Degeling and J Edelman (eds), *Equity in Commercial Law* (Sydney, Lawbook Co, 2005), 185–237.

[9] A Burrows, 'We Do This at Common Law But That in Equity' (2002) 22 *OJLS* 1, 4; see also Elliot, above n 3, 597; A Burrows, 'Remedial Coherence and Punitive Damages in Equity' in Degeling and Edelman, *ibid*, 383; J Edelman, 'A "Fusion Fallacy" Fallacy' (2003) *Law Quarterly Review* 375, 377.

[10] S Hedley, 'Rival Taxonomies Within Obligations: Is There a Problem?' in Degeling and Edelman, *ibid*, 87.

[11] J Getzler, 'Am I My Beneficiary's Keeper?' in Degeling and Edelman, *ibid*, 247; Getzler cited an unpublished paper—M Macnair, 'Judicial Reasoning in Seventeenth Century England'.

disputes should proceed according to law, and that law is a system of principle which is independent of the first-order preferences or idiosyncratic value judgements of the adjudicator. Indeed, Hedley has protested that his defence of the distinctiveness of equity is not a denial of the need to decide cases according to principle. His argument is that the common law's equation of two cases is sometimes wrong and that equity steps in because equity recognises a difference between the two cases which the common law was incapable of recognising.[12] The argument is not about whether like cases should be decided alike so much as it is about what types of similarities justify treating cases alike and what types of differences justify treating cases differently. When that question is asked in the context of the *Mothew* situation, it becomes a question of whether the fact that this breach of duty is a trustee's breach of its duty of care and skill renders the case different, in a way which is relevant to legal justification, from other people's failures to exercise care and skill.

II LAW AS AN EXERCISE IN JUSTIFYING DECISIONS

The controversy about the status of the remoteness rules in relation to a trustee's breach of a duty of care is, to a large extent, a dispute about what types of matters count (or take priority at least) as matters of legal justification. One of the best recent accounts of justification in private law has been the account given by Professor Weinrib. Weinrib said that private law is 'a justificatory enterprise that articulates normative connections between controversies and their resolution'.[13] The idea of law (as opposed to raw power) involves an aspiration that, where two sets of litigants are treated in different ways, that different treatment should be justified by reference to a principle of more general application. Weinrib insisted that private law is 'not an aggregate of isolated and unrelated emanations of official power' but 'strives to avoid contradiction, to smooth out inconsistencies, and to realize a self-adjusting harmony of principles, rules and standards'.[14] Weinrib acknowledged that the law's coherence is 'an aspiration, not a permanent or inevitable achievement'[15] and that private law 'includes a self-critical dimension that manifests itself in overrulings, dissents, juristic commentary, and other indicia of controversy'.[16] Nevertheless, legal criticism and development must take place within the context of a fairly stable framework of legal principle, which is the subject of common acceptance within the relevant legal community. Criticism and development of

12 Hedley, above n 10, 85.
13 E Weinrib, *The Idea of Private Law* (Cambridge, MA, Harvard University Press, 1995), 12.
14 *Ibid*.
15 *Ibid*, 13.
16 *Ibid*, 15.

that framework is necessarily immanent criticism. It is an interpretive exercise which can, in the context of novel fact situations, produce 'fresh nuances in doctrine' and 'reevaluation of the coherence or plausibility of previously settled law'.[17] This type of legal criticism does not refer to concepts external to the law, such as 'economic efficiency', 'social justice' or 'public policy'.

Weinrib's account of private law is founded upon three closely related and mutually reinforcing ideas:

1. Private law is to be understood on its own terms—that is, as providing an internally coherent set of justifications for the recognition of correlative duty-right relationships between certain types of defendants and certain types of plaintiffs as injurers and victims respectively.[18]
2. Private law is concerned with corrective justice—that is, with correcting an injustice which arises where D (a defendant-injurer) has gained at the expense of P (a plaintiff-victim).[19]
3. Private law's conception of justice is informed by the idea of *right* (Kant's *das Recht*)—that is, D is taken to have gained and P is taken to have suffered to the extent that D's doing and P's suffering amount to a departure from the position in which P and D may each exercise a freedom of choice which is compatible with the same freedom of the other.[20]

The interrelationship of these ideas may be seen most clearly in a case where D misappropriates P's property.[21] D's misappropriation causes a subtraction from P's wealth which corresponds with an addition to D's wealth, and the reason for saying that D has gained is the same as the reason for saying that P has lost. P, at the beginning of the story, was entitled to the property to the exclusion of all others (including D), so she is entitled to have it back. D had no entitlement to the property, so was not entitled to appropriate the property for his own use. D cannot resist an attempt by P to reclaim the property. If D resists, D would be asserting a freedom to constrain P's choice while denying to P a similar freedom to constrain his (that is, D's) choice.

[17] *Ibid*; Professor Birks made a similar point: P Birks, 'Equity in the Modern Law: An Exercise in Taxonomy' (1996) 26 *Western Australian Law Review* 1, 25.

[18] '[T]he reasons that justify the protection of the plaintiff's rights are the same as the reasons that justify the existence of the defendant's duty' (E Weinrib, 'Corrective Justice in a Nutshell' (2002) 52 *University of Toronto Law Journal* 349, 352).

[19] Weinrib, above n 13, 63.

[20] *Ibid*, 95; Weinrib quoted the following passage from Kant: 'Right is therefore the sum of the conditions under which the choice of one can be united with the choice of another in accordance with a universal law of freedom' (I Kant, *The Metaphysics of Morals*, M Gregor, ed ((Cambridge, Cambridge University Press, 1996), 24 [6:230]). Kant (at 30 [6:237]) defined 'freedom' as 'independence from being constrained by another's choice'. People have equal freedom to the extent that they cannot be bound by others any more than they themselves can bind those others (24 [6:238]).

[21] Weinrib, above n 18, 354.

The correlativity of loss and gain is less obvious in contract and tort cases, but it is still present. The conclusion that P has lost and D has gained proceeds from the premise that there is an equilibrium position in which both parties have what is due to them.[22] In the case of a contractual relationship, this equilibrium position is reached where the parties have performed their mutual undertakings to confer benefits upon one another. That equilibrium is disturbed where D fails to confer the benefit which she has undertaken to confer upon P.[23] P has lost, in the sense that he has been deprived of the performance of D's undertaking, and D has gained, in the sense that she has exercised a freedom (that is, a freedom not to perform her undertaking) which she does not have. The remedy for a breach of contract restores the equilibrium by either requiring D to perform her undertaking (that is, specific performance) or requiring D to pay to P the monetary value of the performance of the undertaking (that is, damages for breach of contract). Where D, by a negligent act, causes injury to P, there is a departure from an equilibrium position in which neither P nor D is free to inflict harm upon the other. P has less than she deserves because P has suffered a loss for which D is responsible. D is responsible for the loss but does not suffer the harm. Therefore, D must pay to P damages which are measured by reference to the extent to which P is less well off as a result of D's negligence. The law's response is, in each of the aforementioned examples, measured by reference to what needs to be done in order to return the parties to the equilibrium position. The extent to which the defendant is better off will always correspond with the extent to which the plaintiff is worse off. In this way, the defendant's action and the plaintiff's injury are 'not two separate events but the two correlative aspects of the same event'.[24]

Difficulties with Weinrib's account of private law emerge when one considers restitutionary claims, particularly claims for mistaken payments. If these claims are founded on the idea that a defendant's receipt of a mistaken payment constitutes unjust enrichment of the defendant at the expense of the plaintiff, then it is not immediately obvious how the plaintiff's suffering correlates with the defendant's doing. Klimchuk has noted that a mistaken payment is not unjust because of anything which the defendant has done. It is unjust because 'the plaintiff's autonomy was

22 *Ibid*; Weinrib did not use the term 'equilibrium' in his writings on corrective justice, referring instead to 'the equality of the parties' (above n 13, 81) and the entitlement of the parties 'to have what is rightfully theirs' (above n 18, 354). McLachlin J referred to 'the Aristotelian notion of correcting a balance or equilibrium' in *Regional Municipality of Peel v Canada* (1992) 98 DLR (4th) 140, 165. The terms 'equilibrium' and 'disequilibrium' appear at various points in M McInnes, 'The Measure of Restitution' (2002) 52 *University of Toronto Law Journal* 163.

23 Note that Kant described a contractual right as the 'possession of another's choice' (Kant, above n 20, 57 [6:271]).

24 Weinrib, above n 13, 73.

compromised in a way in which the law ought, for that reason, to take an interest'.[25] Weinrib located the plaintiff's suffering in its lack of 'donative intent',[26] but Klimchuk observed that the defendant's infringement of the plaintiff's right would, on that analysis, be the retention of the payment (presumably, after becoming aware of the plaintiff's lack of donative intent) rather than its receipt.[27] Weinrib's account is capable of explaining (in corrective justice terms) how it is that a defendant who knows of the plaintiff's mistake has a duty to make restitution, but it does not explain how the same duty could arise immediately upon receipt—that is, regardless of whether the defendant has yet become aware of the plaintiff's mistake.

There is a possible interpretation of the Kantian underpinnings of Weinrib's account which minimises the impact of this difficulty. The Kantian idea of right is so inextricably tied to the idea of justified coercion that they are really the same thing. Kant said that

> if a certain use of freedom is itself a hindrance to freedom in accordance with universal laws (that is, wrong), coercion that is opposed to this (as a *hindering of a hindrance to freedom*) is consistent with freedom in accordance with universal laws, that is, it is right.[28]

A right can be postulated on the basis that the defendant's exercise of its freedom of action in a particular way in the future would be a wrong use of freedom. It can be said that that plaintiff has a right to restitution of that payment on the basis that it would be wrong (that is, a hindrance to the payer's freedom) for the defendant to refuse to pay it back in the event that a demand is ever made. That right (along with the defendant's correlative duty) would arise at the moment at which the defendant receives the payment. One might say that there is an anticipation of suffering on the plaintiff's part which correlates with an anticipated choice on the defendant's part. Coercion may be justified insofar as it either reverses actual suffering or prevents anticipated suffering.[29]

Notwithstanding that it presents certain difficulties in relation to plaintiff-sided claims (such as the claim for restitution of mistaken payments), Weinrib's account of private law retains considerable explanatory value and is, accordingly, a powerful analytical tool. If Weinrib's account of private law is accurate, certain types of factors are ineligible for use as justifications in the adjudication of a dispute between P and D. One example given by Weinrib was the matter of whether D is insured in relation to the type of liability in issue. A judge might entertain the idea

[25] D Klimchuk, 'Unjust Enrichment and Corrective Justice' in JW Neyers, M McInnes and SGA Pitel (ed), *Understanding Unjust Enrichment* (Oxford, Hart Publishing, 2004), 120.

[26] Weinrib, above n 13, 140–1.

[27] Klimchuk, above n 25, 131.

[28] Kant, above n 20, 25 [6:231].

[29] E Weinrib, 'Kant and Law' (1987) 87 *Columbia Law Review* 472, 498.

that the best solution to P's injury is to spread the burden of the loss from P to D's insurer, which means, in effect, that everyone who is insured bears the burden of the loss, if not directly, perhaps by upward pressure on insurance premiums. Weinrib noted that this factor introduces incoherence into tort law insofar as the insurance consideration is 'overinclusive'—that is, it mandates that P may recover from everyone who is insured rather than merely D, who caused the injury. Furthermore, if it were the case that D was not insured, tort law would not use that as a reason for refusing to allow P to recover from D.[30] Weinrib explained the matter in the following terms:

> From the standpoint of insurance as a device for the spreading of losses, the fact that the defendant has caused the plaintiff's injury is no reason to hold the defendant, rather than some other insured person, liable. Conversely, from the standpoint of causation, the lack of insurance is no reason to exclude the defendant from liability. Causation and insurance are heterogeneous factors, the former dealing with the occurrence of injury, the latter with the alleviation of its effects. The consideration (whatever it is) that justifies the causation requirement must focus on the sequence from the defendant's action to the plaintiff's injury; that sequence has nothing to do with insurance as a mechanism for loss-spreading.[31]

Other factors, which must be excluded from consideration as factors which justify allowing P to recover from D, are P's relative poverty (as compared with D) and any suggestion that D is a "bad" citizen (or, at least, has a prior record of negligently causing injury to others) and P is a "good" citizen. Furthermore, deterring D from engaging in similar conduct in the future will not normally justify a remedy for P, even if deterrence of D may be a by-product of awarding the remedy.

III CORRECTIVE JUSTICE AND TRUSTEES' DUTIES

A Do All Trustees' Breaches Involve the Same Type of Injustice?

One's position on *Mothew* turns upon whether one thinks, on the one hand, that a trustee's duty of care and skill is unlike other duties of trustees (that is, the duty to perform the trust according to its terms and the duty of loyalty) and more like the common law duty of care which is the foundation of the modern tort of negligence or, on the other hand, that a trustee's duty of care and skill is unlike the common law duty of care insofar as it shares certain important attributes with the other duties of

30 Weinrib, above n 13, 36–7.
31 *Ibid*, 37.

trustees. The reasoning of Millett LJ in *Mothew* represents the first view.[32] Proponents of this view insist that one needs more than a difference of historical origin to justify differentiating between equitable duties of care and common law duties of care.[33] Joshua Getzler is clearly in the second camp. Getzler, in a series of articles,[34] has proposed three reasons as to why a trustee's duty of care ought to be treated like the other duties of trustees (rather than like the common law duty of care):

1. It is not always possible to draw a clear line between negligence, on the one hand, and disloyalty or fraud, on the other hand.[35]
2. 'Unreasonably bad management leading to loss of investment' has often been understood as and subsumed within breach of a fiduciary obligation.[36]
3. Less stringent rules of causation in breach of duty of care cases would reduce the 'deterrent pressure' on the trustee.

Each of these arguments appears to give priority (for the purposes of legal justification) to the fact that the relevant duties are trustees' duties.

(i) Negligence versus Unauthorised Actions and Disloyalty

Getzler's first two arguments can be considered together. The essence of Getzler's argument appears to be that a trustee who acts carelessly in the conduct of trust affairs can hardly be said to be loyal to the interests of the beneficiaries. Getzler suggested that

> a tort-like duty to make reasonable efforts at careful performance can be seen to articulate what it means to be a loyal fiduciary devoted to the interests of beneficiaries.[37]

He said that the reason why the duty of care seems like a lesser duty than the duty of loyalty is that the courts, in cases (such as *Speight v Gaunt*[38]) which involved traditional settlements and deceased estates administered

[32] [1998] Ch 1, 17.
[33] *Bank of New Zealand v New Zealand Guardian Trust Co Limited* [1999] 1 NZLR 664, 681 per Gault J, 688 per Tipping J; Elliot, above n 3, 594.
[34] J Getzler, 'Equitable Compensation and the Regulation of Fiduciary Relationships' in P Birks and F Rose (ed), *Restitution and Equity, Volume 1. Resulting Trusts and Equitable Compensation* (London, Mansfield Press, 2000); J Getzler, 'Duty of Care' in P Birks and A Pretto (ed), *Breach of Trust* (Oxford, Hart Publishing, 2002); Getzler, 'Am I My Beneficiary's Keeper?', above n 11.
[35] See also Heydon, above n 8, 226–30.
[36] See also Heydon, *ibid*, 234–5, noting that the High Court of Australia in *Partridge v Equity Trustees and Agency Co Ltd* (1947) 75 CLR 149 described a power of management which involved discretion to postpone pressing for payment of a debt owed to the estate, as a fiduciary power.
[37] Getzler, 'Duty of Care', above n 34, 72.
[38] (1883) 22 ChD 727.

by volunteer trustees, have set the standard of care so low.[39] Heydon (writing extrajudicially) has made a similar argument. He noted that, in cases involving trustees' management of investment of trust funds such as *Cowan v Scargill* [40] and *Harries v Church Commissioners for England* ,[41] the standard of care to be exercised by a trustee 'is inevitably linked to the goal of achieving the best return bearing in mind income yield and capital appreciation'.[42]

The argument is perhaps at its most forceful when considered in the context of investments of trust funds which go wrong. It is reasonable to ask what is the difference (in terms of the injustice done to the cestui que trust) between breaches of trust involving types of investment which are not authorised by law or by the trust instrument and investments of a type which are authorised by law or by the trust instrument, yet the trustee was negligent in the choice of the particular investment or negligent in the way that the investment was carried out. A trustee who fails to take proper care in choosing an investment strategy and putting it into effect is, so the argument goes, not acting in the best interests of the cestui que trust. It is not doing the best it can to achieve the best return for the cestui que trust. If there is no distinction, then trustees ought, in either situation, to be held responsible for any loss which would not have occurred but for the breach of duty.

The problem with the foregoing analysis is that it merges, under the rubric of 'achieving the best return', two conceptually distinct forms of obligation. In the first situation, the trustee has a strict obligation to refrain from engaging in certain types of investments (without the approval of a court, at least[43]). The equilibrium position between trustee and cestui que trust is disturbed by any unauthorised action. If the trustee engages in an unauthorised investment, it should be strictly liable to restore the trust estate to the state in which it would have been had the trustee acted in an authorised way at all times. There is no difference between this type of situation and a situation in which a sum of money in a foreign currency is misappropriated and it just so happens that that currency appreciates against the local currency in between the date of misappropriation and the date of restoration.[44] The trustee is, in effect,

39 Getzler, 'Am I My Beneficiary's Keeper?', above n 11, 264.

40 [1985] 1 Ch 270.

41 [1992] 1 WLR 1241.

42 Heydon, above n 8, 228.

43 In Queensland, see Trusts Act 1973 (Qld), s 94.

44 *Re Dawson* [1966] 2 NSWR 211; so-called 'bare' trusts and trusts where the trustee has powers of management are formally subject to the same rule. Different measures of liability in practice stem from differences in the scope of the trustees' undertakings. A trustee's liability is measured by reference to the particular undertaking of that trustee. It is submitted, on this point, that the decision of the High Court of Australia in *Youyang Pty Ltd v Minter Ellison Morris Fletcher* (2003) 77 ALJR 895 is correct and the comments of Lord Browne-Wilkinson in *Target Holdings Limited v Redferns* [1996] AC 421, 434–5 are misleading, even though the case

liable to reverse all of the consequences of the unauthorised action, no matter how unforeseeable they may have been.

When we say that a trustee (or anyone else) has a duty to exercise care, we are not prescribing or forbidding any particular actions. We are merely telling that person to 'take care' or 'be prudent'. As Heydon has acknowledged, there are many ways in which a person can be careful or prudent.[45] What is being prescribed is a standard of care in relation to the performance of authorised actions. A lack of care has to be alleged in order to convert an otherwise authorised action into a basis for a claim against the trustee. Since the wrongfulness of the trustee's conduct is characterised in terms of a failure to take care, not all of the loss which would not have been suffered by the plaintiff but for the trustee's breach is loss for which the trustee is obliged to compensate the plaintiff. The disturbance to the equilibrium between trustee and cestui que trust consists of the trustee's failure to protect the trust estate against types of harm which it could have and should have taken care to prevent. What a trustee should have and could have prevented may vary according to the characteristics of the trustee. The case law distinguishes, for instance, between a volunteer trustee who administers the estate of a deceased friend or family member and a professional trustee who manages a large investment portfolio and who holds itself out as possessing considerable expertise in doing so.[46] The latter type of trustee is expected to foresee and avoid types of consequences which the former type of trustee would not be required to foresee and avoid. Nevertheless, in either case, it is not the performance or the failure to perform any particular action which disturbs the equilibrium between trustee and cestui que trust. The disturbance is created by the trustee's failure to avoid consequences which it could reasonably be expected to have avoided. Where a trustee's duty consists of refraining from performing a particular action, the correlative right of the cestui que trust is to be returned to the position which they would have occupied but for the unauthorised conduct—that is, it has a right to the restoration of the trust estate to the state in which it would have been had the trustee acted in an authorised manner. Where a trustee's duty consists merely of

was, on its facts, correctly decided. See also C Rickett, 'Equitable Compensation: Towards a Blueprint?' (2003) 25 *Sydney Law Review* 31, 45.

[45] Heydon, above n 8, 228; note also Hayton's comment that 'whether or not a secondary obligation has arisen to make reparation for wrongful losses resulting from the requisite degree of care not having been exercised, is very often a difficult question of degree and so not as clear as the issue whether an act was authorised or was not authorised' (D Hayton, 'Unique Rules for the Unique Institution, the Trust' in Degeling and Edelman, above n 8, 290).

[46] Compare *Speight v Gaunt* (1883) 22 ChD 727 with *Bartlett v Barclays Bank Trust Company (No 1)* [1980] 1 Ch 515; a similar distinction is made in Queensland legislation governing trustees' investments. See Trusts Act 1973 (Qld), s 22. S 1 of the Trustee Act 2000 (UK) requires a trustee to exercise such care and skill as is 'reasonable' bearing in the trustee's knowledge and experience and whether the trustee is acting as a trustee 'in the course of a business or profession'.

exercising care to avoid loss to the trust estate, the correlative right of the cestui que trust to be relieved from the ensuing harm does not extend to those types of consequential harm which were unforeseeable or to harm which stemmed from unforeseeable intervening events. The trustee cannot be taken to have undertaken to avoid harm which it could not foresee or avoid. One might say, adopting the language of Weinrib, that a 'proximate cause' limitation is 'the most plausible construal of the relationship between the parties'.[47]

The decision in *New Zealand Guardian Trust*[48] illustrates the point. New Zealand Guardian Trust ("trustee company"), which was the trustee under a debenture deed relating to advances by a number of banks to a property investment company, failed to detect that the investment company had breached some terms of the deed and, consequently, failed to inform the banks of the breaches at the earliest possible moment. The property investment company attempted subsequently to sell its property, but the property market had fallen and the banks were able to recover less than one-fifth of the amounts they had advanced. While the trial judge found the trustee company to be negligent, both the trial judge and the Court of Appeal found that it was not liable for the banks' losses. The trustee company's negligence had left the plaintiff bank to continue as a lender on the basis of a misunderstanding, but the bank's negligence was not the cause (in the relevant sense) of the banks' losses. The relevant cause of the losses was the downturn in the property market. Gault J said that the scope of a duty to inform another correctly

> has not commonly been found to extend to protect against losses arising from some independent cause where breach of the duty merely creates or preserves the circumstances in which that loss can be incurred.[49]

A trustee's breach of its duty of care may be distinguished from a breach of its duty of loyalty on the basis that the content of the latter duty justifies a much stricter form of liability than the content of the former duty does. Trustees must not use their position as trustees to pursue a benefit for themselves. They must not place themselves in a position where their personal interests potentially conflict with their duties as trustees. The equilibrium is disturbed as soon as a trustee profits from its position or places itself in a position of conflict. Trustees escape liability for breach of these rules only insofar as they have obtained the fully informed consent of the cestui que trust. The primary liability of a trustee is to disgorge any profit it has procured in breach of those rules, but the plaintiff may elect to claim the amount of the loss which it has suffered instead of claiming the

47 Weinrib, above n 13, 221.

48 *Bank of New Zealand v New Zealand Guardian Trust Co Ltd* [1999] 1 NZLR 664.

49 *Ibid*, 683 per Gault J (Richardson P, Henry and Blanchard JJ agreeing); Tipping J wrote a separate concurring judgment.

unauthorised profit.[50] Where the trustee's breach inflicts a loss upon the trust estate, whether the loss is of a foreseeable kind should be irrelevant to the measure of the trustee's liability to pay compensation. The trustee, having acted in an unauthorised way, is responsible for all of the consequences which would not have occurred but for the unauthorised act.

It cannot be denied that the characterisation of a trustee's breach of duty may turn upon subtle factual distinctions. In both *Youyang* and *Mothew*, it would have been better had the funds not been disbursed from the solicitors' trust accounts in the circumstances in which they were disbursed. Both cases involved allegations of negligent acts or omissions. Nevertheless, the two cases involved two quite different disturbances to the equilibrium position between trustee and cestui que trust. In *Youyang*, the act of disbursement itself constituted the breach of duty, while in *Mothew*, the disbursement was an authorised act. Nolan has observed that, while Mr Mothew's authority to disburse the money was certainly revocable, any revocation of that authority could not have retrospectively converted a lawful disbursement into an unlawful one.[51] The breach of duty was to be found in Mr Mothew's lack of care in failing to convey some information (about the proposal to create a second mortgage) to his client. The communication of that information may have led the client to change its instructions in relation to the disbursement of the trust money, but it was also possible that the client may have proceeded with the transaction in any event. Whether the client had suffered loss as a result of Mr Mothew's negligence was a question of fact and, since there was no evidence before the Court of Appeal in relation to whether the client would have changed its instructions, it was appropriate for the question to be remitted to the court of first instance.[52]

(ii) Deterrence

The idea that remedies for breaches of trustees' duties are concerned with deterrence is superficially attractive. Beneficiaries under trusts are in an unusually vulnerable position, so it is desirable that trustees (in common with other fiduciaries) should be deterred from abusing this vulnerability. The law operates as (in Getzler's words) a 'prophylactic defence of guarded

50 *Warman International Ltd v Dwyer* (1995) 182 CLR 544, 559.

51 R Nolan, 'Multiple Duties and Multiple Employment' [1997] *Cambridge Law Journal* 39, 42.

52 [1998] Ch 1, 25 per Orton LJ, 27 per Staughton LJ; note that Millett LJ (at 11) suggested that, since this was a case where the solicitor had given the building society incorrect advice (that there was no proposal to create a second mortgage), the building society would not have to show that it would not have proceeded with the transaction or would have insisted upon different terms. McLauchlan has questioned the validity of his Lordship's distinction between failure to pass on relevant information and giving incorrect advice. See DW McLauchlan, 'A Damages Dilemma' (1997) 12 *Journal of Contract Law* 114, 139.

relationships'.[53] The view that fiduciary obligations and the remedies for breach thereof are to be rationalised in terms of their deterrent fuction has considerable academic and judicial support. Worthington explained the positino of the fiduciary in the following terms:

> The fiduciary is prevented from pursuing his self-interest when all around him are free to take up the relevant opportunities. This only serves to reinforce the point that the duty of loyalty is not designed to deter them from activities which the general law regards as improper, but to deter them from proper activities which the law regards as inimical to the loyal execution of their fiduciary role. The foundation of the rule is a somewhat cynical view of human nature: the assumption is that without such a proscriptive rule the fiduciary would be motivated by self-interest rather than by duty. The remedies are specially designed to remove the incentive to pursue personal interest.[54]

Hayton has also explained the strict liability of trustees to avoid conflicts between their duties and their personal interests in terms of equity's concern with the peculiarly vulnerable position of the beneficiaries. Equity's imposition of strict liability for the consequences of a breach of fiduciary duty functions as 'a positive incentive for the trustee to carry out his duties in the best interests of the beneficiaries.[55]

It is, of course, arguable that the idea of deterrence is not essential to the fiduciary principle. Weinrib has argued that fiduciary obligations protect the principal's entitlement to the fiduciary's loyalty.[56] That entitlement arises because the fiduciary has undertaken to act for the benefit of the principal (and only for the benefit of the principal) in respect of specified matters and, accordingly, the principal has a right that the fiduciary refrain from entering into self-interested transactions which relate to those matters.

Whichever of these views one takes concerning the rationale of fiduciary obligations, it is the mere fact that the fiduciary engages in a proscribed transaction which disturbs the equilibrium between fiduciary and principal and, accordingly, justifies awarding a remedy. Where a trustee breaches its *fiduciary* obligations, whether the trust estate and the beneficiaries suffer an actual loss is irrelevant.

Restoration of the equilibrium position between trustee and cestui que trust requires that the trustee must disgorge any benefit it has derived from

53 Getzler, 'Equitable Compensation and Fiduciary Relationships', above n 34, 244; See also Getzler, 'Am I My Beneficiary's Keeper?', above n 11, 258.

54 S Worthington, *Equity* (2003), 123.

55 Hayton, 'Unique Rules', n 45, 281; See also M Conaglen, 'The Nature and Function of Fiduciary Loyalty' (2005) 121 *Law Quarterly Review* 452, 461; the deterrence view is frequently invoked in Australian case law. See, eg *Warman International Limited v Dwyer* (1995) 182 CLR 544, 557–8; *Maguire v Makaronis* (1997) 188 CLR 449, 492 per Kirby J; and *Say-Dee Pty Ltd v Farah Constructions Pty Ltd* [2005] NSWCA 309, par 184 per Tobias JA.

56 E Weinrib, 'The Juridical Classification of Obligations' in P Birks (ed), *The Classification of Obligations* (Oxford, Clarendon Press, 1997), 54–5.

the proscribed activity. The trustee cannot be allowed to retain any benefit from its disloyalty. When the proscribed activity causes a loss to the trust estate, the trustee ought to be required to pay compensation for the whole of the loss so caused. The loss was the result of the trustee engaging in activity in which it should not have been engaged. The 'exigencies of the marketplace' should, in those circumstances, be borne by the errant trustee/ fiduciary rather than the plaintiff.[57]

To extrapolate from the observation that fiduciary obligations are plausibly explained by reference to the idea of deterrence, so as to say that deterrence is a matter of policy in relation to all breaches of duty by a trustee (or other fiduciary) is to cast the net of deterrence too widely. There can be no doubt that deterrence is often a by-product of private law, insofar as the possibility of being sued provides rational people with an incentive to behave in a way so as to reduce the probability of being sued, but deterrence is not always part of the structure of private law responses. For as much as there might be a plausible argument that incentives and deterrents are an essential part of the structure of the law's reponse to fiduciary disloyalty, it is far from self-evident that incentives and deterrents are an essential feature of the law's response to failures to exercise care and skill. The essence of the law's response in those cases is to compensate the plaintiff in respect of harm of a type which the defendant should have taken care to avoid inflicting and nothing more than that.

One can appreciate the concerns of Getzler and Heydon that trustees should be held to high standards of conduct in all that they do. Nevertheless, it is contended that there are more basic considerations concerning the nature of the duties breached, which should take priority over these concerns. It is possible to identify within the body of case law concerning trustee's duties a number of conceptually distinct types of breaches of trustees' duties. These represent different types of disturbance to the equilibrium position between trustee and beneficiary. The paramount concern of private law is justice between plaintiff and defendant rather than the pattern of distribution of benefits and burdens or incentives or deterrents throughout the community as a whole. The measure of a defendant's liability is limited to that which remedies the disturbance to the equilibrium position between plaintiff and defendant. Different types of disequilibrium point to different measures of liability. The complaint that the *Mothew* measure of liability for breaches of the duty of care and skill reduces the deterrent pressure upon trustees seems to subordinate the essential feature of the disequilibrium between plaintiff and defendant (that is, the defendant's infliction of harm which it could and should have avoided) to the somewhat peripheral consideration of encouraging a better standard of conduct from the defendant (and others) in the future. It is not

[57] *Hodgkinson v Simms* (1994) 117 DLR (4d) 161, 208–9.

the business of adjudicative officials to elevate "policy" matters concerning particular classes of defendants over matters concerning the character of the duty breached.

B Corrective Justice and the Trustee's Duty of Care and Skill

An account of the juridical justification for the legal response to a trustee's failure to exercise care emerges from the foregoing discussion. That account can be summarised in four propositions:

1. An evaluation of whether a duty to exercise care has been fulfilled does not turn upon whether the duty-ower has performed or failed to perform any particular action or whether any particular consequence has or has not occurred. It involves an evaluation of whether the duty-ower's conduct conforms to a standard of conduct.
2. The equilibrium position between the duty-ower and the party to whom the duty is owed is maintained where the duty-ower exercises care in avoiding those undesirable consequences which it could reasonably be expected to take care to avoid.
3. The precise standard of care (and, hence, the types of consequences which ought to be avoided) may vary from case to case, but the relevant question is always whether a prudent person with the knowledge and expertise of the trustee could have been expected to have foreseen and taken care to avoid consequences of the kind which the plaintiff suffered. A trustee who is providing the service of a professional trustee (who can be assumed to have been engaged on account of her or his special skill and expertise) will be expected to take care to avoid a greater range of adverse consequences than a non-professional trustee of a small estate (who agreed to act as a matter of family or social obligation) will be.
4. Where the duty-ower fails to exercise the required standard of care, the disequilibrium to be corrected consists of the harm to the other person of a type which the duty-ower could reasonably have been expected to take care to avoid.

It will be noted that there is, in this account, a continuity of justification linking the applicable liability, causation and remoteness rules. A trustee is not liable unless it has failed to exercise the appropriate standard of care. The compensable harm does not include every consequence which would not have occurred but for the trustee's negligent act. It does not include exacerbations of the harm brought about by subsequent events which the trustee could not have foreseen or avoided and for which the circumstances created by the trustee's negligent act were merely necessary conditions rather than the direct cause. It includes only those kinds of harm in respect of which a prudent person possessing the trustee's level of expertise could have perceived a risk of harm and, consequently, a need to act to avoid that harm.

This analysis of claims which are based upon a person's failure to exercise care conforms to Weinrib's requirement of correlativity between the defendant's duty and the plaintiff's right. The defendant owes a duty to the plaintiff to exercise care to avoid causing harm to the plaintiff, which harm would, from the point of view of a hypothetical careful person in the position of the defendant, be a foreseeable and avoidable consequence of the defendant's failure to exercise care. The plaintiff is entitled to be kept free from harm to the extent that that harm is an event which the defendant could have foreseen and been expected to take care to avoid. Defining the correlative rights and duties in this way treats people as equal, autonomous beings in the sense that they are not responsible for harm to other people which they could not have avoided inflicting without accepting such an extreme restriction upon their personal autonomy as to render them less than equal to the person harmed. People are not really free when any mistake or misjudgement on their part will render them liable for *all* of the consequences which would not have occurred but for the mistake or misjudgement. A stricter form of liability is justified in the case of contractual duties and other specifically undertaken duties to perform (or refrain from performing) a particular action because these duties are themselves the product of the exercise of a person's autonomy freely to undertake (or not to undertake) to perform (or refrain from performing) an action. It is consistent with the idea that private law is about corrective justice between individual legal persons—not deterrence per se or, for that matter, the pursuit of economic efficiency or distributive justice—that the measure of the remedy must reflect the extent of the underlying obligation owed by the defendant to the plaintiff and nothing more (or less) than that.

IV CONCLUSION

The resolution of private law disputes should proceed on the basis that a court should do no more than ensure that the plaintiff is no better off and the defendant is no worse off than they ought to be according to the law's conception of the equilibrium position between those two people. "Policy" issues should not be used as a justification for increasing the liability of a defendant (and the measure of the plaintiff's entitlement to relief) beyond that which is justified by the character of the obligation itself. This means, in relation to breaches of duties of care and skill, that the measure of relief should not exceed that which would place the plaintiff in a position where it is not left worse off by reason of the defendant's failure to foresee and avoid those consequences which a prudent person with the trustee's professed knowledge and expertise would have foreseen and avoided. Trustees are often subject to more extensive forms of liability, but, where this occurs, it is justified by the trustee's undertaking to protect the trust estate from particular consequences or to avoid particular types of transactions which are strictly proscribed by law. The fact that the law takes a strict line with trustees in relation to some types of breaches of duty is not a reason for invoking the same policies or pieties in relation to all breaches of duties by trustees. It is the nature of the duty, and not the office of trustee itself, which counts.

Part IV

Punishment

10

In Defence of Exemplary Damages

JAMES EDELMAN*

I INTRODUCTION

IT HAS BECOME fashionable for private law theorists to condemn exemplary damages as contrary to the structure of private law. This view now has a champion on the House of Lords in the person of Lord Scott. As momentum builds against exemplary damages, it is becoming heresy to suggest that exemplary damages should retain a place, 'infecting' private law. And yet, *e pur si muove*. This heretical essay is intended in support of the counter-revolution, although its aim is modest. It is not a positive case for exemplary damages. It is a defence. Exemplary damages are defended solely on the basis of their goal of deterrence. 'Exemplary' derives from the Latin noun *exemplaris*; an example for others. Although a positive case for deterrence is not made here, the defence is established in three parts. The first part, presented in section II, introduces the moral gap in private law that would exist without a deterrent-based remedy. The second part is more equivocal, but concludes that deterrent-based remedies are too well entrenched in private law to be uprooted without an extremely compelling argument. The third part, and the core of the essay, shows that the main theories that oppose exemplary damages are either flawed or incomplete, and that no compelling argument for their abolition has yet been made.

* Fellow and Tutor in Law, Keble College, University of Oxford; Conjoint Professor of Law (UNSW). I am very grateful to Allan Beever, Joshua Getzler and Robert Stevens and for comments and criticism of an earlier draft of this paper, and to the participants and especially the organisers of the stimulating Obligations III conference: Darryn Jensen, Charles Rickett and Ross Grantham.

II THE MORAL GAP THAT WOULD ARISE IF PRIVATE LAW WERE WITHOUT DETERRENCE

From the time of the early Republic, the XII Tables in Roman law provided for penalties for those who committed the delict of *iniuria*. The statutory penalty for a less serious *iniuria* which did not involve broken bones or maiming was 25 asses (the unit of currency). Changes in the value of money meant that this penalty had become laughable.[1] In *Noctes Atticae* 20.1.13, Aulus Gellius, quoting from Labeo, told the story of Lucius Veratius, who walked around slapping people he did not like. He was followed by his slave, who would dispense 25 asses to the person who Lucius Veratius had slapped.[2]

If Lucius Veratius were alive today he would be an executive at the Ford Motor Company. The story of *Grimshaw v Ford Motor Company*[3] is well known. Ford decided to locate the fuel tank in its Pinto hatchback cars in an economic position on the rear bumper. Management knew that there had been crash tests that had found that there would be a small loss of human life and injuries as a result of explosions from rear-end collisions. In October 1971 they went ahead with production because they made a financial calculation that the risks to life and health could not justify the cost of relocating the fuel tank, which was approximately $4–8 per car. In 1972, Mrs Gray, the driver of a Ford Pinto, was killed and her son Richard, aged 13, suffered severe burns to his face and body as a result of the very explosion that Ford knew could occur in a collision. In an action for negligence against Ford the jury awarded Richard Grimshaw just over $2.5 million in compensation and $125 million in exemplary damages. This exemplary damages award was reduced to $3.5 million on appeal. If the case had been brought as a class action, such a dramatic reduction would not have been made.

The postscript to this story is that in 2002 another case was brought against Ford in *Romo v Ford Motor Company*.[4] This time it involved a Ford Bronco, which had a metal roof above the front seat but a detachable fibreglass roof at the back. Again, Ford knew that there would be very significant safety implications because, after crash tests raised concerns,

[1] W Buckland, *A Textbook of Roman Law*, P Stein, ed (Cambridge, Cambridge University Press, 3rd edn, 1975), 590.

[2] The consequence of this story is a matter of dispute. Some argue that this led to a general Edict and a new remedy: D Daube, 'Ne quid infamandi causa fiat' *Atti del congresso internazionale di diritto romano e di storia diritto* (Verona 1951) 413; Buckland, *ibid*. Others suggest that the Edict must have preceded the story: see P Birks, 'Lucius Veratius and the Lex Aebutia' in A Watson (ed), *Daube Noster: Essays in Legal History for David Daube* (Edinburgh, Edinburgh University Press, 1974), 39.

[3] 119 Cal App 3d 757 (4 Dist 1981).

[4] (2003) 113 Cal App (4th) 738.

Ford considered adding a roll bar and metal reinforcement to the fibreglass section but did not do so in its rush to get the vehicle onto the market. When a top-heavy Bronco rolled, killing the parents and brother of the claimant because of the lack of a roll bar, they sued Ford for negligence and were awarded exemplary damages by the jury of $290 million. This time the award was upheld on appeal. But, after a constitutional appeal to the Supreme Court, it was referred back for failure to comply with Constitutional due process following the decision in *State Farm Mutual Automobile Insurance Co v Campbell*.[5] The award was reduced to $24 million. Again, had the case been brought as a class action then it is unlikely that it would have been reduced.

The Supreme Court of Canada has similarly said that

> as a rule, deterrence can be achieved through the award of compensatory damages and refusal to grant exemplary damages is not condonation of the violation of the rule of law.[6]

This essay begins with the immediate concession that, as a deterrent, exemplary damages will only be needed in exceptional cases. But such awards provide no incentive for the protection of the rights of those like Richard Grimshaw or the Romo family. There is no doubt that a legal system that does not provide a deterrent in these situations provides incomplete protection for the rights of the individual. This hiatus must be addressed. *Grimshaw* and *Romo* are extreme examples. Critics may argue that the gap that exists is simply one in the criminal law. But why should this issue be the sole province of criminal law? Richard Grimshaw and Juan Romo had rights in private law that were not sufficiently protected. Even if it were possible to say that the private law rights in these cases can only be adequately protected by the criminal law, we will see below that a choice might actively be made that it is not appropriate to criminalise private law rights in all tort cases. This would mean that without a deterrent-based award in private law there would be a serious moral gap which would allow a wealthy claimant effectively to appropriate private law rights merely by payment of compensation.

III DETERRENCE IS TOO ENTRENCHED IN PRIVATE LAW TO BE UPROOTED WITHOUT COMPELLING REASON

Justice Windeyer once observed that the origins of exemplary damages depend upon 'how far you wish to go back and how much certainty you demand in the connecting links'.[7] With loose connecting links, exemplary

5 123 SCt 1513 (2003).

6 *Royal Bank of Canada v W Got & Associates Electric Ltd* (2000) 178 DLR 385, 394–5.

7 *Uren v John Fairfax & Sons Pty Ltd* (1966) 117 CLR 118, 152.

damages can be traced back at least 2000 years to Roman law.[8] Exemplary awards of double and treble damages were common in the Lex Aquilia and reflected the long history of punitive awards in Roman private law. An extreme example of the punitive role of the private law of early Rome was that a victim who caught a free man in the act of theft (*furtum manifestum*) had a right to flog and (after judgment of a magistrate) enslave him, whilst a slave, similarly caught, could be flogged and then hurled from the Tarpeian Rock.[9] As Roman law moved away from retribution (*talio*), it developed multiple damages awards.[10] The same pattern existed in English law. For thieves 'caught in the act', the codes of early Anglo-Saxon law recognised the rights of the victim to punish the thief with violence.[11] Again, as the law developed, the necessity to limit recourse to violence and blood-feud resulted in the development of a system involving the payment of *wer* (penalties) to the family of a wrongfully slain man.[12] By the mid-thirteenth century, awards of multiple damages for wrongdoing were common (such as the Statute of Gloucester 1278, which provided for treble damages[13]). These multiple damages awards were commonly recognised in statutes in assize or novel disseisin.[14]

The modern law of exemplary damages arose out of two cases in which the government took heavy-handed action against those involved with John Wilkes's book *The North Briton*, which the government considered to be libelous. In *Wilkes v Wood*,[15] the government agents entered Wilkes's house (breaking his locks) and searched his home under an invalid warrant, seizing his papers. Wilkes sued for trespass and was awarded substantial damages of £1,000 by the jury. In the course of instructing the jury, Pratt LCJ (the later Lord Camden) said that

> A jury have in their power to give damages for more than the injury received. Damages are designed not only as a satisfaction for the injured person but

[9] Possibly further. Roman ideas of multiple damages awards mirrored, in some respects, laws from earlier civilisations. In 1760 BCE the Code of Hammurabi provided in s 8 that if a man stole an ox, sheep, ass or pig from the temple or palace he had to pay 30 times its value.

[10] XII Tables, Table VIII (Delicts) (xv); G III.189; JAC Thomas, *Textbook of Roman Law* (Oxford, North-Holland, 1976), 349.

[11] In our example of manifest theft, an award of four times the value of the stolen goods was subsequently developed in Roman law: G III.189.

[12] J Baker, *An Introduction to English Legal History* (London, Butterworths, 4th edn, 2002), 502. Holdsworth considers this point in a section entitled 'criminal law' although he acknowledges that 'in this period we have not yet arrived at the distinction between the law of crime and the law of tort': W Holdsworth, *A History of the English Law*, Vol II (London, Methuen, 3rd edn, 1923), 43.

[13] Holdsworth, *ibid*, 44–5.

[14] 6 Edw I, c 5. The United States Supreme Court in *BMW of North America Inc v Gore* 517 U.S. 559 (1996), 581 referred to '65 different enactments during the period between 1275 and 1753 [that] provided for double, treble, or quadruple damages'.

[14] J Sayer, *The Law of Damages* (London, Strahan & Woodfall, 1760), 11. See also E Coke 2 Inst 285.

[15] (1763) Lofft 1; 98 ER 489.

> likewise as a punishment for the guilty, to deter from any such proceeding for the future, and as a proof of the detestation of the jury to the action itself.

In the sequel, *Huckle v Money*,[16] the defendants entered the home of the claimant printer under the same invalid warrant. He was arrested and imprisoned for 6 hours, during which time he was treated 'very civilly' and fed 'beef steaks and beer'. A jury awarded him £300 in damages and the defendant sought to set aside the verdict. Again, the Lord Chief Justice emphasised that

> they have done right in giving exemplary damages. To enter a man's house by virtue of a nameless warrant, in order to procure evidence, is worse than the Spanish Inquisition.

The rest of the modern tale of exemplary damages in English law involves twists and turns: exemplary damages grew until 1964, when they were cut back by a series of restrictions over 30 years;[17] then, in 2002, over a powerful dissent by Lord Scott, they were liberated from these restrictions.[18] However, there are recent signs that Lord Scott may yet win the day and that a new era of restrictions may soon begin.[19]

In other Commonwealth jurisdictions exemplary damages followed a consistent pattern of expansion rather than the twisted and tortured path of English law. In Australia they were recognised by the High Court of Australia as a legitimate award in 1920, and the High Court of Australia, like the Court of Appeal in New Zealand,[20] refused to follow the English path of restrictions that began in 1956.[21] By 1985 in Australia, Brennan J was able to comment, in *XL Petroleum (NSW) Pty Ltd v Caltex Oil (Aust) Pty Ltd*,[22] that

> it is now beyond argument that, by the law of this country, it is proper to award exemplary damages by way of punishment of the tortfeasor.

In Canada, exemplary damages were first recognised by the Supreme Court of Canada in 1886[23] and the Supreme Court also consistently refused to embrace the restrictive path of English law.[24] The most recent decision of

16 (1763) 2 Wils 205; 95 ER 768.

17 *Rookes v Barnard* [1964] AC 1129; *Broome v Cassell & Co* [1972] AC 1027; *AB v South West Water Services Ltd* [1993] QB 507

18 *Kuddus v Chief Constable v Leicestershire* [2002] 2 AC 122; *A v Bottrill* [2003] 1 AC 449.

19 See below *Attorney General for Trinidad v Ramanoop* [2006] 1 AC 328 (PC); *Merson v Cartwright* [2005] UKPC 38. See also the discussion of *Watkins v Home Office* [2006] UKHL 17 below.

20 *Donselaar v Donselaar* [1982] 1 NZLR 97; *Daniels v Thompson* [1998] 3 NZLR 22.

21 *Australian Consolidated Press Ltd v Uren* (1966) 117 CLR 185.

22 (1985) 155 CLR 448, 472.

23 *Collette v Lasnier* (1886) 13 SCR 563.

24 See *Vorvis v Insurance Corp of British Columbia* [1989] 1 SCR 1085; *Whiten v Pilot Insurance Company* [2002] 1 SCR 595.

the Supreme Court of Canada has insisted that exemplary damages 'address the purposes of retribution, deterrence and denunciation'.[25]

However, critics of exemplary damages have argued that the longevity of exemplary damages is not, by itself, a sufficient justification for retaining the award. There are two reasons why they say that precedent might not carry the day.[26] The first is because exemplary damages have always been controversial. The opening paragraphs of the first English text on damages, by Serjeant Joseph Sayer, began as follows:[27]

> Damages are a pecuniary recompence for an injury.
>
> It is in the general true, that Damages are not recoverable by a private Person for an Injury to the Publick: For as every private Person is in some Degree injured by an Injury to the Publick, if any private Person could recover Damages for the Injury every one might, the Consequence of which might be an Infinity of Actions.
>
> For the sake of preventing so great an Inconveniency, it has for many Ages a settled Point of Law, that only one Action shall be carried on for one crime, by which Name every Injury to the Publick is called, and that this shall be brought in the Name of the King, who in consequence of his being Supreme Magistrate, is the Guardian and Protector of the Publick Peace and Safety.

Almost 250 years later, doubts still remain. In *Kuddus v Chief Constable v Leicestershire*[28] Lord Scott began his speech with the words

> the function of an award of damages in our civil justice system is to compensate the claimant for a wrong done to him.

Lord Scott then collated the many judicial pronouncements of exemplary damages as an anomaly and observed that, since the expansion of public law, judicial review and remedies such as declarations of right, injunctions and disgorgement of profits (which his Lordship described as restitutionary damages), 'there is . . . no longer any need for punitive damages in the civil law.'[29] Although his Lordship did not need to decide the issue, because the abolition of exemplary damages had not been sought, his antagonism has been echoed in recent observations and developments: the European Court

[25] *Fidler v Sun Life Assurance Co of Canada* [2006] SCC 30 at [61].

[26] Compare Windeyer J in *Uren v John Fairfax & Sons Pty Ltd* (1966) 117 CLR 118, 149–50: 'the roots of tort and crime in the law of England are greatly intermingled. Some things that today are seen as anomalies have roots that go deep, too deep for them to be easily uprooted.' See also 'Over the past 40 years the House has exercised its power to depart from its own precedent rarely and sparingly. It has never been thought enough to justify doing so that a later generation of Law Lords would have resolved an issue or formulated a principle differently from their predecessors . . . But this is not a case in which contracts, settlements of property or fiscal arrangements have been entered into on the faith of a settled legal rule. The criminal law, where certainty is particularly important, will be unaffected if the House departs from *Walkley*. There will be no detriment to public administration.' *Horton v Sadler* [2006] UKHL 27, [29], [31] (Lord Bingham).

[27] Sayer, above n 14, 1–2.

[28] [2002] 2 AC 122, 154.

[29] *Ibid*, 157.

of Human Rights does not make awards of exemplary damages; they are not available for 'Eurotorts' or breaches of the *Human Rights Act* 1998; they are not available in Scotland; and in England, the 'policy of the law is not in general to encourage the award of exemplary damages'.[30]

The second argument by opponents of the exemplary damages argument against a precedent-based defence is that the usual reason for refusing to uproot a well-established rule— that it has become 'so woven into the fabric of the law as to be irremovable without causing serious damage'[31]—does not apply. Those who attack exemplary damages claim that the abolition of exemplary damages would instead bring clarity to the law and *improve* the fabric because exemplary damages belong to public law and are 'foreign to the structure of private law'.[32] We sometimes see bald assertions to this effect:

> "[punitive damages] confuse the civil and criminal functions of the law"[33]; or

> "the function of the civil law which is to compensate with the function of the criminal law which is to inflict deterrent and punitive penalties"[34]; or

> "one fundamental issue has to be resolved: do exemplary damages confuse the civil and criminal functions of the law?"[35]; or

> "exemplary damages are a hybrid between an assertion of ethical indignation and the imposition of a criminal fine"[36]; or

> "the idea [of exemplary damages] is wrong. It is a monstrous heresy. It is an unsightly and unhealthy excrescence, deforming the symmetry and body of the law."[37]

There is a powerful counter-argument which shows why, despite growing judicial antipathy, precedent should not be so easily disregarded. The counter-argument is that there is no sharp divide between private/civil law (which critics commonly assert is based upon claims brought by individuals and has a role of compensation) and public/criminal law (which, it is asserted, is the province of the state and has a role of punishment). In

30 *BB v United Kingdom* (2004) 39 EHRR 635, para 36. See *Watkins v Home Office* [2006] UKHL 17, [26] (Lord Bingham), [32] (Lord Hope), [64] (Lord Rodger). Cf [75] (Lord Walker): 'Exemplary damages, even if anomalous, have a part to play in discouraging abuses of power in a democratic society'.

31 *XYZ v The Commonwealth* [2006] HCA 25, [201] (Callinan and Heydon JJ).

32 A Beever, 'The Structure of Aggravated and Exemplary Damages' (2003) 23 OJLS 87, 105.

33 *Rookes v Barnard* [1964] AC 1129, 1126 (Lord Devlin).

34 *Broome v Cassell*, above n 17, 1086 (Lord Reid).

35 Law Commission (England and Wales), *Aggravated, Exemplary and Restitutionary Damages* (1997, No 247/97), 5.16.

36 *Musca v Astle Corp Pty Ltd* (1988) 80 ALR 251, 262 (French J citing *Haines v Schultz* (1888) 50 NJLR 481). See also *Marsden v Amalgamated Television Services Pty Ltd* [2001] NSWSC 510, [4923] (Levine J).

37 *Fay v Parker* 55 NJU 342, 382 (1873).

criminal law, punishment has never been the exclusive province of the state. We have already seen that in Roman law much of the punitive role of modern criminal law was performed by the more developed private/civil law. Similar examples exist in the history of the common law and have remained. In the seventeenth century, the common law appeal of felony allowed a criminal offence to be prosecuted by individuals rather than the state.[38] This right still exists in many jurisdictions in the form of private prosecution—a private action between persons, for a putative criminal offence straddles both criminal and civil law. Another example of civil application of criminal law is when criminal law generates private rights between individuals, such as in cases where criminal injuries compensation orders can be made against a convicted person in favour of the victim of crime. Those orders are often enforceable as civil debts. Conversely, from the side of civil or private law, the punitive role of criminal law is duplicated in civil penalty provisions which introduce penalties for acts that the legislature considers require deterrence despite considering that those acts are not worthy of criminalisation.[39] For these reasons, it is now a common observation that 'there are dangers in enforcing a system of classification containing but two classes, civil and criminal'.[40] Or, as Gleeson CJ, McHugh, Gummow and Hayne JJ said in *Gray v Motor Accidents Commission*:[41]

> there is an appearance of tension between civil proceedings to compensate a party who is wronged and using the same proceedings to punish the wrongdoer. But there is a tension only if it assumed that . . . a sharp cleavage between criminal law on the one hand and the law of torts and contract on the other is a cardinal principle of our legal system.

For the particular deterrent-based defence of exemplary damages in this essay, there is a further counter-argument why uprooting such a well-established remedy might not be so simple. Deterrence has long been expressed as the basis of the award of an account and disgorgement of profits. It is very common for an account and disgorgement of profits to be awarded for a breach of fiduciary duty where its deterrent role is well recognised: 'to preclude the fiduciary from being swayed by considerations of personal interest and from accordingly misusing the fiduciary position for personal advantage'.[42] The same notions of deterrence are also relied upon when an

[38] Note (1957) 70 *Harvard Law Review* 517, 523.

[39] See also the observations made by Gleeson CJ, McHugh, Gummow and Hayne JJ in *Gray v Motor Accident Commission* (1998) 196 CLR 1, 7–8.

[40] *Chief Executive Officer of Customs v Labrador Liquor Wholesale Pty Ltd* (2003) 201 ALR 1. See also 16 (Kirby J).

[41] (1998) 196 CLR 1, 7. See also *Harris v Digital Pulse Pty Ltd* (2003) 56 NSWLR 298, 308 (Spigelman CJ).

[42] *Meinhard v Salmon* (1928) 164 NE 545 (SCUS) 546 (Cardozo CJ); *Warman International Ltd v Dwyer* (1995) 182 CLR 544, 198–9. See also *Cadbury Schweppes Inc v FBI Foods Ltd* [1999] SCR 142, 164: 'the overriding deterrence objective'.

account and disgorgement of profits is awarded for other equitable wrongs such as a breach of confidence,[43] or even when profits from cynically committed torts are disgorged in equity's auxiliary jurisdiction.[44] Would the abolition of exemplary damages also require abolition of awards requiring an account (and disgorgement) of profits? In *Smith New Court Securities Ltd v Scrimgeour Vickers (Asset Management) Ltd*[45] Lord Steyn said, of the suggestion that the only purpose of the law of tort should be to compensate, that this is 'far too narrow a view' and instead approved the broad view of Professor Glanville Williams that the other roles of tort include appeasement, justice and deterrence.[46] As we saw in the first part of this essay, exemplary damages can have a moral role based solely on deterrence. It is incumbent on those who would seek to uproot such a long-established remedy to show extremely compelling arguments why there is no place for deterrence in private law, especially considering the presence of deterrence in other judicial remedies, the moral demand for deterrence and the strength of precedent.

IV FLAWS IN THE THEORIES THAT REJECT EXEMPLARY DAMAGES

This essay does not seek to justify exemplary damages by reference to a punitive rationale.[47] To the extent that there is a difference between a *rationale* of punishment and an *effect* of punishment, an objection that exemplary damages have the *effect* of punishing a defendant is an objection to many awards of damages. The defendant that is required to reach into her pocket to compensate for loss caused to a claimant suffers the same punitive *effect* on her wealth when satisfying judgment or, if insured, when her insurance premiums rise. The defence of exemplary damages in this

43 *Attorney General v Guardian Newspapers (No 2)* [1990] 1 AC 149, 262: '[disgorgement of profits serves] a useful purpose in lessening the temptation for recipients of confidential information to misuse it for financial gain' (Lord Templeman).

44 *Powell v Aiken* (1858) 4 K & J 343, 351; 79 ER 144, 147; *Jegon v Vivian* (1871) LR 6 Ch App 742, 762.

45 [1997] AC 254.

46 *Ibid*, 280. See also *Standard Chartered Bank v Pakistan National Shipping Corporation (No 4)* [2000] 3 WLR 1692, 1724.

47 Central among arguments against a punishment rationale is the argument that with punishment comes added degrees of protection for the individual which is provided only by the criminal law (see eg *Broome v Cassell*, above n 17, 1087, Lord Reid). One answer to these objections was explained above (no sharp divide exists). Another is that the civil law, like the criminal law, has differing degrees of protection depending upon the nature of the punishment. For instance, reverse onuses for minor offences, which are punishable by only a small fine, are now common. Similarly, in the civil law the more serious an allegation the greater the proof that must be adduced: *Re H (Minors)(Sexual abuse: standard of proof)* [1996] AC 563, 586 (Lord Nicholls); *Three Rivers District Council v Bank of England (No 3) (Summary judgment)* [2001] 2 All ER 513, 577 (Lord Millett); *Briginshaw v Briginshaw* (1938) 60 CLR 336.

essay is not based upon a punitive *rationale*, although the award might have an effect which the claimant considers punitive. The defence here is based upon a rationale of deterrence.

A Functionalism

As soon as it is accepted that a function of tort law is to compensate, then any functionalist argument against deterrence is nothing more than assertion. If it is accepted that tort law has a function which focuses upon repairing injury of a claimant, then why can it not also have a function which focuses upon deterring a defendant? Arguments against deterrence as an alternative function to compensation are simply assertion. For instance, in *Broome v Cassell*[48] Lord Reid said:

> the plaintiff, by being given more than on any view could be justified as compensation, was being given a pure and undeserved windfall at the expense of the defendant, and that in so far as the defendant was being required to pay more than could possibly be regarded as compensation he was being subjected to pure punishment . . . I thought and still think that that is highly anomalous.

Lord Wilberforce, took the opposite approach, seeing Lord Reid's approach (and that of Lord Devlin in *Rookes*) as mere assertion:[49]

> It cannot be lightly taken for granted, even as a matter of theory, that the purpose of the law of tort is compensation, still less that it ought to be an issue of large social import, or that there is something inappropriate, illogical or anomalous (a question-begging word) in including a punitive element in civil damages, or, conversely, that the criminal law, rather than the civil law, is in these cases a better instrument for conveying social disapproval or for redressing a wrong to the social fabric, or that damages in any case can be broken down into the two separate elements. As a matter of practice, English law has not committed itself to any of these theories: it may have been wiser than it knew.

There is a further problem for functionalists who argue against a rationale of deterrence. If they were correct, and compensation were the only rationale for tort law, then, as Professor Heriot has observed, there would be 'no conceptual need for the plaintiff-victim to receive his compensation from the person who inflicted his injury upon him'.[50] If tort law were only concerned with compensation, then it could not explain why the compensation should not come from the deepest pocket of all—the state. Indeed, the functionalist who sees tort law as only concerned with compensation has great difficulty in explaining why tort law should not be abolished

48 *Broome v Cassell*, *ibid*, 1086.
49 *Ibid*, 1114.
50 G Heriot, 'An Essay on the Civil–Criminal Distinction with Special Reference to Punitive Damages' (1996) *Journal of Contemporary Legal Issues* 43, 51; Note, n 38 above, 523.

and replaced with a less costly and more efficient no-fault compensation scheme.[51] A complete functionalist account of tort law requires recognition of both compensation and deterrence in order to explain why it is the defendant that must pay. Functionalists cannot rely only upon a compensation rationale, just as they cannot rely only upon a deterrent rationale:

> nothing about compensation as such justifies its limitation to those who are the victims of deterrable harms, just as nothing about deterrence as such justifies its limitation to acts that produce compensable injury.[52]

B Corrective Justice

The language of corrective justice is that of Aristotle. But there are many different versions of corrective justice, as well as different explanations of what was meant by Aristotle.[53] Some translators of Aristotle, such as JAK Thomson, even eschew the word 'corrective' in favour of 'rectificatory'.[54] Thomson gives, as a reason for this, the desire to avoid moral overtones because with this type of justice Aristotle was concerned only with 'adjustment'.[55] The adjustment with which he was concerned arose 'in involuntary transactions',[56] perhaps more accurately, in cases of breach of a duty.[57] The adjustment was to rectify an imbalance by removing a gain from a defendant and restoring it to the claimant.

51 For years this was the core of a powerful attack of Professor Atiyah, although his solution about how no-fault compensation should be implemented altered in 1998. See P Cane (ed), *Atiyah's Accidents Compensation and the Law* (Cambridge, Cambridge University Press, 6th edn, 2005), ch 7; P Atiyah, 'Personal Injuries in the Twenty-first Century: Thinking the Unthinkable' in P Birks (ed), *Wrongs and Remedies in the Twenty First Century* (Oxford, Clarendon Press, 1996), 1. For a functionalist response, which relies upon the legitimacy of deterrence as a function, see A Burrows, *Understanding the Law of Obligations* (Oxford, Hart Publishing, 1998), ch 6.

52 E Weinrib, *The Idea of Private Law* (Cambridge, MA, Harvard University Press, 1995), 5.

53 For instance, Professor Coleman uses 'corrective justice' in a similar sense to the functionalism discussed above: J Coleman, *Risks and Wrongs* (Cambridge, Cambridge University Press, 1992), 392, speaking of the different values that 'the state may legitimately pursue within the tort system'. Following this criticism by Professor Perry (S Perry, 'Comment on Coleman: Corrective Justice' (1992) 67 *Industrial Law Review* 391), Coleman modified his theory (J Coleman, 'The Mixed Conception of Corrective Justice' (1992) 77 *Iowa Law Review* 427).

54 JAK Thomson was Professor Emeritus of Classics at King's College, London, until his death in 1959. His translation was first published by Allen & Unwin in 1953.

55 JAK Thomson (trans), *Aristotle Ethics* (London, Folio Society, 2003 reprint), 274. The paragraph numbers derive from Bekker's classic collection of Aristotle's works: I Bekker, *Aristotelis Opera* (Berlin, Reimer, 1831). The translation used is that of Thomson.

56 1131b25.

57 At 1131a5, Aristotle defined an involuntary transaction as either a 'secret' transaction (theft, adultery, poisoning) or violent (assault, forcible confinement, murder, robbery, maiming). But the genera 'secret' and 'violent' are not quite accurate translations because the former included testifying falsely and enticement of slaves and the latter included defamation and public insult (part of *iniuria* in Roman law). The more accurate sense, from his context, seems to be that involuntary meant 'in breach of a duty'.

In contrast with corrective justice, Aristotle refers to

> one kind of particular justice . . . [which] is that which is shown in the distribution of honour or money or such other assets as are divisible among the members of the community.[58]

Later, he explains that

> everyone agrees that justice in distribution must be in accordance with merit in some sense, but they do not all mean the same kind of merit: the democratic view is that the criterion is free birth; the oligarchic that it is wealth or good family; the aristocratic that it is excellence.[59]

Professor Cane has written that

> when we make judgments about the fairness of rules of tort law independently of their application to the facts of individual cases, we are commenting on whether the distribution of legal rights and obligations established by those rules is fair.[60]

This is commonly known as 'distributive justice'.

(i) Gains and Losses

Aristotle was concerned with the notion of corrective justice restoring an arithmetic mean or equal.[61] He said that 'it follows that what is just in the corrective sense will be the mean between loss and gain'.[62] In explaining what he meant by gain, Aristotle originally gave examples of a man who defrauded another of property[63] and a man who committed adultery for gain, making money out of it.[64] Confronting cases where there is, in fact, no gain, such as where the defendant physically injures the claimant, Aristotle said that

> the term gain is used generally in such cases, even though it is not the appropriate word for some offences, eg assault.[65]

Many legal theorists have observed the great difficulty this presents for an account of corrective justice based on restoration of a mean.[66] Without some explanation of why a gain is deemed to exist in cases where there is

58 1130b30.

59 1131a25.

60 P Cane, *The Anatomy of Tort Law* (Oxford, Hart Publications,1997), 18.

61 1132a15.

62 1132a19.

63 1132a5.

64 1132a5, recalling the example at 1130a25.

65 1132a10.

66 Eg G Fletcher, 'Corrective Justice for Moderns' (1993) 106 *Harvard Law Review* 1658, 1668; S Perry, 'The Moral Foundations of Tort Law' [1992] *Iowa Law Review* 449, 457; J Coleman, 'Corrective Justice and Wrongful Gain'(1982) 11 *Journal of Legal Studies* 421, 424–5.

no material gain to the defendant, any such theory of pure corrective justice is empty. An insight of Professor Weinrib's was to explain Artistotlean corrective justice by showing that gain does not mean *factual* gain, nor does loss mean *factual* loss. Rather, the concern is with *normative* gains and losses. A person gains when he retains more than he ought. A person loses when he has less than that to which he is entitled.[67] Such normative gains and losses occur when a person violates the right of another as a self-determining agent.[68] There are two difficulties with this theory which correspond with two objections. The first is that the theory cannot explain when a normative gain (and corresponding normative loss) results. The second is that the theory cannot explain how any normative gain or loss is to be quantified. The latter difficulty is directly relevant to the award of exemplary damages.

(ii) The First Objection

Professor Finnis has argued that

> the real problem with Aristotle's account is its emphasis on correction . . . 'Correction' and 'restitution' are notions parasitic on some prior determination of what is to count as a crime, a tort, a binding agreement.[69]

In other words, the objection is that in the law of torts, all primary legal rights arise as a result of non-corrective concerns. A right to compensation is a right a posteriori. It arises because an a priori right has been infringed. Professor Austin called these rights secondary rights and primary rights.[70] He said:

> Those [rights] which I call primary do not arise from injuries, or from violations of other rights and duties. Those which I call secondary or sanctioning (I style them sanctioning because their proper purpose is to prevent delicts or offences) arise from violations of other rights and duties, or from injuries, delicts or offences.

In other words, if I strike you or trespass on your land or lock you in a room I have committed a tort because I have infringed previously existing primary rights of yours. In *Allen* v *Flood*,[71] Viscount Cave said:

67 Weinrib, above n 51, 117.

68 *Ibid*, 122.

69 J Finnis, *Natural Law and Natural Rights* (Oxford, Clarendon Press, 1980), 178.

70 J Austin, *Lectures on Jurisprudence*, Vol II, R Campbell, ed (London, John Murray, 5th edn, 1885), 763. Austin was the first Chair in Jurisprudence at the University of London. The reference is to his revised lectures which were first published in 1832.

71 [1898] AC 1, 29. Professor Hohfeld, whose work built upon Austin's in providing 'jural relations' such as correlatives of rights and duties, described this summary as 'unusually discriminating and instructive': W Hohfeld, *Fundamental Legal Conceptions*, W Cook, ed (New Haven, CT, Yale University Press, 1919), 35. Sir George Cave continued, explaining the difference, which Hohfeld made popular, between a right and a freedom: 'it was said that a man

> The personal rights with which we are most familiar are: 1. Rights of reputation; 2. Rights of bodily safety and freedom; 3. Rights of property; or, in other words, rights relative to the mind, body, and estate.

A theory of corrective justice might be able to explain why I am entitled to recover for violations of my primary rights to reputation, bodily safety or property, but it does not, and cannot, explain the prior distribution of those rights.[72] The reason why I am entitled to rights such as reputation, bodily safety or property and any new addition to that list (such as a right to privacy) is wholly independent of any relationship with someone who might infringe it. Very recently, the same point was made by Crennan J in the leading judgment in the High Court of Australia in *Harriton v Stephens*.[73] The case involved a claim for compensation for 'wrongful life'. Counsel for the appellant claimed that corrective justice required that compensation be paid to the appellant by the doctor who failed to advise her mother that the appellant would be born with severe disabilities (and therefore prevented an abortion). Crennan J rejected this argument, saying this:[74]

> In emphasising "corrective justice", even as added to by his consideration of "distributive justice", Aristotle left unexplored the dependence of "correction" on the prior establishment of principles.[75]

It is not necessary here to consider the theoretical explanations for primary rights, apart from corrective justice (which is plainly inadequate). Such explanations include deontological as well as utilitarian theories of rights within particular epistemological frameworks. The reason that this need not be further explored is because an opponent of exemplary damages might just give a short answer saying simply that corrective justice must underpin secondary rights and, as a secondary right, exemplary damages violate corrective justice. Still, it is very hard to see why corrective justice should underpin secondary rights but not primary rights. This brings us to the second objection to corrective justice theories.

has a perfect right to fire off a gun, when all that was meant, apparently, was that a man has a freedom or liberty to fire off a gun so long as he does not violate or infringe any one's rights in doing so, which is a very different thing from a right the violation or disturbance of which can be remedied or prevented by legal process'.

72 At one point, Professor Weinrib appears to concede this point, saying that 'of course corrective justice presupposes the existence of individual entitlements': Weinrib, above n 52, 80.

73 [2006] HCA 15.

74 *Ibid*, [273].

75 Professor Dagan, a proponent of a functionalist theory of rights, expresses the conclusion that corrective justice cannot explain the distribution of rights by saying that corrective justice rests on a distributive foundation: H Dagan, 'The Distributive Foundation of Corrective Justice' (1999) 98 *Michigan Law Review* 138, 150, 153. See also H Dagan, *The Law and Ethics of Restitution* (Cambridge, Cambridge University Press, 2004), 224.

(iii) The Second Objection

Following Weinrib's explanation of corrective justice, once a normative gain (and corresponding normative loss) occurs, then the value of that normative gain or loss must be the award to which the claimant is entitled. Dr Beever uses this to argue against exemplary damages:

> a claimant cannot justly demand to be put in a better position than she would have been in had she not been wronged. She cannot be owed a windfall.[76]

The flaw in this argument is that, without an explanation of how the normative gain or normative loss is to be calculated, the assertion that exemplary damages are a windfall is tautologous. If a claimant is entitled to exemplary damages, then she is not owed a windfall. This is precisely the attack on corrective justice made by Professor Kelsen in 1957. Kelsen argued that the Aristotelian idea was a tautology because, although corrective justice purports to be based upon rendering to each person that which he is due, it does not explain that which is due.[77] Hence, to the question 'why is an award of damages due?' the answer is 'corrective justice'; to the question, 'why are these damages supported by corrective justice?', the answer is 'because they are (normatively) due'.

Weinrib's answer to this objection is that the theory of corrective justice simply provides a structure which is 'decisive for whatever content one might consider'.[78] What content, then, can be given to this corrective justice analysis, devoid of functionalist considerations, if the theory is to explain the way the structure of tort law *should* operate rather than merely being an empty observation about tort law? Indeed, as a mere observation about tort law corrective justice theory is totally flawed. The presence of awards of exemplary damages as well as subsequent, consequential losses (which focus, respectively, on the defendant and the claimant exclusively) as well as policy reasoning all show that corrective justice has little 'fit' as an explanation of the structure of the existing law.[79] Further, unless content can be given to corrective justice theory then not only does it have little fit with the case law but, as Professor Wright observe, there is

> no reason as a matter of justice for choosing the traditional corrective justice tort liability scheme . . . rather than a more comprehensive no-fault compensation scheme or some other distributive justice scheme.[80]

76 Beever, above n 32, 106.

77 H Kelsen, *What is Justice: Justice, Law and Politics in the Mirror of Science* (Berkeley, CA, University of California Press, 1957), 125.

78 Weinrib, above n 52, 68.

79 R Dworkin, *Law's Empire* (Oxford, Hart Publishing, 1998) 230.

80 R Wright, 'Substantive Corrective Justice' (1992) 77 *Iowa Law Review* 625, 632.

If corrective justice is to be given a substantive role,[81] perhaps a value could be placed upon the right which is infringed. Placing a value on the right infringed might be thought to link both the claimant and the defendant in the award that is made. Although this is not the solution that Weinrib adopts, one might expect that it would follow logically from his view that 'damages are the notional equivalent at the remedial stage of the right that has been wrongly infringed'.[82] The value of the primary right would reflect both the normative gain and the normative loss. For instance, in *Ashby v White*[83] an action was brought by the claimant who had been denied a right to vote by the defendant returning officer. Gould J held, as one reason for refusing the claim, that there was no damage to the claimant because he did not allege that his vote would have made a difference.[84] Powys J held that

> if this refusal of the plaintiff's vote be an injury, it is of so small and little consideration in the law that no action will lie for it.[85]

Powell J said that

> the plaintiff can make no profit of his vote; and it is like the case of a *quare impedit*, in which the plaintiff at common law recovered no damages because he ought not to sell the presentation and so could make no profit of it.[86]

However, Holt CJ dissented and said that an action could be brought:[87]

> My brother Powell indeed thinks, that an action on the case is not maintainable, because there is no hurt or damage to the plaintiff; but surely every injury imports a damage, though it does not cost the party one farthing, and it is impossible to prove the contrary; for a damage is not merely pecuniary, but an injury imports a damage, when a man is thereby hindered of his right.

Holt CJ would have awarded substantial damages because

> the right of voting at the election of burgesses is a thing of the highest importance, and so great a privilege, that it is a great injury to deprive the plaintiff of it.[88]

On 14 January 1703, the House of Lords voted to overturn the decision in favour of the dissent of Holt CJ. The vote was 50 Lords to 16.[89]

[81] The term 'substantive' corrective justice is used by Professor Wright in a different context: R Wright, 'Substantive Corrective Justice' (1992) 77 *Iowa Law Review* 625.

[82] E Weinrib, 'Restitutionary Damages as Corrective Justice' [2000] *Theoretical Inquiries in Law* 1, 4–5.

[83] (1703) 2 Ld Raym 938; 92 ER 126.

[84] *Ibid*, 943/129.

[85] *Ibid*, 944/130.

[86] *Ibid*, 949/133.

[87] *Ibid*, 955/137.

[88] *Ibid*, 953/136.

[89] The vote of the Lords was subsequently overturned by the Commons. See PA Hamburger, 'Revolution and Judicial Review: Chief Justice Holt's Opinion in City of London v Wood' (1994) 94 *Columbia Law Review* 2091, 2143–5.

Such an award of damages in substitution for the value of a right might seem to conform neatly to a theory of corrective justice requiring normative loss and gain. The value of the right reflects the normative loss to the claimant as well as the normative gain to the defendant. Although these awards of damages in substitution for the value of a right are not universal, cases like *Ashby v White* (and the opinion of Holt CJ) are far from uncommon.[90] These substitutory awards are most well known from cases in which the defendant's negligence prevented the claimant's use of a chattel (often a ship) and a substantial award of damages is made notwithstanding that the claimant has suffered no financial loss.[91] Another example of liability for the substitute value of an infringed right is *Solloway v McLaughlin*.[92] McLaughlin instructed a stockbroking company to buy shares. The stockbrokers told him that the shares had been purchased but they had not been. They also sold 14,000 shares that McLaughlin had deposited as security. The share value declined and the company then purchased the shares to fulfil McLaughlin's order (as well as to replace his security) on a rapidly falling market in January 1930. McLaughlin argued that he was entitled to compensation of the full amount of his shares at the time he had provided them to the company as well as the money he had paid for share that were not purchased. In other words, although McLaughlin had ultimately suffered no financial loss, he was entitled to damages for money he paid as a result of the tort of deceit. The Privy Council allowed his claim. There is a powerful case that can be made that this case should be re-explained as an award of restitutionary damages,[93] but at the time it was decided it could arguably be seen as an example that awards of damages reflect the value of a right.

(iv) The Infusion of Deterrence in Assessing the Value of Rights

Although this application of corrective justice appears to exclude awards of exemplary damages, it also excludes awards of consequential losses subsequent to the infringement and awards of disgorgement of profits made

[90] This theme is explored in J Edelman, 'Gain-based Damages and Compensation' in A Burrows and A Rodger (eds), *Mapping the Law: Essays in Honour of Peter Birks* (Oxford, Oxford University Press, 2006) ch 8. It builds on work of Mitchell McInnes: see M McInnes, 'Account of Profits for in S Degeling and J Edelman, *Equity in Commercial Law* (Sydney, Thomson, 2005) ch 16.

[91] *The Mediana* [1900] AC 113. See also *The Greta Holme* [1897] AC 596; *The Marpessa* [1907] AC 241; *Admiralty Commissioners v SS Chekiang* [1926] AC 637; *Admiralty Commissioners v SS Susquehanna* [1926] AC 655; *The Hebridean Coast* [1961] AC 545.

[92] [1938] AC 247 (PC, Canada). Cf *Hiort v London and North Western Railway Company* (1879) 4 Ex D 188; *Borders (UK) Ltd v Commissioner of Police of the Metropolis* [2005] EWCA Civ 197 at [7].

[93] *Kuwait Airways Corporation v Iraqi Airways Company* [2002] 2 AC 883, [63]–[66] (Lord Nicholls; Lords Steyn, Hoffmann and Hope agreeing, re-explaining the case as one of restitutionary damages). See further Edelman, above n 90.

subsequently to the infringement. In other words, the application of this theory of corrective justice can explain a rights-based measure of damages but it cannot explain any award of compensation for causally related loss which is suffered as a result of subsequent external events or disgorgement of causally related profits subsequently made as a result of external events. The same is true of exemplary damages. It has little fit with the rest of private law.

There is a further problem. On the axis of justification even this rights-based analysis cannot be explained purely by corrective justice independent of functionalist concerns. The difficulty can be seen in relation to non-venal rights. How is a price to be put on a right that has no market? For instance, in *R v Governor of Her Majesty's Prison (Brockhill)*[94] the governor calculated the release date of a prisoner in accordance with earlier decisions that the governor thought that he was bound to follow.[95] Those decisions were later overturned, so that the prisoner had served longer than required when she was released on 15 November 1996.[96] The prisoner brought an action for false imprisonment. Like John Wilkes, the prisoner had not suffered any financial loss, or anything that could be translated into financial loss. Nevertheless, the prisoner recovered substantial damages of £5,000 (increased by the Court of Appeal from the trial judge's award of £2,000). The Court of Appeal (whose decision was approved by the House of Lords on this point) said that the trial judge's award of damages for false imprisonment was inadequate and that the award for the infringement of the claimant's right by false imprisonment should be increased from £2,000 to £5,000. But why was this amount chosen? Why £5,000? Why not £20,000?

A recent decision of the Privy Council provides the answer. In *Attorney General for Trinidad v Ramanoop*[97] a police officer beat Mr Ramanoop, humiliated him and then arrested him and locked him up for several hours. The only claim that was brought against the officer, and the State, was for breach of Mr Ramanoop's constitutional rights. For the two-hour deprivation of liberty, Mr Ramanoop was awarded $TT 18,000 (approximately £1,500). The advice of the Privy Council was delivered by Lord Nicholls. Delivering the advice of the Privy Council that this award was too small because it compensated Mr Ramanoop for his (intangible) loss but did not reflect the value of his rights, this is what Lord Nicholls said:[98]

94 [2001] 2 AC 19.

95 *Reg v Governor of Blundeston Prison, Ex parte Gaffney* [1986] 1 WLR 696; *Reg v Secretary of State for the Home Office, Ex parte Read (1987)* 9 CrAppR (S) 206; *Reg v Governor of Styal Prison, Ex parte Mooney* [1996] 1 Cr App Rep (S) 74; *Reg v Secretary of State for the Home Department, Ex parte Woodward & Wilson* [24 June 1996] (unreported).

96 The Divisional Court held that her release date properly calculated was 17 September 1996 and ordered that she be released immediately: [1997] QB 443.

97 [2006] 1 AC 328.

98 *Ibid*, 336, [19]–[20].

> An award of compensation will go some distance towards vindicating the infringed constitutional right. How far it goes will depend on the circumstances, but in principle it may well not suffice. The fact that the right violated was a constitutional right adds an extra dimension to the wrong. *An additional award, not necessarily of substantial size, may be needed to reflect the sense of public outrage, emphasise the importance of the constitutional right and the gravity of the breach, and deter further breaches. All these elements have a place in this additional award.* 'Redress' in section 14 is apt to encompass such an award if the court considers it is required having regard to all the circumstances. Although such an award, where called for, is likely in most cases to cover much the same ground in financial terms as would an award by way of punishment in the strict sense of retribution, punishment in the latter sense is not its object. Accordingly, the expressions 'punitive damages' or 'exemplary damages' are better avoided as descriptions of this type of additional award.
>
> For these reasons their Lordships are unable to accept the Attorney General's basic submission that a monetary award under section 14 is confined to an award of compensatory damages in the traditional sense. Bereaux J stated his jurisdiction too narrowly. The matter should be remitted to him, or another judge, to consider whether an additional award of damages of the character described above is appropriate in this case.

In other words, in valuing the right, the court has regard to functional considerations such as compensation (the gravity of the breach) and deterrence (to deter future breaches) in fixing the award at a value necessary to protect the right. The award is the 'price' that the infringer must pay for the right. If the award is set too low it will not sufficiently discourage infringement or the claimant will not be sufficiently compensated for the gravity of the infringement. Indeed, exactly this approach was taken by Holt CJ in *Ashby* in assessing the value of the right to liberty from governmental interference:

> if publick officers will infringe men's rights, they ought to pay greater damages than other men, to deter and hinder other officers from the like offences.[99]

As the law becomes more transparent, it might be preferable for these 'rights-based awards' to be separated into their respective compensatory and exemplary components. The essential point is that the award cannot be calculated without functional concerns.

(v) Deterrence in Rights-based Substitutionary Awards and Deterrence in Exemplary Damages

We have seen that, in placing a value upon a right, particularly non-venal rights, courts will invariably take a functional approach: how much loss will stem from that violation? What sum of money is required to deter its

[99] Above n 83, 956/137.

breach? Once it is accepted that this immediate valuation of the right can involve such functional considerations, then it follows a fortiori that it must also be legitimate to consider such functions when taking into account subsequent consequential events. In other words, just as further, subsequent consequential losses can enhance a rights-based award by requiring additional compensation, so too can subsequent events which show a need for additional deterrence.

An example is *Merson v Cartwright*,[100] a case heard by the Privy Council at the same time as *Ramanoop*. Ms Merson was treated in a degrading way by the police, who assaulted and falsely imprisoned her and abused her with 'Gestapo-style tactics'.[101] She sued for assault and battery, false imprisonment and deprivation of her constitutional rights. The sole question before the Privy Council was whether the action for damages for infringement of her constitutional rights was cumulative with the damages for the other torts. This required the Privy Council to consider the purpose of the damages award. Lord Scott, delivering the advice of the Board, said:[102]

> The purpose of a vindicatory award is not a punitive purpose. It is not to teach the executive not to misbehave. The purpose is to vindicate the right of the complainant, whether a citizen or a visitor, to carry on his or her life in the Bahamas free from unjustified executive interference, mistreatment or oppression. The sum appropriate to be awarded to achieve this purpose will depend upon the nature of the particular infringement and the circumstances relating to that infringement. It will be a sum at the discretion of the trial judge. In some cases a suitable declaration may suffice to vindicate the right; in other cases an award of damages, including substantial damages, may seem to be necessary.

Although Lord Scott tried to differentiate the award of the value of the right ('vindicatory award') and the award of damages, the essential point is the same. The circumstances of the infringement (and the immediate need for compensation, deterrence) establish the value of the claimant's immediate right. Subsequent events can enhance that award. But, whether considering the value of the immediate violation or the subsequent events, functionalism is inevitable.

C Legitimacy Generally

A final objection to deterrence having a role in private law is that it introduces illegitimate policy concerns into the law of torts. Professor Dworkin is the best-known proponent of this view:[103]

100 [2005] UKPC 38.
101 *Ibid*, [7].
102 *Ibid*, [18].
103 R Dworkin, *Taking Rights Seriously* (London, Duckworth, 1977) 84–5.

> that law should be made by elected and responsible officials, seems unobjectionable when we think of law as policy; that is, as a compromise among individual goals and purposes in search of the welfare of the community as a whole. It is far from clear that interpersonal comparisons of utility or preference through which such compromises might be made objectively, make sense even in theory; but in any case no proper calculus is available in practice. Policy decisions must therefore be made through the operation of some political process designed to produce an accurate expression of the different interests that should be taken into account. The political system of representative democracy may work only indifferently in this respect, but it works better than a system that allows nonelected judges, who have no mail bag or lobbyists or pressure groups, to compromise competing interests in their chambers.

Although there are many examples of judges reaching their decisions by reference to policy concerns, for theorists such as Dworkin such reasoning is illegitimate. Among the judges that would be in Dworkin's cross-hairs, the most obvious contenders are Lord Hoffmann in England and Justice Kirby in Australia. So, for example, in *Fairchild v Glenhaven Funeral Services Ltd*[104] Lord Hoffmann spoke of 'the political and economic arguments involved in the massive increase in the liability of the National Health Service', and in *Gregg v Scott*[105] his Lordship spoke of the 'enormous consequences for insurance companies and the National Health Service'. Justice Kirby is just as explicit. In *Crimmins v Stevedoring Industry Finance Committee*[106] his Honour referred to considerations as diverse as the financial resources of the Stevedoring Industry Finance Committee, the unfairness of levying present stevedores for the defaults of others in the past and the desirability of national minimum standards for the safety of Australian waterside workers.

The political objections to many policy decisions in Australia are compounded by a further legal obstacle in Australia. In the High Court of Australia it is not possible to present evidence (either new or fresh evidence).[107] The difficulty this presents has been acknowledged by Justice Kirby

> if the application of ordinary legal principles is to be denied on the basis of public policy, it is essential that such policy be spelt out so as to be susceptible of analysis and criticism. Desirably, it should be founded on empirical evidence, not mere judicial assertion.[108]

104 [2003] 1 AC 32, 77 [69].

105 [2005] 2 AC 176, 198 [90].

106 (1999) 200 CLR 1, 80–6. See also *Pyrenees Shire Council v Day* (1998) 192 CLR 330, 420–7; *Romeo v Conservation Commission (NT)* (1998) 192 CLR 431, 476–7, 484–5; *Perre v Apand Pty Ltd* (1999) 198 CLR 180, 286–91; *Brodie v Singleton Shire Council* (2001) 206 CLR 512, 604–5.

107 *Mickelberg v The Queen* (1989) 167 CLR 259; *Eastman v The Queen* (2000) 203 CLR 1.

108 *Cattanach v Melchior* (2003) 215 CLR 1, [152].

Such empirical evidence requires considerable foresight by counsel at trial, or before the intermediate appellate court, because of the inability of the High Court of Australia to hear such evidence.

However, Dworkin carefully distinguishes between policy (illegitimate) and principles (legitimate):[109]

> a policy [is] that kind of standard that sets out a goal to be reached, generally an improvement in some economic, political or social feature of the community . . . a principle [is] a standard that is to be observed, not because it will advance or secure an economic, political, or social situation deemed desirable, but because it is a requirement of justice or fairness or some other dimension of morality.

For many of those, such as Dworkin, who oppose the use of policy in private law, an argument of principle stands apart from policy because it is an argument concerned with securing or respecting an individual or group right.[110] As an example of 'principle', Dworkin wrote of the principle that 'no man shall profit from his wrong' using the famous case of *Riggs v Palmer.*[111] That case raised the question of whether an heir named in a will could inherit from the grandfather he murdered. Judge Earl, in the majority, reasoned that the literal construction of the statute was controlled by the principle that no man shall profit from his own fraud or be permitted to take advantage of his own wrong. Although Dworkin acknowledged that the distinction between principle ('no man shall profit from his own fraud') and policy could collapse if the principle is restated as a social goal (for example, reduction of fraud or, in *Riggs*, discouraging murder), this does not mean that the distinction does not exist. Rather, it is that the focus on a public goal, rather than the core value, is illegitimate. A different defence of Dworkin's approach to principles might be simply to say that there is a difference between those policy concerns which judges are ill equipped, both politically and in fact, to decide because they involve balancing conflicting goals or standards and the principled concern of securing the protection of rights which the law has made an ex ante decision must be respected. In the law of torts, all nominate torts involve recognition that a right has been infringed. Securing the protection of that right by an award to deter its breach does

109 Dworkin, above n 103, 22. See also *Cattanach*, *ibid*, [75], McHugh and Gummow JJ quoting from Lord Radcliffe's Rosenthal lectures, published as *The Law & Its Compass* (London Faber & Faber, 1960) 43–4: 'Public policy suggests something inherently fluid, adjusted to the expediency of the day, the proper subject of the minister or the member of the legislature. The considerations which we accept as likely to weigh with them are just not those which we expect to see governing the decisions of a court of law. On the contrary, we expect to find the law indifferent to them, speaking for a system of values at any rate less mutable than this.'

110 Dworkin, *ibid*, 82.

111 115 NY 506; 22 NE 188 (1889). See Dworkin, *ibid*, 22–3.

not raise the illegitimacy objections raised in cases involving the balancing of conflicting goals and standards.[112]

V CONCLUSION

The sole purpose of this essay has been to defend exemplary damages from the growing forces that would see them abolished. The theoretical section of this essay focused upon defending exemplary damages on the basis of one rationale only: deterrence. The problem at the start illustrated how moral *haitûs* can arise in private law without deterrent awards such as exemplary damages and that, based on a rationale of deterrence, exemplary damages have deep and interlocking roots in private law and could not be uprooted without considerable disturbance to other areas of the law. The theoretical defence then showed how those theories that oppose deterrence having a legitimate role in private law are flawed, tautologous (functionalism) or submerge the role for deterrence (corrective justice). The essay concluded by differentiating the use of deterrence as a principle from other (arguably) illegitimate policies sometimes relied upon in judicial decision making.

This essay is purely defensive. No attempt has been made to address those theories that support the deterrent rationale such as theories of tort law based on economic efficiency.[113] Nor has any attempt been made to assess the utility of the deterrent principle. Indeed, it has even been argued by some that if the law were truly committed to deterrence then an award would be far more extreme than the usual profit-stripping or modest exemplary damages awards. If we were truly committed to deterrence, the argument runs, why does private law not allow orders for capital punishment for any breach of duty, no matter how minor? There is an easy answer to this objection. It is that no deterrent-based award will deter everyone. Nor does private law aim for complete deterrence. The award of (generally modest) monetary deterrents is to strike a balance between a concern for sufficient deterrence and a concern for the liberty of the individual.[114] Even a small additional deterrent award, in addition to

112 As Professors Dagan and White observe, 'a legal regime that effectively deters may well be aimed at vindicating the resource holder's control over the infringed resource': H Dagan and JJ Whit,e 'Governments, Citizens, and Injurious Industries' (2000) 75 *New York University Law Review* , 420. The authors, however, express concern at the difficulty in measuring, consistent with a libertarian ideal, a deterrent award which goes beyond profits made by the defendant (or, presumably, where no profits have been made).

113 G Calebresi, *The Costs of Accidents: A Legal and Economic Analysis* (New Haven, CT, Yale University Press, 1970); R Posner, *Law and Legal Theory in the UK and the USA* (Oxford, Clarendon Press, 1996) 52–4.

114 This is well known in the economic literature as a theory of 'appropriate' or 'optimal' deterrence. See, eg KN Hylton, 'Punitive Damages and the Economic Theory of Penalties' (1998) 87 *Georgetown Law Review* 421, 421.

compensation, will deter some people because people's actions are motivated by a panoply of considerations. For some people even a small amount of additional deterrence may therefore be the deciding motivating factor.[115] In other words, although it is true that deterrence will not always work, if an award of $225 million in a class action against Ford Motor Company[116] is one factor which leads to the Ford Motor Company considering its decisions more carefully, then it is very possible that the next Ford Bronco will have a roll bar or the next Ford Pinto will have insulation over its fuel tank. Private law will then have provided justice by protecting the rights of the next Richard Grimshaw or the next Romo family.

115 Compare the contrary argument in W K Viscusi, 'Social Costs of Punitive Damages against Corporations in Environmental and Safety Torts' (1998) 87 *Georgetown Law Review* 285 with T Eisenberg, 'Measuring the Deterrent Effect of (1998) 87 *Georgetown Law Review* 347; D Luban 'A Flawed ase against puitive damaes' (1998) 87 *Georgetown Law Review* 359, 362–4. Cf WK Viscusi, 'Why There Is No Defense of (1998) 87 *Georgetown Law Review* 381.

116 There can be little doubt that such an award would have been upheld if the action were brought by a sufficient class rather than just a single family. US courts have certified class actions demanding over $100 billion in damages: *Walmart Stores v Visa USA Inc* 280 F 3d 124 (2nd cir 2001).

11

Justice and Punishment in Tort: A Comparative Theoretical Analysis

ALLAN BEEVER*

I INTRODUCTION

IN THEIR BEGINNINGS, both the common law of tort and the civil law of delict had 'a strongly criminal flavour'.[1] Both combined punitive and compensatory elements to such a degree that it is impossible clearly to distinguish penal from tort law in those jurisdictions.[2] However, as each developed, the punitive parts of the law of tort gradually separated, giving rise to or completing criminal law.

But the extent of the development differs between the traditions. In most civilian jurisdictions, tort law entirely surrendered its punitive elements.[3] Although this change is difficult to trace historically, according to Pierre Catala it occurred in France in the South, the area most influenced by Roman law, by the middle of the twelfth century but in the North not perhaps until the seventeenth.[4] Moreover, the rejection of punishment as a proper part of private law was emphatic in civilian jurisdictions. As Volker Behr writes with respect to German law, for instance,

> for about a century the nearly unanimous understanding of sections 249 through 255 of the German Civil Code can be summed up in the following way: the exclusive legitimate function of damages is compensation of the victim.

* Reader in Law, University of Durham; von Humboldt Research Fellow, Max-Planck-Institut für ausländisches und internationales Privatrecht, Hamburg. Sincere thanks to the organisers of the Obligations III conference: Darryn Jensen, Ross Grantham and Charles Rickett.

1 R Zimmermann, *The Law of Obligations: Roman Foundations of the Civilian Tradition* (Oxford, Oxford University Press, 1996), 913.

2 *Ibid.*

3 U Magnus, *Unification of Tort Law: Damages* (The Hague, Kluwer, 2001), 9 (Austria), 30 (Belgium), 90 (Germany), 110 (Greece), 145 (Netherlands), cf 117 (Italy); P Tercier and D Dreyer, 'Torts' in F Dessemontet and T Ansay (eds), *Introduction to Swiss Law* (The Hague, Kluwer, 3rd edn, 2004), 145, 159 (Switzerland).

4 P Catala and JA Weir, 'Delict and Torts: A Study in Parallel, Part I' (1963) 37 *Tulane Law Review* 573, 583–4 note 39.

> Consequently, punishment of the tortfeasor is not a legitimate function of damages. German civil law and criminal law are separate. Punitive damages are punishment, and, while a wrongdoer may be punished exclusively under the concept of criminal law, by no means is such punishment allowed under the concept of civil law.[5]

According to Behr, this points to an apparent 'irreconcilable gap' between civil law and common law,[6] a gap that is so wide that German courts have refused to enforce common law courts' awards of exemplary damages because such damages are said to be against German public policy.[7]

On the other hand, common law has retained punishment in the form of exemplary or punitive damages. While there was an attempt to restrict their availability in England,[8] that position has been rejected in the rest of the common law world,[9] and there is considerable support for the maintenance or expansion of exemplary damages even in England.[10]

Moreover, some maintain that the modern civil law, in fact though not in theory, recognises damages that are punitive, suggesting a move away from the traditional civilian approach and a reconciliation between the two traditions.[11]

This article explores one of the reasons the civil and common law developed differently in this regard. It suggests that civil law abandoned punishment, in part, because civilian theorists recognised and elucidated accounts of a form of justice that explained and justified compensation and other similar responses to wrongdoing, but left no room for punishment. I refer to this picture of justice as 'the civilian model'. The article further examines why the common law did not develop in the same way, by exploring the position taken by leading theorists in that jurisdiction. It shows that the account of justice developed by English-speaking theorists—'the common law model'—utilised to explain the law of tort, was compatible with the notion that punishment has a role to play in that law.

[5] V Behr, 'Punitive Damages in American and German Law—Tendencies Towards Approximation of Apparently Irreconcilable Concepts' (2003) 78 *Chicago-Kent Law Review* 105, 106.

[6] *Ibid*, 105.

[7] See, eg BGHZ 118, 312.

[8] *Rookes v Barnard* [1964] AC 1129.

[9] For the rejection in the Commonwealth, see *Uren v John Fairfax and Sons Pty Ltd* (1966) 117 CLR 118; *Donselaar v Donselaar* [1982] 1 NZLR 97; *Vorvis v Insurance Corp of British Columbia* [1989] 1 SCR 1085. For the position in the US, see, eg *Pacific Mutual Life Insurance Co v Haslip* 1 US 15 (US SC 1991); *Cooper Industries Inc v Leatherman Tool Group Inc* 532 US 424 (US SC 2001).

[10] In 1995, the Law Commission for England and Wales questioned interested parties on this matter and found that 72% of respondents favoured retaining (23%) or expanding the availability of (49%) the award. Law Commission for England and Wales, 'Aggravated, Exemplary and Restitutionary Damages' (1997) 247, §§5.14–5.15.

[11] Behr, above n 5, 125–150. See also Magnus, above n 3, 186–7.

After providing this explanation, the article then examines the adequacy of the two models. It suggests that the common law model is deficient, as it is inconsistent with fundamental features of the law. Finally, the article explores recent suggestions that the modern civil law covertly recognises damages that are punitive. It argues that this is a misunderstanding that arises because civilian lawyers are beginning to forget the civilian model. I begin, however, with three preliminary points.

II THREE PRELIMINARY POINTS

A The Role of Natural Law Theory

The civilian model was developed by theorists who argued that the model is justified by the natural law. This may give the impression that the civilian model is inextricably tied to natural law theory, but that is not the case. Both the civilian and the common law models are accounts of justice. According to the natural lawyer, these accounts reflect, in some sense, the nature of the law. For the positivist, on the other hand, the accounts indicate only the way that the law ought to be. This difference is of no importance here. We are interested in the natural lawyers' accounts of justice, not in their ontologies of law.

B What Theory Reveals

The theorists examined below have been chosen both because they present good examples of particular kinds of legal thought and because they were highly influential. But it is not presumed that the influence was one way only. Rather, it is supposed that these theorists both influenced the ways that people thought about the law and were themselves influenced by common perceptions of the law. Therefore, the theories we explore both explain why persons came to think about the law as they did and provide a more or less accurate snapshot of how the law was generally conceived by the theorist's contemporaries.

The civilian model is not intended to capture how modern civilian lawyers conceptualise their law. In my experience, these lawyers have conflicting views on this matter and, as I argue in the sixth section of this article, modern civil lawyers appear to be forgetting the civilian model. The claim is only that the model was influential in the historical development of civil law.

C Compensation, Rectification and Corrective Justice

For reasons that will become apparent, we require a term that refers to what corrective justice demands as a response to an injustice. 'Compensation' is the term most frequently adopted, but it will not do here. This is because that term is now used in a way that implies only part of what corrective justice demands. Accordingly, I have adopted a different term: 'rectification'. The relationship between compensation and rectification is made clear in the following.

The four civilian theorists I examine hold that there are at least two kinds of justice: distributive justice and another kind. The problem is finding an appropriate name for this other kind. Aristotle refers to this kind of justice as *συνάλλαγμα*, which is usually translated as 'corrective' or 'rectificatory' justice. Moreover, the old Latin translation of Aristotle's ethics rendered the term as '*commutativo*', and followers of Aristotle writing in Latin tended to speak of *commutativa justitia*, which is translated into English as 'commutative justice'. But it would be wrong to think that commutative justice is something different from corrective or rectificatory justice. The theorists examined below all take themselves to be referring to the same thing as Aristotle.[12]

In the following, I have chosen to use 'corrective justice' over the other terms. I have done so for three main reasons. First, 'rectificatory justice' is in no way preferable to 'corrective justice' as the same problems exist with respect to both. Secondly, 'corrective justice' is the term used in current legal discourse, while commutative justice is archaic.[13] Thirdly, those who see their work as being part of the tradition outlined below view it in this way because they see it as belonging to the tradition headed by Aristotle. Accordingly, I speak uniformly of 'corrective justice' below.

12 T Aquinas, *Summa theologica*, English Dominicans trans (New York, Benziger Bros, 1947), SS Q61; H Grotius, *The Law of War and Peace*, FW Kelsey, trans (Oxford, Clarendon Press, 1925), I i 8; S Pufendorf, *Of the Law of Nature and Nations*, HC Oldfather and WA Oldfather, trans (Oxford, Clarendon Press, 1934) I vii. See also T Hobbes, *Leviathan* (Oxford, Oxford University Press, 1996), XV 14. According to J Finnis, *Natural Law and Natural Rights* (Oxford, Clarendon Press, 1980), 179, however, Aquinas' allegiance is disingenuous There is insufficient evidence to determine this, but the matter is in part decided by the correct interpretation of Aristotle's views, which are explored below.

13 Finnis, *ibid*, 178.

III THE CIVILIAN MODEL

A Aristotle

As indicated above, no clear distinction between tort and criminal law existed before about the twelfth century. Accordingly, we would expect to find that theorists before this time had not adequately distinguished the concepts of rectification and punishment. This is indeed what we find when we look at the greatest philosopher of the pre-modern age: Aristotle.

In his *Ethics*, Aristotle famously distinguishes between distributive and corrective justice.[14] The first form of justice deals with the overall spread of 'honors or wealth or anything else that can be divided among members of a community'.[15] This form of justice is achieved when goods are divided so that they are held in appropriate amounts by the right persons. This means that those who are equal, according to the appropriate account of equality relevant for distributive justice, have the same while those who are unequal have differing shares.[16] Thus, in more modern language, we can say that distributive justice is concerned with overall distributions of benefits and burdens. It is, as Aristotle puts it, a geometrical justice.[17]

Corrective justice, on the other hand, deals with justice in transactions, with imbalances that arise in dealings between two individuals.[18] Typically, corrective justice is called into play when one person wrongly inflicts harm on another. In such circumstances, a judge

> tries to restore this unjust situation to equality, since it is unequal. For [not only when one steals from another but] also when one is wounded and the other wounds him, or one kills and the other is killed, the action and the suffering are unequally divided [with profit for the offender and loss for the victim]; and the judge tries to restore the [profit and] loss to a position of equality, by subtraction from [the offender's] profit.[19]

Hence, corrective justice is an arithmetic justice.[20]

At this point, it is essential to address the question 'Is corrective justice concerned only with correcting injustices?' Given its name, the answer must appear to be 'Yes'. But the name may be misleading. Of course, Aristotle did not call this form of justice 'corrective justice' but referred to it by the term συνάλλαγμα. Moreover, it must be remembered that

14 Aristotle, *Nicomachean Ethics*, T Irwin, trans (Indianapolis, IN, Hackett, 1999), 1131a–1132b.
15 *Ibid*, 1130b–1131a.
16 *Ibid*, 1131a.
17 *Ibid*, 1131b.
18 *Ibid*, 1131b–1132b.
19 *Ibid*, 1132a (translator's additions).
20 *Ibid*.

Aristotle's work, in this area and in others, was revolutionary. He frequently created new concepts and, indeed, whole areas of thought. Hence, he must relatively often have used terms in a way that did not exactly match their original meanings. This is certainly true of Aristotle's use of the terms translated as 'transaction', 'profit' and 'loss'. As we see below, Aristotle uses these terms to refer to things other than transactions, profits and losses. Why, then, did he choose these terms? The answer is that they would have been the terms closest in meaning to Aristotle's intention that he could find. Hence, Aristotle's' intention in using *συνάλλαγμα* may not correspond to the exact use of the term in contemporary Greek. In using that term, he may have been intending to identify a concept that did not before exist. Therefore, we cannot assume that 'corrective' justice, for Aristotle, is merely about correcting injustices even were 'corrective' a perfect translation for *συνάλλαγμα*.

This point can be brought home by considering the term 'distributive justice'. That term avoids the pitfalls of 'corrective justice' because of an ambiguity in 'distributive'. First, 'distributive' could refer to the act of distribution, as 'corrective' refers to the act of correcting. On this view, distributive justice would be concerned only with how to (re)distribute resources when unjust levels of acquisition have taken place. This is less clear than it might be because of the influence of theorists, such as John Rawls, who ask us to imagine an original state in which all have nothing and must decide how to distribute all available resources.[21] But that is not the real world. In that world, persons already have resources. So, on this understanding, distributive justice could be about how to (re)distribute what persons have when they have too little or too much, but could not tell us about how much persons should have. No amount of reflection on the act of distributing will tell us how much persons should have.

The term avoids this difficulty because 'distributive' can refer not only to the act of distributing, but also to distributive patterns. Hence, on this view, distributive justice is concerned with appropriate patterns of distribution. There is no equivalent reading of 'corrective'. On this view, literally interpreted, distributive justice can tell us about what pattern distributions should take, but nothing about what should be distributed, or to whom. But no one thinks of distributive justice in that way. Everyone allows that distributive justice can and should inform us about these matters. In other words, we do not take 'distributive' too literally in 'distributive justice'. But if that is so, why insist that 'corrective' in 'corrective justice' be understood literally? If distributive justice tells us what should be distributed and why, why cannot corrective justice tell us what should be corrected and why? If distributive justice can tell us about

21 J Rawls, *A Theory of Justice* (Cambridge, MA, Belknap, revised edn, 1999), ch 3.

the just in distributions, why cannot corrective justice be informative about the just in transactions?

None of this would be important if there were no evidence that Aristotle thought that corrective justice was informative about the justice of transactions, but that evidence certainly exists. Though Aristotle naturally spends most of his time discussing corrective justice in the light of practices with which his contemporary audience would have been familiar—the operations of the Greek courts—his discussion ends with this crucial passage:

> [H]aving more than one's own share is called making a profit, and having less than what one had at the beginning is called suffering a loss, in buying and selling, for instance, and in other transactions permitted by law . . . And when people get neither more nor less, but precisely what belongs to them, they say they have their own share and make neither a loss nor a profit. Hence the just is intermediate between a certain kind of loss and profit, since it is having the equal amount both before and after [the transaction].[22]

According to this passage, in a transaction such as buying and selling, persons can end up with more or less than that which rightly belongs to them. There is no suggestion that this can result only as a consequence of a breach of the terms of the transaction. Aristotle maintains that after a sale has taken place the parties can have more, less or as much as justice allows. This appears to be a reference to what became known as the *laesio enormis*, the idea that justice sometimes requires the setting aside (or voidablity) of contracts for sale because the price, though freely agreed to, is unfair. In fact, Reinhard Zimmermann traces the ideas that gave rise to the *laesio enormis* in the ius commune precisely to the passage quoted above.[23]

The idea, then, is that corrective justice determines, inter alia, how much persons should receive in transactions, an amount which will sometimes not equate with what it is for which the parties actually contracted. Now, it does not matter whether corrective justice has exactly this consequence, the crucial point is rather that this takes us well outside the view that corrective justice is informative only about correcting injustices. Aristotle holds that corrective justice tells us how transactions ought to proceed:

> The just in transactions . . . though it is a sort of equality (and the unjust a sort of inequality), accords with numerical proportion, not with the [geometrical] proportion of the other species[24]

22 Aristotle, *Nicomachean Ethics*, above n 14, 74 [1132b] (the addition is the translator's).
23 Zimmerman, above n 1, 266. Note that, against Finnis' claim that Aquinas' allegiance to Aristotle's account of corrective justice was fake (see n 12 above), Aquinas was likely to have interpreted Aristotle's account in the light of this passage, as it reflects important aspects of Aquinas' own view. Aquinas, above n 12, SS Q77 A1.
24 Aristotle, *Nicomachean Ethics*, above n 14, 1132a (translator's addition).

and not merely how transactions that have not proceeded in the way they should have done should be remedied. Accordingly, corrective justice is not merely about correcting injustices, but also about defining justice and injustice in transactions between individuals. In the language used here, we would say that rectification is a part of corrective justice, but not the whole.

'Corrective justice', then, is a proper name for the area of morality that deals with interactions between individuals. It is not a description thereof, and, like other proper names, has no semantic content.

The second thing to notice about Aristotle's formulation of corrective justice is that, although Aristotle defines corrective justice as dealing with 'transactions', this does not imply that corrective justice is relevant only to contracts or agreements more generally. In fact, Aristotle's central case involves situations that we would regard as tortious rather than contractual: trespass to property and to the person, in the language of common law. Thirdly, the kind of rectification ordered by corrective justice is not restricted to the recovery of pecuniary loss. A person who is physically wounded does not suffer only pecuniary loss, but corrective justice nevertheless implies that the person is entitled to complete rectification.

Fourthly, the nature of the equality suggested by Aristotle is problematic. This is because wrongdoers may inflict harm without benefiting or may enjoy a gain without inflicting loss. An example of the former is one who batters another, causing bodily injury. With respect to this case, Aristotle admits this difficulty, claiming that

> in such cases, stating it without qualification, we speak of profit for the attacker who wounded his victim, for instance, even if that is not the proper word for some cases; and we speak of loss for the victim who suffers the wound.[25]

This position can succeed only if it is possible to explain how a wrongdoer who makes no factual gain has made a 'profit'. We do not need to explore that issue here, but we must also notice that there is another related problem: that of the victim who was wronged but suffered no factual loss. An example of this is an owner of land whose land is used by another without permission but without causing damage to that land. If it is possible to show how a wrongdoer who makes no factual gain makes a 'profit', then it may also be possible to show how a victim who suffers no factual detriment suffers a 'loss'. This point is developed by the theorists discussed below.[26]

It is clear that, on Aristotle's understanding, the law of tort is governed by corrective justice. But where does punishment, or criminal law, fit on this view? If distributive and corrective justice are the two forms of justice, and if punishment is rightly inflicted only if it is just to do so, then

[25] *Ibid.*

[26] For a modern solution to this problem, see EJ Weinrib, *The Idea of Private Law* (Cambridge, MA, Harvard University Press, 1995), 76–80.

punishment must belong to one or both forms of justice. Accordingly, the question is whether punishment is a matter of achieving equilibrium in the distribution of benefits and burdens throughout society as a whole, is concerned with rectifying wrongs that one individual has committed against another, or is both. Aristotle gives no clear answer to this question.

The closest Aristotle comes to defining punishment is the following passage from the *Rhetoric*, which distinguishes punishment from revenge.

> Revenge and punishment are different things. Punishment is inflicted for the sake of the person punished; revenge for that of the punisher, to satisfy his feelings.[27]

This claim is difficult to interpret, because it is not clear what it means to say that punishment is for the sake of the person punished. Does this mean, as Plato contended,[28] that all just punishment aims at improving the character of the person punished for that person's benefit or does it mean merely that the justification for punishment refers solely to the person punished and not also to the victim? Key for us, however, is that both interpretations focus on the wrongdoer alone, and that seems to imply that punishment belongs neither to distributive nor to corrective justice. If punishment is justly inflicted 'for the sake of the person punished', then it is neither geometrical nor arithmetical. It neither distributes throughout the community as a whole nor concerns transactions between individuals.

Moreover, Aristotle appears to hold the view that punishment is rightly inflicted as a response to wrongdoing. He defines wrongdoing as 'injury voluntarily inflicted contrary to law',[29] and then divides wrongdoing into two kinds.

> The actions that we ought to do or not to do have also been divided into two classes as affecting either the whole community or some one of its members. From this point of view we can perform just or unjust acts in either of two ways—towards one definite person, or towards the community. The man who is guilty of adultery or assault is doing wrong to some definite person; the man who avoids service in the army is doing wrong to the community.[30]

Apparently, both kinds of wrongdoing merit punishment.

Though Aristotle does not explicitly say so, it appears that the distinction between the two kinds of wrongdoing reflects that between distributive and corrective justice. Wrongs against the whole community are wrongs in the eyes of distributive justice and punishment as a response to those wrongs is justified by distributive justice. On the other hand,

[27] Aristotle, 'Rhetoric' in J Barnes (ed), *Aristotle: The Complete Works* (Princeton, NJ, Princeton University Press, 1984), 2152, 1369.

[28] See, eg Plato, 'Gorgias' in *Gorgias and Phaedrus*, JH Nichols, trans (Ithaca, NY, Cornell University Press, 1998), 1, 468e–473e.

[29] Aristotle, 'Rhetoric', above n 27, 2152, 1368b.

[30] *Ibid*, 1373b.

wrongs against individuals are wrongs in the eyes of corrective justice and are remedied by the application of that form of justice.

However, this does not help us understand how punishment fits Aristotle's account of justice. To begin with distributive justice, if person A wrongs the community and that is a wrong because it upsets distributive justice, then distributive justice calls for a redistribution, but it is hard to see how it demands punishment. Although punishment does distribute 'honors or wealth or anything else that can be divided among members of a community',[31] it is odd to claim that redistribution of such is the point of punishment. For instance, it is hard to see how imprisonment could be justified on this account. Turning now to corrective justice, if person A wrongs person B and must rectify that wrong in accordance with the demands of corrective justice, then what role could punishment play? If, in this context, punishment is the same as rectification, then Aristotle would have no separate theory of punishment—'punishment' and 'rectification' would be synonymous. Conversely, if punishment is not the same as rectification here, then it cannot be justified by corrective justice. Hence, defining this kind of wrongdoing in terms of corrective justice does not help us understand the role and justification of punishment.

This difficulty can also be seen in Aristotle's claim that punishment aims to 'cure' the act of wrongdoing to which it responds.[32] This seems to make sense only if punishment is equated with rectification. Though some think it controversial,[33] it is plausible to suggest that compensating another for an injury cures that injury in an appropriate sense, but it is quite something else to suggest that, to take Aristotle's example, spending time in prison cures draft dodging. It is not even apparent what this could mean. In fact, as this discussion suggests, Aristotle uses 'punishment' to refer to any response that the law makes to wrongdoing, whether that response be (what we would call) punitive or rectificatory. He is, therefore, speaking of sanction rather than of punishment.[34] Hence, his theory is unable properly to distinguish punishment from rectification.

In light of the above, we can see that there are two central problems with Aristotle's account. The first is that it has no place for retributive justice. Instead, Aristotle tries to squeeze punishment into the categories of distributive and corrective justice. In order to explain punishment, however, we need an account of retributive justice as distinct from distributive and corrective justice. This is not necessarily to say that we must

31 Aristotle, *Nicomachean Ethics*, above n 14, 1130b–1131a.

32 Aristotle, 'Rhetoric', above n 27, 2152, 1374b.

33 See, eg J Gardner, 'The Purity and Priority of Private Law' (1996) 46 *University of Toronto Law Journal* 459, 473–4.

34 The *Oxford English Dictionary* defines 'sanction' inter alia as 'A consideration which operates to enforce obedience to any law or rule of conduct'. This would include purely compensatory damages.

understand retributive justice as a third form of justice. It may be that retributive justice is a subset or adjunct of distributive or corrective justice, but it nevertheless possesses a structure that makes it distinct from distributive or corrective justice as described by Aristotle.

The second problem with Aristotle's account is that it inappropriately distinguishes between two types of wrongdoing. Though Aristotle is right to note that a wrong can be committed against an individual or against a community, he is wrong to suggest that one act can correspond only to one type of wrongdoing. Aristotle himself provides a paradigm example of an act that is wrong in both senses: a battery. As Aristotle suggests, a battery wrongs the victim, but there is no need to accept his assertion that it wrongs only the victim. Today, we are quite used to the idea that a battery is both a wrong to the victim and a wrong to the community at large. With these points in mind, we now turn to the legal theory of Aristotle's foremost successor: Thomas Aquinas.

B Aquinas

Aquinas' legal theory is based on Aristotle's distinction between corrective and distributive justice, and he presents no theory of retributive justice.[35] Like Aristotle, Aquinas defines corrective justice as arising in 'the mutual dealings between two persons',[36] but again this is not intended to refer only to contract but includes what we would call tort.[37]

It is clearer in Aquinas than in Aristotle that corrective justice is not merely about correcting injustices. This can be seen in Aquinas' definition of corrective and distributive justice:

> justice is directed to the private individual, who is compared to the community as a part to the whole. Now a twofold order may be considered in relation to a part. In the first place there is the order of one part to another, to which corresponds the order of one private individual to another. This order is directed by [corrective] justice, which is concerned about the mutual dealings between two persons. In the second place there is the order of the whole towards the parts, to which corresponds the order of that which belongs to the community in relation to each single person. This order is directed by distributive justice, which distributes common goods proportionately.[38]

Corrective justice is concerned with 'the order' that regulates the interaction of one individual with another. It determines what is just and unjust within that sphere, and how to respond to injustices when they occur.

35 See especially Aquinas, above n 12, SS Q61.
36 *Ibid*, SS Q61 A1.
37 See, eg *ibid*, SS Q61 A3.
38 *Ibid*, SS Q61 A1.

Hence, for Aquinas, one acts in accordance with corrective justice when one performs a just contract; one does not merely not bring corrective justice into play by not violating a contract.[39] This is also why Aquinas discusses corrective justice and restitution, a synonym for rectification, separately. Restitution is that aspect of corrective justice that deals with correcting injustices, but corrective justice is also involved with defining the kinds of injustices that call for restitution.[40] Accordingly, 'corrective justice' refers to that area of morality that determines how individuals should behave with respect to each other as individuals, 'distributive justice' to that area that determines how individuals should be treated within society as a whole.

Aquinas defines restitution as follows:

> To restore is seemingly the same as to reinstate a person in the possession or dominion of his thing, so that in restitution we consider the equality of justice attending the payment of one thing for another, and this belongs to [corrective] justice. Hence restitution is an act of [corrective] justice, occasioned by one person having what belongs to another, either with his consent, for instance on loan or deposit, or against his will, as in robbery or theft.[41]

Again, like Aristotle, Aquinas does not restrict restitution to the recovery of pecuniary loss. Restitution is an appropriate response to murder and bodily injury, for instance.[42]

The inclusion of robbery and theft within his discussion of corrective justice indicates that Aquinas thought that these forms of wrongdoing were appropriately dealt with by corrective justice and hence, as Aquinas thought they deserved punishment, that punishment belongs to corrective justice.[43] As we have seen, this position is problematic because it is hard to see how punishing the wrongdoer cures the wrong committed against the victim.

Aquinas did not deal with this problem, but he did respond to a related difficulty: squaring Aristotle's account of corrective justice with certain difficult passages in the Bible. At least on their faces, corrective justice and restoration call for an equivalence between the amount that the victim lost and the amount that the wrongdoer must pay. Aquinas expresses this by answering 'Yes' to the question: 'Does it suffice to restore the exact amount taken?'[44] However, Aquinas also notes that Exodus 22:1 states that

39 *Ibid*, SS Q61 A2.
40 See also *ibid*, SS QQ64–6.
41 *Ibid*, SS Q62 A1.
42 *Ibid*, SS Q64–5.
43 See also *ibid*, SS Q65.
44 *Ibid*, SS Q62 A3.

> If a man shall steal an ox or a sheep and kill or sell it, he shall restore five oxen for one ox, and four sheep for one sheep

and Luke 19:8 that 'If I have wronged any man of any thing, I restore him fourfold'.[45]

Aquinas' response to this problem does not refer explicitly to corrective or distributive justice, but instead *covertly* introduces the *idea* of retributive justice.

> Restitution re-establishes equality where an unjust taking has caused inequality. Now equality is restored by repaying the exact amount taken. Therefore there is no obligation to restore more than the exact amount taken . . .
>
> When a man takes another's thing unjustly, two things must be considered. One is the inequality on the part of the thing . . . The other is the sin of injustice, which is consistent with equality on the part of the thing, as when a person intends to use violence but fails.[46]

Like Aristotle, Aquinas identifies two kinds of wrongdoing. Unlike Aristotle, Aquinas holds that a single action can commit both kinds. Moreover, Aquinas defines the kinds differently. One is committed specifically against the victim and is remedied by corrective justice when the wrongdoer restores the victim to the position that the victim would have been in had he not been wronged.

> As regards the first, the remedy is applied by making restitution, since thereby equality is re-established; and for this it is enough that a man restore just so much as he has belonging to another.[47]

However, the wrongdoer also commits 'the sin of injustice', which must be responded to differently: 'as regards the sin, the remedy is applied by punishment, the infliction of which belongs to the judge'.[48]

For Aquinas, then, these wrongs are quite different in character. Because the one committed against the victim is a wrong in the eyes of corrective justice, the obligation to remedy it arises as soon as the wrongdoing occurs. That is, corrective justice itself generates the obligation to rectify the wrong and no judicial pronouncement is required for that obligation to come into existence.[49] Conversely, the authorisation to inflict punishment in response to the 'sin of injustice' arises only when a court says so:

> until a man is condemned by the judge, he is not bound to restore more than he took, but when once he is condemned, he is bound to pay the penalty.[50]

45 *Ibid.*
46 *Ibid.*
47 *Ibid.*
48 *Ibid.*
49 This is consistent with the ideas that the positive legal obligation to rectify comes into existence only upon judicial pronouncement and that judicial pronouncement gives the wrongdoer an additional obligation to rectify.
50 Aquinas, above n 12, SS Q62 A3.

What is this second wrong, this 'sin of injustice'? In the eyes of what kind of justice is the sin a sin? Aquinas' answer to these questions is contained in his earlier discussion of sin, where he claims that

> man can be punished with a threefold punishment corresponding to the three orders to which the human will is subject. In the first place a man's nature is subjected to the order of his own reason; secondly, it is subjected to the order of another man who governs him either in spiritual or in temporal matters, as a member either of the state or of the household; thirdly, it is subjected to the universal order of the Divine government. Now each of these orders is disturbed by sin, for the sinner acts against his reason, and against human and Divine law. Wherefore he incurs a threefold punishment; one, inflicted by himself, viz. remorse of conscience; another, inflicted by man; and a third, inflicted by God.[51]

On this view, the relevant punishment is warranted because the wrongdoer violated human law.

That can be only a partial justification for punishment, however, because it does not explain the point of punishment. That issue is never addressed systematically, but Aquinas' discussion of particular categories of wrongdoing contains some suggestions. For instance, Aquinas justifies capital punishment as a response to murder on the ground that

> if a man be dangerous and infectious to the community, on account of some sin, it is praiseworthy and advantageous that he be killed in order to safeguard the common good.[52]

Similarly, punishing those who cause physical injury to others is justified because,

> as the whole of man is directed as to his end to the whole of the community of which he is a part . . . it may happen that although the removal of a member may be detrimental to the whole body, it may nevertheless be directed to the good of the community, in so far as it is applied to a person as a punishment for the purpose of restraining sin. Hence just as by public authority a person is lawfully deprived of life altogether on account of certain more heinous sins, so is he deprived of a member on account of certain lesser sins.[53]

As indicated above, Aquinas' account of punishment is found in his discussion of restoration and corrective justice. Moreover, his analysis of murder and battery and the appropriateness of punishment as a response thereto occurs under the heading: 'Vices Opposed to Corrective Justice'. Despite this, however, the above analysis has revealed two main reasons why punishment cannot belong to corrective justice on Aquinas' view.

51 *Ibid*, FS Q87 A1.
52 *Ibid*, SS Q64 A2.
53 *Ibid*, SS Q65 A1.

First, Aquinas holds that restitution calls for the wrongdoer to return what he has taken and no more: 'for this it is enough that a man restore just so much as he has belonging to another'.[54] Hence, the need for restitution cannot justify punishment. Given, then, that restitution is the part of corrective justice that responds to the commission of injustice, punishment cannot be warranted by corrective justice.

Secondly, Aquinas holds that an obligation to restore comes into existence as soon as an act of wrongdoing has been committed, because corrective justice is a form of justice and so independent of the positive law. Hence, the wrongdoer would be obliged to restore even in the state of nature. On the other hand, the authorisation to inflict punishment exists only when a judge brings it into existence. Accordingly, there can be no obligations to pay fines, for example, in the state of nature. Those obligations depend on the pronouncements of judges in accordance with human law. For this reason, Aquinas insists that private individuals have no right to exact punishment, even if they obtain the consent of the wrongdoer.[55] With respect to capital punishment, this is because

> the care of the common good is entrusted to persons of rank having public authority: wherefore they alone, and not private individuals, can lawfully put evildoers to death.[56]

Here, then, the relevant wrong was not against a private individual, but against the community as a whole because it violated human law, and the response must be meted out by a representative of that community. Were the individual victim (of the different wrong) to attempt to exact punishment, then he would commit another wrong. In effect, the killing of a murderer with the murderer's consent would be an act of (illegal[57]) assisted suicide rather than one of capital punishment.

This reveals that, despite Aquinas' claims and categorisations, punishment for him does not belong to corrective justice. Corrective justice is defined as existing as between two individuals, but punishment essentially involves the community. It may be the case that punishment is based on a kind of justice that mirrors corrective justice very closely but where the justice exists as between the community and an individual, but that is another matter. Clearly, then, though one could not say that Aquinas presents an account of retributive justice, because he does not adequately distinguish punishment from corrective justice, we are seeing the emergence of notions of retributive justice in Aquinas' writings.

[54] *Ibid*, SS Q62 A3.
[55] *Ibid*, SS Q64 A3, Q65 A1.
[56] *Ibid*, SS Q64 A1.
[57] *Ibid*, SS Q64.

C Grotius

Unfortunately, Grotius' account of justice is confusing and confuses the views of his predecessors. First, he claims that Aristotle held that corrective justice applies only to contracts and criticises Aristotle on the ground that that definition is too narrow as it does not include tortious actions such as the taking of property.[58] As we have seen, this criticism of Aristotle is misplaced. Furthermore, Grotius identifies corrective justice with his preferred term 'expletive justice' and distributive justice with his preferred 'attributive justice', but he then goes on to define expletive justice as the kind of justice that can be legally enforced and attributive justice as extra-legal justice.[59] This would be fine if Grotius also felt that only corrective justice could be legally enforced, but, as we see below, that is not the case. And finally, though Grotius purports to replace 'corrective justice' and 'distributive justice' with 'expletive justice' and 'attributive justice' respectively, he continues to speak of corrective justice as something distinct from expletive justice. It is perhaps not coincidental that corrective justice and expletive justice part company in Grotius' exploration of punishment.

However, despite these difficulties, some things are clear. First, expletive justice is not concerned merely with correcting injustices but also with defining the nature of justice and injustice. According to Grotius, this is done by enunciating a set of rights that owe their origin to expletive justice.[60] Therefore, although the connection between expletive and corrective justice is obscure in Grotius, it seems safe to say that Grotius' version of corrective justice also defines a person's rights and does not merely dictate how to respond to the violation thereof. Secondly, we can also be sure that, for Grotius, corrective justice is not restricted to contract but includes tort. Moreover, it is plain that corrective justice is not restricted to the recovery of pecuniary loss. Grotius maintains that corrective justice demands that one 'make good' damage caused by one's fault, and defines damage as any interference with another's right.[61] This allows Grotius to maintain that one is able to recover for violations of one's rights to life, the body, limbs, reputation, honour and acts of will.[62] Hence, Grotius maintains that striking another calls not only for compensation for the physical injury inflicted, but also for the injury to the victim's honour, and he insists that compensation can appropriately be in money.[63]

58 Grotius, above n 12, I i 8.
59 *Ibid.*
60 *Ibid*, II xvii 2.
61 *Ibid*, II xvii 1–2.
62 *Ibid*, II xvii 2i.
63 *Ibid*, II xvii 22.

Also important is Grotius', at first obscure, claim that one who takes another's property is 'bound to restore the thing taken together with its *natural increase*, and make good the resulting loss or failure to secure gain'.[64] It is not immediately apparent what 'natural increase' refers to, but this is elucidated in Grotius' discussion of property. Briefly, the position is that the taker of someone else's property must surrender to the rightful owner any profits made with that property, though certain exceptions to this principle exist.[65] For Grotius, this is an ordinary consequence of corrective justice.

> The reason for this obligation [to disgorge the profits] arises from ownership. For the person who is the owner of a thing is likewise naturally the owner of the income derived from it.[66]

Accordingly,

> if you have been made richer through possession of my property, while I did not have possession of it, you are under obligation to the extent that you have been enriched. The reason is that in the degree that you have been enriched from my property you have more while I have less.[67]

Because you are in possession of the profits made with my property and because those profits rightly belong to me as the owner of that property, you have more than you should have with respect to me and I have less than I should have with respect to you. Hence, corrective justice demands that those profits be surrendered by you to me. We return to these themes below.[68]

Like Aquinas, Grotius accepts that an action can be a wrong in two different senses, one wrong calling for rectification and the other for punishment.[69] However, Grotius more clearly brings out the distinction between these two categories. This can be seen most prominently in that Aquinas discusses punishment while exploring corrective justice, while Grotius examines rectification and punishment in two separate chapters, XVII and XX, of Book II of *The Law of War and Peace*.

Moreover, Grotius claims that rectification is justified by corrective justice and so the obligation to rectify exists even in the state of nature.[70] Hence, the point of rectification is to cure a wrong that lies between two individuals. On the other hand, Grotius holds that punishment is justified because it rehabilitates the offender[71] and protects from further harm the

64 *Ibid*, II xvii 16 (emphasis added).
65 *Ibid*, II x 2–9.
66 *Ibid*, II x 4.
67 *Ibid*, II x 2.
68 Note that my rights to the profits are primary, not secondary, rights. Again, this shows that corrective justice is not merely concerned with correcting injustices.
69 Grotius, above n 12, II xx 1.
70 *Ibid*, II xvii 1.
71 *Ibid*, II xx 7 ii.

victim[72] and society generally.[73] Hence, unlike rectification, punishment is an entirely social institution.

Again, however, we cannot say that Grotius presents a theory of retributive justice. For Grotius, punishment belongs to expletive justice,[74] which is hardly surprising given that punishment can be, and must be able to be, legally enforced. However, despite Grotius' identification of expletive justice with corrective justice, he insists that punishment is not a form of corrective justice. He notes that persons are inclined (as they are today) to say that punishment is *owed*, and hence punishment may appear to belong to corrective justice, but responds that

> This is plainly 'misleading'. For he to whom something is properly owed has a right against another. But when we say that punishment is due to some person we mean nothing more than that it is proper for him to be punished.[75]

Pufendorf makes this point more clearly.

> Some of those who refer penalties to [corrective] justice, take the view of the matter that a penalty is meted out to a criminal in the manner usual in contracts [ie in accordance with corrective justice]. They have been led to this error through the habit which we have of saying that a 'punishment is owed him who offends', which, however, is an *ἄκυρος* [improper] way of speaking. For he to whom something is owed in the strict sense has a right over the debtor whereby he can require of the other his due. But who would say that a criminal has the right to demand that the magistrate inflict a punishment upon him? Therefore, the real meaning of the expression is that the magistrate can properly require of a guilty person the penalty defined in the laws.[76]

If A injures B in the eyes of corrective justice, then A gains an obligation to compensate B for B's injury. This obligation is identical to a right in B to demand the compensation from A. Hence, B is owed and A owes compensation, as B has a right against A to that compensation. However, when we say that an offender is owed punishment, we do not mean that the offender has a right against someone to be punished. Importantly, the point here is not really about the use of the verb 'to owe', but rather to reveal an asymmetry between corrective justice and the justification for punishment. Corrective justice brings into existence a bilateral and bidirectional relationship: the wrongdoer owes the victim and the victim is owed by the wrongdoer. But the justice relevant to punishment—for which Grotius has no name other than the unhelpful 'expletive justice'—brings into existence a bilateral but unidirectional relationship. The community has a warrant to punish the offender, but the offender gains no rights or duties against the

[72] *Ibid*, II xx 8.
[73] *Ibid*, II xx 9.
[74] *Ibid*, II xx 2.
[75] *Ibid*, II xx 2 ii.
[76] Pufendorf, above n 12, VIII III 5.

community. Hence, because punishment involves an individual and the community and because it involves uni- rather than bidirectional norms, the justification for punishment cannot be corrective justice.

Grotius further explores the ways in which the justification for punishment resembles corrective justice,[77] but nowhere does he provide an account of that justification. A discussion of this topic must wait for Pufendorf.

D Pufendorf

Pufendorf's account also begins with Aristotle's distinction between corrective and distributive justice.[78] Strangely, however, he at first appears to define corrective justice solely in terms of contract.[79] But that definition must be only provisional, because Pufendorf later recognises that Aristotle's account of corrective justice encompasses tortious actions and Pufendorf endorses that view.[80] Also, Pufendorf holds that corrective justice is a complete normative order that exists as between individuals, not merely a method of correcting injustices defined independently. Hence, the just performance of a contract is an instance of corrective justice.[81] Like Grotius, Pufendorf identifies wrongdoing in the eyes of corrective justice as the violation of a right in another determined in accordance with corrective justice, and infers that wrongfully caused personal injury demands compensation for physical damage, pain and suffering, cure, cessation from work and the disgrace occasioned by the injury.[82] Clearly, then, corrective justice is not restricted to the recovery of pecuniary loss. Moreover, like Grotius, Pufendorf maintains that one who takes another's property wrongly must surrender the 'natural increment' gained from the property.[83] Again, the meaning of this is made clear in the discussion of property and it is a simple consequence of corrective justice:

> [A] thing, dominion over which I have lost neither by my consent nor by my misdeed or right of war, still belongs to me, as does also whatever comes of it. Therefore, when it has fallen into the hands of another, and he has profited by its consumption . . . he can on no excuse retain the profit which he has made, when I demand it, since that is a part, as it were, or the fruit still remaining, of a thing that belongs to me.[84]

77 Grotius, above n 12, II xx 2 iii–iv.
78 Pufendorf, above n 12, I vii.
79 *Ibid*, I vii 10.
80 *Ibid*, I vii 12.
81 *Ibid*, I vii 10.
82 *Ibid*, III i 8.
83 *Ibid*, III i 11.
84 *Ibid*, IV xiii 6.

The fruits of an asset belong to the owner of that asset. Hence, if they are possessed by another without the owner's consent, then that other has more than he should have vis-à-vis the owner and the owner has less than he should have vis-à-vis the possessor. Therefore, corrective justice demands that the profits be surrendered by the possessor to the owner.

Like those before him, Pufendorf accepts that a single action can be wrong in two different senses. The first involves wrongdoing specifically to an individual. That is a wrong in the eyes of corrective justice and calls for rectification.[85] Because the wrong violates corrective justice, the obligation to correct that wrong belongs to the law of nature and would exist in the state of nature.[86] However, the second wrong is a wrong to society in general; it calls for a penalty to be imposed and that penalty can be imposed rightly only on the authority of an appropriate public body, such as a court.[87] Accordingly, like Aquinas, Pufendorf concludes that punishment must be exacted by a representative of the state. If an individual attempts to punish another, that is simply an act of war.[88]

Unlike his predecessors, however, Pufendorf accounts for the justice of punishment. First, he rejects the idea that punishment is based either on corrective or distributive justice, and infers that

> nothing remains for us but to conclude that punishments belong to neither species of justice, but fall under a branch of justice peculiar to itself.[89]

This must refer to what Pufendorf earlier calls 'vindictive justice', or what we prefer to call 'retributive justice'.[90] As will be clear from the discussion above, this form of justice exists as between an individual and the community at large.

Like corrective justice, retributive justice is bilateral in that it operates as between two entities, but unlike corrective justice these entities are not two individuals but one individual and the community as a whole. Like distributive justice, retributive justice involves the whole community, but while distributive justice treats all the members of the community together, retributive justice singles out one individual and does justice to him as between himself and the community. Hence, though retributive justice shares similarities with both corrective and distributive justice, it has a structure of its own and is independent of the others.

85 *Ibid*, VIII iii 5.
86 *Ibid*, III i 1.
87 *Ibid*, VIII iii 2, 4–5.
88 *Ibid*, VIII iii 2–3.
89 *Ibid*, VIII iii 5.
90 *Ibid*, I vii 10.

E Consequences of the Civilian Model

We have seen the development of the following position. There are two kinds of wrongs: one committed against an individual as an individual, the other against society as a whole. The first wrong is defined in accordance with corrective justice. This form of justice determines the rights that we hold against each other as individuals. Violations of these rights are appropriately remedied by requiring the wrongdoer to rectify his wrong, standardly by compensating the victim. This is also done in accordance with corrective justice, and corrective justice is itself the point of the remedy. Moreover, corrective justice is not limited to contract, to the recovery of pecuniary loss or even to compensation, but can include disgorgement of profits. On the other hand, the second wrong—the wrong to society as a whole—is defined in accordance with distributive justice and is appropriately remedied by punishing the wrongdoer, a response that involves retributive justice. This serves various functions, most importantly including protection of the community as a whole.

It would not, I think, be right to regard retributive justice as a third form of justice on this model. Rather, it is better to think of it as the justice that relates to the enforcement of those rules designed to achieve distributive justice, and hence as a product of distributive justice. It may help to imagine the following picture. Take, for example, taxation legislation. We might describe this as consisting of first- and second-order rules. The first-order rules determine how much tax individuals have to pay. These rules are determined in accordance with distributive justice. The second-order rules deal with those who violate the first-order rules. Ultimately, these rules are designed to preserve and protect the distributive justice at which the first-order rules aim. One way in which they might do so is by deterring persons from violating the first-order rules. On this view, this deterrence is justified by distributive justice; however, the rules that deter have not the structure of distributive justice but, rather, that of retributive justice. The rules aim directly at deterrence, not at distributing benefits and burdens appropriately. In other words, if one were to ask 'Why is this offender being punished?', the answer would be 'Because the offender violated the rules'. This refers to retributive justice rather than to distributive justice. However, if one were to ask 'Why are offenders, in general, punished?', the answer would be 'Because doing so is ultimately socially beneficial'. This refers to distributive justice. Hence, although the structure of retributive justice and distributive justice differ, retributive justice is ultimately part of distributive justice, because the point of retributive justice is the overall achievement of distributive justice. Crucially, though, retributive justice is quite distinct from corrective justice.

Though none of the figures discussed explore this point explicitly, they conclude that, as corrective and retributive justice are quite different and possess distinct structures, they should not be combined in one area of the law. Moreover, as the wrongdoing to which these kinds of justice respond is different, different areas of the law should deal with them. The first wrong is committed against a particular person who must be recompensed in accordance with corrective justice. This requires a legal procedure that allows the victim to establish a case against the wrongdoer to gain rectification. The second wrong is committed against the society as a whole (including, perhaps, an individual victim) and the perpetrator must be punished in line with retributive justice. This calls for a legal procedure in which a representative of the community establishes a case against the wrongdoer in order to have that person punished. It would be illogical to combine these actions, because the structures of corrective and retributive justice are so different. There are times when corrective justice calls for correction but retributive justice does not call for retribution and others when retributive justice calls for retribution but corrective justice does not call for correction. Combining corrective and retributive justice in one cause of action, then, necessarily leads to incoherence.[91] Moreover, combining the actions would confuse the role of the person who opposes the wrongdoer. The community has no place attempting to gain 'recompense' from the wrongdoer for the wrong against an individual victim and the individual victim has no place attempting to punish the wrongdoer. That, as Pufendorf notes, would be an act of war.

In conclusion, civilian lawyers came to believe that punishment had no role to play in private law, in part because they adopted the view that private law possesses a normative structure—corrective justice—that allows no room for punishment. Rather, punishment belongs to retributive justice and so must be exacted by an area of the law that can deal with retributive justice in a coherent fashion. That became criminal law. Despite suggestions to the contrary,[92] this is no mere dogmatism but a reflection of an extremely well thought out account of justice and law. With that in mind, it is time to turn to common law.

IV THE COMMON LAW MODEL

The relationship between abstract theory and legal scholarship is much looser in common than in civil law. Because of this, I begin by examining changes in the way that legal scholars have viewed the law of tort, before locating one of the reasons for this change in the ideas of leading English-speaking moral and political theorists.

91 I have analysed this incoherence in A Beever, 'The Structure of Aggravated and Exemplary Damages' (2003) 23 *OJLS* 87, 105–10.

92 See, eg Behr, above n 5, 106.

A The Legal Scholars

Perhaps surprisingly, the civilian model also played an important role in the development of common law and helped to produce the separation of tort and criminal law. The model was adopted by some of the most prominent common law commentators. For instance, Coke distinguished criminal from private law by remarking that, unlike the latter, the former

> concerneth the safety of his majestie, the quiet of the common-wealth, and the life, honour, fame, liberty, blood, wife, and posteritie of the party accused besides the forfeiture of his lands, goods, and all that he hath.[93]

In other words, unlike private law, the commands of criminal law are instituted in accordance with the interests of society as a whole (distributive justice) and the response to the violation of those rules is punishment (retributive justice). Similarly, Hale defines private law in terms of rights persons possess in and of themselves or in respect to things and defines these rights before turning to discuss the state.[94] Hence, those rights could only be ones of corrective justice.

Perhaps the clearest example of the influence of the civilian model, however, is seen in Blackstone.

> Wrongs are divisible into two sorts of species: *private wrongs* and *public wrongs*. The former are an infringement or privation of civil rights belonging to individuals considered as individuals; and are thereupon frequently termed *civil injuries*: the latter are a breach and violation of public rights and duties, which affect the whole community, considered as a community; and are distinguished by the harsher appellation of *crimes* and *misdemeanours*.[95]

This adopts the distinction between corrective justice on the one hand and distributive and retributive justice on the other, and defines tort law in terms of the former and criminal law in terms of the latter.

However, although traces of this view can still be found in mainstream analyses of the law, it has largely disappeared. This can be seen in PH Winfield's attempt to define the difference between tort law and criminal law. According to Winfield, the two areas of law are distinguished by the fact that they deliver different sanctions: punishment for a crime, damages for a tort.[96] This immediately raises the problem of the availability of exemplary or punitive damages in tort, but Winfield attempts to avoid this problem by defining punishment as that 'which, when once liability to it

93 E Coke, *The Institutes of the Laws of England* (London, W Clarke, 1817), Part III intro para 2.

94 M Hale, *The History of the Common Law of England; and, an Analysis of the Civil Part of the Law* (London, Henry Butterworth, 1820), II §1.

95 W Blackstone, *Commentaries on the Laws of England* (New York, Garland, 1978), III i.

96 PH Winfield, *The Province of the Law of Tort* (Cambridge, Cambridge University Press, 1931), 201.

has been decreed, is not avoidable by any act of the party offending'.[97] This distinguishes 'punishment' from exemplary damages, because the victim can decline to insist on receiving the latter in response to some action of the wrongdoer, but cannot rescue the defendant from 'punishment' once decreed by a court. This definition of 'punishment' is obviously strategic. It is no part of our ordinary understanding of punishment, but is rather designed to exclude exemplary damages from the definition simply in order to avoid the problem encountered above. As such, it could not possibly reveal anything substantive about the distinction between tort and crime. Moreover, while the fact that the victim has more power in tort than in criminal law may point to an important difference between those laws, Winfield does nothing to reveal it. Finally, even putting the problem of exemplary damages aside, the mere observation that tort law deals out damages while criminal law responds with 'punishment' tells us little of interest. What we need to know is why those areas of the law respond in that way.[98]

Interestingly, in developing his account, Winfield explores Blackstone's view and reproduces the passage from Blackstone quoted above.[99] However, while Winfield develops Blackstone's comments concerning punishment, he ignores the central feature of Blackstone's analysis: the notion that private law deals with 'civil rights belonging to individuals considered as individuals' while criminal law polices 'public rights and duties, which affect the whole community, considered as a community'. Apparently, Winfield had no use for these ideas. Why not?

The answer is that Winfield adopts what I call 'the common law conception of tort'.[100] There are two parts to this conception. The first part consists of a general principle, according to which persons are responsible for the injuries they cause others. The second part holds that the strict application of this principle would lead to overly extensive liability and so the principle must, for reasons of broad social and economic policy, be accompanied by a long list of exceptions. On Winfield's version of this conception, 'the law of tort is based upon a general principle that all harm to another person is presumptively unlawful'.[101] Against this, Winfield notices that not all acts that cause harm to others are actionable, but responds that

> To say that all unjustifiable harm is actionable is a totally different thing from saying that all harm is actionable.[102]

97 *Ibid*, 200.
98 See also WVH Rogers, *Winfield and Jolowicz on Tort* (London, Sweet & Maxwell, 16th edn, 2002), §§1.1, 1.4.
99 Winfield, above n 96, 193.
100 The relationship between this and the common law model is explored below. I argue that the conception follows from the model.
101 Winfield, above n 96, 36.
102 *Ibid*, 37.

In other words, if A harms B and does not have to compensate B, this must be because A's action was justified by something that warrants an exception being made to the general principle of liability.

I call this the common law conception of tort because it, or a near version of it, is shared by the vast majority of modern tort lawyers.[103] Tony Weir, for example, claims that

> All systems of law from the earliest times onwards seem to have afforded a person injured by someone else a claim to some reparation, subject to whatever conditions seemed appropriate in that society.[104]

Here again, the default rule is recovery for all injury, but this rule is subject to a list of exceptions.[105] It is also exemplified by the almost ubiquitous description of the various stages of the negligence enquiry—the duty of care, remoteness, etc—as 'control mechanisms' designed to cut back on liability for reasons of social and economic policy. Consider, for instance, Stephen Todd's analysis of the law of negligence:

> The duty requirement exists because the potential scope of negligence as a basis for legal liability is virtually unlimited. On its face, 'negligence' looks only to the quality of the defendant's conduct and not to factors such as the likely or possible number of plaintiffs, the likelihood that loss would be caused, the nature and extent of particular loss, and the circumstances in which the loss came to be inflicted. Thus the courts have had to devise principles to delimit the boundaries of liability. To this end, they have instituted a requirement in every case of foreseeability of damage to the person bringing the action, and have also taken account of these other factors in deciding whether, for reasons of policy, liability ought to be especially restricted or denied altogether. The language of duty provides the formula for expressing these conclusions of policy. It operates as a 'control device' or filter through which any particular claim must pass. It is apparent, then, that the function of the duty of care is not so much to identify cases where liability is imposed as to identify those where it is not.[106]

Many would accept this description.

We must now explore what this conception of the law means in terms of the accounts of justice explored above. For many common lawyers, the general principle of liability is understood as an instantiation of corrective justice. This position has prominently been taken by Lord Steyn[107] and echoed by WVH Rogers:

103 The notion of fault is sometimes added to the general principle.

104 T Weir, *Tort Law* (Oxford, Oxford University Press, 2002), 1.

105 The view is also clearly stated by Rogers, above n 98, §1.3.

106 S Todd, 'Negligence: The Duty of Care' in S Todd (ed), *The Law of Torts in New Zealand* (Wellington, Brookers, 3rd ed, 2001), 140, §4.1 (citation omitted), quotation from *Smith v Littlewoods Organisation Ltd* [1987] 1 AC 241, 280.

107 See especially *Macfarlane v Tayside Area Health Board* [2000] 2 AC 59, 82; *Rees v Darlington Memorial Hospital NHS Trust* [2003] UKHL 52, [2004] 1 AC 309, [4]; Lord Steyn, 'Perspectives of Corrective and Distributive Justice in Tort Law' (2002) 37 *Irish Jurist* 1, 1–7.

> [T]he law cannot even go so far as to order every person whose action may be regarded as 'faulty' to make redress to those who suffer by it: paradoxical as it may seem, the law of tort is as much about non-liability as it is about liability . . . Corrective justice (the principle that wrongs should be righted) points towards liability where a loss has been inflicted but the demands of distributive justice (the principle that there should be a fair allocation of assets and losses) also have to be taken into account.[108]

Allied to this view is the idea that corrective justice has no content without an account of harm, an account that corrective justice cannot provide. To put this another way, corrective justice tells us how to correct wrongs, but it does not inform us about wrongdoing itself. In Grotius' and Pufendorf's terms, corrective justice dictates how we should respond to rights violations, but cannot justify those rights. That can be achieved only by distributive justice.[109]

This view assumes that only distributive justice can provide accounts of harm, wrongdoing and rights. For instance, Weir maintains that underlying the whole of private law 'is an idea about how people in society should behave towards each other', clearly intending, in context, to refer to distributive justice.[110] Rogers maintains that tort liability 'is most generally concerned with the allocation or prevention of losses, which are bound to occur in our society'.[111] The 'allocation' of losses is a reference to distributive justice. And John Fleming defines the law of tort with respect to such elements of distributive justice as deterrence, loss spreading, insurance and economic efficiency.[112]

An excellent example of this view is found in the decision of the High Court of Australia in *Harriton v Stevens*.[113] In that case, the plaintiff's mother had contracted rubella when she was pregnant with the plaintiff. She was negligently informed that the disease posed no risk to her foetus. Had she correctly been informed that her foetus was at serious risk of deformity, she would have had the pregnancy terminated. As it was, however, her child, the plaintiff, was born with 'catastrophic disabilities', including blindness, deafness, mental retardation and spasticity.[114] The plaintiff claimed damages for 'wrongful life', that is, that she ought not to have been born. In doing so, counsel for the plaintiff argued that corrective justice demands that the plaintiff recover. In response, Crennan J replied:

108 Rogers, above n 98, §1.3 (citation omitted).
109 For a prominent example of this view, see P Cane, 'Distributive Justice and Tort Law' [2001] *New Zealand Law Review* 401.
110 Weir, above n 104, 1.
111 Rogers, above n 98, §1.2.
112 J Fleming, *The Law of Torts* (Sydney, LBC Information Services, 9th edn, 1998), 8–14.
113 [2006] HCA 15.
114 *Ibid*, [20].

> Aristotelian notions of 'corrective justice', *requiring somebody who has harmed another without justification to indemnify that other*, and 'distributive justice', requiring calculation of benefits and losses and burdens in society, were referred to by Lord Steyn in *McFarlane v Tayside Health Board*, for the purpose of explicating the dynamic interrelationship between differing values, which values need to be considered when faced with a novel claim in negligence . . . However, there remains a problem in Aristotle's analysis, relevant to this submission. In emphasising 'corrective justice', even as added to by his consideration of 'distributive justice', Aristotle left unexplored the dependence of 'correction' on the prior establishment of principles. As Finnis puts it, '"[c]orrection" and "restitution" are notions parasitic on some prior determination of what is to count as a crime, a tort, a binding agreement, etc'. The values of fairness, coherence, and the corporate welfare of the community or community expectations . . . are not considered singly, in isolation from each other or from relevant matters, particularly the doctrines and well-established principles determining what constitutes negligence.
>
> [Hence,] a need for 'corrective justice' alone could never be determinative of a novel claim in negligence.[115]

The 'corporate welfare of the community or community expectations' are references to distributive justice.

It is important to notice that all these views assimilate corrective justice to the common law conception of tort. That is, corrective justice is seen as identical to the general principle of liability. As Crennan J put it, corrective justice requires 'somebody who has harmed another without justification to indemnify that other'.[116] On this view, corrective justice is interpreted merely as the demand that wrongs be corrected. This view completely denudes corrective justice of the positive content it has according to the civilian theorists examined above, none of whom would have accepted that all physical injuries constitute damage in the eyes of corrective justice. This is most clear in Grotius and Pufendorf, who insist that a wrong in the eyes of corrective justice is a violation of a right.[117] For all of the thinkers, these rights are determined in accordance with corrective justice, which is, in part, a theory about the rights and obligations that persons owe to each other as persons. Thus, it is possible to conclude that corrective justice 'requires somebody [ie everybody] who has harmed another

115 *Ibid*, [274]–[275] (emphasis added, citations omitted). Quotation from Finnis, above n 12, 178–9.

116 *Harriton v Stevens* [2006] HCA 15 [274].

117 For discussion of this point in relation to the recovery of economic loss in negligence, see P Benson, 'The Basis for Excluding Liability for Economic Loss in Tort Law' in D Owen (ed), *Philosophical Foundations of Tort Law* (Oxford, Oxford University Press, 1995), 427; R Brown, 'Still Crazy After All These Years: *Anns, Cooper v Hobart* and Pure Economic Loss' (2003) 36 *University of British Columbia Law Review* 159; R Brown, 'Justifying the Impossibility of Recoverable Relational Economic Loss' (2004) 5 *Oxford University Commonwealth Law Journal* 155; A Beever, 'A Rights-based Approach to the Recovery of Economic Loss in Negligence' (2004) 4 *Oxford University Commonwealth Law Journal* 25.

without justification to indemnify the other'[118] only if we forget what 'corrective justice' meant to those who discovered it. Moreover, according to Grotius and Pufendorf, the reason that the plaintiff in *Harriton v Stevens* could not recover would have been because the plaintiff had no right not to have been born and the absence of that right would itself have been a consequence of corrective justice. Crennan J's comments concerning corrective justice demonstrate a failure to come to terms with the tradition to which corrective justice theory belongs.

At this point, it is crucial to notice that the common lawyer's conception of corrective justice and tort law exactly matches the civilian theorists' account of *criminal* law. According to that account, rules are put in place in accordance with distributive justice and, when those rules are violated, retributive justice comes into play to respond to the wrongdoing. According to most modern scholars of common law, the law of tort possesses precisely that structure, though they tend to call the second 'corrective', rather than 'retributive', justice.[119] Consider also the claim made by Peter Cane and others that tort law must be seen as an institution of distributive and corrective justice, where the former tells us what our rights are and the latter how violations of those rights should be dealt with.[120] Again, this precisely matches the civilian account of criminal law. It is hardly surprising, then, that common lawyers are more receptive to the idea that punishment has a role to play in private law than are civil lawyers.

Moreover, because the common law conception of tort maintains that tort and criminal law possess the same structure, theorists find it extremely difficult to provide a substantive distinction between the two areas of the law. That task has largely been abandoned. Instead, the modern trend is to attempt a functional, rather than substantive, distinction. That is what Winfield did by suggesting that the distinction lies in the fact that tort gives damages while criminal law 'punishes', and that view is echoed by Rogers,[121] Fleming[122] and Todd.[123] This leaves it quite unclear why the two areas of law should have different functions and leaves open the—from this perspective quite plausible—notion that the functions of the laws should not strongly be separated.

118 *McFarlane v Tayside Area Health Board* [2000] 2 AC 59, 82.

119 See, however, P Cane, 'Retribution, Proportionality, and Moral Luck in Tort Law' in P Cane and J Stapleton (eds), *The Law of Obligations: Essays in Celebration of John Fleming* (Oxford, Oxford University Press, 1998), 141.

120 Cane, above n 109. See also D Klimchuk, 'On the Autonomy of Corrective Justice' (2003) 23 *OJLS* 49; R Mullender, 'Corrective Justice, Distributive Justice, and the Law of Negligence' (2001) 17 *Professional Negligence* 35; SR Perry, 'On the Relationship Between Corrective and Distributive Justice: Fourth Series' in J Horder (ed), *Oxford Essays in Jurisprudence* (Oxford, Oxford University Press, 2000), 237.

121 Rogers, above n 98, §1.13.

122 Fleming, above n 112, 5.

123 Todd, above n 106, 140, 1.1.2.

None of the above should be seen as criticism of the common law conception of tort. Though I think it plain that the conception is inadequate on its face, it has not been my task to criticise it, merely to document it. I now turn to examine how we came to it; how our understanding of the law shifted from Blackstone to Winfield. One of the reasons was a shift in theoretical thought both exemplified by and caused by the thinkers examined below. I examine the adequacy of the common law conception of tort in the fifth section of this article.

B The Philosophers

It is one of the peculiarities of common law that, historically, many of its most famous philosophers of law have been uninterested in theorising about substantive law. For most, 'philosophy of law' is about ontology: defining the nature of law in the abstract rather than the nature of, say, the law of tort or contract. Accordingly, there are no equivalents of Aquinas, Grotius or Pufendorf in the common law tradition. Instead, for ideas about the nature of justice and law, one must turn to those normally regarded as political or moral, rather than legal, philosophers. I examine, Hobbes, Locke, Bentham and Sidgwick.

(i) Hobbes

There can be no doubt that Hobbes dominates the way English-speaking lawyers, and theorists more generally, think about legal and political issues. Hobbes provided the framework that others adopted even while rejecting aspects of Hobbes's account. And as we see, Hobbes's approach helps us to understand the gulf between civilian and common law views of justice and private law.

Hobbes was writing at a time of great political and social upheaval in England. His most famous work, *Leviathan*, was published in 1651, during the period of the English Civil Wars and only two years after the execution of King Charles I. Moreover, English society appeared to be in serious threat of disintegration, with conflict between groups representing views as far ranging as ultra-conservative Royalists to egalitarian Levellers and the even more radical Diggers. Unsurprisingly, then, in *Leviathan* Hobbes focused on theoretical and practical problems concerning the state. In particular, Hobbes's concern was to show why Englishmen were obliged to obey the decisions of the current English sovereign, which was Oliver Cromwell's Commonwealth government, just as in the earlier *De Cive* he had argued that Englishmen were obliged to obey the commands of the King.

The general features of Hobbes's political philosophy are well known. He argues that, because of our natural fear and mistrust of other persons, the state of nature—of which the state of civil war is an example—is a condition in which life is awful. Because of this, it is rational and necessary for persons to surrender their natural freedom to a sovereign—this is known as the social contract—whose task is to lay down publicly accessible norms, laws, by which persons govern their lives. When this is achieved, persons behave, not always according to their own private judgements, but also according to publicly accessible laws that bind everyone except the sovereign itself.[124]

This picture leads Hobbes to define law as

> those rules, which the commonwealth hath commanded him, by word, writing, or other sufficient sign of the will, to make use of, for the distinction of right, and wrong; that is to say, of what is contrary, and what is not contrary to the rule.[125]

In other words, law is the command of the sovereign and it trumps the agent's own moral judgments.[126] This is not to say that Hobbes rejects the existence of natural law. In fact, he elucidates 18 different natural laws[127]—the dictates of reason—and maintains that statutes must be interpreted in the light of them.[128] But Hobbes insists that subjects have no authority to appeal to the natural law to escape the commands of the sovereign.

For Hobbes, then, law possesses a 'top-down' structure. It is a command given by the sovereign to his subjects. Moreover, the sovereign passes laws in the interests of the community as a whole (as he sees it). In other words, law is concerned with distributive justice and not with corrective justice as defined in the civilian tradition.

Additionally, Hobbes maintains that those who violate the commands of the sovereign deserve punishment, and that the point of punishment is 'the preservation of them all', ie the welfare of the whole society.[129] Accordingly, all law is based either on distributive justice or responds to violations of law based on distributive justice by punishing the offender. In other words, all law is based on distributive or retributive justice. As Hobbes explicitly says, all law is either distributive or penal.[130]

124 Hobbes, above n 12.

125 *Ibid*, XXVI 3.

126 Of course, this view is also reflected in the influential work of John Austin. See especially J Austin, *The Province of Jurisprudence Determined* (Union, NJ, Lawbook Exchange, 1999).

127 Hobbes, above n 12, XIV–XV.

128 *Ibid*, XXVI 14, 17, 26.

129 *Ibid*, XXVIII 2.

130 *Ibid*, XXVI 38.

That said, however, there is one odd exception to this picture. Hobbes maintains that the social contract argument implies not only that one must keep the social contract but that one must keep all contracts.

> From that law of nature, by which we are obliged to transfer to another, such rights, as being retained, hinder the peace of mankind, there followeth a third; which is this, *that men perform their covenants made*: without which, covenants are in vain, and but empty words; and the right of all men to all things remaining, we are still in the condition of war.[131]

This is a curious argument, because it appears to derive the obligation to contract from two distinct and competing sources. The second is the idea that the social contract can be binding only if all contracts are, and hence all contracts must be binding on pain of remaining in the condition of war, ie the state of nature. But this argument is clearly invalid, as it is possible that there are special reasons why the social contract is binding that do not apply to other contracts and Hobbes gives such reasons. The first argument, on the other hand, is a direct appeal to the natural law (and a very Kantian one at that) which appears to have no place within Hobbes's philosophy as a whole.

In any case, the notion that contracts must be kept allows Hobbes to claim—despite his explicit avowal of the contrary seen above—that not all law is the command of the sovereign. For Hobbes, the obligation to keep one's contracts is conceptually prior to the state. Hence, Hobbes recognises the existence of a kind of law based on corrective justice.[132] However, for Hobbes, corrective justice is relevant only to the law of contract.[133] Because all law arises in the sovereign except the law that one must keep one's covenants, the only law relevant to corrective justice is contract law, and then only that part of contract law that insists that one keep one's covenants.

It follows that, according to Hobbes, even if the sovereign has not spoken, it is an act of injustice to violate an agreement made with person A. However, in the absence of a command from the sovereign to the contrary, it is not an act of injustice to kill A or to inflict serious bodily harm on A.[134] This position is surely highly unintuitive. If corrective justice exists, as Hobbes accepts, then it must demand more than that one keep one's agreements. Fairness between the parties cannot insist that they keep their mutual agreements but allow them to kill each other.

Because Hobbes recognises scope for corrective justice, he follows the civilian theorists in maintaining that two kinds of wrongdoing exist. Hence,

131 *Ibid*, XV 1.
132 *Ibid*, XIV 14.
133 *Ibid*, XV 14.
134 *Ibid*, XIV 4.

private men may remit to one another their debts; but not robberies or other violences, whereby they are endamaged; because the detaining of debt, is an injury to themselves; but robbery and violence and injuries to the person of the commonwealth.[135]

According to this view, if A breaches a contract with B, then A wrongs specifically B and no one else. However, if A robs B, then A wrongs the whole society and, as Hobbes makes clear in *De Cive*, not specifically B.[136] The reason for this, according to Hobbes now speaking of battery, is that

if he who receives the hurt should expostulate the mischief, and he that did it should answer thus: what art thou to me; *why should I rather do according to yours, than mine own will, since I do not hinder but you may do your own, and not my mind?*[137]

Again, this view is quite implausible. As Pufendorf notes,

men would judge that a person had lost all common sense, if he thought he could turn aside another's complaints with such a reply.[138]

The notion that a person who batters another does not hinder the other in doing as he likes is preposterous. The basic problem here is the one encountered above: if corrective justice exists, then it must demand more than that one keep one's covenants.

A further problem for Hobbes' account is that it cannot explain why A's violation of his contract with B injures only B. Surely, contract law is as much a part of the legal system as other areas of law. It is, therefore, part of the sovereign's commands, and hence Hobbes ought to have concluded that a violation of a contract injures both B and everyone else. But Hobbes appears to hold the Aristotelian view that one act can commit only one kind of wrongdoing.

A consequence of the above is that Hobbes is unable to account for the role of private law—specifically tort law—in the legal system. Setting in place a distinction that still dominates the way English-speaking lawyers think, Hobbes divides law into the distributive and the penal.[139] The distributive is that area of the law that defines the rights of subjects, such as property law, and the penal responds to violations of those rights. Accordingly, the function of the law of tort can be understood only to be penal.[140] In the language of the civilian lawyers, the law of contract aside,

135 *Ibid*, XV 12.

136 'So also in a civil government, if any man offend another with whom he hath made no contract, he [factually] damages him to whom the evil is done; but he injures [ie violates justice with respect to] none but him to whom the power of government belongs.' T Hobbes, *De Cive* (London, Royston, 1651), III 4.

137 *Ibid.*

138 Pufendorf, above n 12, I vii 13.

139 Hobbes, above n 12, XXVI 38.

140 On this model, it also has an implicit distributive function, that of recognising rights to the person. See Beever, above n 117, 26–7.

all law is based either on distributive justice or on retributive justice, which is itself a response to violations of distributive justice. With the exception of contract, corrective justice has disappeared. Hence, at this level of generality, the law of tort has no function distinct from criminal law.

The demotion of corrective justice was not a necessary consequence of Hobbes's social contract theory. It was open to Hobbes to maintain that corrective justice rightly governs the law of tort as well as contract. But Hobbes's understandable obsession with the state meant that he largely ignored issues of private law. Only contract receives any attention, and then only because of its connection with the social contract. Accordingly, not only does corrective justice disappear from the conceptual map, private law also slips under Hobbes's radar. And as we see, this becomes a trend.

(ii) Locke

Locke was also writing at a time of great political upheaval in England. When Locke wrote the *Two Treatises of Government*, he had lived through the Civil Wars, the Interregnum, the Protectorate and the Restoration of Charles II, and was deeply concerned with, and involved in, the Exclusion Crisis. Again, then, it is not surprising that Locke focused on issues concerning the state rather than on matters of private law.

Like many who followed him, Locke was not happy with Hobbes's justification of absolute sovereignty. Instead, Locke argued that the power of the sovereign was limited in terms of certain natural rights possessed by citizens, and that this limitation meant that, in certain circumstances, the people were entitled to replace the sovereign.[141]

At the heart of Locke's theory is an account of natural rights that exist even in the state of nature. The following is Locke's description of that state.

> But though this be a state of liberty, yet it is not a state of licence: though man in that state have an uncontrollable liberty to dispose of his person or possessions, yet he has not liberty to destroy himself, or so much as any creature in his possession, but where some nobler use than its bare preservation calls for it. The state of nature has a law of nature to govern it, which obliges every one: and reason, which is that law, teaches all mankind, who will but consult it, that being all equal and independent, no one ought to harm another in his life, health, liberty, or possessions . . .[142]

141 I continue to speak of the sovereign here, though Locke prefers to speak of the legislative and to hold that sovereignty lies in the people.

142 John Locke, *Two Treatises of Government and a Letter Concerning Toleration* (Stilwell, KS, Digireads.com, 2005), II §6.

This description is crucial because Locke insists that the power given to the sovereign by the people can be 'no more than those persons had in a state of nature before they entered into society'.[143] Hence, because persons in the state of nature had no power to destroy themselves or over the life, health, liberty or possessions of others, the sovereign cannot have that power either.[144] Furthermore, Locke maintains that persons leave the state of nature in order to have their lives, possessions, etc protected. Accordingly, power is given to the sovereign on condition that it protects those things. In other words, the power of the sovereign is fiduciary and so the sovereign can be removed if it abuses that power.[145]

Unlike Hobbes, then, Locke does not accept a top-down view of the law which sees (almost) all legal standards emanating from the sovereign. Locke adds to the Hobbesian picture the notion that there are norms that bind the sovereign. Nevertheless, for both Hobbes and Locke all law is 'vertical' in the sense that it exists only as between the sovereign and its subjects. For both theorists, the area of concern is the relationship between individuals and the state, and the relationship between individuals per se is almost entirely neglected. In other words, both Hobbes and Locke present theories of distributive justice and ignore corrective justice.

One difficultly for Locke's account lies in his claim that rights and obligations exist in the state of nature. What is the origin and justification of these norms? Given that we are talking about a state in which there is no sovereign, the civilian lawyers would have argued that the norms could have one source only: corrective justice. As, by definition, there is no community in which to do distributive justice in the state of nature, the only kind of justice that could apply there is corrective justice. But this was not Locke's view.

According to Locke, norms in the state of nature exist because they are the commands of God.

> [F]or men being all the workmanship of one omnipotent, and infinitely wise maker; all the servants of one sovereign master, sent into the world by his order, and about his business; they are his property, whose workmanship they are, made to last during his, not one another's pleasure: and being furnished with like faculties, sharing all in one community of nature, there cannot be supposed any such subordination among us, that may authorize us to destroy one another, as if we were made for one another's uses, as the inferior ranks of creatures are for ours.[146]

Accordingly, God's pleasure is the justification for the norms that exist in the state of nature. Given Locke's description of humans as God's property,

143 *Ibid*, II §135.
144 See generally *ibid*, II xi.
145 *Ibid*, II §149.
146 *Ibid*, II §6.

it seems natural to conclude that God takes pleasure in the good of the property as a whole rather than in the good of its individual parts.[147] Hence, for Locke, the norms that exist in the state of nature are, in fact, justified by distributive justice.

Moreover, Locke argues that the appropriate response to those who violate these norms is penal:

> And that all men may be restrained from invading others rights, and from doing hurt to one another, and the law of nature be observed, which willeth the peace and preservation of all mankind, the execution of the law of nature is, in that state, put into every man's hands, whereby every one has a right to punish the transgressors of that law to such a degree, as may hinder its violation . . .[148]

Importantly, this picture also influences Locke's account of rectification.

> [I]n the state of nature, one man comes by a power over another; but yet no absolute or arbitrary power, to use a criminal, when he has got him in his hands, according to the passionate heats, or boundless extravagancy of his own will; but only to retribute to him, so far as calm reason and conscience dictate, what is proportionate to his transgression, which is so much as may serve for *reparation* and restraint: for these two are the only reasons, why one man may lawfully do harm to another, which is that we call punishment.[149]

For Locke, wrongdoing amounts to the violation of a law given (by God or by the sovereign) for the governance of the community generally. In appropriate cases, the response to wrongdoing will call for reparation to be paid to the victim. But that is not because reparation is owed to the victim in accordance with an interpersonal morality, but simply because God or the state has so ordained for reasons of retributive justice. Accordingly, for Locke, rectification is part of retributive justice, not corrective justice.

Again, none of this was demanded by Locke's social contract argument. Locke could have maintained that the rights and obligations that exist in the state of nature are justified by corrective justice (and that is why they are ordained by God) and that private law is rightly governed thereby. In fact, his position may have been considerably strengthened if he had taken this route. But Locke's focus on the state meant that he did not pay attention to issues of corrective justice. Again, then, corrective justice and private law disappear from sight.

147 The point here is that, in defining human beings as property, Locke implicitly rules out the idea that human beings have rights with respect to each other simply in virtue of being human beings (as opposed to the creations of God who so ordains). If I choose to keep one article of property that is damaging a second, that is because I value the first more than the second, not because that first has some entitlement as against the second. Items of property are not rights holders.

148 *Ibid*, II §§7.

149 *Ibid*, II §§8 (emphasis added).

(iii) Bentham

Though Bentham lived in a more settled age than Hobbes or Locke, it was nevertheless one of great social change. Of particular importance was the Industrial Revolution and the problems English society had coming to terms with it. Bentham's life's work centred on trying to respond to these problems, in particular by arguing that antiquated institutions should be replaced with ones able to cope with the modern age. As he saw it, the law was the antiquated institution *par excellence*.[150]

Because of this, Bentham's concerns were not the same as Hobbes's or Locke's. While the older theorists focused on questions about the justification of the state, Bentham concentrated on asking how the state—assuming that it is per se just—should treat its citizens. But like Hobbes and Locke, Bentham shares the focus on distributive justice. First, he defines morality in terms of the now famous principle of utility:

> that principle which approves or disapproves of every action whatsoever, according to the tendency which it appears to have to augment or diminish the happiness of the party whose interest is in question.[151]

This leads Bentham to define just governmental action as that

> conformable to or dictated by the principle of utility, when in like manner the tendency which it has to augment the happiness of the community is greater than any which it has to diminish it.[152]

This in turn leads Bentham to say that the purpose of law 'is to augment the total happiness of the community'.[153] Clearly, this refers to distributive justice and there is no place for corrective justice in Bentham's account. In fact, Bentham maintains that claims not based on the principle of utility are meaningless, and so it must follow that, for Bentham, corrective justice is itself meaningless.[154]

Again, none of this was necessary. Bentham could have claimed that corrective justice has its own form and that some law is based on the interpersonal morality that belongs to it. But he passes over this possibility because of his exclusive focus on issues of distributive justice.

As we have seen, Bentham maintains that the function of law is to promote happiness in the community in general. It does so mainly by preventing acts that would produce disutility or, as Bentham prefers to put it, preventing mischief.[155] It achieves this goal by punishing in order to

150 See in particular J Bentham, *A Fragment on Government* (London, Payne, 1776).

151 J Bentham, *The Principles of Morals and Legislation* (Amherst, NY, Prometheus Books, 1988), I §2.

152 *Ibid*, I §7.

153 *Ibid*, XIII §1.

154 *Ibid*, I §4.

155 *Ibid*, XIII §1, XIV §1.

deter the wrongdoer and others from committing offences.[156] It is entirely unsurprising that Bentham adopts this view given his general account of justice. First-order rules of law are designed to promote distributive justice, and the response to violations of those laws are designed to preserve or regain distributive justice. In other words, violations of the law call for the application of retributive justice.

For Bentham, therefore, compensation, too, is part of retributive justice. In perhaps the most obscure passage from *The Principles of Morals and Legislation*, Bentham claims with respect to compensation that

> This property of punishment, if it be *vindictive* compensation that is in view, will, with little variation, be in proportion to the quantity: if *lucrative*, it is the peculiar and characteristic property of pecuniary punishment.[157]

This appears to mean the following. First, wrongdoers should be required to pay compensation when that would deter them and others from committing offences (vindictive compensation). This idea has been developed very considerably by the modern law and economics movement.[158] Secondly, if the wrongdoer's act was aimed to realise monetary gain, then the requirement to pay compensation is particularly appropriate because it takes away the very thing that the wrongdoer was trying to gain, thus clearly teaching the wrongdoer that wrongdoing does not pay (lucrative compensation). On either view, compensation is an element of retributive justice and is conceptualised by Bentham as a form of punishment.

Consequently, when Bentham divides offences into various kinds—private offences, offences against the state, etc[159]—this cannot be read to imply two kinds of wrongdoing in the sense explored by the civilian theorists. For Bentham, there simply is no area of morality that corresponds to corrective justice. Hence, like Hobbes and Locke, corrective justice is ignored. It is not explored and rejected, its possibility does not even arise.

Unlike Hobbes and Locke, however, Bentham does explore private law and attempts to account for the distinction between public and private law. But, given his account of justice and law, it is unsurprising that he has great difficulty in doing so.

In particular, for Bentham, criminal law and tort law possess exactly the same normative structure. Both respond to violations of laws set up in accordance with distributive justice and both respond to those violations in line with retributive justice. It is not surprising, then, to find Bentham claiming that the distinction between private and criminal law is 'The most

156 *Ibid*, XIV §§3–6.

157 *Ibid*, XV §21.

158 See, eg W Landes and R Posner, *The Economic Structure of Tort Law* (Cambridge, MA, Harvard University Press, 1987); RA Posner, *Economic Analysis of the Law* (New York, Aspen Law & Business, 5th edn, 1998).

159 Bentham, above n 151, XVI.

intricate distinction of all'.[160] What was absolutely plain for the civilian theorists is totally obscure for Bentham. Moreover, the first edition of *The Principles of Morals and Legislation* ended immediately after Bentham set out the question as to the nature of this distinction. It is as if, after elucidating the question, Bentham realised that he did not have the theoretical resources to answer it. However, he returned to the question nine years later, to provide an answer perfectly consistent with, in fact suggested by, his theory of law and justice, and yet totally implausible.

This position relies on the distinction Bentham draws between imperative, punitive and expository laws. An imperative law demands that persons do or refrain from doing certain things. A punitive law dictates certain consequences for the violation of an imperative law. To use Bentham's example, the law 'Do not steal' is imperative, whereas the law 'Those who steal shall be hanged' is punitive.[161] Bentham acknowledges, however, that these laws are meaningless unless a definition of stealing is provided. He notes that the contemporary definition is 'the taking of a thing which is another's, by one who has no TITLE so to do, and is conscious of his having none'.[162] But this definition is, in turn, unhelpful unless the nature of title is explained. That is the job of expository laws.[163]

Now, it is plain that private law contains all three of Bentham's laws,[164] but Bentham maintains that we must put this fact aside. In fact, Bentham insists that the distinction between private and criminal law, rightly understood, cannot be found in the positive law because, due to its casuistical development, that law is thoroughly confused. Instead, a large rethink of the law is required. For Bentham, this implies that private law, properly understood, is concerned only with the expository. On this view, then, the role of criminal law is to define our rights in general terms and how the violation of those rights will be dealt with, while the function of private law is to fill in the definitions of our rights given by criminal law.

Although this, or some similar, reconceptualisation of the law is demanded by Bentham's theory, it is entirely radical. It would mean that not only the law of tort, but also that part of the law of contract that deals with (not merely responds to) breach of contract would belong to criminal law.[165] It is a reconceptualisation that would shatter the common lawyer's understanding of her subject, and yet it or a near equivalent is demanded by the abandonment of corrective justice in favour of a position based

160 *Ibid*, XVII §29.
161 *Ibid*, XVII §21n1 §6.
162 *Ibid*, XVII §21n1 §10.
163 *Ibid*.
164 That is, if we assume with the common law model that tort is in fact punitive.
165 See also H Sidgwick, *The Methods of Ethics* (London, Macmillan & Co, 7th edn, 1907), III *v* §7 para 4, who claims that breach of contract calls for a penalty.

entirely on distributive justice, a position held by the majority of modern common lawyers.

From Hobbes onwards, English-speaking theorists have generally ignored both corrective justice and private law. However, while corrective justice disappears from consciousness, private law remains an important institution. Bentham, then, could not ignore it in a work dealing with the law. But the disappearance of corrective justice from the intellectual toolbox means that theorists find themselves no longer able to deal properly with private law. Questions that once had clear answers appear now to have no answers or answers that are 'The most intricate . . . of all'.[166] There is a lesson in this, to which we return later.

(iv) Sidgwick and the Reconceptualisation of Corrective Justice

Unsurprisingly, utilitarians after Bentham continued the tradition of recognising only distributive justice, with retributive justice a subset thereof. Accordingly, it is not necessary to examine their views here. However, it is worth briefly exploring Henry Sidgwick's interesting investigation of corrective justice.

After discussing the view (that he rejects) that evil should be inflicted on wrongdoers even if it leads to no good, Sidgwick claims that

> This, then, is one element of what Aristotle calls Corrective Justice, which is embodied in criminal law. It must not be confounded with the principle of Reparation, on which legal awards of damages are based.[167]

I do not think that this should be read to imply that reparation is not based on corrective justice. Rather, the 'it' that must not be confounded with the principle of reparation is not corrective justice per se, but that part of corrective justice that demands that wrongdoers suffer evil even if no good comes of it. Corrective justice is also relevant to reparation. That said, the key thing to notice about this account is that it connects corrective justice to punishment. And here we see a transformation in the meaning of the term 'corrective justice'. For the civilian lawyers, and even for Hobbes, it referred to an area of interpersonal morality that both defined rights possessed by persons and dictated how one should respond to violations of those rights. For Sidgwick, on the other hand, 'corrective justice' is concerned with correcting injustices that are, and must be, defined independently, for Sidgwick by the principle of utility and hence by distributive justice. Accordingly, 'corrective justice' comes to mean what 'retributive justice' meant to the civilian theorists.

166 Bentham, above n 151, XVII §29.
167 Sidgwick, above n 165, III *v* §5 para 6.

As indicated above, this view is very widespread today and has given rise to the perfectly understandable, but entirely erroneous, view that corrective justice cannot account for private law because it is unable to define the rights upon which tort law operates.[168] That claim is true of retributive justice, but not of corrective justice—a point that is generally missed because the modern understanding of 'corrective justice' mirrors the civilian theorist's understanding of retributive justice. In fact, most modern common lawyers have no conception of corrective justice, properly understood, at all.

(v) Compensation and the Common Law Model

One objection to the argument presented here is that the common law model does not, in fact, fit the common understanding of the law of tort because compensation is the function of that law, and compensation is clearly distinct from punishment.

However, the discussion above, particularly that of Hobbes and Bentham, has warned us against the assumption that 'compensation' cannot be intended with punitive connotations. Moreover, compensation has always been a poor explanation for the law of tort, because there are large classes of deserving victims whom tort law does not even try to compensate. The point here is not the notorious one, that tort law does a bad job of compensating,[169] but rather that compensation does not seem to be even an aim of tort law. Take, for instance, the case of two persons sitting on adjacent park benches. One is struck by a negligently driven vehicle, the other by an innocently driven one. There is nothing in respect of these persons in themselves that demonstrates that one is more deserving of compensation than the other, yet tort law tries to compensate only one of them. Notice that this point has nothing to do with lawyers' fees, delays in getting to court, difficulties of proving causation, or other transactions costs. It is not that tort law is doing a bad job of compensating here; rather, compensation is not the job that it is trying to do. If it were, it would at least try to compensate both persons in the example above and in the many similar ones.

The obvious reply is to insist that I have misinterpreted the claim that compensation is the goal of tort law. On this view, 'compensation' is not intended to mean compensation per se, as if tort law were like New Zealand's accident compensation regime. Rather, it is compensation *for*

[168] See text at nn 109–17.

[169] See, eg D Dewees, et al, *Exploring the Domain of Accident Law: Taking the Facts Seriously* (Oxford, Oxford University Press, 1996). See also J Morgan, 'Tort, Insurance and Incoherence' (2004) 67 *Modern Law Review* 384, who thinks that this is the primary objection to the idea that compensation is at the heart of tort law.

wrongdoing that is the goal of tort law.[170] But now we have come full circle. For which kind of wrongdoing does tort law compensate? For violations of laws that protect distributive justice or for those that reflect corrective justice? If the former, then 'compensation' is indeed punitive.

This seems to be a very widely held, though perhaps often unarticulated, view. Consider, for instance, the claim that exemplary damages should be awarded only when the quantum of compensatory damages is insufficient to punish the defendant.[171] This makes sense only if compensatory damages are viewed as at least quasi-punitive. It makes no sense on the civilian model. It also lies behind the quest many have undertaken to show that even those found liable apparently when not at ethical fault are, in fact, somehow ethically responsible.[172] That quest would be unmotivated unless one thought it necessary to show that the defendant is deserving of punishment.

The view also surely helps to explain why common law took so long to recognise the law of unjust enrichment. As the defendant in an unjust enrichment case had usually committed no wrong, it was hard to account for his liability on the view that general liability in private law was based on retributive justice. Instead, the defendant's liability had to be said to lie in quasi-contract. In other words, the defendant was said to have been responsible either because he had violated a pretend agreement or because, if he did not pay, he would have violated a pretend agreement. Only in this way could unjust enrichment be seen to fit with retributive justice.

(vi) Implications of the Common Law Model

Even though not all English-speaking legal and political theorists have been utilitarians, until recently one would have searched in vain for a theorist of any stripe discussing private law in terms of corrective justice, though many speak of 'corrective justice' when meaning retributive justice.[173] It is the retributive justice model that dominates.[174] This is the common law model

170 Another possible reply is that tort law does not attempt to compensate the person in the example above, because compensation is not the sole function of tort law. But this reply explains nothing. The mere fact that tort law may have functions other than compensation does not explain why it does not even attempt to compensate some of the deserving. The position is equivalent to arguing that it is understandable for a waitress to have no intention to serve waiting customers in her section because it is also her job to clear tables.

171 See, eg *Broome v Cassell & Co Ltd* [1972] AC 1027, 1089; *John v MGN Ltd* [1997] QB 586, 619; *Thompson v Metropolitan Police Commissioner* [1988] QB 517, 517.

172 For recent leading examples of this view, see T Honoré, *Responsibility and Fault* (Oxford, Hart Publishing, 1999); P Cane, *Responsibility in Law and Morality* (Oxford, Hart Publishing, 2002), chs 2–3.

173 The outstanding modern counter-example is Weinrib, above n 26, which has, entirely unsurprisingly, often been greeted with misunderstanding precisely because its thesis is based on a conception of justice that, as a conception, has been out of the minds of common lawyers for centuries: corrective justice.

174 This view is adopted explicitly by Cane, above n 119, 141.

for understanding tort law. The rights upon which tort law is based are justified by distributive justice and responses to the violation of those rights proceed in accordance with retributive justice. Tort law has the same structure as criminal law. It is no surprise, then, that many common lawyers think that punishment has a legitimate role to play in private law and greet the view that punishment is necessarily out of place in that law with bewilderment.

Note also that the idea of corrective justice disappeared from English legal thought, not because good theoretical objections to it were raised, but rather because corrective justice did not reflect the chief concerns of the major thinkers in the English-speaking tradition. It was simply not what Hobbes, Locke, Bentham, Mill, Sidgwick and so on were interested in. But lack of interest is not disproof. It may be that corrective justice still has much to tell us about our law.

V THE MODELS AND THE COMMON LAW OF TORT

As the above has hinted, although the common law model is accepted by most common lawyers, it does a very bad job of explaining common law. Take, for instance, the seminal case, *Palsgraf v Long Island Railroad Co.*[175] The defendant's employees negligently pushed a man onto a moving train, dislodging a package the man was carrying. The defendant's employees did not know, and could not reasonably have known, that the package contained fireworks. These exploded, causing scales far down the platform to fall onto the plaintiff, resulting in personal injury.[176]

A majority of the New York Court of Appeal decided that the defendant was not liable. This result is easy to explain based on the civilian model. The defendant wronged the man carrying the package but not the plaintiff. No reasonably foreseeable risk was created to her at all. Hence, the plaintiff was not wronged and had no complaint in corrective justice against the defendant. As Cardozo CJ said:

> The conduct of the defendant's guard, if a wrong in its relation to the holder of the package, was not a wrong in its relation to the plaintiff, standing far away. Relatively to her it was not negligence at all. Nothing in the situation gave notice that the falling package had in it the potency of peril to persons thus removed.[177]

175 162 NE 99 (NY CA 1928). See also *Bourhill v Young* [1943] AC 92 (HL).

176 In the following, I ignore the issue of vicarious liability and imagine that it was the defendant himself who pushed the man.

177 *Palsgraf*, above n 175, 99.

However, the result is much harder to explain based on the common law model. The defendant did violate one of society's rules—he acted negligently. Hence, he was a wrongdoer. As Andrews J claimed in dissent:

> The proposition is this. Every one owes to the world at large the duty of refraining from those acts that may unreasonably threaten the safety of others. Such an act occurs. Not only is he wronged to whom harm might reasonably be expected to result, but he also who is in fact injured, even if he be outside what would generally be thought the danger zone.[178]

This analysis fits the common law model perfectly. But why, then, was the defendant not found liable to the plaintiff? The answer, the only one available within the common law model, was the one given by Andrews J:

> because of convenience, of public policy, of a rough sense of justice, the law arbitrarily declines to trace a series of events beyond a certain point. This is not logic. It is practical politics.[179]

In other words, findings of no liability where the defendant was negligent cannot be explained by the common law model, but must be accounted for by something else. We have come to call this something else 'policy'. As I said earlier, in practice, common lawyers have claimed that the duty of care, remoteness, etc are restrictions on liability—'control mechanisms'—designed for reasons of social and economic policy to prevent liability from occurring too frequently.

We can now see that what I called above 'the common law conception of tort' is a natural consequence of the common law model. According to the conception, there is a general principle of liability for causing harm to others. This is thought to follow from the fact that causing harm to others is not in society's interests (distributive justice) and therefore calls for the defendant to be brought to account (retributive justice, though it is often called 'corrective justice'), standardly by being required to compensate the plaintiff. However, it is thought intolerable to apply this principle strictly, so exceptions to the principle must be created, themselves based on distributive justice.

We can now see the enormous superiority of the civilian model even for common law, and the bankruptcy of common law's own model. What the civilian model can explain without difficulty,[180] the common law model

178 *Ibid*, 103.

179 *Ibid*, 103–4. In fact, Andrews J would have allowed recovery in *Palsgraf*. However, Andrews J accepted that recovery must have some limits and argued that the limits should be provided by policy.

180 At first glance, it may appear odd that the common law actually appears to adopt the civilian rather than the common law model, but this is not as strange as it appears. Recall that the civilian model holds that private law is to be understood in terms of an account of justice that focuses on interactions between individuals. Accordingly, the civilian model for understanding tort law understands that law as being about the interactions between the perons who find themselves in courts, ie plaintifs and defendants. That, of course, exactly mirrors the

can do only with the addition of policy arguments. This is just another way of saying that the common law model does not really explain common law. The common law model asserts a rule (that one is liable for acting against society's interests by causing harm) coupled with a list of exceptions to that rule (such as the duty of care, remoteness, causation, the defences). But the exceptions are much more important than the rule. This is like defining sheep as mammals simpliciter, and then listing dogs, dolphins, rats, cats, mice, elephants, humans and so on as exceptions to that principle. That would be nonsensical, but no more so than the common law model for understanding common law. The common law conception of tort needs to rely on policy arguments because of the inadequacy of the model from which that conception arises. Both should be rejected.

The widespread belief that punishment has a place in private law is a symptom of our misunderstanding of our own law. We believe that tort law is based on retributive justice (whatever we call it), and yet retributive justice possesses a structure not reflected in the law of tort.[181] We will come to comprehend that law only when we see that punishment has no place in it.

VI THE DETERIORATION OF THE CIVILIAN MODEL IN THE CIVILIAN LAW

Some allege that, although punitive damages do not officially exist in civilian jurisdictions, civilian courts do, in fact, award damages that punish the defendant.[182] This allegation, too, is a result of a decline in the appreciation of corrective justice, a decline that is now occurring in continental Europe. I briefly explore the reasons for this decline before examining this symptom further.

Civil law has been blest with the attention of the Western world's most distinguished theorists of substantive law. However, the focus of these theorists was almost exclusively the Roman law rather than the indigenous laws of the various European states.[183] As a result, when the ius commune was replaced by civil codes, studies associated with Roman law came to be

structure of litigation in both civilian and common law jurisdictions. It is not surprising, then, that common law judges—who have been largely uninterested in theory—have found themselves reflecting the civilian accout of justice in their decisions. The problem in the common law, then, has not so much concerned what we do, but how we understand what we do. In most cases, the common law of tort achieves corrective justice, and, I submit, is felt to be right because it does, though it cannot understand itself as doing so.

181 This is analysed in more detail in Beever, above n 91, 105–10.

182 In the following, I refer to these as 'punitive damages'. We are interested, not in the label, but in whether courts actually award damages that are punitive.

183 This is true also of the natural lawyers, though they sought to reform Roman law.

seen as merely historical and no longer relevant to the study of modern law. Reinhard Zimmermann has documented the decline in the perceived importance of legal history over the period of codification,[184] and there has also been a similar decline in the perceived importance of legal theory.

In the absence of legal theory, it is perhaps natural to think that European private law is based on distributive justice, as it is—at least nominally—contained in statutory codes promulgated by the state. The inference seems clear: as it was the state that passed the civil code, the code must reflect the state's justice, ie distributive justice. But, of course, this is a non sequitur. It is quite possible that the state chose to implement a code designed to achieve corrective justice. This is particularly plausible when one remembers that the civil codes were largely designed to preserve the law and its values as they existed before codification.[185] Certainly, no lawyer of the ius commune would or could have accepted the idea that the law emanated from the state; it would have seemed, rather, the other way around. So, despite the apparent paradox, it is likely to be the case that if one wants to understand the state's statute (ie the civil code) one must ignore the state's justice (ie distributive justice) and see instead that the state wanted the code to reflect corrective justice. There is no sense in which it is odd to say that the state would be concerned to ensure that justice was being done as between individuals.

As indicated earlier, however, it is increasingly common for civilian lawyers to see the law through different eyes. A symptom of this is found in the claim that civil law covertly recognises damages that are punitive. This position is the direct consequence of forgetting about corrective justice.

Civil law is said to recognise punitive damages for four main reasons: the law allows for the recovery of non-pecuniary loss;[186] an award of damages is viewed as a sanction and hence as punitive;[187] the law sometimes calculates awards, in part, by looking to the degree of fault exhibited by the defendant;[188] and the law allows profit stripping or disgorgement.[189] None of these, so it is claimed, can be compensatory and so must be punitive. I examine these claims in turn.

I begin with the surprisingly common claim that damages for non-pecuniary loss cannot be compensatory and must therefore be punitive and that, as civilian jurisdictions allow damages for non-pecuniary loss, those jurisdictions must in fact recognise punitive damages. There are two errors

184 R Zimmermann, *Roman Law, Contemporary Law, European Law: The Civilian Tradition Today* (Oxford, Oxford University Press, 2001), lecture 1.

185 For discussion, see J Gordley, 'Myths of the French Civil Code' (1994) 42 *American Journal of Comparative Law* 459; Zimmermann, *ibid*, 3–4.

186 See, eg Behr, above n 5, 130–1; Magnus, above n 3, 77, 81, 94–5, 186.

187 Magnus, *ibid*, 186–7.

188 Eg Behr, above n 5, 131, 134–5; Magnus, *ibid*, 81.

189 Eg Behr, above n 5, 136–8.

in this argument. One is the invalid inference from the notion that an award is non-compensatory to the claim that it is punitive. That is passed over here, however, because it is dealt with in more detail below with respect to profit stripping. The other error is the false premise that non-pecuniary damages cannot be compensatory. This premise is normally supported by arguing that there is an incommensurability between, say, physical damage to the body and quantities of money, such that it is impossible to assess monetary awards as responses to bodily injury.

This view would certainly have been regarded as mistaken by the civilian theorists we explored earlier, for all of whom rectification for non-pecuniary loss is clearly compensatory, and it is not difficult to see why they thought this way. We all recognise someone who has had his finger amputated to be worse off than he was before, just as we recognise someone who has been given $10,000 to be better off than he was before. Why, then, does it become impossible to think of someone who is given $10,000 as a response to having his finger cut off as being compensated? Moreover, though it is impossible to fix an exact amount as fair compensation, we all recognise that there are limits. For the loss of a finger, $10 would be too small an amount whereas $10 million would be too much. There is nothing to be said for the view that non-pecuniary loss is incompensable.

According to the second argument, awards of damages are sanctions on the defendant's behaviour, and sanction implies punishment.[190] But this argument relies on an equivocation in the use of the term 'sanction'. According to the *Oxford English Dictionary*, 'sanction' has both a narrow legal and a wider ethical meaning. According to its narrow meaning, a sanction is 'The specific penalty enacted in order to enforce obedience to a law'. On its wider meaning, however, a sanction is 'A consideration which operates to enforce obedience to any law or rule of conduct'. Another way of putting this is as follows. On its narrow meaning, a sanction is a punishment. On its wider meaning, a sanction is (or includes) any response to the violation of a norm, rule or law. Accordingly, on its wider meaning, an award of damages that are purely compensatory is a sanction. But, clearly, this does not imply that it is punitive.

The idea of sanction in tort law seems to follow from the notion that damages are imposed on the wrongdoer because the wrongdoer did something that he should not have done. Hence, the award of damages is a response to that wrongdoing. On any view that neglects corrective justice, it will be natural to see this response as a sanction in the punitive sense, because the account of wrongdoing that the view adopts is the same account as that used to explain wrongdoing in criminal law. As it were, in awarding damages, the court is taken to say to the wrongdoer: 'You have

190 Magnus, above n 3, 186–7.

violated the norms that protect our society (distributive justice) and so must pay damages in consequence (retributive justice)'. But this is not the only analysis available. The court could also be saying, as it were: 'You violated the victim's rights (the right defining aspect of corrective justice) and so have an obligation to make good that wrongdoing (the rectification aspect of corrective justice), an obligation that we will ensure you honour'. Both views hold that the court is imposing a sanction, but only the former sees this as punitive. It does not follow from the fact that tort law imposes sanctions that tort law is punitive.

The third argument is that sometimes courts take into account the degree of the defendant's fault in assessing damages, and that this implies that courts are imposing punishment. That inference, however, is invalid. Above, we saw Grotius claiming that corrective justice demands compensation for injury to the victim's 'honour'[191] and Pufendorf insisting that corrective justice demands compensation for any 'disgrace' suffered by the victim at the hands of the wrongdoer.[192] But it is impossible to recognise injury to honour or disgrace without looking at the fault of the wrongdoer. As Aquinas said, 'the injury of the deliberate transgressor is greater [than that of the merely negligent one], for internal contempt is added to the external damage'.[193] I have argued elsewhere that aggravated damages in common law respond to a violation of the plaintiff's dignitary interest that flows from being treated, not as a rights-bearing individual worthy of respect, but as a mere thing. The damage to this dignitary interest can be observed only by looking at how the defendant actually treated the plaintiff, and that in turn is observable only by looking at the defendant's fault.[194] A simple example should be sufficient here.

Imagine that A kisses you against your will but in the honest belief that you want to be kissed. Imagine also that B kisses you against your will knowing that you do not want to be kissed. It is clear that B's violation of your rights is more serious than A's, and hence that B's kissing makes you worse off than A's—ie one is more violated by B than by A—but it is impossible to ascertain this without looking at the kisser's intention.[195]

191 Grotius, above n 12, II xvii 2i.

192 Pufendorf, above n 12, III i 8.

193 T Aquinas, *Commentary on the Nicomachean Ethics*, CI Litzinger, trans (Chicago, IL, Henry Regnery Co, 1964), §970.

194 Beever, above n 91, 88–94. See also EJ Weinrib, 'Punishment and Disgorgement as Contract Remedies' (2003) 78 *Chicago-Kent Law Review* 55, 91.

195 Notice that the right in the plaintiff violated in this case was the right to bodily integrity. Hence, the objection to aggravated damages raised in this volume by James Edelman—that persons do not possess a right to dignity at common law—is not compelling, even if there were no such right. The defendant is liable because he violated the plaintiff's right to bodily integrity. He is required to pay aggravated damages because his violation of the plaintiff's bodily integrity caused the plaintiff to be worse off, in part, by infringing her dignity. Liability is one thing, damages another.

The cases in which civilian courts look to the defendant's fault in determining the quantum of damages is readily explained on this model.

The fourth argument is based on the idea that damages involving profit stripping must be punitive. For example, Behr discusses a case in which

> a journal published a fake interview with former empress Soraya of Iran . . . The Federal Supreme Court no longer relied on the idea of damages for pain and suffering . . . the Federal Supreme Court expressly stated that the amount [of damages] had to be determined in such a way that the commission of similar torts would be deterred. To this goal, the profits of the tortfeasor had to be taken from him. Such outcomes are the result of purely punitive damages argumentation.[196]

Behr also explores intellectual property cases in which the German courts take a similar approach.[197]

In fact, however, profit stripping cannot be explained on punitive grounds. This is because stripping profits never punishes. A defendant who has the profit he made from a wrong taken from him does not benefit from the commission of the wrong, but that is far from saying that he is thereby punished for it. Imagine that I start with assets worth $100,000 and then commit a wrong that brings me a further $10,000. A court then takes this $10,000 from me and hence I am left with what I started with: $100,000. It is not possible to regard this as punishment, as I am no worse off than I was before.

Moreover, as our exploration of the civilian theorists above revealed, it is wrong to think that non-compensatory awards must be punitive. Although Aristotle was not entirely clear on the point, Aquinas, Grotius and Pufendorf were explicit that corrective justice sometimes demands the surrender of wrongly made gains. The paradigm example occurs when a defendant profits by wrongly appropriating the plaintiff's property. Because the property and its fruits rightly belong to the owner of the property, the defendant must surrender them to the plaintiff. This is sufficient to dispose of the intellectual property cases. It is more difficult to explain the case involving Empress Soraya on this model, but if it is appropriate to see the journal as having taken from Soraya something that rightly belonged to her—her reputation, life story, etc—then the profits from that something rightly belong to Soraya and so must be disgorged. Though this is not compensation—at least in the sense in which we are in the habit of using the word—it is in accordance with corrective justice and is not punitive. It is rectificatory.

The support for the notion that civil law recognises punitive damages arises because scholars neglect the theoretical basis upon which that law was built: corrective justice. It is most disappointing to see civilian lawyers

196 Behr, above n 5, 136.
197 *Ibid*, 137–8.

begin to make the same errors as common lawyers, who at least have the excuse of not having benefited from centuries of legal theory based on corrective justice.

VII CONCLUSION

The different attitudes to the role of punishment in private law exhibited by civil and common lawyers is explained, in part, by different understandings of the kind of justice relevant to that law. For the civil lawyer, at least traditionally, private law was concerned with corrective justice and so allowed no room for punishment. For the common lawyer, on the other hand, private law is about a mixture of distributive and retributive justice. Accordingly, the common lawyer tends to find the idea that punishment has a place in private law quite intuitive. However, the idea that the law is based on distributive and retributive justice fits very poorly with substantive law, indicating a serious deficiency with this understanding of common law. Peter Birks once claimed that the study of Scots law may lead (English) common lawyers better to understand their law.[198] The study of civilian legal theory would do likewise.

198 P Birks, 'More Logic and Less Experience: The Difference between Scots Law and English Law' in DC Miller and R Zimmermann (eds), *The Civilian Tradition and Scots Law* (Berlin, Duncker & Humblot, 1997), 167, 190.

Part V

Restitution and Disgorgement

12

Restitutionary Remedies for Wrongs: Causation and Remoteness

GRAHAM VIRGO

IT IS A fundamental principle that no wrongdoer should profit from the commission of a wrong,[1] and the law of restitution for wrongs exists to deprive the defendant of gains made from wrongdoing.[2] Even though the award of gain-based remedies is clearly recognised where the defendant has profited from a wrong, the actual assessment of these remedies is something which has received insufficient attention in the cases and secondary literature. But this is a very important matter. It is all very well to assert that no wrongdoer should profit from a wrong, but how do we determine what profit has arisen from a wrong? This raises important and difficult issues concerning the definition of profits and determining which profits were caused by the commission of the wrong, which in turn involves consideration of the appropriate tests of causation and remoteness of profits.

At the outset we need to be clear about three particular issues: what do we mean by restitutionary remedies for these purposes, what do we mean by profit and how do compensatory and restitutionary remedies relate to each other? The law of restitution can be defined as that body of law which is concerned with the award of gain-based remedies. Consequently, restitutionary remedies should be assessed by reference to the gain made by the defendant rather than the loss suffered by the claimant. A distinction appears to be emerging, in the academic literature at least,[3] between gain-based remedies which are literally restitutionary and gain-based remedies which involve disgorgement. The former category of remedy is relevant where the defendant's gain derives directly from the claimant as a result of the commission of a wrong; so the function of the remedy is to reverse the transfer of value from the claimant to the

[1] *Attorney-General v Guardian Newspapers Ltd (No 2)* [1990] 1 AC 149, 286 (Lord Goff); *Attorney-General v Blake* [2001] 1 AC 268, 278 (Lord Nicholls of Birkenhead).

[2] See generally G Virgo, *The Principles of the Law of Restitution* (Oxford, Oxford University Press, 2nd edn, 2006), pt IV.

defendant. Disgorgement remedies operate where the defendant is required to give up a gain made from the commission of the wrong, even though that gain was not obtained directly from the claimant. Although this distinction between restitutionary and disgorgement remedies has not been recognised explicitly in case law, there is growing evidence, especially in England, of the distinction emerging in the guise of distinct remedies of account of profits[4] and the measure of relief involving a hypothetical bargain to waive rights.[5] Nevertheless, the distinction between restitutionary and disgorgement remedies remains controversial, partly because it remains unclear as to when each category of remedy will be awarded. Edelman considers that restitutionary remedies are generally available to deprive a wrongdoer of a gain, but disgorgement remedies should be awarded only where the defendant has committed a wrong deliberately and cynically,[6] although this appears to be contradicted by aspects of the decision of the House of Lords in *Attorney-General v Blake*.[7] For the purposes of this paper, however, it is sufficient to recognise that both categories of remedy can be characterised as broadly restitutionary, in the sense of being gain-based, regardless of whether they actually operate to restore or disgorge benefits to the claimant. What does matter, for present purposes, is whether the principles of causation are to be interpreted differently when the defendant restores or disgorges a benefit.

A second preliminary question concerns the interpretation of 'profits' for the purposes of determining the gain which was caused by the commission of the wrong. In particular, is this confined to a positive benefit or does it encompass money saved by virtue of the commission of a wrong? There has been a tendency in case law to assume that the appropriate restitutionary remedy for wrongdoing is the account of profits, which apparently requires proof of an actual gain.[8] But it is clear that there are a wide variety of circumstances where a defendant has obtained a benefit negatively, through the saving of expense as a result of committing a wrong, and this should be treated as a relevant gain for the purposes of the operation of restitutionary remedies. This even appears to have been acknowledged by Lord Nicholls, who is reported to have said extra-judicially[9] that

3 See Smith, 'The Province of the Law of Restitution' (1992) 24 *Canadian Business Law Journal* 121; and Edelman, *Gain-based Damages* (Oxford, Hart Publishing, 2002), 66.

4 See p 307, below.

5 See pp 310 and 318, below.

6 Edelman, above n 3, p 86.

7 Above n 1. See also *WWF—World Wide Fund for Nature v World Wrestling Federation* [2006] EWHC 184 (Ch) and [2007] EWCA Civ 286, [2008] 1 WLR 445. See p 312, below.

8 *Blake*, above n 1, 284 (Lord Nicholls).

9 In Burrows and Peel (eds), *Commercial Remedies: Current Issues and Problems* (Oxford, Oxford University Press, 2003), 129.

> the measure of recovery could extend from expense saved through to stripping a proportion of the profits made through to stripping all of the profits made from the breach [of contract].

This broad approach to the identification of a gain must be correct. It follows that, when assessing restitutionary remedies for wrongs, we should be focusing on benefits obtained rather than literal profits received, so we should ask simply which benefits obtained by the defendant derive from the commission of the wrong, and these benefits can encompass both profits obtained and money saved through the commission of a wrong.[10]

One final introductory point to emphasise is that, in this area of the law of restitution, there is some evidence that the award of restitutionary remedies is subordinate to the award of compensatory remedies, but the operation of this principle of subsidiarity is not consistent in its operation. Where this principle operates, it follows that the award of restitutionary remedies should only be relevant where compensatory damages are inadequate, typically because no loss can be identified or the loss cannot be valued. This is important when assessing the significance of causation because the issue will then only arise where compensatory damages are first shown to be inadequate. In other words, the question of loss caused by the wrong, using the 'but for' test of causation, must be considered before the question of gain can be examined. However, it is first necessary to consider when, and why, this principle of subsidiarity is relevant.

This paper will focus on three distinct but related questions. First, it will identify the key principles of causation and remoteness for all types of restitutionary claims for wrongs. Secondly, it will assess the application of these principles to different types of restitutionary remedy to determine whether the nature of the remedy affects the application of the principles of causation. Finally, it will assess the application of these principles to different types of wrongdoing, to determine whether the different policies underpinning particular wrongs affect the application of the principles of causation.

I THE PRINCIPLES OF CAUSATION

Regardless of the nature of the restitutionary remedy which is sought following the commission of a wrong, it must be shown that the receipt of a benefit by the defendant was caused by the commission of the wrong.

10 In *Blake* Lord Nicholls did use the language of 'benefit' as well as 'profit': above n 1, 284. See also *Warman International Ltd v Dwyer* (1995) 182 CLR 544, 558; *Say-Dee Pty Ltd v Farah Constructions Pty Ltd* [2005] NWSCA 309, para 196 (Tobias JA).

A The General Principle of Causation

In *CMS Dolphin Ltd v Simonet*[11] Lawrence Collins J recognised that there must be 'some reasonable connection' between the wrong and the benefit which was obtained as a result of it. Traditionally, the test of causation which has been used in respect of restitutionary claims founded on wrongdoing is the but for test. Consequently, the defendant will only be liable to make restitution where the claimant can show that the defendant would not have obtained the particular benefit but for the commission of the wrong.[12] Presumably the but for test of causation will be established by showing that the relevant wrong was the principal cause of the benefit being obtained, but it need not be the sole cause. Further, it appears that the burden of proving causation is placed on the claimant, although there are certainly exceptions to this where, for policy reasons, the burden is placed on the defendant.[13]

B Assessing the Defendant's Contribution

The fact that the benefit arose partly due to the contribution of the defendant does not mean that it was still not caused by the commission of the wrong, but in such circumstances the defendant's contribution should affect the assessment of the remedy which the claimant is awarded. This may occur by apportioning the profits which arose from the wrong, to reflect the fact that some part of the profits were made by virtue of the defendant's contribution.[14] Alternatively, where the defendant is liable to account for all of the profits made as a result of the commission of the wrong, he or she may be awarded a personal allowance to reflect the reasonable value of his or her contribution, at least where his or her conduct is not reprehensible.[15] A further option is to conclude that the claimant is only entitled to receive the profits made by the defendant for a certain period, after which the profits are deemed not to have derived from the commission of the wrong.[16]

11 [2001] 2 BCLC 704, para 97.

12 See Farnsworth, 'Your Loss or My Gain? The Dilemma of the Disgorgement Principle in Breach of Contract' (1985) 94 *Yale Law Journal* 1339, 1343.

13 See, eg breach of fiduciary duty. See p 321, below.

14 See *Guardian Newspapers*, above n 1, 266 (Lord Brightman).

15 *Boardman v Phipps* [1967] 2 AC 46; *Guinness v Saunders* [1990] 2 AC 663; *Warman*, above n 10.

16 See *Warman*, *ibid*.

C The Principle of Remoteness of Benefit

In the same way that remedies which seek to compensate the claimant for loss suffered are subject to a principle of remoteness of loss, the award of restitutionary remedies are limited by a principle of remoteness of benefit. Without such a limiting principle, all benefits which accrue to the defendant as a result of the wrongdoing would be liable to be transferred to the claimant. This could constitute overprotection of the claimant from the effects of the defendant's wrongdoing by focusing on the principle that no wrongdoer should benefit from the commission of the wrong, without sufficient consideration of whether the whole of this benefit should be transferred to the claimant. The nature of the problem is illustrated by the following example. If the defendant took £10,000 from the claimant without consent, it is obvious that the benefit which was obtained by the defendant as a result of the tort of conversion was £10,000. But what if the defendant used part of the money to buy shares and the value of the shares increased? Can the claimant successfully argue that this increase in value arose from the wrongdoing or should this profit be regarded as too remote from the commission of the wrong? This depends on how the notion of remoteness is defined.

This principle of remoteness of benefit is less significant if the focus is on awarding a literal restitutionary remedy rather than disgorgement, since such a remedy should be assessed by reference to the value of the benefit which was received by the defendant directly from the claimant, so that the defendant's gain is reflected by an equivalent loss suffered by the claimant. There may still be an issue of remoteness of benefit, as illustrated by the example above, if an additional question is asked, namely whether the claimant would have made the same profit as that made by the defendant had the claimant had the money to invest. Further, the suggestion that remoteness is not relevant to literal restitutionary remedies assumes that such remedies are confined to restoring precisely what the claimant had lost. But that is not necessarily the right approach to adopt. Instead, it might be sufficient to show that the defendant has obtained a benefit and the claimant has suffered a loss, but the remedy is then assessed by focusing on the defendant's gain and it is irrelevant whether or not the claimant would have made the same gain if he or she had retained the benefit. This must be the preferable approach, for otherwise the courts will be forced to engage in meaningless speculation as to what the claimant might have done[17] and, even more importantly, it diverts attention from the crucial fact that we are here concerned with gain-based remedies, which are only concerned with the benefit obtained by the defendant and

[17] See also the problems of speculation involving the assessment of the hypothetical amount for waiving a right. See p 310, below.

not with the claimant's circumstances. Remoteness questions should therefore be relevant even to the award of literal restitutionary remedies.

Regardless of the nature of the restitutionary remedy, the appropriate test of remoteness should, at least as a general rule, focus on whether the benefit arose directly from the commission of the wrong,[18] even if those benefits arose after the wrong was committed. Benefits which arise indirectly from the commission of the wrong should be considered to be too remote and so do not need to be disgorged. The application of this principle of remoteness can be illustrated by the following example. The defendant wrongfully took the claimant's car. All the benefits which the defendant gained from the use of the car should be considered to arise directly from the wrongdoing. So, if the defendant hired the car to third parties, any money obtained from such hiring should be disgorged to the claimant. Similarly, if the defendant used the car and so saved necessary expenditure which would have been incurred had he or she hired a car instead, this is also a relevant benefit for the purposes of the restitutionary claim. If, however, the defendant obtained £500 from the use of the car and bought shares with this money, then any dividends paid in respect of those shares to the defendant need not be disgorged to the claimant, since it did not arise directly from the wrongful use of the claimant's car.[19] The only qualification to this will arise if the claimant could establish a proprietary claim to the profits obtained by the defendant, as would occur if the profits are found to be held on constructive trust, for then the claimant would be able to claim all the profits made from the use of the car, regardless of whether they arose directly or indirectly from the commission of the wrong.[20]

Support for this principle that indirect benefits are too remote can be found in the decision of the Court of Appeal in *Halifax Building Society v Thomas*.[21] One of the issues in that case concerned whether a restitutionary claim could be made in respect of the proceeds of sale of a flat which had been purchased by the defendant with a loan from the claimant building society. This loan had been made as a result of the defendant's fraudulent misrepresentation as to his identity. When the flat was sold by the claimant there was a surplus after the loan had been discharged. It was held that the defendant could claim this surplus because it had not been made at the claimant's expense.[22] In other words, the

[18] This test of remoteness was endorsed by the Court of Appeal in *Attorney-General v Blake* [1998] Ch 439, 459. The matter was not considered by the House of Lords.

[19] Similarly, if the car had increased in value while the defendant was using it.

[20] See, eg *Attorney-General of Hong Kong v Reid* [1994] 1 AC 324. See p 316, below.

[21] [1996] Ch 217. See also *Boyter v Dodsworth* (1796) 6 TR 681, 101 ER 770; *Ex p Vaughan* (1884) 14 QBD 25; *Chief Constable of Leicestershire v M* [1989] 1 WLR 20.

[22] *Halifax, ibid*, 227 (Peter Gibson LJ). In fact, the main reason for the failure of the claim was because the claimant was held to have affirmed the mortgage by relying on its contractual rights in selling the flat. This appears to have been treated as a waiver of tort, although the conclusion is dubious. See Virgo, above n 2, 474.

surplus was not obtained directly from the commission of the wrong, but was indirectly obtained once the defendant had used the loan to purchase the flat, by virtue of the fact that the value of the flat had increased. Similarly, in *Chief Constable of Leicestershire v M*,[23] the defendant had made profits from the sale of properties he had purchased with the assistance of a mortgage advance which he had obtained by deception. Hoffmann J did not accept that these profits derived from the deception, but concluded that they arose from the loan which was obtained by deception. In other words, the profit was too remote from the wrong and did not have to be disgorged.

Interestingly, in *Halifax Building Society v Thomas* Peter Gibson LJ justified his conclusion on remoteness in the language of whether a gain was obtained at the claimant's expense. This is unfortunate language, since it suggests that the restitutionary claim is founded on the reversal of unjust enrichment, rather than on the wrong itself. But does the language of 'at the claimant's expense' have any residual use when considering the remoteness principle? The better view is that it does not. It is certainly unhelpful where the benefit was obtained from a third party rather than from the claimant. Even where the defendant's gain has resulted in some loss to the claimant it is better to focus on whether the defendant's gain derived directly from the wrong rather than to focus on whether it came directly from the claimant. The language of remoteness of benefit is consequently preferable to that of 'at the claimant's expense'.

II APPLICATION OF THE PRINCIPLES OF CAUSATION TO DIFFERENT TYPES OF RESTITUTIONARY REMEDY

A Account of Profits

The order of an account of profits has a long pedigree in equity as the primary remedy following the commission of an equitable wrong, but it is increasingly being recognised in the common law as well, since it is clearly available in respect of some torts[24] and for breach of contract.[25]

When an account of profits is ordered, this is actually a mechanism to require the taking of an account to determine the profits made and to deduct the expenses incurred, subsequent to which the defendant will be required to disgorge the net profit made as a result of committing the

23 Above n 21.
24 See, in particular, the torts which involve interference with intellectual property rights. See p 317, below.
25 *Blake*, above n 1. See p 317, below.

wrong. The but for test of causation generally applies.[26] An account of profits should be compared with other forms of account, such as surcharge and falsification, which are concerned with compensating a trust for loss suffered as a result of breach, and which raise different issues of causation.[27] The remoteness of benefit principle applies to an account of profits, at least as a general rule, so that the defendant is only liable to account for those benefits which derive directly from the commission of the wrong.

An account of profits straddles both the literal restitutionary function and the disgorgement function of restitutionary remedies. For, where the claimant has paid money to the defendant as the result of the commission of a wrong, the appropriate remedy may be an account of the profits. Equally, where the defendant has obtained a profit from a third party, he or she may be liable to account for this profit too. Indeed, in *Murad* v *Al-Saraj*,[28] a case involving breach of fiduciary duty, Arden LJ described the remedy as a 'procedure to ensure the restitution of profits which ought to have been made for the beneficiary'. However, Jonathan Parker LJ in the same case[29] described the remedy as being neither restitutionary nor compensatory, but designed to strip the fiduciary of profits. A remedy which is focused on the stripping of the defendant's profits is properly analysed as restitutionary in the sense of its being a gain-based remedy, albeit a remedy which may sometimes operate to disgorge profit rather than being literally restitutionary. The remedy cannot be characterised as compensatory because it has long been recognised that it is irrelevant that the claimant could not have obtained the profit him or herself.[30]

It is often difficult to ascertain exactly what profits the defendant made as a result of the wrongdoing, since usually the profits will have been increased by the contribution of the defendant's own ideas, property and money. Consequently, the courts do not require absolute accuracy in the determination of the profits which derived from the commission of the wrong.[31] As Lord Nicholls recognised in *Blake*:[32]

> Despite the niceties and formalities once associated with taking an account, the amount payable under an account of profits need not be any more elaborately or precisely calculated than damages.

26 *Warman*, above n 10. Cp *Murad v Al-Saraj* [2005] EWCA Civ 959, p 323, below.

27 *Target Holdings Ltd v Redferns (a firm)* [1996] AC 421. See Millett, 'Equity's Place in the Law of Commerce' (1998) 114 *LQR* 214, 226.

28 Above n 26, para 85.

29 *Ibid*, para 108.

30 See, eg *IDC v Cooley* [1972] 1 WLR 443; *Murad*, above n 26, para 59 (Arden LJ).

31 *Watson, Laidlaw and Co Ltd v Pott, Cassels and Williamson* (1914) 31 RPC 104, 114 (Lord Atkinson). See also *My Kinda Town Ltd v Soll* [1982] FSR 147, 159 (Slade J). Cp the account of profits following the commission of an equitable wrong. See p 321 below.

32 Above n 1, 288. See also *Warman*, above n 10, 558.

A problem with ordering an account of profits to be taken is that requiring the defendant to give up all profits made might unfairly benefit the claimant,[33] especially where all the profit made cannot be attributed to the commission of the wrong. Two mechanisms have been identified which can assist in the assessment of the profits for which the defendant should account to the claimant.

1. Limiting the period for which the account must be taken.

Where the nature of the wrong is such that the defendant earns a profit over a period of time, and is still earning the profit at the time of the trial, a difficult question arises as to whether the defendant should be required to account both for all the profits which have already been made and those which may be made in the future. This was a matter which was examined in *Warman International Ltd v Dwyer*,[34] where the High Court of Australia recognised that, where it is equitable to do so, the defendant may only be required to account for the profits generated over a specified period of time. This was the type of account which was ordered in *Warman* itself. The defendant in that case was an employee who had breached his fiduciary duty by taking a business opportunity for himself. It was held that the defendant was only required to account for those profits which he would not have incurred but for the breach of fiduciary duty,[35] which was found to be two years' profits made from the exploitation of the business opportunity.

2. The equitable allowance

Alternatively, the defendant may be awarded an equitable allowance in respect of those profits which were earned by virtue of the defendant's own efforts and this sum will be deducted from the amount for which the defendant has to account to the claimant.[36] The preferable explanation of this allowance is that, where the defendant has made a profit as a result of the exercise of his or her time and skill, it is not possible to say that all of the defendant's profits derived from the commission of the wrong. It follows that the equitable allowance seeks to apportion profits so that the claimant only recovers those profits which derive from the wrong and the defendant is allowed to retain those profits which can be considered to derive from his or her work and skill. It will, of course, be very difficult to apportion the profits exactly, but at least the existence of the allowance

[33] See *Fyffes Group Ltd v Templeman* [2000] 2 Lloyd's Rep 643, 672 (Toulson J).

[34] Above n 10. See also *Murad*, above n 26, para 115 (Jonathan Parker LJ).

[35] The High Court also suggested that the profits might be split between the claimant and the defendant but that this would normally be appropriate only where there was an antecedent profit-sharing arrangement.

[36] See *Re Jarvis, deceased* [1958] 1 WLR 815, *Boardman*, above n 15; *Warman*, above n 10, para 33. See also *Docker v Somes* (1834) 2 My and K 655, 39 ER 1095.

gives the court the opportunity to determine in general terms how much of the profits derived from the defendant's input, so that the defendant is not required to account for those profits because they did not derive from the commission of the wrong.[37] However, the award of the allowance is not automatic, since the decision to award it and the amount awarded depend on the operation of judicial discretion, which will be influenced by a variety of factors, including the good faith of the defendant.[38] Despite this, the existence of the allowance is still preferably analysed as being grounded on principles of causation, albeit that the award will be tempered by judicial discretion.

B Hypothetical Bargain Measure

As an alternative to an account of profits, the defendant wrongdoer may instead be required to pay a sum of money to the claimant which is measured by reference to what the claimant could legitimately have demanded from the defendant to secure the claimant's permission for the defendant's conduct by means of a hypothetical bargain. Consequently, this remedy focuses on money saved rather than money gained. This remedy is clearly available for a variety of wrongdoing, but its interpretation and rationale remain a matter of some controversy.

The leading case on the award of this type of remedy is *Wrotham Park Estate Co Ltd v Parkside Homes Ltd*.[39] The defendant had built houses in breach of a restrictive covenant and it was held that the appropriate remedy was damages in lieu of an injunction to demolish the houses. The claimant had suffered no obvious financial loss as a result of the breach, because the value of its land was unaffected by the development. The remedy which was awarded was assessed by reference to the price which the claimant would reasonably have demanded of the defendant to agree to a waiver of the covenant. This bargain was most definitely hypothetical because it was acknowledged that the claimant would not have agreed to relax the covenant on any terms.[40] The price was assessed as 5% of the defendant's profit from building the houses, though it is unclear how this figure was determined. Further, it is unclear whether this hypothetical bargain measure should be characterised as compensatory, by reference to what the claimant had lost in not being able to bargain with the

37 *Warman*, *ibid*, para 33.

38 *Boardman*, above n 15; *Guinness*, above n 15; *Warman*, *ibid*. See also *Say-Dee*, above n 10, para 252 where it was recognised that dishonesty, surreptitious conduct and bad faith would not necessarily disentitle the claimant to an equitable allowance but should mean that the allowance would not be liberal.

39 [1974] 1 WLR 798.

40 This was recognised by Brightman J at *ibid*, 815.

defendant,[41] or restitutionary, by reference to what the defendant had saved in avoiding the bargain. This question of characterisation of the remedy is vital to the assessment of the role of causation, since the crucial issue concerns what was caused by the wrong—either loss suffered, for which a compensatory remedy would be awarded, or benefit obtained, for which a restitutionary remedy would be awarded—although the correct characterisation is only of practical significance where the amount of loss and gain are different. Following the decision of the House of Lords in *Blake*,[42] it appears that the *Wrotham Park* measure is properly characterised as restitutionary.[43]

A further crucial question concerns why the defendant in *Wrotham Park* was not liable to account for all of the profits which it had made as a result of the breach of the covenant. This was presumably because it could not be established that all of these profits derived from the breach, since most of the profits arose from the defendant's contribution to the building of the houses. Consequently, the defendant could only have been liable to disgorge those profits which would not have been made but for the breach, but in a case such as this it is virtually impossible to determine which profits derived from the breach. The formula which was adopted, namely 5% of the profits, is artificial, but it is at least realistic since it represents a reasonable sum which would have been demanded by somebody in the position of the claimant before agreeing to relax the covenant. Subsequent cases have expanded on how this reasonable sum should be assessed. In *Gafford v Graham*[44] Nourse LJ emphasised that assessment of the reasonable sum was a matter of judgement which was incapable of strict rational and logical exposition. In *O'Brien Homes Ltd v Lane*[45] David Clarke J emphasised that it is the defendant's expected profit which is taken as the starting point for the assessment, so clearly this is restitutionary in approach. This case concerned breach of a contract to build no more than three houses. It was held that the hypothetical bargain should be determined when the defendant sought to be released from the contract, rather than when the contract was made. This was significant because when the contract was made it was not clear whether planning permission for a fourth house would be given. However, when the defendant would have wished to be released from the restriction the

41 This was how Megarry V-C explained the case in *Tito v Waddell (No 2)* [1977] Ch 106, 335, as did Millett LJ in *Jaggard v Sawyer* [1995] 1 WLR 269, 291. See also Sharpe and Waddams, 'Damages for Lost Opportunity to Bargain' (1982) 2 *OJLS* 290 and Stoljar, 'Restitutionary Relief for Breach of Contract' (1989) 2 *Journal of Contract Law* 1.

42 Above n 1.

43 *Ibid*, 283–4 (Lord Nicholls of Birkenhead). See also *Experience Hendrix LLC v PPX Enterprises Inc* [2003] EWCA Civ 323, [2003] 1 All ER (Comm) 830, 839 (Mance LJ). Cp *Blake*, *ibid*, 298, where Lord Hobhouse explicitly characterised this measure as compensatory.

44 [1999] 3 EGLR 75, 80.

45 [2004] EWHC 303 (QB).

planning permission had been granted, so the defendant would have been willing to pay more for the release. The judge also recognised that the award need not be limited to a relatively small percentage of the defendant's profit. The claimant was awarded £150,000 in a case where the defendant's profit from breaching the contract was considered to be £280,000.

Two recent cases have examined the method of assessing this remedy further. In *Horsford v Bird*[46] the claimant had sued the defendant for the tort of trespass to his land. The defendant had built a boundary wall purportedly between his property and that of the claimant, but in fact the defendant had encroached on the claimant's land and added 455 square feet to the defendant's property. The Privy Council concluded that two remedies should be awarded: first, mesne profits to compensate the claimant for the defendant's use of the claimant's land until the point when the trial judge determined that damages should be awarded in lieu of an injunction to remove the wall; and secondly, damages in lieu of an injunction representing the price which the claimant would reasonably have demanded for the defendant to purchase part of the claimant's property, by virtue of the *Wrotham Park* measure. This price was initially assessed by reference to the value of the land which the defendant had appropriated, but this amount was then doubled because the appropriation of the land had enhanced the amenity value of the defendant's own property by providing vehicular access and a garden, plus the defendant had saved money in not having to demolish the wall and rebuild it along the proper boundary. It appears that this remedy was considered to be restitutionary in effect, because there was explicit reliance on the benefit obtained by the defendant in committing the tort. It is unclear, however, why double the value of the land was considered to be the benefit which derived from the commission of the tort. There was no analysis of the nature of the test of causation or how the hypothetical bargain would have been made.

In *WWF—World Wide Fund for Nature v World Wrestling Federation Entertainment*[47] Peter Smith J, in a hearing on a preliminary issue, sought to add some flesh to the bones of the *Wrotham Park* hypothetical bargain measure. The *WWF* case arose from a dispute between the World Wide Fund for Nature and the World Wrestling Federation concerning the use of the initials WWF. The parties had entered into a settlement which had been breached by the defendant. It was agreed that the basis for the assessment of damages was the *Wrotham Park* hypothetical bargain measure, namely what the claimant would reasonably have demanded from the defendant

46 [2006] UKPC 3.

47 Above n 7. See further Virgo, 'Hypothetical Bargains: Compensation or Restitution?' (2006) 65 *CLJ* 272. See now [2008] EWCA Civ 286, [2008] 1 WLR 445, where the Court of Appeal characterised this remedy as compensatory.

to relax its rights under the agreement. The claimant asserted that this should be 12% of the defendant's gross receipts. The judge rejected this amount on the ground that its calculation was a 'complete mystery' and sought instead to identify a number of key principles to assist with the assessment of the appropriate sum. He emphasised that the essence of this remedy was to determine what the parties would have agreed had each been making reasonable use of their bargaining positions without holding out for unreasonable amounts and having regard to their knowledge at the time of the negotiation. Although the award of the remedy lay in the discretion of the court[48] having regard to the circumstances of the case, two factors were particularly significant, namely whether damages, presumably meaning compensatory damages, would be an inadequate remedy, and whether the innocent party would obtain 'just recompense' for the wrongdoer's breach in doing what it agreed not to do. The bargain was explicitly acknowledged to be hypothetical, since it was irrelevant that the innocent party would not have entered into such an agreement. Nevertheless, the parties could adduce evidence which would have been used in the hypothetical negotiations. So, for example, the claimant could use evidence that its reputation had been tarnished by the defendant using the abbreviation WWF and the defendant could adduce evidence that profits made from the use of the abbreviation may have arisen in part from its own efforts. The wrongdoer's conduct was irrelevant, since this would incorporate a punitive element to the award of damages for breach of contract.

Crucially, the judge considered that the reasonable price was to be treated as compensatory damages rather than as a punitive award, because it seeks to compensate the claimant for the loss of the opportunity to bargain with the defendant for an appropriate price to relax its rights. This has been recognised in some other cases, such as *Severn Trent Water Ltd v Barnes*,[49] where damages for trespass to land were awarded specifically to compensate the claimant for the loss of the opportunity to bargain with the defendant for the price of interfering with the claimant's land rather than to deprive the defendant of any gain made by committing the tort. Such a compensatory analysis might sometimes be justified, at least where the claimant would have been willing to enter into a bargain with the defendant, but a principle of lost opportunity to bargain cannot be used to explain the function of the remedy in every case where this measure has been awarded. This is because this remedy has sometimes been awarded even though there was no evidence that the claimant would have bargained with the defendant,[50] and sometimes it is clear that the claimant

[48] As is true of the remedy of an account of profits.

[49] [2004] EWCA Civ 570. See also *Strand Electric and Engineering Co Ltd v Brisford Entertainments Ltd* [1952] 2 QB 246, Somervell and Romer LJJ.

[50] See the analysis in *The Mediana* [1900] AC 113, 177 (Earl of Halsbury LC); *Watson, Laidlaw and Co Ltd v Pott, Cassels and Williamson* (1914) 31 RPC 104, 119 (Lord Shaw).

would definitely not have bargained with the defendant.[51] If the remedy which was awarded in these cases is to be treated as compensatory rather than restitutionary, it is necessary to introduce a fiction that the claimant would have been prepared to bargain with the defendant, even though this might be contradicted by the evidence.

A further danger in analysing these remedies as operating only to compensate the claimant for loss suffered is that such an analysis depends on a strange and artificial notion of loss to ensure that the claimant obtains a remedy. Where the defendant has obtained a benefit as a result of the commission of a wrong but the claimant suffered no real financial loss, it is appropriate to consider the award of a restitutionary remedy which explicitly focuses on the defendant's benefit rather than create a constructive loss.[52]

In the *WWF* case itself, the judge's analysis of this remedy is fundamentally flawed by his characterisation of the remedy as compensatory without acknowledging even the possibility of a restitutionary analysis. This causes a number of problems. First, there is an obvious inconsistency since the principles which the judge identified implicitly acknowledge a restitutionary slant, particularly as to whether benefits obtained by the defendant arose from the breach of contract or from the defendant's legitimate work. Secondly, there is a clear conflict with the approach of the Privy Council in *Horsford v Bird*, and other cases.[53] Thirdly, the emphasis on a compensatory analysis seems misplaced, and liable to mislead, where it is clear that the claimant would not have entered into the hypothetical bargain. For, where no bargain would have been made, how can the claimant have suffered loss from the failure to bargain? Surely in such circumstances it is more sensible to focus on the benefit which was actually obtained by the defendant in not paying the claimant to alter the settlement? Indeed, it has been assumed in a number of cases that the hypothetical bargain is the preferable mode of analysis of the remedy even though this is by definition a fiction, and, like all fictions, there are dangers of confusion and incoherence, as illustrated in the law of restitution by the absurdities created by the implied contract theory.[54] Fourthly, the emphasis on the inadequacy of damages as being a significant factor in assessing the hypothetical bargain award is potentially confusing. If compensatory damages are inadequate, it is presumably because there was no loss which could be identified or valued. But if a hypothetical bargain can be identified and a price for relaxation of the contract assessed, then, if

51 See in particular *Strand Electric and Engineering Co Ltd v Brisford Entertainments Ltd* [1952] 2 QB 246; *Penarth Docks Engineering Co Ltd v Pounds* [1963] 1 Lloyd's Rep 359; *Gondall v Dillon Newspapers Ltd* [2001] RLR 221.

52 See *Attorney-General v Blake* [2001] AC 268, 279 (Lord Nicholls). See also *Experience Hendrix*, above n 43, 842 (Mance LJ), 849 (Peter Gibson LJ).

53 *Ibid.*

54 Virgo, above n 2, 19–21.

this is characterised as compensation for the failure to bargain, it must follow that compensatory damages are adequate and so this factor becomes logically irrelevant. This paradox can be avoided if it is acknowledged that there is a restitutionary dimension to the hypothetical bargain and nothing can be gained by treating it solely as compensatory.

It is clear that the hypothetical bargain measure should be characterised as having both compensatory and restitutionary characteristics, since any bargain would take into account losses suffered by the claimant and gains made by the defendant. In many situations the appropriate characterisation is of no significance since the loss suffered by the claimant is the same as the benefit obtained by the defendant in not making the bargain. Sometimes, though, as both *Horsford v Bird* and *WWF* show, the proper characterisation will affect the amount awarded, and it is therefore unhelpful to treat the hypothetical bargain measure as absolutely compensatory. In fact, this hybrid characterisation of remedies has been previously recognised by the Privy Council in *Inverugie Investments Ltd v Hackett*[55] in the context of assessing damages for the tort of trespass. In that case the defendant had excluded the claimant for 15 years from apartments which the claimant had leased from the defendant. During this period the defendant leased the apartments itself but only achieved an occupancy of about 40%. It was held that damages should be assessed by reference to a reasonable rental value of all of the apartments which the claimant had leased whilst the defendant was committing the trespass, after deduction of what the claimant had saved in not having to pay rent as a result of the defendant's trespass. It was irrelevant that the premises had not been fully occupied. Crucially, the court said of the award of the damages in this case that it 'need not be characterised as exclusively compensatory, or exclusively restitutionary; it combines elements of both'.[56] This was not a case involving the hypothetical bargain measure, but it does support a more sophisticated approach to the characterisation of remedies. In *Inverugie* the award could not be considered to be solely compensatory, because the claimant's actual loss was confined to the income which it did not receive from the apartments, and, since the occupancy throughout the 15 year period was only about 40%, awarding the claimant the full rental value of the apartments would have overcompensated him. Similarly, the remedy could not be characterised as purely restitutionary because, as the Privy Council recognised, the defendant had not derived a benefit from all of the apartments all of the time, but it was still expected to pay a reasonable rent for the use of the apartments throughout the period during which the tort had been committed.

[55] [1995] 1 WLR 713.
[56] *Ibid*, 718.

I have previously criticised the hybrid analysis of the remedies in *Inverugie* as absurd,[57] but perhaps there is more truth in this analysis than I had originally anticipated. Perhaps, as the hypothetical bargain measure suggests, we are moving towards a more sophisticated approach to the law of obligations where there is less emphasis on the division between restitution and compensation and more emphasis on a holistic approach.[58] If this holistic approach is recognised, it follows that a much more sophisticated approach to causation needs to be adopted for the hypothetical bargain measure, since loss and gain are both relevant arising from the defendant's failure to enter into a bargain with the claimant. Crucially, for present purposes, the hypothetical bargain measure shares restitutionary characteristics but it does not appear to be limited by them.

C Proprietary Restitutionary Remedies

Sometimes, primarily where the defendant has committed an equitable wrong, the courts recognise that profits obtained by the defendant as a result of the breach of duty will be held on constructive trust for the claimant. Where such a trust is recognised, it follows that the claimant has an equitable proprietary interest in the profits which were obtained by the defendant and the claimant can vindicate this property right by means of proprietary restitutionary remedies. These remedies have a number of advantages, including that the claimant will gain priority over the defendant's unsecured creditors if the defendant becomes insolvent, but also the claimant is entitled both to the profits directly received and to the fruits of those profits. In other words, the principle of remoteness of benefit does not apply where the claimant seeks a proprietary remedy. This is particularly well illustrated by the decision of the Privy Council in *Attorney-General for Hong Kong v Reid*.[59] The defendant fiduciary held a number of public offices in Hong Kong, including that of Director of Public Prosecutions. He had accepted bribes to induce him to frustrate the prosecution of some criminals. He purchased land with this bribe money and the claimant asserted that it had an equitable proprietary interest in this land. The Privy Council agreed and declared that the land was held by the defendant on constructive trust for the claimant, which meant that the claimant could recover the land itself.

Of course, a disadvantage of these proprietary restitutionary remedies is that, if the property and its fruits fall in value or are dissipated, the remedy

[57] Virgo, above n 2, 469.
[58] Cp Cunnington, 'The Border Between Compensation, Restitution and Punishment' (2006) 122 *LQR* 382, 386.
[59] Above n 20.

is much less attractive. In such circumstances an account of profits would be preferable.

III APPLICATION OF THE PRINCIPLES OF CAUSATION TO DIFFERENT TYPES OF WRONG

A Torts

Where the defendant has tortiously interfered with the claimant's proprietary rights it is clear that the hypothetical bargain measure will be available. This was recognised in *Strand Electric and Engineering Co Ltd v Brisford Entertainments Ltd*[60] for the tort of detinue, and also, more recently, in *Horsford v Bird*[61] as regards the tort of trespass to land. Other restitutionary remedies are available as well, including account of profits.[62]

B Breach of Contract

Following the decision of the House of Lords in *Blake*,[63] it is now clear that restitutionary remedies can be awarded following a breach of contract. In *Blake* an account of profits was awarded to ensure that the defendant did not profit from his wrong. It was acknowledged that this remedy is only available in exceptional circumstances, although sometimes the notion of what is exceptional has been interpreted rather liberally. The essential rationale of this remedy was identified by Lord Nicholls as follows:

> When, exceptionally, a just response to a breach of contract so requires, the court should be able to grant the discretionary remedy of requiring a defendant to account to the plaintiff for the benefits he has received from his breach of contract.[64]

60 [1952] 2 QB 246.
61 [2006] UKPC 3, p 312 above. See also *Severn Trent Water Ltd v Barnes* [2004] EWCA Civ 570.
62 See, in particular, the intellectual property torts: copyright (Copyright, Designs and Patents Act 1988, s 96(2)); design rights (Copyright, Designs and Patents Act 1988, s 229(2)); patents (Patents Act 1977, s 61(1)); deliberate passing off (*My Kinda Town Ltd v Soll* [1982] FSR 147); deliberate interference with trademarks (*Edelsten v Edelsten* (1863) 1 De GJ and S 185; 46 ER 72). However, in *Murad*, above n 26, para 46, Arden LJ described the award of the equitable remedy of an account of profits for the common law tort of deceit as 'novel'. In fact, the award of an account of profits was justified on the facts because the defendant had committed the different wrong of breach of fiduciary duty. See p 323, below. But cp at para 164 Clarke LJ, who contemplated the order of an account of profits in respect of the tort of deceit.
63 Above n 1.
64 *Ibid*, 284.

It was held that the facts of the *Blake* case were exceptional and justified the award of an account of all the profits made from the sale of his autobiography, amounting to £70,000 of royalties. This was for a variety of reasons, including that compensatory damages were not adequate and the claimant had a legitimate interest in preventing the defendant's profit-making activities and so in depriving the defendant of his profit.[65] More specifically, a full account of profits was justified because the defendant had deliberately and repeatedly breached his contract in publishing his autobiography, because the contractual obligations owed by him were considered to be closely akin to those of a fiduciary,[66] and because he had compromised national security and committed a serious criminal offence.[67]

An account of profits was subsequently awarded in a commercial context in *Esso Petroleum Co Ltd v Niad Ltd*.[68] The case arose from a pricing agreement made by Esso with dealers who sold their petrol, whereby dealers agreed both to report to Esso the prices of petrol sold by local competitors and to abide by the prices set daily by Esso, which were intended to match the competition. The dealers received financial support from Esso in recompense. This agreement was deliberately breached by Niad, which charged higher prices than had been agreed but still received the financial support from Esso. Esso obtained a full account of the profits made by Niad in breach of agreement because the facts were considered to be exceptional within the principle recognised in *Blake* since, amongst other reasons, the defendant's breach of contract was deliberate and repeated, and compensatory damages was not an adequate remedy.

In other commercial contexts, however, an account of profits has not been awarded for breach of contract. So, for example, in *The Sine Nomine*,[69] the owners of a ship had wrongfully withdrawn the vessel from charter after the market had risen, making the contract less profitable. It was accepted that no account of profits was available. This was surely right because compensatory damages were an adequate remedy in the circumstances. Similarly, in *WWF World Wide Fund for Nature v World Wrestling Federation Entertainment Inc*[70] no account of profits was awarded where the World Wrestling Federation had used the initials WWF in breach of an agreement, since the breach was not considered to be exceptional within the *Blake* principle.

As an alternative to the remedy of account of profits, it has been recognised, post-*Blake*, that the hypothetical bargain measure still applies where

65 *Ibid*.
66 *Ibid*, 287 (Lord Nicholls), 292 (Lord Steyn).
67 *Ibid*, 292 (Lord Steyn).
68 [2001] All ER (D) 324.
69 [2002] 1 Lloyd's Rep 805. See also *University of Nottingham v Fishel* [2001] RPV 367.
70 [2002] FSR 32. Subsequently the hypothetical bargain measure was awarded. See p 312, above. Now see [2007] EWCA Civ 286, [2008] 1 WCR 445.

a contract has been breached, as had previously been recognised in *Wrotham Park* in respect of the breach of a restrictive covenant. However, it remains unclear when each remedy will be awarded.

One of the most important modern cases on the hypothetical bargain measure is the decision of the Court of Appeal in *Experience Hendrix*.[71] In that case a hypothetical bargain remedy was awarded where the defendant had repeatedly breached a settlement agreement made in 1973 relating to the use of master recordings made by Jimi Hendrix without paying royalties. A restitutionary remedy was justified because other remedies were inadequate: there was no evidence of financial loss suffered by the claimant as a result of the breach,[72] so a compensatory remedy would be inadequate and, since the claim related to past profits, the remedies of specific performance and injunction were not available. Further, as in *Blake*, the defendant did what it had promised not to do by deliberately and flagrantly[73] breaching the contract, and the claimant was considered to have a legitimate interest in preventing the defendant from profiting from the breach. However, the Court did not order the defendant to account for all the profits which derived from the breach since the case was not considered to be exceptional within the *Blake* formula because it was not concerned with a sensitive subject such as national security, the defendant was not in a fiduciary or quasi-fiduciary relationship[74] and the case arose in a commercial context. Rather, the sum awarded was assessed with reference to what the claimant would reasonably have demanded of the defendant for the defendant's use of the recordings in breach of the agreement. The Court was, however, unable to reach a final conclusion on the evidence before it as to what the appropriate sum should be.

Some commentators have suggested that there is now a sliding-scale of remedies available for breach of contract, ranging from a full account of profits, through the hypothetical bargain measure which can deprive the defendant of some of the profits made, and on to a compensatory award.[75] The earlier analysis that the hypothetical bargain measure is properly analysed as being a hybrid remedy[76] which shares both compensatory and restitutionary functions might support this sliding-scale approach, since the hypothetical bargain measure straddles both the restitutionary and the compensatory function. But the sliding-scale characterisation is still misleading, because it ignores the fact that restitutionary remedies, in the context of breach of contract at least, are subsidiary to compensatory

[71] Above n 43.
[72] *Ibid*, p 845 (Mance LJ).
[73] *Ibid*, p 848 (Peter Gibson LJ).
[74] *Ibid*.
[75] See the report of Lord Nicholls' comments in Burrows and Peel, above n 9, 129. See also Burrows, *Remedies for Torts and Breach of Contract* (Oxford, Oxford University Press, 3rd edn, 2004), 401–4; Graham, 'Restitutionary Damages: The Anvil Struck' (2004) 120 *LQR* 26.
[76] See p 315, above.

remedies. This is made clear in all the cases on the award of restitutionary remedies for breach of contract, which emphasise that such remedies should only be available if compensatory damages are inadequate. The availability of compensatory remedies needs to be considered first and then the restitutionary remedies can be considered, with account of profits only being available in particularly exceptional circumstances.

Once it is recognised that there is a basket of remedies which are available where the defendant has committed a breach of contract, it is necessary to determine when the hypothetical bargain measure should be adopted, as opposed to awarding a full account of profits. Edelman[77] has suggested that a full account of profits should only be available where the breach of contract was deliberate and cynical. However, the significance of the defendant's conduct in breaching the contract was specifically rejected as a factor in assessing damages by Peter Smith J in *WWF*.[78] In addition, we know from both *Blake* and *Experience Hendrix* that account of profits is an exceptional remedy. The notion of what is exceptional remains vague, but it is clear that the full context of the case needs to be assessed. One of the key factors for so characterising the claim is in treating the relationship between the parties as akin to a fiduciary relationship. Where the circumstances are not truly exceptional, then the hypothetical bargain measure can be considered. But when should it be available? Analysis of the cases where this remedy has been awarded suggests that the hypothetical bargain measure is appropriate whenever the defendant has interfered with the claimant's property rights in some way. The policy of the law is to prevent such proprietary interference by ensuring that the wrongdoer does not profit from the wrong. This explains why this remedy was awarded in, for example, *Wrotham Park* (breach of a restrictive covenant over land), and *WWF* and *Experience Hendrix* (interference with intellectual property rights). The remedy was also awarded in *O'Brien Homes Ltd v Lane*,[79] but that is difficult to justify because there was no interference with any of the claimant's property rights since the breach was of a collateral contract which was not a restrictive covenant. The proprietary rights requirement is a particularly useful condition to impose to limit the application of the hypothetical bargain measure, with the remedy of an account of profits being confined to very exceptional circumstances which has fiduciary connotations. In all other cases compensatory remedies would be available and, if no loss had been suffered, there would be no significant remedy at all. This respects the subsidiarity principle, which is of particular importance in the context of breach of contract.

[77] Above n 3, 86.
[78] Above n 7.
[79] [2004] EWHC 303 (QB).

C Equitable Wrongs

The key equitable wrongs are breaches of trust and fiduciary duty. The orthodox approach to the award of restitutionary remedies for such wrongs is to require the defendant to account to the claimant for all the profits which he or she obtained as a result of the breach,[80] whether this breach involved a gain or benefit arising from a conflict between the fiduciary's personal interest and duty or arose from taking advantage of the fiduciary's position.[81] The remedy is clearly restitutionary rather than compensatory because it does not depend on whether the principal suffered loss from the breach[82] or whether he or she could have made the profit.[83] The defendant is required to disgorge the value of the profits obtained from the breach of duty but is not required to disgorge all profits made regardless of the source.[84] When taking the account, it is necessary to ascertain what profits derive from the commission of the equitable wrong by means of establishing a reasonable connection between the breach of duty and the profits obtained.[85] It is appropriate, however, to deduct expenses incurred by the defendant in making the profit, as well as a sum to represent reasonable overheads.[86] The burden is placed on the defendant to show that a particular profit did not derive from the breach of duty.[87] This shift in the burden of proof is presumably justified by the stringent policy that fiduciaries should not profit in any way from their breach of duty. Consequently, it is presumed that all profits were derived from the breach, and it is for the defendant to show that this was not the case. If the defendant is unable to distinguish the profits made from the breach with the profits made legitimately from other sources, he or she will be liable to disgorge all the profits, because of the policy, reflected in the law of tracing as well, that everything is presumed against a fiduciary in breach.[88]

It appears that the principle of remoteness of benefits, whereby the defendant is only liable to account for profits which derive directly from the commission of the wrong, is interpreted differently where the

[80] *Nocton v Lord Ashburton* [1914] AC 932, 956–7 (Viscount Haldane VC). See also *Regal (Hastings) Ltd v Gulliver* [1967] 2 AC 134n; *Boardman*, above n 15; *Hong Kong v Reid*, above n 20).

[81] See *Chan v Zecharia* (1984) 154 CLR 178, 1989–99 (Deane J); *Warman*, above n 10, 557.

[82] *Murad*, above n 26, para 58 (Arden LJ). See also *Warman International Ltd v Dwyer* (1995) 182 CLR 541, 557. Cp *WWF v World Wrestling Federation Entertainment Inc*, above n 70, para 58 (Chadwick LJ).

[83] *Murad*, *ibid*, para 59 (Arden LJ). See also *Regal*, above n 80, 144 (Lord Russell of Killowen).

[84] *Murad*, *ibid*, para 62 (Arden LJ); *Blythe v Northwood* [2005] NSWCA 221, para 194 (Mason P).

[85] *CMS Dolphin*, above n 11, para 97 (Lawrence Collins J). See also *Swain v The Law Society* [1982] 1 WLR 17.

[86] *CMS Dolphin*, *ibid*, para 97 (Lawrence Collins J).

[87] *Murad*, above n 26, para 77 (Arden LJ).

[88] *Warman*, above n 10.

defendant has profited from a breach of fiduciary duty, so that the fiduciary is also liable to account for profits which arise indirectly from the commission of the wrong. So, for example, in *Gwembe Valley Development Co Ltd v Koshy (No 3)*,[89] the defendant fiduciary was held liable to account for all the profits he had made from unauthorised loan transactions. The account included those profits which derived directly from the commission of the wrong in the form of payments made to him, and also indirect benefits arising from the increase in the value of his shareholding in the company. It would follow from this, for example, that if a fiduciary has received a bribe, he or she should be liable to account for the value of the bribe and any income obtained from its investment.[90] This relaxation of the rules on remoteness is presumably justified by the policy to deter breaches of fiduciary duty because such breaches are considered to be especially culpable,[91] by ensuring that the fiduciary is deprived of all benefits which derive from the commission of the wrong. It would follow that the defendant in *Attorney-General for Hong Kong v Reid*,[92] who was held liable to hold the land which had been purchased with bribe money on constructive trust for the principal, could have been held liable to account instead for the value of the land, since this represented a benefit received indirectly from the commission of the wrong. This would have avoided the unfortunate proprietary connotations of recognising a constructive trust, which gives the principal priority over the defendant's unsecured creditors if the defendant became insolvent.

In addition to the qualified notion of remoteness in the context of breach of fiduciary duty, it appears that the test of causation is interpreted much more flexibly than the usual but for test. This is supported by the important, but difficult, decision of the Court of Appeal in *Murad*,[93] where it was held that the court was not concerned with what would have happened but for the breach, but only with whether the fiduciary had profited following the breach. Consequently, a defendant fiduciary will be liable to account to the claimant for profits made from the breach of fiduciary duty even if the profit would have been made had the defendant not committed the wrong. The justification for this stringent approach to causation was that, for policy reasons, the courts refuse to speculate about what would have happened had the breach of duty not occurred;[94] it was

89 [2003] EWCA Civ 1048, [2004] 1 BCLC 131.

90 *Murad*, above n 26, para 85 (Arden LJ).

91 See *Hong Kong v Reid*, above n 20, 330 (Lord Templeman).

92 *Ibid*. See also *Ocular Sciences Ltd v Aspect Vision Care Ltd* [1997] RPC 289, 412–13 (Laddie J); *Fyffes Group*, above n 33; *Daraydan Holdings Ltd, v Solland International Ltd* [2004] EWHC 622 (Ch), [2005] Ch 119.

93 Above n 26.

94 *Ibid*, para 76 (Arden LJ). See also *Ex parte James* (1803) 8 Ves 337, 345 (Lord Eldon); *Brickenden v London Loan and Savings Co* [1934] 3 DLR 465, 469 (Lord Thankerton); *Gwembe Valley*, above n 89, para 145 (Mummery LJ).

also due to the need to deter defendants from the temptation of abusing a relationship of trust and confidence.[95]

In *Murad*[96] a majority of the Court of Appeal recognised that the fiduciary, who had failed to disclose a material fact to his principals in breach of fiduciary duty, was liable to account for the whole profit he made as a result of the principals entering into a joint venture with him, even though some profit might still have been made had the fiduciary made the relevant disclosure. The fiduciary would only not have been liable to account for other profits which had arisen from a different transaction. The claimants and the defendant had entered into a joint venture to buy a hotel. The defendant fraudulently told the claimants that the purchase price was £4.1 million when it was actually £3.6 million, and that he would contribute £500,000 in cash. However, this contribution actually took the form, in part, of a secret commission for introducing the claimants to the vendor, and a set-off of certain non-enforceable obligations. The trial judge found that, had the actual purchase price and the set-off been disclosed, the claimants would still have agreed to the joint venture but with a higher profit share for themselves. The majority held that this was irrelevant and the defendant was liable to disgorge all the profits, both revenue and capital, which he had made from the joint venture following the sale of the hotel, even though some profit would have been made had the defendant not breached his fiduciary duty.[97] Arden LJ cited the decision of the House of Lords in *Regal (Hastings) Ltd v Gulliver*[98] as authority for this proposition, although it is difficult to see how that case is of any relevance to the determination of the causation issue, other than to affirm that the profits must have been made 'by reason and in course of the fiduciary relationship'.[99] Other cases were cited by Jonathan Parker LJ,[100] but they just affirm that the fiduciary should not profit from the breach and that loss suffered by the principal need not be established; they do not engage with the question of what profit does derive from the breach. The majority appears to have assumed that, since but for causation is relevant to establishing loss for the purposes of equitable compensation[101] and because loss is not relevant to the account of profits, it must follow that but for causation is not relevant either.[102]

95 *Murad*, above n 26, para 107 (Jonathan Parker LJ). See also *Bray v Ford* [1896] AC 44, 51 (Lord Herschell); *Consul Development Pty Ltd v DPC Estates Pty Ltd* (1975) 132 CLR 373, 397 (Gibbs J).

96 *Ibid.* See also *United Pan-Europe Communications NV v Deutsche Bank AG* [2002] 2 BCLC 461, para 47 (Morritt LJ); *Gwembe Valley*, above n 89.

97 *Murad*, above n 26, para 62 (Arden LJ).

98 [1967] 2 AC 134n, particularly the dictum of Lord Russell of Killowen at 144–5.

99 *Ibid*, p 143. See also p 153; *Swain v The Law Society* [1982] 1 WLR 17, 36 (Fox LJ): *Warman*, above n 10, 559; *Blake*, above n 1, 280 (Lord Nicholls).

100 See, eg *Parker v McKenna* (1874) LR 10 Ch App 96, 118.

101 See *Swindle v Harrison* [1997] 4 All ER 705.

102 See also Conaglen, 'Strict Fiduciary Loyalty and Account of Profits' (2006) 65 *CLJ* 278.

But this conclusion does not follow. Nevertheless, the conclusion is consistent with the earlier decision of the Court of Appeal in *United Pan-Europe Communications NV v Deutsche Bank AG*,[103] where Morritt LJ[104] said:

> I see no justification for any further requirement that the profit shall have been obtained by the fiduciary 'by virtue of his position'. Such a condition suggests an element of causation which neither principle not the authorities require.

This is clearly inconsistent with the decision of the House of Lords in *Regal v Gulliver*, where this 'further requirement' was recognised.[105] To confuse matters further, this requirement was even recognised by Jonathan Parker LJ in *Murad*[106] itself.

Clarke LJ dissented from the majority's approach on the basis that the question of whether the defendant would have made the profit even had there not been a breach of fiduciary duty is relevant to the extent of the account of profits, although he accepted that it was not relevant to whether there was any liability to account at all.[107] Clarke LJ preferred to treat the assessment of the profits as being dependent on what was an equitable result. But that way confusion and uncertainty lies.

A similar approach was adopted by the New South Wales Court of Appeal in *Say-Dee Pty Ltd v Farah Construction Pty Ltd*.[108] This case involved a joint venture to purchase and redevelop a property. The defendant controller of Farah Construction, who owed fiduciary duties to the claimant, obtained information that the property could not be redeveloped because the site was too small, but he did not disclose this information to the claimant. Instead he arranged for the acquisition of two adjoining properties by his associates and did not invite the claimant to participate in the investment. This was held to constitute a breach of two fiduciary duties, namely the duty to avoid a conflict of interest and the duty not to profit from his fiduciary position. The defendant was held liable to account for all the benefit or profit made from the acquisition of the properties,[109] even though it was inherently improbable that the claimant would have participated in the purchase of those properties for financial reasons. As in *Murad v Al-Saraj*, the New South Wales Court of Appeal emphasised that the reason for this conclusion was that the remedy for breach of fiduciary duty focuses on the defendant's gain rather than the

103 [2000] 2 BCLC 461.

104 *Ibid*, para 47.

105 As it was in *Warman*, above n 10, 559. See p 324, below.

106 Above n 26, para 116 (Jonathan Parker LJ).

107 *Ibid*, para 141.

108 Above n 10. Reversed by the High Court: [2007] HCA 22 on the ground that informed consent had been given following full disclosure by the fiduciary.

109 Through the mechanism of a constructive trust by virtue of which the properties were held on constructive trust for the joint venture.

claimant's loss. Causation needed to be established, but this was done by focusing on the nature of the breach of fiduciary duty, namely the failure to disclose a material fact to the claimant. It was held that the defendant's profit arose from that absence of disclosure. This appears to raise similar problems as regards the interpretation of causation as in *Murad v Al-Saraj*, since in both cases there was evidence that, even if there had been disclosure, the claimants would not have entered into that particular transaction. The cases are distinguishable, though, because of the precise nature of the breach of fiduciary duty. In *Say-Dee* it is true that the claimant was not able to contribute to the purchase of the additional properties for financial reasons, but this was not significant because the breach of fiduciary duty related to the failure to obtain the claimant's informed consent to the defendant purchasing the properties. The claimant would not have given that consent and so any profit made by the defendant was made as a direct result of the breach of fiduciary duty. *Murad v Al-Saraj* was different because in that case there was evidence that the claimants would have consented to the transaction, albeit on different terms, had there been disclosure. In other words, the claimants would have consented to the transaction in principle. It is this fact which makes it difficult to conclude that the but for test of causation was satisfied. This distinction based on the significance of informed consent also explains why there was liability to account for breach of fiduciary duty in some of the leading cases even though the claimant was unable to participate in the transaction itself, because the defendant's breach involved the failure to obtain the fully informed consent of the claimant.[110]

The decision of the majority in *Murad v Al-Saraj* creates real difficulties when determining the extent of the account of profits. In assessing its validity, it is useful to return to first principles. It is clear that the remedy of an account of profits is the usual remedy where a defendant has breached his or her fiduciary duty. The alternative remedy is that of equitable compensation. To assess that remedy it is necessary to show that, but for the commission of the wrong, the claimant would not have suffered loss. To obtain an account of profits, however, it is not necessary to show that the claimant had suffered any loss. But it also clear that the fiduciary who has breached his or her duty need not account for all profits made from whatever source;[111] some link to the breach of duty must be established. It would be absurd to say, for example, that a defendant who has breached his or her fiduciary duty and who at the same time won a large sum in a lottery would have to account for that lottery win. Some causative link needs to be shown between the breach and the profit. It is for this reason that a defendant who has profited from breach of fiduciary

110 See, eg *Keech v Sandford* (1726) Sel Cas t King 61, 25 ER 223; *Regal (Hastings) Ltd v Gulliver* [1967] 2 AC 132n; *Boardman*, above n 15.

111 *Murad*, above n 26, para 62 (Arden LJ).

duty can be awarded an equitable allowance to reflect the fact that the defendant's services and skills contributed to the profit,[112] because that part of the profit did not relate to the breach of duty. Similarly in *Warman*[113] the High Court of Australia limited the account to two years' profits to reflect the policy that the defendant should account for the profits 'made within the scope and ambit of his duty'.[114] This limitation on the account of profits also arose because the principal's business opportunity, which was exploited by the defendant fiduciary, was only anticipated to last for about one further year, although it was concluded that some advantages, such as goodwill and the experience of employees, would have lasted beyond that time.[115]

So if causation is relevant and, as the Court of Appeal in *Murad v Al-Saraj* recognised, the profit must arise 'within the scope and ambit of the relevant fiduciary duty',[116] what profit derived from the breach of fiduciary duty? Surely, if the defendant would have made a profit anyway had there not been a breach of fiduciary duty, then the only profit which was caused by the breach must be the difference between the profit which was made and that which would otherwise have been made. Now it is true that equity has been reluctant to speculate about what might have happened had there not been a breach of duty,[117] but such speculation is perfectly acceptable for the hypothetical bargain measure at common law[118] and, further, in *Murad v Al-Saraj* the trial judge had been able to conclude that the claimants would have been willing to enter into a joint venture, albeit on different terms, had there been no breach of fiduciary duty. Further, the question of what might have happened but for the breach has to be considered for the assessment of equitable compensation,[119] so there is no technical reason why equity cannot speculate about this when ordering an account of profits.[120] Consequently, there is no justification for the rejection of the but for test of causation when accounting for profits following a breach of fiduciary duty. It must be shown that, but for the breach,[121] the profit would not have been made.

112 See *Boardman*, above n 15. Such an allowance was awarded in *Say-Dee*, above n 10.

113 Above n 10.

114 *Ibid*, 559.

115 *Ibid*.

116 *Murad*, above n 26, para 116 (Jonathan Parker LJ).

117 See *Brickenden v London Loan and Savings Co* [1934] 3 DLR 465, 469 (Lord Thankerton) (Privy Council); *Gray v New Augarita Porcupine Mines Ltd* [1952] 3 DLR 1, 15 (Privy Council).

118 See p 310, above.

119 *Murad*, above n 26, para 110 (Jonathan Parker LJ). See *Bristol and West Building Society v Mothew* [1998] Ch 1, 17 (Millett LJ); *Target Holdings Ltd v Redferns* [1996] 1 AC 421, 436 (Lord Browne-Wilkinson).

120 The High Court of Australia was willing to engage in such speculation for the purposes of taking an account in *Warman*, above n 10, 565–6.

121 The language of but for causation was used by Clarke LJ in his dissenting judgment in *Murad*, above n 26, para 160.

This does not involve the watering down of the policy of deterring breaches of fiduciary duty; it is simply a matter of ensuring that the profit which must be disgorged derives from the breach of duty.

That a but for test of causation should be applied even in the context of breach of fiduciary duty is supported by the decision in *Fyffes Group Ltd v Templeman* of Toulson J,[122] who refused to order a briber to account for the profits he had made from a transaction which the principal had entered into following the bribing of the principal's agent. This was because the agent's principal would have entered into the transaction with the briber even if the agent had not been bribed, so the briber's profit was not caused by the bribery of the agent. The cause of action in this case was that of dishonestly assisting a breach of fiduciary duty, rather than breach of fiduciary duty itself, but that is no reason to treat this case as distinct from that of *Murad*. The defendant in *Fyffes Group* had still committed an equitable wrong, but no restitutionary remedy was awarded because of the absence of a nexus between the profit which arose from the provision of services under the agreement and the wrong of paying the bribe. Arden LJ sought to distinguish this case on the basis that the wrongdoer was entitled to an allowance for his services.[123] But this is unconvincing.

This analysis of the recent cases concerning the remedies for breach of fiduciary duty and the policies underpinning the award of such remedies indicates that there is no justification for watering down the usual test of but for causation, since it is vital to show that there is a causative link between the breach of duty and the profit made, for otherwise it is not possible to determine the profits for which the defendant should be accountable. As the High Court of Australia emphasised in *Warman*:[124]

> In determining the proper basis for an account of profits, it is of first importance in this, as in other cases, to ascertain precisely what it was that was acquired in consequence of the fiduciary's breach of duty.

However, the policy of deterring breaches of fiduciary duty suggests that a much weaker test of remoteness should be adopted to encompass gains made both directly and indirectly as a result of the breach of duty. It is only where some form of proprietary link to the profit made can be established that the constructive trust should be recognised, for then the profit can legitimately be considered to belong to the claimant in equity.[125]

122 [2002] Lloyd's Rep 643.

123 *Murad*, above n 26, para 69.

124 Above n 10, para 40.

125 Although the trend of recent authorities, primarily in England, suggests a more extensive use of the constructive trust, extending possibly to any case where the defendant has profited from a breach of fdicuiary duty: see *Hong Kong v Reid*, above n 20; *Daraydan Holdings Ltd v Solland International Ltd* [2004] EWHC 622 (Ch), [2005] Ch 119.

D Unconscionable Receipt

Where the defendant has received property which has been transferred in breach of trust or breach of fiduciary duty, and in circumstances where the defendant can be considered to have acted unconscionably,[126] the defendant will have committed the wrong of unconscionable receipt and will be held liable to account as if he or she was a constructive trustee.[127] The language of constructive trusteeship is liable to confuse since it has proprietary connotations, but the liability of the defendant is a personal one to restore the value of the property received rather than to restore property itself.[128] That the remedy is personal and not proprietary was recognised by Millett LJ in *Paragon Finance plc v DB Thakerar and Co*:[129]

> the expressions 'constructive trust' and 'constructive trustee' are misleading for there is no trust and usually no possibility of a proprietary remedy; they are nothing more than a formula for equitable relief.

The inappropriateness of the proprietary language of the constructive trust is emphasised by the fact that if the defendant has received and retained property in which the claimant has an equitable proprietary interest, then the claimant will be able to bring a proprietary claim to vindicate his or her property rights and recover the property which has been retained. The true function of the action for unconscionable receipt is that it provides for a remedy where there are no longer rights in specific property to be vindicated and, although that remedy uses the language of accounting as if the defendant was a constructive trustee, the defendant is simply liable to account for the value of the property received.

However, should the language of constructive trusteeship be dismissed so readily, or might it have an effect on the interpretation of the principles of causation and remoteness for this cause of action? In particular, should the account be taken at the time of receipt of the property or should any change in the value of the property whilst it is being retained be taken into account? Certainly, if the action for unconscionable receipt is considered to be the equitable counterpart of the common law action for money had and received,[130] the remedy should be assessed at the point of receipt, when the

126 *Bank of Credit and Commerce International (Overseas) Ltd v Akindele* [2001] Ch 437. See also *Kalls Enterprises Pty Ltd (In Liq) v Baloglow* [2006] NSWSC 617.

127 See, in particular, *Gwembe Valle*, above n 89, para 88.

128 Cp *Say-Dee*, above n 10, where it was held that where a party had received property which had been transferred in breach of fiduciary duty that property would be held on a constructive trust.

129 [1999] 1 All ER 400, 408. See also *Dubai Aluminium Co Ltd v Salaam* [2002] UKHL 48, [2003] 2 AC 366, 404.

130 As advocated by Lord Nicholls of Birkenhead writing extra-judicially: 'Knowing Receipt: The Need for a New Landmark' in Cornish, Nolan, O'Sullivan and Virgo (eds), *Restitution: Past, Present and Future* (Oxford, Hart Publishing, 1998), 231.

defendant is enriched at the claimant's expense. However, the traditional language of constructive trusteeship, as opposed to that of the constructive trust, might support a wider interpretation of the remoteness principle, in the same way as that principle should be interpreted more widely as regards the determination of the remedy for breach of fiduciary duty. Indeed, in *Crown Dilmun v Sutton*[131] Peter Smith J held that a defendant who had unconscionably received property in breach of fiduciary duty was liable to account for all the profits which it had received or would subsequently make. The only restriction was that the account would have to be taken before the end of the six-year limitation period after the claimant first became aware of its claim.[132] Further, the judge recognised that in taking the account the defendant could be awarded an allowance to reflect his or her own contribution, but this would probably not be awarded by virtue of the defendant's fault in receiving property in breach of trust. Although this case did not deal specifically with the principles of causation and remoteness, it is at least consistent with the approach adopted for causation and remoteness as regards primary breaches of fiduciary duty. Consequently, the language of constructive trusteeship, as opposed to the constructive trust, is significant by virtue of its fiduciary connotations to require the defendant to account for all benefits received, both directly and indirectly.

E Criminal Offences

By virtue of the principle that no wrongdoer should profit from his or her wrong, it should follow that any criminal who profits from his or her crime should be liable to make restitution to the victim. Such a general principle has been recognised in English law,[133] and this also extends to third parties who obtain the proceeds of crime.[134] Despite this fundamental principle, there is little evidence in the cases of a general liability to make restitution of the proceeds of crime at common law. This is primarily because of the development of statutory schemes to confiscate the proceeds of crime by the state, through fines or statutory confiscation mechanisms, rather than allow the victim to recover the proceeds at common law.[135] The existence of an additional claim for restitution at common law has been doubted,[136] primarily because the confiscation of the proceeds of crime is considered to

131 [2004] EWHC 52, [2004] 1 BCLC 468, para 27.

132 *Ibid*, para 30.

133 *St. John Shipping Corp v Joseph Rank Ltd* [1957] 1 QB 267, 292 (Devlin J). See also *Guardian Newspapers*, above n 1, 286 (Lord Goff).

134 *Bridgeman v Green* (1757) Wilm 58, 65; 97 ER 22, 25 (Lord Commissioner Wilmot).

135 In England this statutory scheme is now provided for by the Proceeds of Crime Act 2002.

136 *Halifax*, above n 21, 229 (Glidewell LJ).

be a matter for Parliament.[137] The preferable view is that there is a subsidiary power at common law for judges to deprive a criminal of the proceeds of crime where the statutory powers of fines and confiscation are inadequate, because, for example, of the nature of the crime, or because the defendant has not been convicted.[138]

Once it is recognised that there is a role for restitutionary relief to deprive a criminal of the proceeds of the crime, it is necessary to consider what form that relief should take. Normally where the criminal has profited from the crime the remedy will be an account of those profits. However, the court might conclude that the profits should be held on constructive trust for the victim, particularly where the proceeds derive from the commission of fraud or theft.[139]

Where the remedy of an account of profits is awarded, the normal test of but for causation will presumably apply, so it is necessary to show that, but for the commission of the crime, the defendant would not have obtained the benefit. Likewise, the normal rules of remoteness of benefit appear to apply as well, so that the defendant is only liable to account for profits which directly arise from the commission of the wrong.[140] Where, however, the proceeds of crime are held on constructive trust, all the defendant's profits will be held on trust, regardless of whether they arose directly or indirectly from the commission of the crime.[141]

There is, however, a case to be made that the normally strict test of remoteness should be relaxed where the victim claims an account of profits in respect of the proceeds of a particularly heinous crime, such as murder,[142] by virtue of the policy that no criminal should profit in any way from such a crime.[143] So, for example, if a murderer has published his or her autobiography, the royalties might be considered to be an indirect benefit of the crime, but should still be given up to the victim and no allowance should be made for the defendant's contribution to the book.

137 *Ibid*, 229 (Peter Gibson LJ); *M*, above n 21, 23 (Hoffmann J).

138 *Halifax*, above n 21, 230 (Glidewell LJ).

139 See *Westdeutsche Landesbank Girozentrale v Islington LBC* [1996] AC 669, 716 (Lord Browne-Wilkinson).

140 *Halifax*, above n 21. See also *M*, above n 21.

141 *Hong Kong v Reid*, above n 20.

142 Note the similar principle that the court will never allow a claimant to obtain restitution on the ground of unjust enrichment where he or she has committed a serious crime, simply for reasons of public policy. See *Tappenden v Randall* (1801) 2 Bos and Pul 467, 471, 126 ER 1388, 1390 (Heath J); *Kearley v Thomson* (1890) 24 QBD 742, 747 (Fry LJ).

143 Although, because of the decision in *Halifax Building Society v Thomas* [1996] Ch 217, this would not extend to crimes involving fraud.

IV CONCLUSIONS

This survey of the law of restitutionary remedies reveals that the principles of causation and remoteness have a vital part to play regardless of the nature of the wrong. Despite recent developments in the law relating to equitable wrongs, the preferable view is that the but for test of causation should apply to all claims for restitution for wrongdoing. However, the test of remoteness should vary depending on the nature of the wrong. Normally the defendant will only be required to make restitution of benefits received directly from the commission of the wrong, save where there is a clear policy which supports claims to indirect benefits.

However, this survey reveals other currents within the law of restitution for wrongs. One of the most significant is that the law of restitution is in danger of subverting the established order in many areas of private law, but especially within the law of wrongs. This subversion can be controlled in two ways. First, through the recognition of a more sophisticated approach to the analysis of remedies; one which recognises the notion of hybrid remedies, in the sense that certain remedies may have both compensatory and restitutionary functions. Secondly, restitutionary remedies for wrongs are sometimes the norm and sometimes subsidiary to other remedies, particularly compensatory remedies, depending on the nature of the wrong. A distinction, justified primarily for historical reasons, appears to exist between equitable wrongs and common law wrongs. In equity there is no principle of subsidiarity as regards the award of restitutionary remedies, but this principle does operate at law, so that no restitutionary remedy, even a hybrid restitutionary remedy, can be awarded if compensatory remedies are adequate. Restitutionary remedies for common law wrongs should, therefore, remain the exception rather than the rule.

13

Subtractive and Wrongful Enrichment: Identifying Gain in the Law of Restitution

DUNCAN SHEEHAN*

TRADITIONALLY RESTITUTION HAS been divided between autonomous unjust enrichment and restitution for wrongs. In the latter the normative reason for a remedy is the wrong. There is a breach of duty for which a remedy, a secondary right, is awarded. In the former there is no wrong. There is no breach of duty and the claimant's right is a primary right to the return of the asset transferred. We are concerned with both here, but in slightly different, albeit interconnected, ways.

At a minimum, three questions need to be answered to establish a claim of unjust enrichment. Is the defendant enriched? Is the defendant enriched at the expense of the claimant? Is there an unjust factor, a reason for restitution?[1] We focus mainly on identifying the recoverable gain in this paper. There is an overlap between the enrichment and the 'at the expense of' questions. The defendant may have obtained a gain from a third party, but the claimant may still argue that it should be attributable to his expense.

Other unjust enrichment theorists have approached this question. According to Barker, there is, or should be, no difference between different measures of gain.[2] He attempts to create an integrated framework for

* Senior Lecturer in Law, University of East Anglia. I should like to thank James Edelman for reading the penultimate draft and helping me to sharpen some of the arguments. Thanks are also due to the Society of Legal Scholars for providing funding to enable me to present this paper at the Obligations III conference in Brisbane.

1 PBH Birks, *An Introduction to the Law of Restitution* (Oxford, Clarendon Press, revised edn, 1989), 21. This third requirement has become controversial. Birks has repudiated it. PBH Birks, *Unjust Enrichment* (Oxford, Clarendon Press, 2nd edn, 2005), ch 4; see also T Krebs, *Restitution at the Crossroads* (London, Cavendish Publishing, 2001). We cannot enter this debate here.

2 K Barker, 'Riddles Remedies and Restitution: Quantifying Gain in *Unjust Enrichment* Law' [2001] *Current Legal Problems* 255.

quantifying gain in both unjust enrichment cases and restitution for wrongs cases. He rejects the difference between Birks's measures of value received and value surviving,[3] and suggests that the defendant can only claim to be in one position as regards the claimant. He must be returned to the status quo ante. Barker therefore does not accept the difference between disgorgement and restitutionary damages.[4] That is the difference between a measure based on the value of a transfer to the defendant and one based on the actual profit made. He accepts, however, that there may be reasons to restrict recovery of the defendant's gain, primarily the avoidance of a windfall to the claimant.[5]

Edelman, by contrast, not only insists upon the distinction between the two forms of damages, but also insists that restitutionary damages should be treated separately from restitution for unjust enrichment.[6] Edelman also introduces his distinction into unjust enrichment as a way of distinguishing between permissible and impermissible unjust enrichment awards. Birks has described Edelman's work as irrefutable[7]; however, his own thinking has cast doubts on how the scheme can hold up, and renders the interplay between the concepts discussed very much more complex. There is a necessary terminological preliminary. We use the terms restitutionary and disgorgement damages here in the same way as Edelman, and the term gain-based damages as a neutral term to cover both.

I RESTITUTION OF UNJUST ENRICHMENT

Money is the measure of benefit. However, we also find non-money enrichments, which are discussed in the first part of this paper. The second part examines the distinction between abstractly and traceably surviving enrichment, and between value received and retained.[8] There is also an important question as to the availability of relief in cases of indirect enrichment. In the final part we look at issues of causation, remoteness and tracing.

A Non-money Enrichments

Non-money enrichments come in two forms: goods and services. We call this 'enrichment in kind'. These cases are not as simple as money cases. The

[3] Birks, *Law of Restitution*, above n 1, 75–6.
[4] Barker, above n 2, 258.
[5] *Ibid*, 292–4.
[6] J Edelman, *Gain-based Damages* (Oxford, Hart Publishing, 2002), 80, 93–9.
[7] Birks, *Unjust Enrichment*, above n 1, 282.
[8] *Ibid*, ch 5.

default position is that enrichment can be measured by its market value.[9] That implies that anything with a market value can in principle be enriching. This causes controversy in the context of pure services. They are sometimes argued to be non-enriching,[10] or enrichment subject to instantaneous disenrichment.[11] However, the willingness of a reasonable person to pay for something renders it objectively enriching. In *BP v Hunt (No 2)*[12] Robert Goff J accepted that, but for the Law Reform (Frustrated Contracts) Act 1943, he would have held services enriching in themselves. It is hard to see why the ephemeral nature of the benefit should make a difference. If pure services are enriching because people would pay, the question when a service is received disappears: if only two notes are played, has the symphony been received?[13] The question when a service is received is comprehensible only if the law of unjust enrichment is concerned with reversing transfers. But even then it makes little sense. It seems more plausible that the law reverses enrichments rather than transfers.[14]

This is subject to the principle of subjective devaluation, and to the principle that agreed contract prices should remain, even where the contract itself does not.[15] Subjective devaluation derives from the principle that we should be able to choose how we spend our money.[16] The defendant should be able to say he does not value the benefit as does the market. He may be disentitled from subjective devaluation. He may have freely accepted. This indicates a failure to reject a returnable benefit, where he still has the asset,[17] or where there was an opportunity to reject that he failed to take. His behaviour may also be such as to disentitle him from relying on his lower valuation.

9 Barker, above n 2, 264; AS Burrows, *The Law of Restitution* (London, Butterworths, 2nd edn, 2002), 17; G Virgo, *The Principles of the Law of Restitution* (Oxford, Oxford University Press, 1999), 62; Birks, *Law of Restitution*, above n 1, 109–10; Birks, *Unjust Enrichment*, above n 1, 47–48; M McInnes, 'Enrichment Revisited' in J Neyers (ed), *Understanding Unjust Enrichment* (Oxford, Hart Publishing, 2004), 165, 169.

10 J Beatson, 'Benefit, Reliance and the Structure of *Unjust Enrichment*' in J Beatson (ed), *The Use and Abuse of Unjust Enrichment* (Oxford, Clarendon Press, 1991), 21, 38.

11 Birks, *Unjust Enrichment*, above n 1, 62–3. Consequently enrichment is sometimes thought to be a narrower concept than transfer. Edelman, above n 6, 70.

12 [1979] 1 WLR 783, 801–2 (Robert Goff J).

13 Barker, above n 2, 257.

14 Virgo, above n 9, 739; see Edelman, above n 6, 70.

15 See A Skelton, *Restitution and Contract* (Oxford, Mansfield Press, 1998).

16 *Gidney v Shank* [1995] 5 WWR 385; *Olchowy v McKay* [1996] 1 WWR 36; *Club 7 Ltd v EPK Enterprises* (1993) 15 Nfld & PEIR 271; *McDonald v Coys of Kensington* [2004] EWCA Civ 47, [26]–[40]. *Peel (Regional Muncipality) v Canada* [1992] 3 SCR 762, (1992) 98 DLR (4th) 140 does not use the phrase but does place emphasis on 'the right to choose how to spend one's own money'.

17 *McDonald v Coys of Kensington* [2004] EWCA Civ 47; Barker, above n 2, 264–7.

B Measures of Enrichment

Birks argues that there are two ways of contemplating wealth in the unjust enrichment context. The first sees it as a single fund expressable in money. The second sees it as a list of assets. The first is the abstract conception, the second the traceable conception.[18] Jaffey denies this distinction, and rolls the abstract and traceable conceptions together. The side effect is that a proprietary claim is a claim in the abstract, not to any specific asset.[19] This runs against the tide of traditional opinion,[20] and is too great a side effect. Here we accept the Birksian view that one can be traceably enriched, but not abstractly so. We therefore also accept the traditional view that a proprietary claim is a claim to a specific identifiable asset, and consequently there is a need to separate traceable and abstract enrichment. This is important. To avail himself of a proprietary remedy, the claimant must show that the defendant has in his hands assets traceably the product of assets previously his, the claimant's, and that he has not lost those proprietary rights. The law cannot create proprietary rights by magic. That lies at the heart of its hostility to the remedial constructive trust, a discretionary proprietary response.[21]

The defendant may disenrich himself as a result of having received the enrichment.[22] He may, for instance, after receiving the payment, make a charitable donation he would not otherwise have made. Birks has posited a wider availability for the defence.[23] Under this wider view, the defendant need not consciously rely on the receipt; he need only lose the enrichment. If the defendant were mugged walking across the street, he could avail himself of the defence. The purpose of the wider defence is to ensure that receipts are not sterilised by parties taking greater care not to lose the enrichment than they would take with their own property.[24] Birks has correctly pointed out that abstract enrichment must trump traceable. This prevents differing results, depending on whether the defendant retains traceably surviving value, but has causally disenriched himself elsewhere.[25] If not, there would be a stampede to a proprietary claim, which would provide recourse to the traceably surviving value even where there had

18 Birks, *Unjust Enrichment*, above n 1, 69.

19 P Jaffey, *The Nature and Scope of Restitution* (Oxford, Hart Publishing, 2000), 282.

20 S Worthington, *Proprietary Interests in Commercial Transactions* (Oxford, Oxford University Press, 1996), 189; K Barker, 'Review Article—The Nature and Scope of Restitution' [2001] *Restitution Law Review* 232, 237.

21 *Re PPI (No 2)* [1998] 3 All ER 812 (CA).

22 R Goff and G Jones, *The Law of Restitution* (London, Sweet & Maxwell, 6th edn, 2002), 808–18.

23 PBH Birks, 'Change of Position and Surviving Enrichment' in WJ Swadling (ed), *The Limits to Restitutionary Claims* (London, UKNCCL, 1997), 36; Birks, *Unjust Enrichment*, above n 1, 209–10.

24 *Ibid*, 50–1.

25 Birks, *Unjust Enrichment*, above n 1, 210.

been abstract disenrichment. Lionel Smith has claimed that there are personal claims that are dependent on tracing where the claimant cannot claim value received. Tracing identifies the value of the claim.[26] Smith identifies a number of claims where this will be so, such as a claim for the return of money lent to a party without the capacity to borrow. Tracing can be relevant to this process, but a party might, as Smith realises, disenrich himself so that traceably surviving enrichment remains.[27]

Barker wishes to have only one measure of gain and to integrate tracing.[28] Barker sees no reason, especially given the interplay between them, for abstractly and traceably surviving enrichment to be treated separately. The relevance of both causation and tracing to some personal claims makes his point. That single measure of gain would be the same for both unjust enrichment and wrongs claims. His argument is that the defendant can only claim to be in one position vis-à-vis the claimant—the pre-transaction position. The aim behind the wrong should go some way to identify whether gains ought to be stripped.[29] Unjust enrichment cases, however, demand the full enrichment be reversed.[30]

Barker has suggested that maintaining change of position as a separate defence apart from abstractly surviving enrichment causes conceptual multiplication.[31] The difficulty with this argument is that it is not clear now that there can never be non-disenriching changes of position.[32] There may also be cases of disenrichment where the defendant is disentitled from relying on the disenrichment, and cannot therefore claim change of position. Barker has criticised Jaffey's attempt to integrate causation and tracing.[33] Tracing will continue to be treated differently to identify the title link.[34] Despite this, he argues that tracing and subrogation 'are techniques for obtaining monetary remedies, not remedies as such . . . their involvement ought not to affect the quantification of the award.'[35] There is, according to Barker, a danger that a purely causal approach may lead to overextensive proprietary relief. Tracing can though be supplemented 'where the evidence presents a convincing case for the existence of a factual causal link' with the defendant's gain.[36] Barker, however, here

26 LD Smith, *The Law of Tracing* (Oxford, Clarendon Press, 1997), 29–33.

27 *Ibid*, 32.

28 Barker, above n 2, 262.

29 M McInnes 'Disgorgement for Wrongs: An Experiment in Alignment' [2000] *Restitution Law Review* 514; K Barker and LD Smith '*Unjust Enrichment*' in D Hayton (ed), *Law's Futures* (Oxford, Hart Publishing, 2000) 411, 414.

30 McInnes, above n 9, 198.

31 Barker, above n 2, 277.

32 *Commerzbank v Gareth Price-Jones* [2003] EWCA Civ 1663.

33 Barker, above n 20, 236–7.

34 LD Smith, '*Unjust Enrichment* Property and the Structure of Trusts' (2000) 116 *LQR* 412, 417–18; Barker, above n 2, 280.

35 Barker, above n 2, 262.

36 *Ibid*, 280.

discusses personal claims. Tracing's role in proprietary claims requires it be treated separately.

C Indirect Enrichment

We address a number of interlinked questions here. The first is the question whether an unjust enrichment claim can reach remote recipients. We restrict liability to the immediate enrichee and forbid leapfrogging to remoter defendants.[37] Virgo refers to this as a principle of privity,[38] but this is at best confusing, given the concept of the same name in contract. The usual rule must be that purely personal claims do not reach beyond the initial recipient.[39] A proprietary claim is required. Birks has argued that a relatively weak non-proprietary link can explain some leapfrogging cases.[40] He prays the German rule to his aid.[41] He relies on a group of agency cases,[42] and *Lipkin Gorman v Karpnale*.[43] In that case Cass, a partner in the claimant firm, used money from the client account to gamble at the defendant's club. The firm subsequently claimed the money back from the club, Cass being bankrupt. The agency cases can be confined to their context, and *Lipkin Gorman* is only explicable as a legal power to revest title.[44] It is hard to explain Lord Goff's references to the firm's tracing 'their money', given his insistence that title had passed, except as a proprietary claim of some sort.

The second issue is whether English law insists upon a corresponding loss in the hands of the claimant. Birks maintains that English law does not insist on a corresponding loss.[45] Birks also allows claims for secondary profits on the basis of interceptive subtraction. Grantham and Rickett see this as impermissibly including wealth received from third parties.[46] We also look at interest claims.

37 PBH Birks, 'At the Expense of the Claimant: Direct and Indirect Enrichment in English Law' in R Zimmermann and D Johnson (eds), *Unjustified Enrichment: Key Issues in Comparative Perspective* (Cambridge, Cambridge University Press, 2001), 493.

38 Virgo, above n 9, 106–7; Burrows, above n 9, 31.

39 A Tettenborn, 'Lawful Receipt—A Justifying Factor' [1997] *Restitution Law Review* 1; *Agip (Africa) Ltd v Jackson* [1990] Ch 265.

40 PBH Birks, 'Overview' in PBH Birks (ed), *Laundering and Tracing* (Oxford, Clarendon Press, 1995), 289, 311; Birks, *Unjust Enrichment*, above n 1, 94–98.

41 Birks, above n 37, 510–11; § 822 BGB.

42 *Bannatyne v D&C MacIver* [1906] 1 KB 103; *B Liggett (Liverpool) Ltd v Barclays Bank* [1928] 1 KB 48; *Re Cleadon* [1939] Ch 286; *Butler v Rice* [1910] 2 Ch 277. Birks admits this last case can be explained on the basis of voidable title.

43 [1991] 2 AC 548 (HL).

44 D Sheehan, 'Proprietary Responses to Mistake and Ignorance: An Unseen Equivalence' [2002] *Restitution Law Review* 69, 74–7.

45 Birks, above n 37, 509.

46 R Grantham and C Rickett, 'Disgorgement for *Unjust Enrichment*?' [2003] *CLJ* 158, 171.

(i) *Capping Relief at the Claimant's Loss*

Birks correctly points out that relief available in unjust enrichment cannot be capped by the loss to the claimant.[47] Compensation is not a remedial goal of unjust enrichment.[48] There are a number of factors that point to this conclusion, although they do not compel the conclusion that Birks ultimately draws from them.

The defence of passing on is not part of English law.[49] Where B is enriched at the expense of A, who passes the loss to C, Degeling posits a cause of action in C against A where A recovers in unjust enrichment from B.[50] That prevents A from accumulating recoveries from both B and C. The defence of passing on would prevent A from recovering from B. The absence of the defence from English law is said to demonstrate that loss and gain need not correlate.[51] Grantham and Rickett argue that this misses the point that the central concern is with the claimant's overall wealth position.[52] However, the linkage that Grantham and Rickett posit with the 'expense' requirement suggests instability in the cause of action, and when it arises. This has implications for defences such as limitation. The cause of action must be fully formed at the point of the payment or transfer. This is implicit in *Kleinwort Benson v Birmingham CC*.[53] In that case the bank entered into hedging transactions mirroring hedges made elsewhere so as to ensure they never made a loss. Saville LJ argued that mitigation was irrelevant, and that 'at the expense of' referred to immediate expense.[54] Obviously the existence of the cause of action cannot be affected by subsequent credits and debits. If passing on is a defence separate from the initial expense requirement, the law suffers from unnecessary conceptual multiplication. The defence is used to give effect to a requirement of 'expense' inherent in the unjust enrichment principle. Two principles are in use rather than one. There are also practical reasons of proof why the defence should not be allowed.[55] The gains from

47 Contrast M McInnes, 'Interceptive Subtraction, *Unjust Enrichment* and Wrongs—A Reply to Professor Birks' [2003] *CLJ* 697; the Canadian position is different requiring a 'corresponding impoverishment', *Pettkus v Becker* (1980) 117 DLR (3d) 257 (SCC).

48 *Royal Brompton Hospital NHS Trust v Hammond* [2002] UKHL 14 at [33], [2002] 1 WLR 1397, 1413 (Lord Steyn).

49 Birks, *Unjust Enrichment*, above n 1, 219–21; *Kleinwort Benson v Birmingham CC* [1997] QB 380 (CA).

50 S Degeling, 'The Defence of Passing On and Policies against Accumulation: Consumers and *Unjust Enrichment*' [2004] *Restitution Law Review* 25, 29.

51 *Ibid*, 27.

52 Grantham and Rickett, above n 46, 170; LD Smith, 'Restitution: The Heart of Corrective Justice' (2001) 79 *Texas Law Review* 2115.

53 [1997] QB 380 (CA).

54 *Ibid*, 394–5; *Roxborough v Rothman Pall Mall of Australia* (2002) 208 CLR 513 (HCA), 528–30 (Gleeson CJ), 541 (Gummow J); *Commissioner of State Revenue v Royal Insurance Australia* (1994) 126 ALR 1.

55 M McInnes, '"Passing On" in the *Law of Restitution*: A Re-Consideration' (1997) 19 *Sydney Law Review* 179, 199; R Grantham and C Rickett, *Enrichment and Restitution in New Zealand* (Oxford, Hart Publishing, 2000), 379.

third parties would have to be attributable to the original relationship. At best this would be rare, and hard to prove.[56] The lack of the defence may reflect recognition that it will never be so; all third party receipts only incidentally recoup the loss.

The issue of whether the gain must correspond to the loss can, however, be decoupled from the defence of passing on, although Saville LJ seems to have assumed otherwise. Lionel Smith accepts that passing on should not be a defence,[57] yet maintains a need for a corresponding loss. According to Smith, there is no need to find a wrong to characterise the gains and losses as normative. It suffices that the claimant had not, for example, consented.[58] The transfer unites the parties and turns material losses into normative losses, and material gains into normative gains. The measure of the transfer is the measure of the claim.[59] This explains why secondary profits are not available in a personal unjust enrichment claim. English law has, however, chosen to prevent defendant windfalls, where the defendant values the asset or service transferred more highly than the claimant. Smith cannot explain subjective revaluation, where the defendant can be shown to value something objectively valueless, or where the defendant values the service higher than the cost of providing it.[60] Smith calls the assumption that the defendant's gain is the measure of recovery an oversimplification caused by the conflation of unjust enrichment and wrongs.[61] However, subjective revaluation would be impossible to explain as a wrong.

Cases that are said to prove the correspondence theorists' point fail to do so. In *Re BHT*,[62] for example, a receiver made payments to a debenture holder on the grounds he had a fixed charge. The liquidator sought directions as to whether it was floating and claimed the money back on the basis that it was in fact a floating charge, and therefore a mistaken payment. The court argued that the preferential creditors had a claim to the whole sum; the company had suffered no loss; its balance sheet was not affected. On payment to the company, however, the company would, outside insolvency, have title. Therefore, on payment the liquidator had title. The immediate claimability of the money by third parties is irrelevant. Kevin Garnett QC, however, brought in the rights of the preferential

56 Barker, above n 2, 302–4.

57 Smith, above n 52, 2153–4.

58 *Ibid*, 2140; other possible causes of action suffice 2143–6.

59 *Ibid*, 2147–8.

60 Virgo, above n 9, 86–8; *BP v Hunt (No 2)* [1979] 1 WLR 783, 803; this would call into question the result in *Greenwood v Bennett* [1973] QB 195.

61 Smith, above n 52, 2147; see also Grantham and Rickett, above n 46, 169, criticising *Roxborough* for precisely this.

62 [2004] EWHC 201, [2004] 1 BCLC 568; see A Berg, 'The Cuckoo in the Nest: Some Aspects of the Spectrum Case' [2006] *Journal of Business Law* 22, 50–1. Mitchell points to *Gnitrow v Cape Plc* [2000] 3 All ER 763 (CA) in C Mitchell, 'The New Birksian Approach to *Unjust Enrichment*' [2004] *Restitution Law Review* 260, 267. But see *BP v Hunt (No 2)* [1979] I WLR 783, 826–7; Birks, *Unjust Enrichment*, above n 1, 80.

creditors to claim ahead of the members as a relevant factor.[63] There is no rule that gain and loss must correspond.

Nonetheless we must be careful not to take the point too far. Edelman argues that unjust enrichment cannot legitimately strip the defendant's secondary profits.[64] It is meaningless to suggest a mistaken payee can or should be deterred. That must be right where the claim is a personal one. Grantham and Rickett posit a case of a mistaken payment which is used to buy a winning lottery ticket. The winnings are not recoverable.[65] Proprietary rights allow the claimant to reach remote recipients and secondary profits because they enable the claimant to point to continuing rights in the asset and rights to accretions in value. Smith does, however, deny that these are properly unjust enrichment claims; a different kind of 'expense' is at issue; it is a vindicatio.[66] We cannot deal in detail with this argument here. It suffices to say the claimant can only claim the lottery win by retaining proprietary rights in the original money taken.[67]

(ii) Interceptive Subtraction

Initially Birks conceived interceptive subtraction in terms of the defendant taking an asset that was legally or factually bound to go to the claimant, as where I hand you £100, a thief runs by and grabs it. He now suggests that this is direct subtraction, because I have done everything I could to transfer title, and equitable title vests in you.[68] McInnes argues that the best example of interceptive subtraction is the obsolete doctrine of usurpation of office.[69] In those cases the claimant is entitled as of right to certain fees. The defendant collects those rents or fees. There is no tort in English law. It is an action in unjust enrichment. Others have argued that there is no subtraction, interceptive or otherwise, unless the claimant loses a cause of action against the third party.[70] This seems likely. What matters is the

63 [2004] EWHC 201, [25].

64 Edelman, above n 6, 38–9, 200–4; but see *Say-Dee Pty v Farah Constructions* [2005] NSWCA 309; on whether this type of case is properly unjust enrichment, see Smith, above n 34.

65 Grantham and Rickett, above n 46, 165; M McInnes, '"At the Plaintiff's Expense": Quantifying Restitutionary Relief' [1998] *CLJ* 472.

66 Smith, above n 52, 2158; see to the contrary PBH Birks, 'Knowing Receipt: Re Montagu's Settlement Trusts Revisited' (2001) 1 *Global Jurist Advances* issue 2; Sheehan, above n 44, 85–86.

67 *Re Tilley' WT* [1967] Ch 1167; *FC Jones v Jones* [1997] Ch 159 (CA); *Foskett v McKeown* [2001] 1 AC 102 (HL); this is consistent with resulting trust doctrine. See against this S Worthington, 'Justifying Claims to Secondary Profits' in E Schrage (ed), *Unjust Enrichment and the Law of Contract* (The Hague, Kluwer, 2001), 451.

68 Birks, above n 37, 508; *Re Rose* [1952] Ch 78 (CA).

69 *Arris v Stukely* (1677) 2 Mod 660, 86 ER 1060; McInnes, above n 47, 698–9. See also *Official Custodian v Mackay (No 2)* [1985] 1 WLR 1308; *Shamia v Joory* [1958] 1 QB 448; Goff and Jones, above n 22, 41–43.

70 LD Smith, 'Three Party Enrichment: A Critique of Birks' Theory of Interceptive Subtraction' (1991) 11 *OJLS* 481; Virgo, above n 9, 109; Burrows, above n 9, 37. See *LAC Minerals v International Corona Resources* (1989) 61 DLR (4th) 14.

discharge of the debt to the claimant. This analysis can also be applied to the usurpation of office cases, and would lead to the enrichment being in all cases direct. This requirement for Smith[71] explains the requirement that remedies against the executors be exhausted in *Re Diplock*.[72] The executors of a will mistakenly paid money out to a number of charities. The next of kin brought an action against the charities. That action was dependent on exhaustion of remedies against the executors. Without that the charities were not enriched at the expense of the next of kin. Birks thinks this indefensible, and that the liability of the executors should be made secondary to that of the charities, who interceptively subtracted the payments.[73]

Even accepting Birks's explanation of *Re Diplock*, his new explanation of interceptive subtraction seems misconceived. It is now conceived in terms of money made from the use of another's asset. Birks draws support from *Jones*.[74] The trustee in bankruptcy, he says, cannot justify receipt of additional funds unless ownership of the original fund carries with it wealth-creating opportunities.[75] Jones withdrew cheques from the firm's account and gave them to his wife. His wife opened an account at Raphael's and successfully played the potato futures market, making a considerable profit. The account was owned by the trustee in bankruptcy. Birks's position is that the trustee did not just receive restitution of the chose in action whatever it was worth; the initial fund and the proceeds of the investment were distinct.[76] The transfer of the chose of action is restorative, and the proceeds disgorging. Similarly, in *Foskett v McKeown*[77] the trustee misappropriated money to pay life insurance premiums. The trust beneficiaries were entitled to take a proportionate share in the life insurance proceeds, not just to recover the premiums.

Birks's position that the additional gain is separate from the initial transfer finds no support in Millett LJ's judgment in *Jones*. His lordship felt that restitution was of the chose whatever it was worth.[78] Judgment recognised that the trustee had title to the chose in action and consequently the balance. Birks's view is correct in the sense that some enrichment was directly from the firm, and other enrichment, although factually received from third parties, is attributable to that original receipt. Yet there was no mixture, merely a series of clean substitutions. Common law tracing was therefore possible, which made it unnecessary to see the profits as separate. McInnes is procedurally correct to say that the decision

71 Burrows, above n 9, 497–500.
72 [1948] Ch 465 (CA); contrast Birks, above n 37, 509.
73 Birks, *Unjust Enrichment*, above n 1, 77.
74 Above n 67.
75 Birks, above n 37, 509–10.
76 *Ibid*, 510–11; McInnes, above n 47, 710–11.
77 [2001] 1 AC 102 (HL).
78 Above n 67, 167–70; *Foskett v McKeown* [2001] 1 AC 102 (HL), 116 (Lord Hoffmann).

was an interpleader action.[79] That said, the decision retains implications for unjust enrichment. Mrs Jones was also claiming the money. The court had to decide that Mrs Jones would otherwise be unjustly enriched at the expense of the trustee.[80] Without a reinterpretation of the trustee's proprietary rights, though, the case has intolerable effects. Raphael's had no way of knowing that Mrs Jones could give no good receipt for the money. The true justification for *Jones* is that the trustee in bankruptcy exercised a restitutionary legal power to revest title.[81]

Birks also pleads in aid *Hambly v Trott*.[82] In *Hambly* the question arose as to whether there could be a claim for the use made of a horse which was taken from the claimant ridden and returned, none the worse for the exercise. A use claim was available, giving the claimant a sum for the reasonable hire of the horse, that is, a sum for the gain made from another's property. Birks believes that an unjust enrichment claim would also reach any secondary profits derived from the misappropriated 'earnings potential' had the defendant hired the horse to a third party. It would not. Grantham and Rickett suggest that these are cases of indirect vindication of property rights.[83] That may be right, but it does not follow that they are not 'restitution for wrongs' cases. The unjust enrichment claim only reaches secondary profits where the claim is that the profits are owned, not merely owed. The property element of *Jones* comes to the fore more than Birks allows.

Grantham and Rickett are right to refer to the difficulty of seeing how any claim for disgorgement for wrongs could not be recharacterised as unjust enrichment on Birks's view.[84] Worse still, unjust enrichment could have a wider ambit than disgorgement for wrongs. McInnes implies the existence of cases where a disgorgement remedy is unavailable for the wrong, but available in unjust enrichment. In some cases, therefore, the remedy will be starkly different;[85] greater for the not-wrong than the wrong. Birks denies total overlap between wrongs and unjust enrichment, but the overlap is at best much greater than he admits; he cites *AG v Blake*[86] as an example of where unjust enrichment will not lie 'for want of a not-wrong connection'.[87] There are two separate reasons why there may be no unjust enrichment action: there may be no enrichment at the expense of the claimant, or there may be no unjust factor. As we see later, if Birks is

79 McInnes, above n 47, 701.
80 *Jones*, above n 67, 168.
81 Sheehan, above n 44, 78; this is the same interest the claimant firm possessed in *Lipkin Gorman*, above n 43; Sheehan, above n 44, 75–7.
82 (1776) 1 Cowp 371, 98 ER 1136.
83 Grantham and Rickett, above n 46, 174.
84 *Ibid*, 174.
85 McInnes, above n 47, 713–15.
86 [2001] AC 268 (HL).
87 Birks, *Unjust Enrichment*, above n 1, 81.

to maintain the view that there is no overlap in this case, he must do so on the basis of a lack of cause of action, and this seems hard to do on his new 'absence of basis' view.

(iii) Interest Claims

The term 'compound interest' comprises both restitutionary and disgorgement claims.[88] English law also allows for the award of simple interest. Section 35A of the Supreme Court Act 1981 allows for simple interest in any case where judgment is given for a debt or damage. Two questions arise. First, there is the question whether compound interest ought to be available, and for what causes of action. Secondly, there is the question what purpose interest serves.[89]

Interest serves a number of purposes. It can be restitutionary, but also compensatory. In many wrongs cases, interest is seen as a type of damages.[90] It is not a freestanding cause of action. Interest is seen as serving a compensatory function.[91] It may also serve a restitutionary function where the interest claim relates to a debt, because the loss that the claimant has suffered by not having the use of the money is mirrored by the defendant's gain. Interest, however, does not serve as a freestanding and distinct benefit.[92]

In *Westdeutsche Landesbank Girozentrale v Islington LBC*[93] a local authority had entered into swaps contracts, only to discover that they were void. This led to a spate of cases seeking to rewind the transactions. It was an unjust enrichment claim. It was not a wrong. By the time the matter came before the House of Lords, the only question was whether compound interest was available on the sum recoverable from the local authority. The majority decided that simple interest was available. Statutory interventions about the availability of interest had rendered it impossible to develop it further in equity.[94] Lords Goff and Woolf, in dissent, would have allowed compound interest. Edelman argues that they opened the door to a disgorgement remedy in unjust enrichment.[95] Lord Goff quite correctly pointed out that the jurisdiction to award compound interest cannot be confined to cases where it has been recognised so far.[96] Interest should be,

[88] Edelman, above n 6, 88.

[89] Burrows, above n 9, 55–6; FD Rose, 'Interest' in FD Rose and PBH Birks (eds), *Lessons of the Swaps Litigation* (Oxford, Mansfield Press, 2000), 291, 303–5. Rose has a third question relating to the timing of interest.

[90] *London Dover and Chatham Rly Co v South Eastern Rly* [1893] AC 429.

[91] *Hungerfords v Walker* (1989) 84 ALR 119.

[92] K Mason and J Carter, *Restitution Law in Australia* (Sydney, Butterworths, 1995), para 2807.

[93] [1996] AC 669 (HL).

[94] *Ibid*, 717–18.

[95] Edelman, above n 6, 89–91; Burrows, above n 9, 54–6.

[96] *Westdeutsche*, above n 93; Virgo, above n 9, 27.

according to Lord Goff, available in all cases where the defendant has acquired a benefit through a wrongful act, or been unjustly enriched.

Lord Goff approved comments by Hobhouse J at first instance.[97] Had the council not received the money, they would have had to borrow. In the Court of Appeal, relying on *Wallersteiner v Moir (No 2)*,[98] Leggatt LJ said that the money was 'worth to him the equivalent of compound interest at commercial rates'.[99] Lord Woolf did talk, in error, of compound interest as an award 'to reflect a profit made, or presumed to have been made'.[100] In other words, the claimant can recover gains not actually made. This is punitive, and out of place in unjust enrichment. Similarly, compound interest in unjust enrichment contexts cannot strip the secondary profits; it cannot strip money made from lending the funds. Lord Goff commented, however, that, had the council had to borrow the money, it would have paid compound interest, and therefore an award of compound interest is appropriate in unjust enrichment.[101] The council saved expense and this was a gain directly referable to the bank's payments. It is not disgorgement. There is a critical distinction to be made between the borrowing and the lending rates of interest.

D Causation, Tracing and Remoteness of Gain

This section is linked to the section on measures of enrichment, as it is also to that on interceptive subtraction. Both touched on personal and proprietary claims, as here. The causation inquiry needs to be unpacked. To date it has primarily focussed on one particular question. Let us take the example of a mistaken payment. The question has been whether the fact I was mistaken as to owing you the money caused me to make the payment.[102] There has been some debate as to precisely what causation test should be applied.[103] It is now agreed to be a 'but for' test. There are difficult problems, relating to multiple sufficient causes, as human decision making usually proceeds on the basis of a basket of variables. These can be solved by analogy to tort cases.[104]

97 [1996] 1 AC 669 (HL), 712, approving [1994] 4 All ER 890, 955; Burrows, above n 9, 54.

98 [1975] 1 All ER 745.

99 [1994] 4 All ER 890 (CA), 966–7.

100 *Westdeutsche*, above n 93, 723; J Edelman, 'Claims to Compound Interest in Restitution: Awakening the Sleeping Giant' (1999) 27 *Australian Business Law Review* 211, 222.

101 *Ibid*, 698; Virgo, above n 9, 27; Barker, above n 2, 293.

102 *Kelly v Solari* (1841) 9 M&W 54, 152 ER 24; *Barclays Bank v Simms* [1980] QB 677; *Nurdin & Peacock v DB Ramsden & Co* [1999] 1 WLR 1249.

103 PBH Birks and C Mitchell, 'Unjust Enrichment' in PBH Birks (ed), *English Private Law* (Oxford, Oxford University Press, 2000), para 15.57; Burrows, above n 9, 23–27.

104 S Arrowsmith, 'Mistake and the Role of 'Submission to an Honest Claim'' in AS Burrows (ed), *Essays on the Law of Restitution* (Oxford, Clarendon Press, 1991), 17, 22–3. For the tort law, see *Clerk and Lindsell on Torts* (London, Sweet & Maxwell, 18th edn, 2001), ch 2.

That a gain is causally related to an initial receipt does not mean it is traceable. Still less does it mean that it is recoverable. Birks initially commented that autonomous unjust enrichment had a built-in remoteness rule in that the claimant could only ever recover that enrichment which was in fact subtracted from him.[105] This must be right. It does, however, beg the question what is subtracted from the claimant. How far does causation go, and how doctrinally do we control it? The winnings from the lottery ticket discussed above are causally related to the mistake. A causal justification for non-recovery might be that the payee's acts were a novus actus interveniens. His act in purchasing the lottery ticket, or in using skill and effort in generating investment profits, cuts the causal connection between the receipt of the payment and the ultimate profit. Novus actus interveniens cannot mean the same thing here as it does in tort law, but there is something of a parallel. Clerk and Lindsell comment that the 'more voluntary the act . . . the more potent its causative effect'.[106] Buying the ticket is completely voluntary; it has a potent causal effect.

It is now necessary to pause and take stock of where we have reached. Tracing provides a substitutional link, and a proprietary claim can be made over the final asset. Barker's highly integrative agenda cannot be taken as far as he claims, although he is right to view both tracing and causation as attributive techniques. We can illustrate the point. In *Foskett v McKeown*[107] the beneficiaries of the trust were entitled to a proportionate share of the proceeds of a life insurance policy paid for partly from trust funds. Berg has asked why only a proportionate share was awarded.[108] To take a greater proportion would be confiscatory. That may be justified in a wrongs claim; causally related profits are claimable in wrongs. The beneficiaries of the policy were not wrongdoers. It was an unjust enrichment claim. However, there is an important caveat. The misappropriation in *Foskett* was not a sine qua non condition of the payout to the beneficiaries.[109] Causally related secondary profits greater than those traceably surviving should not be reached by a proprietary claim in unjust enrichment, and profits not a sine qua non certainly ought not. Abstract and traceable enrichment need to be kept separate.

There are different facets to this question, captured by differing theorists. There is an earnings opportunity, the potential to invest the trust money. The ultimate secondary profits do come from a third party—in *Foskett* the insurance company. The 'interceptively subtracted' enrichment is derived from the immediate; it is only available, however, in proprietary

105 Birks, *Law of Restitution*, above n 1, 352.

106 Clerk and Lindsell, above n 104, para 2.37.

107 [2001] 1 AC 102 (HL).

108 A Berg, 'Permitting the Trustee to Retain Profits' (2001) 117 *LQR* 366.

109 AS Burrows, 'Proprietary Restitution: Unmasking *Unjust Enrichment*' (2001) 117 *LQR* 412, 420; see eg [2001] 1 AC 102 (HL), 112 (Lord Steyn). This need not prevent recovery in a wrongs claim.

unjust enrichment claims. Personal claims never reach secondary profits, and only in comparatively rare cases, for instance involving services, will recovery exceed the claimant's loss.

II GAIN-BASED DAMAGES FOR WRONGS

We first set out Edelman's scheme. The quantum awarded in any particular case may be consistent with several measures.[110] The Law Commission assume as much in their report.[111] Burrows suggests Edelman's sharp distinction does not capture the complexity of the law.[112]

A Edelman's Scheme

Edelman argues that restitutionary damages refer to a monetary award reversing a transfer of value. This is measured by the objective value of the asset transferred. Where the transfer is of money, the transfer is equivalent to the loss suffered.[113] Subjective devaluation of the award may be possible, although Edelman accepts that this will be exceptional.[114] Edelman argues that user of land or other property gives rise to restitutionary damages, because value in the form of the use, or right to use, has been transferred. Edelman equates this requirement with the requirement for a transfer in the law of unjust enrichment.[115] These are always available on corrective justice grounds; in some, perhaps most, cases there may also be an alternative analysis in terms of compensation.[116] Disgorgement damages ignore any transfer that may, or may not, have taken place. They concentrate on profits actually made by the defendant.[117] There may be a greater or lesser transfer of value, or no transfer at all. The value might be generated from a third party or from the defendant's own skill and initiative. The claimant may even have benefited already.[118] These damages are available to deter breaches in cases of cynical wrongdoing, or in cases of fiduciary duties where the breach need not be cynical.

110 S Worthington. 'Reconsidering Disgorgement for Wrongs' (1999) 62 *MLR* 218, 219.

111 Law Commission, *Aggravated, Exemplary and Restitutionary Damages* (Law Comm No 247 1997), paras 3.59–63.

112 Burrows, above n 9, 462.

113 Edelman, above n 6, 66; J Edelman, 'The Compensation Strait-jacket and the Lost Opportunity to Bargain Fiction' [2001] *Restitution Law Review* 104; for a contrary view see *Stoke on Trent CC v Wass* [1988] 1 WLR 1406; *Inverugie v Hackett* [1995] 1 WLR 713.

114 Edelman, above n 6, 71.

115 *Ibid*, 67–8.

116 M McInnes, 'Account of Profits for Common Law Wrongs' in J Edelman and S Degeling (eds), *Equity in Commercial Law* (Sydney, Law Book Co, 2005), 405.

117 Edelman, above n 6, 72.

118 *Boardman v Phipps* [1967] 2 AC 46 (HL).

B Disgorgement as the Product of Restitution

Where restitutionary damages are available, any profits liable to be disgorged are derived from this putative transfer of value. Dagan[119] argues that entitling the claimant to net profits undoes the forced transfer. It vindicates the value of control over entitlements. Dagan suggests that fair market value protects another value, the utility value of the asset.[120] Dagan's normative position, while not without its difficulties, does suggest agreement with Edelman. They are not, however, separate premises of relief. From a normative perspective, this draws some support from the work of Ernest Weinrib. He has argued that both restitutionary and disgorgement damages, which he includes within the term 'restitutionary damages', are explicable, on corrective justice grounds, as reversing the value received by the defendant and derived from the wrong.[121] Edelman's measures do not, therefore, have separate purposes; each can serve, at least in part, a corrective justice rationale.

(i) Common Law Claims: Contract and Tort

Some English cases are said to stand against the acceptance of gain-based remedies for torts.[122] Many are said to allow only what Edelman would call restitutionary damages. However, as Barker has said, the door is open for profits awards to be made.[123] Up until recently, there was little scope for gain-based remedies for breach of contract in English law. These claims are all personal. The common law knows no proprietary right that it can award.

AG v Blake[124] recently allowed gain-based damages for breach of contract, but only where there was a legitimate interest in performance. Lord Nicholls, in concluding that gain-based damages were permissible, relied[125] heavily on *Wrotham Park Estate v Parkside Homes*.[126] That case involved the construction of a number of houses in breach of a restrictive

119 H Dagan, *The Law and Ethics of Restitution* (Cambridge, Cambridge University Press, 2004), 214.

120 *Ibid*, 215.

121 E Weinrib, 'Restitutionary Damages as Corrective Justice' (2000) 1 *Theoretical Inquiries in Law* 1, 16–18.

122 *Phillips v Homfray* (1883) 24 Ch D 439 (CA) *Stoke on Trent CC v Wass* [1988] 1 WLR 1406 (CA); *Halifax BS v Thomas* [1996] Ch 217 (CA); these are effectively dealt with by Burrows, above n 9, 473–6.

123 Barker, above n 2, 267–8; *Lamine v Dorrell* (1701) 2 Ld Ray 1216; 92 ER 303; *Oughton v Seppings* (1830) 1 B&Ad 241, 109 ER 776.

124 [2001] AC 268 (HL); *Esso v Niad* [2001] All ER (D) 324 (Nov); J Beatson 'Courts, Arbitrators and Restitutionary Liability' (2002) 118 *LQR* 377; *Experience Hendrix v PPX Enterprises* [2003] 1 All ER (Comm) 830 (CA).

125 [2001] AC 268 (HL), 283.

126 [1974] 1 WLR 798; *BMTA v Gilbert* [1951] 2 All ER 641; *Bracewell v Appleby* [1975] 1 Ch 408.

covenant. Brightman J held that it would be wasteful to order their destruction, and ordered that damages be assessed on the basis of a reasonable fee for relaxing the covenant to allow the construction to go ahead. That was calculated on the basis of 5% of the anticipated profit.[127]

Lord Nicholls did not see the distinction between restitutionary and disgorgement damages, and decided that an award stripping Blake's profits could be made.[128] He seems to have wrongly seen the distinction as a historical jurisdictional accident. He is right, however, not to make the distinction; there is, as Graham suggests, only one gain-based remedy, reaching all the profits only in egregious cases.[129] It would be strange to draw a strict line in this context when the main case Lord Nicholls relies on is, on Edelman's view, an example of a different type of damages. Graham refers to *Experience Hendrix v PPX Enterprises*,[130] which involved a breach of a licence and a related compromise agreement, and a consequent claim for damages. Mance LJ said,

> The law can in such cases act either by ordering over a percentage of any profit, or in some cases by taking the cost which the wrongdoer would have had to incur to obtain . . . equivalent benefit from another source.[131]

This gave rise to the suggestion of the sliding scale.[132] That is the suggestion that there is a scale of gain-based remedies from a proportion to full account of profits, essentially a structured discretion.[133] Some support for this can be drawn from Lord Nicholls's speech in *Blake*. He sometimes elides damages and account, and refers to them in discretionary terms. He talks of 'reasonable payment in respect of the benefit' and in the next breath of 'the discretionary remedy of requiring the defendant to account for the benefits from . . . breach of contract'.[134]

A wide-ranging discretion would be unattractive, but Edelman's analysis suffers from the strained use of the word 'transfer'. He himself acknowledges the objection that the transfer is metaphysical.[135] He explains,

127 *Wrotham, ibid*, 811–13.

128 [2001] AC 268 (HL), 279–80; P Jaffey, 'Disgorgement Damages for Breach of Contract' [2000] *Restitution Law Review* 578.

129 M Graham, 'Restitutionary Damages: The Anvil Struck' (2004) 120 *LQR* 26, 28; *Experience Hendrix v PPX Enterprises* [2003] EWCA Civ 323, [2003] 1 All ER (Comm), 830, 840–2 (Peter Gibson LJ).

130 *Ibid.*

131 *Ibid*, at [26]; *Caxton Publishing v Sutherland Publishing* [1939] AC 178 shows similar reasoning in the tort context (damages assessed as proportion of profits made minus expenses).

132 AS Burrows and E Peel (eds), *Commercial Remedies: Current Issues and Problems* (Oxford, Oxford University Press, 2003), 129.

133 Barker, above n 2, 262–3.

134 [2001] AC 268 (HL), 283–5; see also *Experience Hendrix v PPX Enterprises* [2003] EWCA Civ 323, [58].

135 Edelman, above n 6, 67–8.

however, that the word directs attention 'to the fact that the objective value received by the defendant must come *from* the claimant'.[136] There are two problems with this.

The first may be more semantic than actual, but helps to make the second. It is that a transfer would normally be premised on an identifiable thing, which existed before the transfer in the hands of the claimant coming into the hands of the defendant. The Crown had the right to publish; it would never have done so. To say Blake appropriated the right implies that he did, in fact, have the right. He did not. Edelman merely restates that Blake did the Crown a wrong. The appropriation of the right is that wrong, and there are some cases, as we will see, where it is impossible to see a right transferred even on Edelman's view.

The question, however, as it is in unjust enrichment cases, is an attributive one. George Blake made use of certain 'earnings potential' to make his profits. The profits physically moved from the purchasers of the book to the publisher and on to him, but they could not have been made without the earnings potential. As such, they are derivative. One cannot therefore be a separate premise to the other. Birks denies that there is an unjust enrichment claim in *Blake*. He cannot do so on the basis of lack of enrichment. If he accepts Edelman's analysis that there is a transfer of the right to publish, he must accept the presence of earnings potential. Birks need not, however, concede the existence of a cause of action in unjust enrichment. There may be no unjust factor, and it is hard to identify one, although perhaps easier to see the lack of a juristic basis. Birks's analysis, however, despite its unattractive consequences if applied to personal unjust enrichment claims, can be applied to gain-based remedies for wrongs to demonstrate that disgorgement and restitution are not separate premises or measures of relief.

In *Edwards v Lee's Administrator*[137] the defendant allowed entrance to a cave that was partly underneath the claimant's land, but the entrance to which was on his. He charged entrance, built a hotel and made a substantial amount of money. Many of the more popular sights were underneath the claimant's land. The court made an award of one-third of the profits from the venture. That is, they awarded a third of the profits from the visits to the cave; the profits from the hotel business were exempt from claim. The court did not make much of the cynical nature of the breach.[138] Edelman does, and describes the award as one of disgorgement damages.[139] This is what distinguishes *Edwards* from *Beck v Northern*

136 *Ibid*, 67.

137 96 SW (2d) 1028 (1932); see also *Martin v Porter* (1839) 5 M&W 351, 151 ER 149; *Livingstone v The Rawyards Coal Co* (1880) 5 App Cas 25 (HL).

138 96 SW (2d) 1028, 1031.

139 Edelman, above n 6, 139.

Gas Co.[140] There the defendant's gas seeped under the claimant's land, enabling the defendant to store some $12m worth of extra gas. It was not deliberate. Only a rent claim for use was available.

Edelman maintains all the profits are recoverable in disgorgement. If they are not, then the award has nothing to do with profits. Yet it is untrue to say that all the profits factually derived from the trespass were given up in *Edwards*. At least some of the profits from the hotel would not have been made but for the trespass. If disgorgement damages are available to deter, they ought to capture the hotel profits as well. The answer seems to be that the right infringed by the defendant did not entitle the claimant to profits from activities purely on the former's land. The explanation is, at least in part, a corrective justice explanation.[141] In *Beck* the defendant could have done little, if anything, to prevent the seepage. The gain was therefore not due to a conscious denial of the claimant's rights, and a profits-based recovery is not justified by corrective justice.[142] The availability of a corrective justice explanation supports the thesis that these are not different premises of relief. This is borne out by Weinrib's talk of the value of the use, the court's valuation, or a purchaser's subjective valuation as the quantum of relief.[143]

(ii) Equitable Wrongs

These often provide a proprietary response. They need not do so. Account of profits is a personal remedy. The question arises whether quantification of the remedy will differ between personal and proprietary. Edelman seems to assume not,[144] but a claimant choice between them will never arise. It is impossible to both own something and be owed it. Equity has a ready-made proprietary response to wrongs in the form of the constructive trust, and this often allows gain-based relief through a tracing process. Tracing is a process normally associated with unjust enrichment cases. In wrongs cases there are two possibilities. 'Normal' transactional tracing may be possible. A fiduciary may have misused or misappropriated property of the trust, such as funds in bank accounts or shares.[145] That an actual asset has changed hands shows that alternative analysis as unjust enrichment.[146]

140 170 F (3d) 1018 (1999); see also *Whitwham v Westminster Brymbo Coal* [1896] 2 Ch 538; *Penarth Docks Engineering v Pounds* [1963] 1 Lloyds Rep 359; *Swordheath Properties v Tabet* [1979] 1 WLR 285; *Strand Electric v Brisford* [1952] 2 QB 246.

141 Weinrib, above n 121, 11–13.

142 *Ibid*, 27–8.

143 *Ibid*, 17–18.

144 Edelman, above n 6, 262–4.

145 *Foskett v McKeown* [2001] 1 AC 101 (HL).

146 For an account of the unjust factor of ignorance see Burrows, above n 9, ch 4; ignorance is though a highly controversial unjust factor.

There remains, of course, the difficult question of what will count as an asset for these purposes.

Breach of confidence cases involve the defendant obtaining and misusing or selling on information in which the claimant has an interest. That interest is a right to control the information and the use made of it.[147] Information is a definable 'thing'[148] and, as such, it can be traced. Information, however, has a different normative character to other assets. It cannot be substituted in the same way.[149] The transferor still retains knowledge of the information; his memory is not wiped clean. There is, therefore, a necessary causal step at the beginning, but, once information can be traced into a more traditional asset, transactional tracing rules can apply.[150] They do, and a proprietary response is available. However, the important point for present purposes is that the value of the information, or the right to use it, would be the value of restitution in Edelman's terms. The profits are disgorgement, albeit proprietary disgorgement, but they are derived from the former in much the same way as disgorgement from restitution in the common law claims.

C Profits, Transfers of Value and Expense Saved

Edelman must identify whether relief is restitutionary or disgorgement, and whether any particular measure of recovery, profits or expense saved, counts as disgorgement or restitution. In other words, expense saved may be disgorgement or restitution. This creates a set of unnecessary, interlocking and criss-crossing categories. In almost all of these cases there is only one possible gain recoverable.

(i) No Profits but High Value Transfer

Edelman's example is *Inverugie v Hackett.*[151] In *Inverugie* the claimants had had title to a set of flats adjacent to a hotel. The hotel owners had cynically occupied the flats and attempted to run them as an adjunct to the hotel. The hotel, however, ran at a loss. There were no profits. Profits made would have been the product of the right to use the flats. Edelman argues

147 D Sheehan, 'Information, Tracing Remedies and the Remedial Constructive Trust' [2005] *Restitution Law Review* 82.

148 *Ibid*, 93; R Heverly, 'The Information Semi-Commons' (2003) 18 Berkeley Tech LJ 1127, 1144.

149 *Ibid*, 94–7.

150 *ABK v Foxwell* [2002] EWHC 9; *Morrison v Moat* (1851) 9 Hare 241, 68 ER 492; *Thomas v Pearce* [2000] FSR 718; R Pattenden, *The Law of Professional-Client Confidentiality* (Oxford, Oxford University Press, 2003), para 7.20.

151 [1995] 1 WLR 713; Edelman, above n 6, 87.

that disgorgement damages were not available, but restitutionary damages were awarded on the basis that the defendants could have rented them out.

The gain the defendants make in these cases is the higher of the value of the profits made or the market rent, but it depends on the type of market rent. Friedmann describes the award in *Inverugie* as one of attributed gain.[152] This is a gain that has not in fact been realised. This gains support from Lord Lloyd's own suspicions that there was no actual gain in *Inverugie*.[153] Like interest claims, *Inverugie* fails to distinguish two 'reasonable market values'. There is, first, the reasonable rate at which the defendants would have rented the premises, and the reasonable (higher) rent at which they could have sub-rented them. Friedmann's position that these were attributed gains suggests that he is considering the latter. Indeed, he comments that a commercial operator would surely negotiate a lower rate.[154] If there were an actual gain, it would be the saved expense, the equivalent of the borrowing rate. There is only one gain. It may, of course, be extremely difficult factually to distinguish these cases, but the distinction does exist. The likely explanation for the result of the case is, as Barker hints, confusion between these two measures.[155] Any attributed profits, or profits not actually made, should only be imposed in quasi-punitive cases; indeed, it may be difficult to distinguish these cases from exemplary damages. It seems clear that exemplary damages are available for cynical breach, aimed at making a profit where no profit is actually made.[156]

(ii) No Transfer but Profits Made

Edelman's example is *Boardman v Phipps*.[157] As an example, it is not obviously apt, but it does in fact work. There is a transfer. Where profits are made, using confidential information in an unauthorised fashion, the profits are, according to Smith, the fruit of the right to use the information.[158] It may be the fruit of the information, but that does not matter. The fact of a tracing process being available supports, as we have seen, the argument that disgorgement is a product of restitution.[159] However, were a

152 D Friedmann, 'Restitution for Wrongs: The Measure of Recovery' (2001) 79 *Texas Law Review* 1879, 1885.

153 [1995] 1 WLR 713 (PC) 718.

154 Friedmann, above n 152, 1886.

155 Barker, above n 2, 286.

156 D Harris, D Campbell and R Halson, *Remedies in Contract and Tort* (London, Butterworths, 2nd edn, 2002), 607; actual profits can be stripped by restitutionary (or disgorgement) damages. See *Kuddus v Chief Constable of Leicestershire* [2001] UKHL 29, [2002] 2 AC 122.

157 [1967] 2 AC 46 (HL); Edelman, above n 6, 72.

158 Smith, above n 26, 362.

159 *ABK Ltd v Foxwell* [2002] EWHC 9; *Morrison v Moat* (1851) 9 Hare 241, 68 ER 492; Sheehan, above n 147, 94–6.

person in a fiduciary relationship to be allowed to use information in this way, he would no longer be a fiduciary. Such profits are incompatible with a fiduciary relationship.[160] The party buys a release from his fiduciary position.

The best example is assault. *R v Brown*[161] decided that it was no defence to a charge of assault occasioning actual bodily harm that the victim consented to sado-masochistic sex. The decision was a public policy decision to prevent the glorification of violence and tolerance of a cult of violence.[162] One cannot normally consent to having oneself beaten up, yet if the defendant is paid £100 to beat you up, he has made a profit. Restitutionary damages are unavailable on Edelman's model because that would imply that the right to physically harm another person was saleable. Equally this type of case could not attract unjust enrichment liability. Edelman would allow disgorgement damages in this case.[163] Exemplary damages would also be available. The gain that B makes is the £100 payment. There is no other gain.

(iii) Expense Saved Alone

Edelman's example is *White Arrow Express Ltd v Lamey's Distribution Ltd.*[164] The claimants had paid for a deluxe delivery service and received the most basic. No profit was made. At first instance it was decided that only nominal damages were available. However, Beale has suggested that damages based on the loss of performance ought to be available.[165] The Court of Appeal[166] decided that, in principle, damages were available on the basis of the difference in the value of what was tendered and what was contracted for—that is, a measure of damages based on lost performance.

In *City of New Orleans v Firemen's Charitable Association*[167] the claimants had saved expense by not providing the number of fire engines and firemen they promised. However, nobody was hurt. All fires were put out expeditiously. In that case the expense saved was the hire of the firemen and engines. The decision was that the city was entitled to no

160 *Armitage v Nurse* [1998] Ch 241; *Walker v Stone* [2000] 4 All ER 412; D Hayton, 'The Irreducible Core of Trusteeship' in AJ Oakley (ed), *Contemporary Trends in Trusts Law* (Oxford, Clarendon Press, 1996), 49 discuss the analogous question of when an exclusion clause renders the 'fiduciary' no longer a fiduciary and the clause invalid.

161 [1993] 2 All ER 75 (HL).

162 *Ibid*, 90–1 (Lord Jauncey); B Bix, 'Assault Sado-Masochism and Consent' (1993) 109 *LQR* 540.

163 Edelman, above n 6, 74, but see Weinrib, above n 121, 34–5.

164 [1995] CLC 1251.

165 H Beale, 'Damages for Skimped Performance' (1996) 112 *LQR* 205; *AG v Blake* [2001] 1 AC 268 (HL); *Alfred McAlpine Construction Ltd v Panatown Ltd* [2001] 1 AC 518 (HL); E McKendrick 'The Common Law at Work: The Saga of Alfred McAlpine Construction Ltd v Panatown Ltd' [2003] *Oxford University Commonwealth Law Journal* 145.

166 [1995] NLJR 1504.

167 9 So 486 (1891).

more than nominal damages, as no damage was caused.[168] The essential element of the contract was the extinguishment of the fires. The court could have awarded the difference between the value of what was provided and requested. That would have been an award of performance damages. That is not necessarily the same as the market value of the right to skimp, which would have been Edelman's restitutionary damages award, nor was it the same as the profits made, the disgorgement award.

The Court of Appeal in *AG v Blake* would have awarded the extra profits made.[169] Lord Woolf's sense here is correct. Lord Nicholls suggests that expense saved does not fall within the traditional notion of account of profits.[170] In principle, this does not matter; negative gain is as much gain as positive gain. In any case, there should be no action to recover expense saved where a loss has been made, or would be made were the action successful. Economic arguments stand strongly against forcing the defendant to make a loss.

(iv) Profit Made and Expense Saved

Edelman argues that the two measures of calculating disgorgement damages are in competition, and gives as an example *Seager v Copydex*, where the defendant made profits, through the use of confidential information acquired from the claimant, in manufacturing a carpet grip.[171] The defendant was liable for breach of confidence and was 'not at liberty to make use of the information . . . without paying for it'.[172] Expense saved may also be the measure of restitutionary damages, and seemingly, therefore, may represent either restitutionary or disgorgement damages.

In *Dart Industries v Décor Corp*[173] the action related to the breach of a patent on seals for plastic containers. In the High Court of Australia argument revolved around quantification of the damages. The court referred to the question of opportunity cost,[174] that is, the cost of an alternative method of making the profits. McHugh J pointed out that some of the variables are peculiarly within the knowledge of the defendant. It would be hard to get accurate information. Expense saved can therefore refer to the alternatives to the wrongdoing. In *Seager v Copydex (No 2)* the cost of buying the information was accepted as the effective value of the rights transferred.[175] Lord Denning MR did indicate that there was a choice. Where the information was not special, damages would be the

168 *Ibid*, 488.
169 [1998] 1 All ER 833 (CA) 845 (Lord Woolf).
170 *AG v Blake* [2001] 1 AC 268 (HL) 286.
171 Edelman, above n 6, 75; [1967] 1 WLR 923 (CA).
172 [1967] 1 WLR 923 (CA) 932 (Lord Denning MR).
173 (1993) 179 CLR 101 (HCA).
174 *Ibid*, 114 (Mason CJ), 123–124 (McHugh J).
175 [1969] 1 WLR 809 (CA).

consultancy fee required, but if the information was unique it was the price a willing buyer would pay,[176] which Lord Denning assumed would be higher. If possible, we should compare the expense incurred against the expense incurred in carrying out the obligations, rather than making the profits some other way.[177] The remedy must correct the injustice done to the claimant. The claimant has no right or interest in the defendant's making profits some other way, merely in the defendant's not using his, the claimant's, assets to do so. It is this that Laddie J decided in *Celanese International Corpn v BP Chemicals*,[178] where the defendant wrongfully used the claimant's patented method of production, but another non-infringing method was available. The availability of this method was deemed not relevant to calculating damages. Expense saved can therefore be used as a proxy measure for the profits made. The measures are not in reality in competition.

Edelman highlights *Tang Man Sit v Capacious Investments*.[179] An election was required. In that case the defendants had agreed to assign properties to the claimant. They failed to do so, and made a profit by wrongfully letting them out. The claimants claimed for an account of profits and for damages. One head of those damages was for the reasonable market value of the flats which the claimant could have received (A), another head for the wear and tear, and damage caused by the tenants (B). Lord Templeman did not see the two heads of damages as inconsistent[180]—and, indeed, they are not. The claimant was, however, asked to elect between account of profits and damages.[181] However, the election was not all or nothing: if the claimant chose account of profits, it could have damages so far as they were not inconsistent with account. Edelman argues that restitutionary damages (head A) were greater than account of profits and incidentally performed their function. The loss caused (head B) was different again, and not inconsistent with either other measure of relief, except to the extent that damages for loss incidentally perform another head's function.[182] The correct position is that the actual gain was measured by head A of the damages. Head B is not inconsistent with that, but may incidentally perform the same function. The choice is between different end results, not different premises of relief.

176 *Ibid*, 813.
177 Weinrib, above n 122, 19–20.
178 [1999] RPC 203.
179 [1996] AC 512 (PC); *Esso v Niad* [2001] All ER (D) 324 (Nov).
180 *Ibid*, 526.
181 *Ibid*, 525.
182 Edelman, above n 6, 246–7; see generally S Watterson, 'Alternative and Cumulative Remedies: What is the Difference?' [2003] *Restitution Law Review* 7.

D Causation, Tracing and Remoteness of Gain

The Canadian Federal Court of Appeal has commented,

> Just as in a reference on a claim for damages issues of fact relating to causality and remoteness may properly be explored, so may they be likewise on an accounting of profits.[183]

Causality, remoteness and tracing are not coextensive.[184]

(i) Causation and Tracing

Edelman divides gain-based damages into restitutionary and disgorgement. He correctly observes that there may be some situations in which a transfer is procured as a result of a wrong, but some part of the transfer or profits would have occurred in any event.[185] This is not recoverable. If disgorgement damages are derivable from restitutionary, the way in which they are dealt with should be similar—and they are, although questions of culpability, for instance, increase or reduce recovery. That causal questions are treated the same is hard to demonstrate. If restitutionary damages are a perfect parallel to restitution of unjust enrichment, they should not reach secondary receipt; that would be profit, but these damages do, as we see, reach secondary receipts. This question becomes most difficult in the area of fiduciary gains. Some of these cases can only be analysed as proprietary unjust enrichment cases. *Foskett v McKeown* is an example. The beneficiaries of the life insurance policy had committed no wrong. Other cases can be analysed as either, but the general rule allowing all profits to be taken points to a wrong.[186] Some can only be wrongs, and others relating to information and business opportunity are a curious hybrid. Whether they, too, are proprietary unjust enrichment claims depends at least in part on how far we are prepared to reify information and opportunity as trust property.

In wrongs cases the test will normally, but need not, be a but for test. It has been described in breach of fiduciary duty cases as 'an adequate or sufficient connection'.[187] There will be other causes of the profit, or elements of profit, not attributable to the wrong. *Potton v Yorkclose*[188]

183 *Imperial Oil v Lubrizol* (1996) 71 CPR (3d) 26, 30; *My Kinda Town v Soll* [1983] RPC 407 (CA) 431; *Hodgkinson v Simms* [1994] 3 SCR 377; Law Comm, above n 111, paras 3.59–60.

184 Smith, above n 34, 417.

185 Edelman, above n 6, 103–4.

186 *Scott v Scott* (1963) 109 CLR 649 (HCA) 658–60; see also Lord Millett, 'Book Review' [2002] *Oxford University Commonwealth Law Journal* 281, 295; Lord Millett, 'Proprietary Restitution' in J Edelman and S Degeling (eds), *Equity in Commercial Law* (Sydney, Law Book Co, 2005), 309, 324, suggesting something akin to agency liability.

187 *Maguire v Makaronis* (1997) 188 CLR 449 (HCA) 468; *IDC v Cooley* [1972] 1 WLR 443.

188 [1990] FSR 11.

provides a good example. Millett J did not allow the claimant to include profit, made independently of the wrong.[189] This attributive process can be very complex; we can only give a taste of the complexity here. Terrell comments that a useful guide may be that profits should be apportioned in the same proportion as the costs attributable to that particular element of the larger enterprise.[190] There are different sorts of costs. Variable costs differ, depending on production; overheads or fixed costs do not, and questions of deduction arise. Deductions of overheads may not be available to wilful wrongdoers.[191] Where this type of apportionment is inappropriate or impossible, the court is released from mathematical constraints to come to a fair approximation.[192] Barker suggests that, in some cases, there is a quasi-punitive award where profits are disgorged whether they are a gain as a result of the wrong or not.[193] The defendant may be able to recover an allowance for skill and effort.[194] These may be recovered in cases both of restitutionary damages and disgorgement damages in Edelman's senses.[195]

Warman Intl v Dwyer[196] was a breach of fiduciary duty case. It involved the defendant agents setting up a business exploiting a relationship with Bonfiglioli. Warman had employed the defendants partly to run a relationship with Bonfiglioli which came to an end at the same time the defendants left. They had previously been in discussions with Bonfiglioli. That was a breach of their fiduciary duty, but obviously the running of that business took considerable skill. The High Court of Australia noted that there were two means of dealing with skill and effort. It could award an allowance. Alternatively, a profit-sharing process could take place; this is a more generous approach to the defendant, but the onus is on the defendant to show it is appropriate.[197] The defendants in *Warman* were ordered to account on the basis least favourable to them.[198] The claimant could only recover gains made two years after the breach.[199]

189 *Ibid*, 17.

190 *Terrell on the Law of Patents* (London, Sweet & Maxwell, 15th edn, 2000), para 13.47.

191 *Dart Industries v Décor Corporation* (1993) 179 CLR 101 (HCA) 116 (Mason CJ), 130 (McHugh J).

192 *Copinger and Skone James on Copyright* (London, Sweet & Maxwell, 15th edn, 2005), para 22.175–6; Goff and Jones, above n 22, 761.

193 Barker, above n 2, 284; *Boardman v Phipps* [1967] 1 AC 47 (HL).

194 *Re Jarvis* [1958] 1 WLR 815; *Boardman v Phipps* [1967] 1 AC 47 (HL); *Re Berkeley (Applegate) Ltd* [1989] Ch 32; *Say-Dee Pty v Farah Constructions* [2005] NSWCA 309 at [252]; D Sheehan, 'Negotiorum Gestio: A Civilian Concept in the Common Law?' (2006) 55 *International and Comparative Law Quarterly* 253.

195 *World Wide Fund for Nature v World Wrestling Federation* [2006] EWHC 184 at [120–121].

196 (1995) 128 ALR 201 (HCA).

197 Barker, above n 2, 284–5; *Maguire v Makaronis* (1997) 188 CLR 449, *Murad v Al-Saraj* [2005] EWCA Civ 959 at [85].

198 (1995) 128 ALR 201 (HCA) 212.

199 *Ibid*, 215.

This seems to have been a fairly crude attempt to estimate the causal effect of the breach.[200] This is not inconsistent with the granting of an allowance. The causal effect of the breach disappeared after two years,[201] but within that two-year period Dwyer's skill and effort had some effect to which the allowance gave effect.

In *Livingstone v The Rawyards Coal Co*[202] the claimants had purchased an area of land, believing the rights to the minerals to be reserved. They had not been. The defendants worked out the coal under the claimant's land, not realising they were not entitled to do so. The House agreed that a just sum for expenses was allowable. Mala fide defendants seem not to be entitled. No attempt was made, for instance ,to value Blake's literary efforts.[203] McKendrick has suggested that the rules of causation and the availability of allowances depend on culpability. He comments that a party's skill and effort might be a novus actus interveniens, cutting the causal link.[204] This is not quite right; the party's skill can only with difficulty be called an act separate from the wrong.

Barker discusses these issues at length, and his paper is largely devoted to identifying the policy issues relevant to deciding these issues. His division of the question into factual and legal causation[205] is, although necessary, a difficult one. The two merge imperceptibly into one another. He suggests it can explain the differences between some cases. In *Peter Pan Manufacturing v Corsett Silhouette*[206] the design of the claimant's bra was used by the defendant. He was ordered to pay the full profits. In *Seager* the information had a more limited role and a user fee was payable. Barker suggests there was no factual causal link between the misused information and the profits in the latter case. Yet, if this is so, why was there any relief at all? Additionally, profits could have been apportioned. The real explanation seems to be twofold: the lack of real culpability on the defendant's part and a sense that the information was of little value. Edelman's sense that cynical wrongdoers and fiduciaries do attract more severe remedial consequences is right.

Some cases are inexplicable except on the basis of relative culpability. In *MoD v Ashman*[207] a family remained in MoD housing after their

200 *Ibid*, 216; M McInnes, 'Account of Profits for Breach of Fiduciary Duty' (2006) 122 *LQR* 11, 14; *Murad v Al-Saraj* [2005] EWCA Civ 959 at [78], [85]–[88].

201 *3464920 Canada Inc v Strother* [2005] BCCA 35 at [60] (Newbury JA).

202 (1880) 5 App Cas 25.

203 *AG v Blake* [2001] 1 AC 268 (HL); *Martin v Porter* (1839) 5 M&W 351, 151 ER 149; Barker, above n 2, 284–5.

204 E McKendrick, 'Breach of Contract, Restitution and Punishment' in AS Burrows and E Peel (eds), *Commercial Remedies: Current Issues and Problems* (Oxford, Oxford University Press, 2003), 93, 117; *AG v Blake* [1998] 3 All ER 833 (CA), 846 (Lord Woolf MR); Barker, above n 2 above, 270; see also *Maguire v Makaronis* (1997) 188 CLR 449 (HCA).

205 Barker, above n 2, 282; for the contrary view Goff and Jones, above n 22, 758.

206 [1964] 1 WLR 96.

207 (1993) 66 P&CR 195 (CA); Edelman, above n 6, 72; Barker, above n 2, 271.

entitlement expired. They were trespassers, but had little choice. They were allowed to subjectively devalue the market value of the dwelling to the actual amount saved from the MoD.[208] The argument that there is a fundamental distinction between the objective valuation of the benefit received and the profits, which are provable, and a subjective valuation[209] of the benefit is undermined by the recognition that, at least in some, albeit rare, cases, the objective valuation is subjectively devaluable. Change of position will more frequently apply. Indeed, it is hard to see how a distinction could be drawn. Subjective devaluation is justified by the logic of change of position.[210] Birks acknowledges the pressure to apply change of position to wrongs, but argues that it will be hard to 'hold the line, but also hard to know how to cross it'.[211] It seems increasingly plausible that we will allow innocent[212] wrongdoers to avail themselves of the defence of change of position. Innocent converters, and trespassers, will be the beneficiaries of this change of heart. They will not have 'reprehensibly sought out' the benefit.[213]

(ii) Remoteness of Gain

The initial suggestion was that of Birks, that relief reach no further than the first 'non-subtractive' receipt.[214] This is at best somewhat arbitrary. Edelman has argued that the rules of remoteness in restitutionary damages cases are the rules of tracing. He does not discuss tracing in reference to disgorgement. Disgorgement by implication is purely causal; it is not. Disgorgement damages may yield profits from the sale of assets; restitutionary damages may yield the same.[215] These, then, are secondary receipts recoverable in restitutionary damages. Edelman argues that it is important to distinguish these cases, just as it is important to distinguish cases of disgorgement and unjust enrichment claims contingent on tracing. Yet many of these claims for 'tracing based' restitutionary damages are common law claims; Edelman talks of money had and received. Tracing is normally used to identify assets prior to a proprietary claim in unjust enrichment. The reasons why we allow recovery of the proceeds of sale are different in wrongs cases to unjust enrichment cases. No proprietary remedy is available in these common law wrongs cases. Tracing does, as we

208 *Ibid*, 201.

209 Weinrib, above n 122, 17–18.

210 Birks, *Law of Restitution*, above n 1, 441; Virgo, above n 9, 726; A Spence, 'In Defence of Subjective Devaluation' (1998) 43 *McGill Law Journal* 889, 913.

211 Birks, *Unjust Enrichment*, above n 1, 93.

212 Including negligent wrongdoers, *State Bank of New South Wales v SBC* [1996] RLR §30, and 110.

213 See Burrows, above n 9, 458–9.

214 Birks, *Law of Restitution*, above n 1, 351–5; *AGHK v Reid* [1994] 2 AC 342 (PC).

215 Edelman, above n 6, 107.

have seen, prepare the way for proprietary remedies in wrongs cases; the typical example is breach of confidence. There tracing has the same role as in unjust enrichment (albeit with an injection of causation), yet Edelman describes it as a proprietary disgorgement claim. Indeed, arguably all tracing claims disgorge. Analytically, the difference is that one type of claim is common law and personal, and the other equitable and proprietary. It does nothing but confuse the issue to make further distinctions.

Edelman suggests that in disgorgement cases the defendant should be forced to disgorge all reasonably foreseeable gains.[216] In *CMS Dolphin v Simonet* Lawrence Collins J said there had to be a reasonable connection between the breach and the profit in account claims.[217] The claimant recovers the full gain in cases where he has acted fraudulently or cynically. This does not fill the field, because it allows innocent fiduciaries to claim the benefit of the rule.[218] Edelman and Elliott maintain that there are many cases where

> although the defendant has been entitled to recover value transferred, if the defendant has not acted in bad faith the claimant has been unable to recover actual profits made.[219]

There is, however, no clean cut-off between causation, remoteness and the sharp distinction that Edelman tries to draw throughout his work between disgorgement and restitution.

III CONCLUSION

The focus of this paper has been twofold: I have explored the question of identification of the gain in restitution law, but also the interplay between the several different possible claims. The end result will depend on whether the claim is in unjust enrichment or wrongs, personal or proprietary. Edelman draws a distinction between disgorgement and restitution. Barker's position that the distinction between restitution and disgorgement makes no sense as different premises of relief, rather than as conclusions, is correct. Barker is also right that much of the quantification debate can be reduced to policy. Edelman's solutions are not often wrong; his point that in cases of cynical wrongdoing more extensive gain-based relief is available is correct. The claim here is merely that, after dividing restitutionary and

216 *Ibid*, 108–10, but see *Target v Redferns Ltd* [1996] AC 421 (HL) 434 (Lord Browne-Wilkinson).

217 [2001] 2 BCLC 704, [97]; *UPE v Deutsche Bank* [2000] 2 BCLC 461 (CA), 481 (Morritt LJ).

218 By analogy with *Doyle v Olby* [1969] 2 QB 158 (CA); *Smith New Court v Scrimgeour Vickers* [1997] AC 254 (HL); *Maguire v Makaronis* (1997) 188 CLR 449; *Kao Lee & Yip v Koo* [2003] HKC 113, [157].

219 J Edelman and S Elliott, 'Money Remedies against Trustees' (2004) 18 *TLI* 116, 127.

disgorgement damages, he needs to look at all the same questions examined in this paper. The division obscures the way causal and tracing questions are answered in the same way across his divide; it is analytically and semantically an unnecessary complication.

Personal unjust enrichment claims can only reach as far as the value of the immediate receipt in the hands of the defendant. Only a proprietary claim can reach secondary profits or receipts. Personal claims for wrongs can reach secondary profits and receipts. Causation and remoteness rules influenced by differing policy factors then quantify the gain recoverable. Barker has a highly integrationist agenda. He suggests that the same policy factors can explain the results in both unjust enrichment and wrongs. There are certainly parallels between the claims, but also dangers in taking these parallels too far.

14

Equitable Relief from Forfeiture: Performance or Restitution?

MICHAEL BRYAN*

I INTRODUCTION

A GREAT DEAL has been written in recent years about the place of equity in unjust enrichment. In the first *Restatement of Restitution*, the reporters, Seavey and Scott, proposed that restitution for unjust enrichment embrace equity, as well as the common law.[1] The relationship between equity and restitution has been debated ever since.[2] Equitable restitution, in the broad sense of assessing the measure of relief by reference to the defendant's gain rather than the plaintiff's loss,[3] is commonplace, particularly if restitution is taken to include the disgorgement of gains.[4] But equitable restitution for unjust enrichment is another matter. All candidates for admission to this category are closely scrutinised, and few are allowed in.[5]

The relationship between equity and unjust enrichment can be examined from various perspectives, but for present purposes it is convenient to

* Faculty of Law, University of Melbourne. I am grateful for the comments of Fred Ellinghaus, Bill Rimmer and Lionel Smith on this paper. The usual disclaimers apply.

1 WA Seavey and AW Scott, *Restatement of Restitution* (St Pauls, MN, American Law Institute Publishing, 1937); WA Seavey and AW Scott, 'Restitution', 29 (1938) *LQR* 29.

2 The *Restatement* is, of course, based on earlier materials, many of which are examined in D Ibbetson, *An Historical Introduction to the Law of Obligations* (Oxford, Oxford University Press, 1999), ch 14.

3 To be distinguished from the concept of restoration, or restitution, awarded for loss caused by a breach of trust: *Caffrey v Darby* (1801) 6 Ves 488; *Re Dawson Dec'd* [1966] 2 NSWR 211; *Target Holdings v Redferns (A Firm)* [1996] 1 AC 421; *Youyang Pty Ltd v Minter Ellison Morris Fletcher* (2003) 212 CLR 484. J Edelman and S Elliott, 'Money Remedies Against Trustees' (2004) 18 *Trust Law International* 116.

4 LD Smith, 'The Province of Restitution' (1992) 17 *Canadian Bar Review* 672; J Edelman, *Gain-based Damages* (Oxford, Hart Publishing, 2002).

5 G Virgo, 'Restitution Through the Looking Glass: Restitution Within Equity and Equity Within Restitution' in J Getzler (ed), *Rationalizing Property, Equity and Trusts: Essays in Honour of Edward Burn* (LexisNexis, London, 2003), 82.

distinguish four types of claim that have been made.[6] The first, and most ambitious, is that all applications of a particular doctrine belong to the law of unjust enrichment. Arguments that the resulting trust, claims based on tracing, reviving subrogation and the liability as constructive trustees of recipients of property transferred in breach of fiduciary duty respond to unjust enrichment all belong to this category. The claims in each case have been asserted and contested with equal vigour. Judicial support is claimed by both sides. The debates generated by these claims have highlighted the indistinct boundaries between unjust enrichment, on the one hand, and property and wrongdoing, on the other.

The second claim is that equitable rescission for mistake, misrepresentation, undue influence or unconscientious conduct is an application of the unjust enrichment principle. This is also a strong claim—and is, strictly speaking, is no more than an example of the first type of claim—but the characteristics of rescission in equity require distinct analysis. Acceptance of the claim ultimately depends on whether the proposition that rescission is a restitutionary remedy is accepted.[7]

A third claim, often overlooked by the unjust enrichment writers, is that equity will sometimes intervene in order to prevent unjust enrichment. Possible examples of this kind of anticipatory unjust enrichment include the doctrine of relief against penalties and the constructive trusteeship imposed in order to prevent a wrongdoer from profiting from the commission of the wrong.[8] The claim is marginalised by most unjust enrichment writers because the equitable response is not restitutionary but preventative. But restitution does in fact have a role to play. If the rationale for equitable intervention is prophylactic, in the sense of taking steps to prevent the occurrence of a mischief, equity must sometimes have to respond to the failure of prophylaxis. Compensation for the losses caused by the mischief is one such response; restitution of the benefits accruing to the benefits accruing to the wrongdoer is another. One of the aims of this paper is to show how restitution for unjust enrichment reinforces the

[6] This paper is concerned only with equity in the sense of the doctrines and principles developed by the Court of Chancery, and other courts administering equity jurisdiction. See R Grantham, 'The Equitable Basis of the Law of Restitution' in S Degeling and J Edelman (eds), *Equity in Commercial Law* (Sydney, Thomson, 2005), ch 14, 349.

[7] A Burrows, *The Law of Restitution* (London, Butterworths LexisNexis, 2nd edn, 2002), 56–60. The principal points of controversy here are (i) whether rescission of a wholly executory contract reverses unjust enrichment; and (ii) whether an order that a contract be rescinded and re-formed on different terms is consistent with a restitutionary analysis of rescission: see *Solle v Butcher* [1950] 1 KB 671, *Grist v Bailey* [1967] Ch 532, overruled in *Great Peace Shipping Ltd v Tsavliris (International) Ltd* [2002] EWCA Civ 1407, [2003] QB 679 on the question of the availability of equitable relief, but not on the question of whether rescission on reformed terms can be granted.

[8] K Mason and JW Carter, *Restitution Law in Australia* (Sydney, Butterworths, 1995), ch 19, [1903]. The references in S Waddams, *Dimensions of Private Law* (Cambridge, Cambridge University Press, 2003) to 'restitution in its general sense' or 'considerations of unjust enrichment' are mostly to this form of anticipatory unjust enrichment.

prophylactic aims of the doctrine of penalties where the penalty sum has been paid and prophylaxis has failed.

The fourth type of claim is that the reversal of unjust enrichment is one among several aims that the application of an equitable doctrine can achieve, even if the aim is concealed by the language and practice of equity. The claim recognises the plurality of objectives that equitable relief fulfils. They include the specific enforcement of a legally complete transaction, the perfection of an incomplete transaction, compensation or disgorgement for wrongdoing, and restitution for unjust enrichment. The constructive trust, although not a doctrine in the sense discussed in this paper, illustrate the variety of equitable responses. Not all constructive trusts reverse unjust enrichment, but some do.[9] Likewise, relief in estoppel cases is multi-functional: it is usually fashioned so as to enforce expectations or to compensate for reliance expenditure incurred, but there is no reason in principle why it should not also entitle a claimant who has transferred value to his detriment in reliance on a representation to personal or proprietary restitution for unjust enrichment.[10] The discretionary nature of relief awarded in cases belonging to this category is reflected in the terminology of 'doing equity', 'achieving substantial justice' and having regard to the 'matrix of the circumstances'.

The fourth claim is modest. It is a limited proposition that restitution for unjust enrichment is one of the discretionary remedial goals of equity. The claim does not identify a cause of action in unjust enrichment because equity has its own framework for identifying, barring and remedying claims. But where the defendant has been enriched, the tension between a plaintiff's right to restitution and the defendant's interest in security of receipt, which was historically mediated at common law through actions such as the action for money had and received, will be resolved through equity's distinctive processes for determining the availability of relief. The distinctiveness of the processes does not prevent the claim from being in substance one of unjust enrichment.

Unjust enrichment writers have difficulty accepting the fourth type of claim. One response has been to deplore appeals to discretion where the certainty that comes from the articulation of rules is attainable.[11] Another has been to suggest that appearances deceive: although equitable principle can be expressed in terms of fashioning generous, discretionary relief, the fundamental aim of the relief is in practice more confined to the pursuit of

9 G Elias, *Explaining Constructive Trusts* (Oxford, Clarendon Press, 1990); R Chambers, 'Constructive Trusts in Canada', 37 (1999) *Alberta Law Review* 173.

10 E Cooke, *The Modern Law of Estoppel* (Oxford, Oxford University Press, 2000); A Robertson, 'Equitable Estoppel Remedies after Verwayen', 20 (1996) *Melbourne University Law Review* 805.

11 P Birks, 'Equity in the Modern Law: An Exercise in Taxonomy', 26 (1996) *University of Western Australia Law Review* 1, 97–9.

limited ends.[12] Rather than rejecting or minimising the role of discretion, a more realistic approach would be to accept the discretionary, multi-functional nature of equitable relief, and to examine how inquiries into restitution for unjust enrichment are handled within its framework of structured discretion.

The central purpose of the law of unjust enrichment is to identify those situations in which someone who has parted with, or been deprived of, value is entitled to its restitution.[13] The law has to reconcile the claimant's interest in restitution with the recipient's interest in security of receipt. The reconciliation is as relevant to applying equitable discretion as it is to adjudicating a common law claim in unjust enrichment. It is arguably harder to achieve in equity because the restitutionary applications of relief compete with equity's enforcement and compensatory goals, though it also reinforces them. Nonetheless, the applications of an equitable doctrine which reverse unjust enrichment can be isolated and examined separately from its other applications.

This paper examines restitution for unjust enrichment as one of the objectives of equitable relief from forfeiture. Its purpose is to contribute to an understanding of how unjust enrichment questions are answered as part of the exercise of 'doing equity'. The restitutionary aims of equity in forfeiture cases were identified by Lionel Smith in an important article.[14] Smith noted in the article that the restitution approach to awarding equitable relief from forfeiture is an alternative to performance, or enforcement, of the terminated contract where termination would result in the loss of a proprietary interest.

An Australian development since Smith wrote his paper has been the recent decision of the High Court in *Tanwar Enterprises Ltd v Cauchi*,[15] which confirmed that the circumstances in which a purchaser of land can obtain specific performance where he is in breach of an essential time stipulation in the contract are strictly limited. As a result of *Tanwar*, the relief allowed to a party in breach will only rarely include performance of the contract, although the restitution of benefits conferred under the terminated contract can be ordered. The problem with this solution is that the unjust enrichment issues are hidden behind the veil of 'doing equity' or 'achieving substantial justice'. The veil conceals instances of inconsistent treatment of benefits conferred by purchasers on vendors of property under terminated contracts. The cases have failed to draw a rational distinction between benefits entitling the purchaser to restitution and

12 P Birks, *An Introduction to the Law of Restitution* (Oxford, Clarendon Press, revised edn, 1989), 290–3, analyses estoppel as promise enforcement in equity.

13 *Ibid*, ch 1; P Birks, *Unjust Enrichment* (Oxford, Clarendon Press, 2nd edn, 2005), ch 1.

14 L Smith, 'Relief against Forfeiture: A Restatement', 60 (2001) *CLJ* 178. The doctrine is analysed in the context of enforcing personal property security agreements in jurisdictions which do not have Article 9 UCC-type security registration legislation.

15 [2003] HCA 57, (2003) 217 CLR 315.

so-called 'windfall benefits' which are part of the rough justice of contract termination and which cannot be recovered. Indeed, line-drawing is eschewed in favour of determining the availability of restitution on a case-by-case basis. In *Tanwar* itself it was assumed without argument that instalment payments, not being deposits, were recoverable 'in equity' but that a development approval obtained by the purchaser for the benefit of land retained by the vendors was a windfall benefit in respect of which the purchaser was entitled to no relief. The paper argues that restitution should in principle be available for both types of benefit. Where equitable relief from forfeiture is in substance restitution for unjust enrichment it is not sufficient to announce judicial determinations in terms of the mystical process of 'doing equity'; it requires instead the application of a structured unjust enrichment inquiry, including the identification of an appropriate ground of restitution (or 'unjust factor') found elsewhere in the law of unjust enrichment.

Section II outlines the principles of equitable relief from forfeiture applied in Australia prior to the High Court decision in *Tanwar v Cauchi*. Section III summarises the decision in *Tanwar*. Section IV examines the circumstances in which restitution for unjust enrichment will be awarded as part of the jurisdiction to grant equitable relief, and identifies the principles which ought to apply in these cases. The final section summarises the conclusions of the paper.

II EQUITABLE RELIEF FROM FORFEITURE

Equitable relief can be granted against the loss or determination of an interest in property occurring as a result of a breach of contract or upon the occurrence of an event, not amounting to a breach, which would result in loss or determination of the interest. The earliest form of relief was afforded to mortgagors who failed to meet the stringent deadlines for repayment of the loan stipulated in mortgage agreements. The mortgagor was entitled to specific performance upon terms that the outstanding principal, interest and costs owed under the mortgage agreement were paid. The routine award of specific performance in these cases was the chrysalis of the mortgagor's equity of redemption.

Equitable relief for non-mortgage purchasers was fashioned along the lines of the relief granted to defaulting mortgagors. But, in contrast to the mortgage cases, it was never routinely granted, and so never met the threshhold precondition for transformation into a full equitable proprietary interest. Courts showed greater respect for security of bargain in the non-mortgage cases, and were less inclined to rationalise the vendor's right to forfeit the purchaser's interest in the property as security for the latter's performance. Sanctity of bargain sometimes yielded to countervailing policy concerns, but it took until the twentieth century to organise the concerns on a principled basis.[16]

Although equitable relief from forfeiture is not confined to cases of failure by a purchaser of property to make payment on a stipulated date, these cases nowadays provide the doctrine's most common field of application. Whereas the common law treated all time stipulations in contracts as conditions, entitling the vendor to terminate the contract, retain the deposit and sue for damages for loss of bargain, equity allowed the purchaser to sue for specific performance notwithstanding the breach. The vendor was still entitled to damages, if loss could be proved, but late completion was permitted provided that all the outstanding moneys owing were paid. Equity, however, followed the common law in characterising time provisions as conditions if time was stated to be of the essence of the contract.

The critical question raised in several recent decisions has been whether equitable relief from forfeiture can be granted where time is stated to be of the essence of the contract. Opposing philosophies of contractual ordering are at stake here. Respect for contractual autonomy ought to mean that the vendor is entitled to forfeit any interest the purchaser has acquired in the subject-matter of the contract as well as instalments of the purchase price paid before termination, if the contract so provides. On the other hand, the purchaser's late payment will often, though not invariably, occasion the vendor no financial loss (or perhaps a loss easily compensable in damages), and justifies allowing the purchaser to complete. Indeed, a vendor who is permitted to retain the property together with instalments of the purchase price paid, or alternatively to keep the benefit of improvements made to the property by the purchaser, will be unjustly enriched at the expense of the purchaser. Nineteenth and early twentieth century authorities oscillated between the policies of enforcing bargains strictly according to their terms and preventing the unjust enrichment which could result from insisting on the letter of the contract.[17] The majority judgments in the leading High Court decisions of *Legione v Hateley*[18] and *Stern v McArthur*[19] favoured performance of the contract as the best means of preventing unjust enrichment, but there was no consensus as to the basis of that relief.

16 The key decision is *Shiloh Spinners Ltd v Harding* [1973] AC 691, particularly the judgment of Lord Wilberforce.

17 The authorities are fully examined by C Harpum, 'Relief Against Forfeiture and the Purchaser of Land' [1984] *CLJ* 134. Although some of the cases raised true issues of restitution for unjust enrichment most are cases of anticipatory unjust enrichment, preventing the conferral of unbargained-for and unpaid-for benefits which, but for equitable intervention, would otherwise occur.

18 (1983) 152 CLR 406.

19 (1988) 165 CLR 489.

A legal system committed to enforcing bargains strictly, which is prepared to allow purchasers to take all the consequences, however catastrophic, of failing to comply with the letter of the contract, will refuse relief to defaulting purchasers whenever time is stated to be of the essence of the contract. Even the most fervent believer in sanctity of contract, however, would presumably allow the purchaser to complete where the vendor's conduct was the cause of the late payment. To allow relief on any other ground subordinates the policy of security of bargains to some other policy consideration, and it then becomes necessary for the law to articulate what that consideration is.

Lionel Smith has identified two approaches to granting relief. The first is the 'restitution solution', which permits the vendor to terminate the contract for breach but applies the law of unjust enrichment to compel the vendor to make restitution for windfall benefits received under the partly performed contract.[20] The solution respects the parties' contractual bargain but modifies the consequences of non-performance by allowing restitution in some situations where strict contractarians might allow losses and benefits to lie where they fall.

The other approach is the perfection (or performance) solution, which permits a purchaser who has failed to comply with a time stipulation to complete the contract provided that any arrears in payments and costs are paid off. The solution equates the essentiality of time provisions with the mortgagor's equitable right to redeem a mortgage. The equity entitles the mortgagor to perform the mortgage agreement after the contractual date for repayment has passed until a foreclosure or sale order extinguishing the equity has been made. The interest that the mortgagee holds in the property is a security, not a beneficial, interest. The performance solution is inconsistent with the express terms of the parties' agreed bargain, and for this reason some equitable intervention into mortgage agreements has been condemned by diehard contractarians as being ill-considered judicial paternalism,[21] but it is a perfectly sound application of the principle that equity looks to the substance of a transaction and not to its form. Lionel Smith, whose paper is primarily directed to the application of the doctrine to personal property sales contracts in jurisdictions which do not require registration of security agreements, favours performance of the agreement on the ground that the primary purpose of inserting time stipulations into personal property sales agreements is to provide non-collateral security for the purchaser's performance.

20 Smith, above n 14, 182.

21 *Salt v Marquess of Northampton* [1892] AC 1, Lord Bramwell at 19; cf the current uncertain status of the equitable prohibitions of clogs on the equity of redemption: *Westfield Holdings Ltd v Australian Capital Television Pty Ltd* (1992) 32 NSWLR, 194,202, Young J; *Re Modular Design* (1994) 35 NSWLR 96, 103–4, Santow J.

The various approaches to awarding equitable relief where the purchaser is in breach of an essentiality of time provision can be summarised as follows:

A. Performance

(1) where the vendor's conduct has caused the purchaser's breach; or alternatively

(2) upon payment of arrears of principal, interest and costs.

B. Restitution

(1) if performance is never permitted; or alternatively

(2) where performance can be ordered but the criteria for either A(1) or A(2) have not been met.

C. No relief

permitting losses and gains to lie where they fall.

Examples of both A and B can be found in Australian law,[22] but the modern High Court decisions of *Legione*[23] and *Stern*[24] preferred performance of the contract to termination mitigated by restitution. In *Legione* a majority of the High Court held that the purchaser under a contract for the sale of land was entitled to specific performance, notwithstanding the essentiality of time provision, if the misstatement made by the vendor's agent as to the materiality of that provision constituted 'exceptional circumstances'[25] justifying equitable relief.

In *Stern* a co-purchaser under a terms contract who had built a property on the land, not expressly provided for by the contract, was also held to be entitled to specific performance in spite of falling into arrears of payments, even though time had, by virtue of a notice to complete, been stated to be of the essence. Two of the majority judges, Deane and Dawson JJ, held that the time stipulation was in substance security for repayment of the loan, analogous to the repayment date in a common law mortgage. This is the characterisation advocated by Lionel Smith in his analysis of equitable relief. Gaudron J placed relief on a broader basis by holding that termination would be unconscionable if it conferred significant windfall benefits on the vendors. The vendors had argued for the restitution solution by offering to pay for the purchaser's improvements as a condition of being permitted to terminate the contract. The High Court, however, rejected the

22 Examples of the restitutionary approach include *Pitt v Curotta* (1932) 41 NSWWN 107, *Berry v Mahony* [1933] VLR 314 and *Real Estate Securities Ltd v Kew Golf Links Estate Pty Ltd* [1935] VLR 114.

23 (1983) 152 CLR 406.

24 (1988) 165 CLR 489. See NY Chin, 'Forfeiture: Windfalls and Conscience', (1995) 25 *University of Western Australia Law Review* 110, a valuable examination of these issues in *Stern*.

25 (1983) 152 CLR 406, 449, Mason and Deane JJ.

offer in favour of allowing the purchaser to perform provided that she paid all moneys owing under the contract.

III *TANWAR ENTERPRISES PTY LTD V CAUCHI*[26]

The High Court in *Tanwar* held that relief from forfeiture will only be granted upon proof of one of the equitable grounds of fraud, accident, mistake and surprise. It will not be awarded solely because it would, in the opinion of the court, be unconscionable for the vendor to terminate the contract. The case concerned three contracts to purchase land, each stipulating that time was to be of the essence. Two of the contracts required the purchaser to obtain development consents for the benefit of adjoining land retained by the vendors. These consents were obtained. Having failed to meet several previous completion dates, the purchaser had paid part of the purchase price in order to keep the contracts on foot. The remainder of the money due was sourced from funds paid from Singapore. Upon being issued with the final notice to complete, the purchaser was unable to pay this amount because the Singapore authorities refused to authorise the transfer until further checks were made. The money was received the next day but the vendors declined to accept payment and gave notice of termination. The trial judge and the New South Wales Court of Appeal rejected the purchaser's claim for equitable relief. Upon further appeal to the High Court, relief was also refused.

The reasoning of the joint judgment[27] of Gleeson CJ, McHugh, Gummow, Hayne and Heydon JJ accepted the following propositions:

1. The critical question is whether the purchaser should be granted specific performance, notwithstanding his failure to pay the purchase price on the settlement day, where time is of the essence of the contract.
2. The purchaser will be entitled to specific performance where fraud, accident, mistake or surprise,[28] or analogous conduct on the part of the vendor not falling under one of these heads,[29] makes it inequitable for the vendor to rely on its termination of the contract as a defence to specific performance. Specific performance would therefore have been justified in *Legione* if, upon remission to the Supreme Court, it had been shown that the vendor's agent had 'surprised' the purchaser by representing that payment after the date of settlement would be accepted.

26 [2003] HCA 57, (2003) 217 CLR 315. See also the companion decision of *Romanos v Pentagold Pty Ltd* [2003] HCA 58, (2003) 217 CLR 367.

27 In addition to the joint judgment, Kirby J and Callinan J delivered separate judgments.

28 These ground of relief were identified by Lord Wilberforce in *Shiloh Spinners v Harding* [1973] AC 691, 723.

29 *Tanwar*, above n 15, [58].

3. The fact that termination confers benefits on the vendor not provided for in the contract (so-called 'windfall benefits') is not, without more, a reason for granting the purchaser specific performance.[30]
4. The purchaser company in *Tanwar* was not entitled to specific performance because it could not show that any of the established heads of equitable relief were applicable to the facts of the case. More specifically, there was no 'accident' because the fortuity of the purchase-moneys being held back by the Singapore authorities was reasonably within the contemplation of the parties. The time stipulation could have been made subject to the willingness of the authorities to release money on that day.

The judgment clearly explains how the principles of equitable relief applied to the contracts in *Tanwar*, but it leaves some loose ends. In particular, two matters remain obscure.

First, it is uncertain whether under Australian law a vendor who has not been paid the full purchase price under a specifically performable contract becomes a constructive trustee of the subject-matter of the contract for the purchaser.[31]

It is not easy to extract a clear principle from the discussion of the vendor–purchaser constructive trust in the joint judgment, but in any event the question was irrelevant to the determination of the case. The 'interest' of the purchaser under such a contract was held not to be proprietary but only commensurate with the availability of specific performance. Property language was said to be unhelpful in this context: '[r]eliance upon the "interest" . . . does not assist; it is bedevilled by circularity'.[32] But obituaries of this species of constructive trusteeship may be premature. *Tanwar* emphasises that the central question in this kind of case is whether the purchaser is entitled to specific performance of the contract. The reference to 'circularity' means only that a purchaser cannot base his claim to specific performance on the fact that he has acquired an equitable interest under a constructive trust upon entry into the contract. Where time is of the essence of the contract the claim to performance can only be based on the heads of equitable intervention listed in the second proposition above.

Some indirect support for this interpretation can be found in the recent High Court decision in *Halloran v Minister Administering National Parks and Wildlife Act 1974*,[33] where one of the questions was whether a claimant of compensation for the compulsory purchase of land was entitled to an equitable interest in the land. The claimant had agreed to buy an equitable interest in return for an allotment of shares in the

30 *Ibid*, [62].

31 R Chambers, 'The Importance of Specific Performance' in S Degeling and J Edelman (eds), *Equity in Commercial Law* (Sydney, Thomson, 2005), ch 17, 448–62.

32 *Tanwar*, above n 15, [53].

33 [2006] HCA 3.

vendor's unit trust. In his separate judgment, Heydon J held that the claimant had acquired an equitable interest upon entry into the contract:

> At that moment a constructive trust arose and the beneficial interest in [the vendor's] equitable interest changed, at least to some extent. The interest of [the purchaser] was commensurate with its ability to protect that interest by obtaining specific performance. In the present circumstances there was no impairment of that ability by reason of any termination of the contract by [the vendor]. Hence there is no circularity, and no other difficulty, in viewing [the purchaser] as having obtained an interest under a constructive trust in such a way as to change the beneficial ownership of [the vendor's] equitable interest to some extent.[34]

On this analysis, a purchaser of an interest in land is entitled to the benefit of a constructive trust before the purchase money has been paid in full, except in cases, exemplified by *Tanwar*, where the availability of specific performance is the very question in issue.

The majority judgment in *Halloran* was content to leave open the question whether the contract entitled the purchaser to an interest under a constructive trust.[35] Nonetheless, it is suggested that the approach of Heydon J is correct in principle: a purchaser of land, or under some other specifically enforceable contract, has the benefit of a constructive trust upon entry into the contract provided that there are no bars to specific performance. The termination of a valid contract where fraud, accident, mistake, surprise or some similar factor cannot be shown precludes specific performance and deprives the purchaser of any equitable interest to which he would otherwise have been entitled.

The discussion of constructive trusteeship in *Tanwar* was therefore a red herring. It distracted attention from the only relevant inquiry in that case, being whether the criteria for the award of specific performance had been satisfied.

The second question left open in *Tanwar* is more pertinent to the theme of this paper. In what circumstances will a forfeiture provision in a specifically enforceable contract, where time is of the essence, be treated as security for the purchaser's performance? In *Stern* Deane and Dawson JJ characterised the terms contract in that case as being in substance a mortgage. The purchaser was therefore entitled to the equitable relief available to a mortgagor in default once she had shown that she could pay off the arrears of her instalment payments. In *Tanwar*, however, there was no discussion of this question beyond an observation in the joint judgment that there was no parallel between the contracts in that case and a

[34] *Ibid*, [93], references omitted.

[35] *Ibid*, [72]–[73]. The emphasis of the majority judgment was on the fact that ss 29(2) and s 44 (2) of the Stamp Duties Act 1920 (NSW) did not permit proof of the transaction to be adduced for the purpose of establishing a right to compensation.

purchase with the aid of a mortgage.[36] The mortgage analogy, although not repudiated, is likely now only to apply to instalment purchase agreements where the purchaser takes possession immediately after signing the contract. This is consistent with some state legislation which treats a terms contract as being in substance a mortgage, thereby enabling the purchaser to exercise the rights and remedies of a mortgagor.[37]

Let us recapitulate the analysis so far. A purchaser who is in breach of a time stipulation entitling the vendor to terminate the contract will, after *Tanwar*, only rarely be granted specific performance. A purchaser who defaults in making a payment under an instalment contract, being in substance a mortgage, will be entitled to performance on payment of the outstanding arrears. In all other cases relief will be limited to the traditional heads of equity—fraud, accident, mistake and surprise—and perhaps to some analogous cases, such as estoppel, to the extent that they are not covered by the traditional heads. The fact that the vendor derives some incidental benefit from exercising the right to terminate the contract does not by itself justify the award of specific performance in favour of the purchaser.

If *Tanwar* restricts the circumstances in which a purchaser in breach of a time stipulation can obtain specific performance, it also increases the significance of restitutionary relief. Termination is the trigger for quantifying the benefits received, as well as the losses incurred, under the uncompleted contract. In *Tanwar* the unpunctual purchaser had conferred two benefits on the vendors prior to termination: it had paid part of the purchase price, in excess of the agreed deposit, prior to the settlement date and it had obtained development approvals in respect of land retained by the vendors. It was not disputed at trial that the part-payment of the purchase price was recoverable 'in equity', an assumption that the High Court did not challenge, but it was held that the development approval was a 'windfall benefit' which the vendor could keep without making restitution. The principles for granting or withholding restitutionary relief in forfeiture cases were not examined. If equity is going to be parsimonious in allowing a purchaser in breach of a time stipulation to perform the contract the restitutionary consequences of the vendor's termination merit closer examination than they received in *Tanwar*.

36 *Tanwar*, above n 15, [34].

37 Sale of Land Act 1962 (Vic), s 4. K Nicholson, 'Stern v McArthur – the Jurisdiction to Relieve against Forfeiture and Instalment Contracts' (1990) 2 *Journal of Contract Law* 148, 156.

IV RESTITUTION AND RELIEF FROM FORFEITURE

Where V has exercised a right to terminate a contract for the sale of land as a result of P's breach of an essential time stipulation, P may have conferred either or both of the following enrichments on V under the partly performed contract:

1. P has paid part payment of the purchase price for the land, not being an irrecoverable deposit[38] or consideration for an extension of the payment deadline. The critical case here will be a contract which entitles V to retain the part payment on breach.
2. P has conferred on V a tangible benefit, such as a house built on the land, or an intangible benefit, such as a development approval, which is realisable in money.

It used to be argued that termination enabled V to obtain P's equitable interest in the land but, as we saw in the previous section, P's breach of the essential condition will usually mean that he cannot obtain specific performance, and therefore no longer has an equitable interest which can be protected from forfeiture. Accordingly, no question of restitution of the equitable interest need be considered.

A Restitution of Part Payments

The joint judgment in *Tanwar* noted the fact that the purchaser was entitled 'in equity' to repayment of the advance payment of part of the purchase price, should it fail to obtain orders of specific performance of the contracts, was not in dispute.[39] There is nothing new about sourcing the right to restitution to equity: a similar statement had been made by the High Court in *McDonald v Dennys Lascelles Ltd*.[40] But why is an equitable right to restitution needed? At first sight the purchaser has a common law claim in unjust enrichment, based on failure of consideration, for restitution of the advance payments. Indeed, *McDonald* is a leading authority for the existence of the common law claim. Why, then, the recourse to equity?

The cases suggest two reasons for sourcing the purchaser's claim to repayment to equity:

1. Equitable restitution overcomes the established common law hurdle that a failure of consideration must be total.

38 *Howe v Smith* (1884) 27 ChD 89; *Mayson v Clouet* [1924] AC 980; *Workers Trust & Merchant Bank v Dojap Investments Ltd* [1993] AC 573.

39 *Tanwar*, above n 15, [12]

40 (1933) 48 CLR 457, Starke J at 470, Dixon J at 478.

This rationale was advanced in *Real Estate Securities Ltd v Kew Golf Links Estate Pty Ltd*,[41] where a contract for the sale of land subdivided into allotments provided that the purchase money was to be payable in instalments, and that on the purchaser's default all moneys previously paid would be forfeited to the vendor. The contract permitted the purchaser to go into possession and resell the land before all the instalments had been paid. After the purchaser had gone into possession and sold off some of the land the vendor terminated the contract for the purchaser's non-payment. Lowe J held that the purchaser was entitled in equity to restitution of the instalments paid, though the amount was offset by the vendor's damages award for breach of contract.[42] Equitable relief was preferred to recovery in a common law action for money had and received because, it was said, in equity failure of consideration did not have to be total.[43]

This is not a convincing reason. Under Australian law restitution of money paid will only be granted where the failure of consideration is total.[44] But the totality requirement has been cogently criticised,[45] and its abolition would be preferable, while making due allowance for any counter-restitution conferred by the vendor. The difficulties caused by the absence of a doctrine of partial failure of consideration, or basis for payment, are not eliminated by making a jurisdictional leap into equity. Equity supplements the common law where the latter is inadequate, but the basis of supplementation is that the common law is adequate where the criteria for equitable relief are not met. It is not part of equity's jurisdiction to fashion relief where the common law is defective in all the circumstances to which it might apply. Structural defects in the common law are matters for the law reformer, not for equity.

2. The consideration, or basis, of the payment has not failed, and restitution on this ground is therefore not available.

A payer is entitled to restitution under Australian law if the basis, or assumption, on which the payment was made has failed.[46] The basis need not be contractual, but where the payment has been made pursuant to a valid contract it will be determined by reference to the terms of the agreement.[47] In the first example the contract permits V to retain instal-

41 [1935] VLR 114.

42 See also *Berry v Mahony* [1933] VLR 314, where an award was made in similar circumstances, the Victorian Full Court applying at 322 Sir Leo Cussen's aphorism that 'he who seeks equity must do common law'.

43 [1935] VLR 114, 122.

44 *Baltic Shipping Co v Dillon (The Mikhail Lermontov)* (1993) 176 CLR 344.

45 Birks, *Introduction*, above n 12, 242–8; Burrows, above n 7, 333–6.

46 *Roxborough v Rothmans of Pall Mall Australia Ltd* [2001] HCA 68 (2002), 208 CLR 516, Gleeson CJ, Gaudron and Hayne JJ at 525. Birks, *Introduction*, *ibid*, 223.

47 Mason and Carter, above n 8, [1113]–[1114] emphasise the need for a failure of the agreed return, rather than a failure of consideration or basis.

ments of the purchase price paid prior to breach. When V exercises the contractual right of retention the consideration, or basis, of the contract has not failed: on the contrary, the legal consequences of the purchaser's breach were foreseen by the parties and expressly provided for in the contract.

This reasoning was applied by Farwell J in *Mussen v Van Diemen's Land Co*,[48] where a contract to purchase land in Tasmania provided that time was of the essence of the contract, and that upon breach of this provision all moneys previously paid were to be forfeited. The vendor terminated the contract as a result of the purchaser's failure to pay an instalment. Farwell J held, crucially, that the vendor's retention of the money already paid was not a penalty since it was an integral part of the purchase arrangement, and that it was not recoverable by the purchaser for failure of consideration. Relief was refused because the purchaser had agreed that the vendor could keep the instalments already paid in the event of a breach. Relevantly, Farwell J held that the claim to restitution fared no better in equity than at common law: the basis of a contract must be ascertained by construing its terms, and the techniques of construction at and in equity are identical.

But P's right to restitution will not always be defeated by V's contractual right to retain the instalments; statute authorises repayment in some cases.[49] Legislation apart, support for a restitutionary claim can be found in a well-known, if controversial, dictum of Denning LJ in *Stockloser v Johnson*:

> Suppose a buyer has agreed to buy and necklace by instalments, and the contract provides that, on default in payment of any one instalment, the seller is entitled to rescind the contract and forfeit the instalments already paid. The buyer pays ninety per cent of the price but fails to pay the last instalment. He is not able to perform the contract because he simply cannot find the money. The seller thereupon rescinds the contract, retakes the necklace, and resells it at a higher price. Surely equity will relieve the buyer against forfeiture of the money on such terms as may be just.[50]

In *Stockloser v Johnson* Somervell LJ agreed with Denning LJ but the third judge, Romer LJ, took a more restricted view of the scope of possible equitable intervention. In the absence of some vitiating factor such as fraud or undue influence, he thought that equitable relief would be limited to giving the buyer more time to pay the last instalment.

Denning LJ's analysis of his own hypothesis has had a mixed reception, the differences of opinion largely reflecting the differences in the Court of

48 [1938] Ch 253.
49 Eg *Trade Practices Act 1975* (Cth) s75A (3).
50 [1954]1 QB 476, 491.

Appeal as to the permissible limits of equitable discretion.[51] It is generally accepted that equity can intervene on the side of the purchaser. Even on Romer LJ's analysis equity can extend the time for payment, but the availability of a claim in unjust enrichment (whether in equity as Denning LJ suggests, or at common law) has been disputed.

The critical question is whether an established legal basis for restitution exists (the 'unjust factor' inquiry). Australian law requires proof of an identified ground of restitution, such as mistake or failure of consideration, in spite of Birks's eloquent argument that what makes an enrichment unjust is the absence of any explanatory basis for making it.[52] In *Introduction* Birks rationalised Denning LJ's hypothetical as an example of restitution for 'inequality', based on the seller's exploitation of a purchaser relying on instalment purchase.[53] He later doubted whether 'inequality', or any such defendant-sided ground of restitution, could ever justify a claim in unjust enrichment.[54] But even if restitution of benefits conferred under unequal or exploitative transactions can be ordered, the ground does not really explain Denning LJ's example. Unless legislation has identified specific instalment purchase contracts as being actually or potentially exploitative, there is no good reason for supposing that an instalment payer is vulnerable or subject to the payee's oppressive conduct.

Restitution of advance payments should only be ordered where the provision entitling the vendor to retain the payments would have been struck down as being a penalty, had the contract been executory.[55] Where a contract provides that a sum of money payable upon breach is not a genuine pre-estimate of the loss suffered by the other party to the contract in consequence of that breach, the provision will be unenforceable in

51 The authorities are considered in detail by Mason and Carter, above n 8, [1141]–[1144]. As the authors point out, the correctness of the dictum was left open in *Legione*, above n 18, 443–4, and *Scandinavian Trading Tanker Co AB v Flota Petrolera Ecuatoriana* [1983] 2 AC 694, 702–3.

52 Birks, *Unjust Enrichment*, above n 13.

53 Birks, *Introduction*, above n 12, 212–13. Birks did not necessarily consider this ground to be 'defendant-sided'. It can be justified on the basis that consumers do not rationally assess the potential gains and losses involved in entering into some transactions. As he stated at 208, in these cases 'personal happiness is too much at stake for ordinary wisdom to exercise any restraint'.

54 There is no discussion of the *Stockloser v Johnson* hypothetical in *Unjust Enrichment*. Birks later took a limited view of the role of 'defendant-sided' grounds of restitution: P Birks, 'In Defence of Free Acceptance' in A Burrows (ed), *Essays on the Law of Restitution* (Oxford, Clarendon Press, 1991), 105.

55 The analogy with the penalties doctrine was applied in *In Re Dagenham (Thames) Dock Co, Ex Parte Hulse* (1873) LR 8 Ch App 1022, though performance was ordered in that case. Compare Mason and Carter, above n 8, [1142], who, in addition to applying the penalties doctrine, require unconscionable conduct on the part of the payee as a precondition to relief. As the authors point out, whereas the status of a payment as a penalty is determined at the time the contract is entered into, an inquiry into unconscionable conduct is decided at the time of forfeiture. The view taken in this paper is that the unjust enrichment inquiry can be carried out without reference to considerations of conscience.

equity.[56] The relevant date for determining whether a provision constitutes an enforceable liquidated damages clause or an unenforceable penalty is the date of entry into the contract. Although the contract may have been partly or wholly executed, the inquiry will be entirely prospective.

Where restitution of the advance payment is claimed, however, the inquiry is necessarily retrospective. The court will know, by reference to the actual payments made prior to breach, whether the vendor's retention of the payments confers a disproportionate benefit in comparison to the loss he has suffered, having regard to the damages he would have obtained in the absence of the retention clause. If the retention of the money is considered to be an excessive and disproportionate benefit in comparison to the loss (which will not necessarily be the case simply because the payments exceed, perhaps by a small amount, the damage suffered by the vendor) the retention clause should be just as unenforceable as a result of this *ex post* inquiry as a penalty clause would be in consequence of an *ex ante* inquiry.[57]

The consequence of the unenforceability of the retention of payments clause will be that the purchaser can obtain restitution of the payments made. Restitution for unjust enrichment steps in to assist the penalty payer where equitable prophylaxis, in the form of the penalties doctrine, has failed. The difficult question is to identify the precise ground of restitution. Given that the law of unjust enrichment is here reinforcing the doctrine of penalties, which in turn is grounded in the policy of preventing overcompensation for breach of contract, recovery of the advance payment can reasonably be characterised as an example of policy-motivated restitution.

B Restitution for Services Provided by the Purchaser

In *Tanwar* the High Court held that the development approvals which the purchaser had obtained for the vendors' retained land neither justified the claim for enforcement of the contract nor entitled the purchaser to payment for the services performed. The costs of obtaining them were held to be irrecoverable. The judgments contain no real discussion of why restitution was refused. This is regrettable because pre-termination service expenditure is a common feature of the cases on equitable relief from forfeiture. *Tanwar*

[56] The classic statement on the distinction between penalties and liquidated damages clauses is the judgment of Lord Dunedin in *Dunlop Pneumatic Tyre Co Ltd v New Garage and Motor Co Ltd* [1915] AC 79, 86–7, approved in *Ringrow Pty Ltd v BP Australia Pty Ltd* [2005] HCA 71.

[57] In *Stockloser v Johnson* Denning LJ stated that relief in his example was not against a penalty, but against forfeiture of a sum already paid. Nonetheless, whether characterised as a penalty or as relief against forfeiture, it is an application of the penalties principle of preventing overcompensation for breach of contract: *Workers Trust & Merchant Bank Ltd v Dojap Investments Ltd* [1993] AC 573 (PC).

can be contrasted on this point with *Legione* and *Stern*, where in each case the purchaser's construction of a house on the land to be bought influenced the decision to grant relief. Development approvals do not invariably enhance the value of the land in respect of which they have been obtained, but improvements conferring value on the vendor should not be treated as the vendor's windfall benefit.[58]

If relief by way of specific performance is unavailable, service providers must look to other branches of the law for payment. In *Tanwar* the High Court assumed, without deciding, that no basis for payment existed. But that conclusion is not inevitable. The performance of services may justify a claim in estoppel or unjust enrichment. As the following analysis shows, the requirements of unjust enrichment will usually be easier to satisfy than those of estoppel.

(i) Estoppel

Estoppel can ground a claim to specific performance where the purchaser has relied on the vendor's representation that the time stipulation will not be insisted upon. *Legione*, where the representation was made by the vendor's agent, was a case of this kind. The doctrine will also be relevant where the vendor has encouraged the purchaser to improve the land or has acquiesced in the improvements. Indeed, the 'improvement of the defendant's land' cases are the very heartland of proprietary estoppel, and it could be argued that a vendor who has encouraged an intending purchaser of land to improve land or to obtain development approvals should be estopped from denying the purchaser's claim to payment. Following *Tanwar*, the purchaser will not be entitled to specific performance, but could not the cost of the improvements justify an award of equitable compensation?[59] Although estoppel might seem at first sight to provide the improver with a promising avenue to payment, it may in practice be difficult to satisfy the equitable criteria in a *Tanwar*-type claim.

Where the purchaser has enhanced the value of the vendor's land prior to termination a fine but distinct line separates an estoppel claim from one based on unjust enrichment. The former will fail in the absence of a representation or other conduct on the part of the vendor which induces the purchaser to improve the vendor's property. The recent Privy Council decision in *Blue Haven Enterprises Ltd v Tully*[60] illustrates both the need

58 The point was explicitly noticed in *Romanos*, above n 26, where it was noted, at [24], that at trial it was assumed, but not proved, that the development approvals were valuable. *Romanos* is also distinguishable from *Tanwar* in that Special Condition 22 of the contract of sale entitled the vendor to the 'use and benefit of all engineering, architectural and survey plans' upon termination of the contract, thereby excluding by contract any right to restitution for services performed in drawing up the plans.

59 *Giumelli v Giumelli* (1999) 196 CLR 101.

60 [2006]UKPC 17.

for some kind of inducing conduct to be established and the confusion caused when insufficient attention is paid to the discrete requirements of estoppel and unjust enrichment. The vendor had sold land in Jamaica suitable for development as a coffee plantation. A protracted dispute then ensued between the parties as to the size of the estate to be sold and the price to be paid for it. The dispute was settled in favour of the purchaser, who obtained an order of specific performance. Meanwhile, the vendor had sold the same estate to the plaintiffs, who proceeded to develop it as a coffee plantation. The plaintiffs eventually conceded that the earlier purchaser was entitled to the estate, but they brought a claim in unjust enrichment against him based on the work they had done in developing the plantation. Although framed in unjust enrichment, the claim was in substance one of estoppel and was treated as such by the Privy Council. It was rejected because the earlier purchaser had done nothing to encourage the plaintiffs to develop the plantation. On the contrary, he had taken active, though unsuccessful, steps to prevent the plaintiffs from undertaking the work.[61]

The elements of estoppel will rarely be established in a forfeiture case. This is because the assumption upon which the purchaser acts when improving the property is that he will be entitled to that property upon full payment of the purchase price, not that he will be entitled to it in any event. The reason why assumption is not fulfilled is not because the vendor has gone back on his word but because the purchaser's late payment entitles the vendor to terminate the contract. It is the purchaser's own conduct, not that of the vendor, which has defeated the expectation of acquiring the land.

(ii) Unjust Enrichment

The purchaser has better prospects of success in an unjust enrichment claim than in estoppel. The relevance of such a claim to a purchaser who has improved property under a terminated contract was examined by the Privy Council in *Union Eagle Ltd v Golden Achievement Ltd (Hong Kong)*.[62] A contract for the sale of a flat provided that the purchase money had to be paid by 5.00 pm on the date of completion. The messenger bringing the purchase money arrived at the office of the vendor's solicitors at 5.10 pm. The vendor refused to accept the money and terminated the contract. The Privy Council held that the purchaser was not entitled to specific performance. The decision has been said to illustrate the different philosophies adopted by English and Australian courts in exercising discretion to grant

61 *Ibid* [28].
62 [1997] AC 514.

relief from forfeiture,[63] but it is consistent with the principles laid down in *Tanwar.* Like *Tanwar*, the *Union Eagle* decision allows a vendor to terminate the contract where the purchaser has broken an essentiality of time stipulation unless an established head of equitable intervention, such as fraud, mistake, accident or surprise, can be shown.

Obiter dicta in the Privy Council opinion recognise the availability of an unjust enrichment claim in respect of services performed which benefit the vendor. The conclusion, derived from an analysis of *In re Dagenham (Thames) Dock Co, Ex Parte Hulse*[64] and *Legione*,[65] was that these decisions:

> could be regarded as cases in which it might have been expected that the purchaser should be entitled to relief way of restitution rather than by way of being allowed to keep the benefit of the bargain in spite of his breach of an essential term. In neither case, however, was restitutionary relief considered; partly, no doubt, because of the state of the authorities on this branch of the law and partly because there was no suggestion that the value of the land so exceeded the purchase price as to make a practical difference between restitution and specific performance.[66]

The High Court in *Tanwar* implicitly rejected this analysis of *Legione*; specific performance in that case was justified by reference to the 'surprise' caused by the representation made by the vendor's agent that strict compliance with the time stipulation was unnecessary. The rationalisation is correct if the retention of the old heads of equitable relief is accepted. Nevertheless, the case that the Privy Council makes for restitution is convincing. A purchaser whose work on the vendor's land enriches the vendor is entitled to restitution for unjust enrichment notwithstanding his breach of contract. Services enrich even if their performance does not result in an end-product.[67] It is immaterial for this purpose whether the enrichment assumes a tangible form, such as a house, or is intangible, such as obtaining a development consent which can be realised in the enhancement of the value of the property.

The facts of *Ex parte Hulse* demonstrate why a party in breach of a time stipulation needs restitution. The purchaser had been in possession of the land pending completion for five years, and by the time of breach had constructed a dock at its own expense. Specific performance was granted on the facts of the case, but, following *Tanwar*, the award of this remedy could not now be justified under any of the established heads of equity.

63 *Tanwar v Cauchi* (2003) NSW Conv R ¶ 56-948, Handley JA.
64 (1873) LR 8 Ch App. 1022.
65 (1983) 152 CLR 406.
66 [1997] AC 514, 522 [16].
67 Cf J Beatson, 'Benefit, Reliance, and the Structure of Unjust Enrichment' in *The Use and Abuse of Unjust Enrichment* (Oxford, Clarendon Press, 1991), ch 2, 45.

Only a claim in unjust enrichment will entitle the purchaser to payment for the work done.

The only serious difficulty concerns the identification of the precise ground of restitution. In *Pavey & Matthews Pty Ltd v Paul*[68] the High Court justified an award of a quantum meruit for services performed under an unenforceable contract on the ground that the recipient had freely accepted the performance of the services. The principle of free acceptance would presumably also apply to unjust enrichment claims based on services performed under a terminated contract. But there is also a strong case for arguing that the ground of restitution is failure of consideration: the assumption (or consideration) on which the performance of the services was carried out, being the acquisition of the improved land, has failed.[69] It is not the aim of this paper to debate the merits of free acceptance and failure of consideration as competing justifications for a claim to a non-contractual quantum meruit. It is enough to show, as the Privy Council in *Union Eagle* recognised, that, unless the contract has allocated the risk of the performance of services under a teminated contract,[70] an established ground of restitution can readily be found.

V CONCLUSION

This paper has analysed the equitable principles of relief from forfeiture as an example of how restitution can occur within the framework of an equitable doctrine. It does so by adopting concepts and using language far removed from the concepts and language of the unjust enrichment theorist. The point is not that equity and unjust enrichment represent opposing analytical frameworks, or that unjust enrichment is in some sense superfluous to the inquiry into the exercise of equitable discretion. The appeal, well known to anyone who teaches the law of unjust enrichment in Australia, that one should 'let equity be equity' needs to be resisted. Where benefits have been conferred under contracts which have been terminated, and the contract has not allocated the risk of conferral or there are recognised public policy reasons for ignoring the contractual allocation, the competing policies of balancing a claimant's right to recover an enrichment and a recipient's interest in security of receipt require the same analytical framework of resolution in equity as at common law.

After *Tanwar v Cauchi* it ought to be clearer to Australian courts than perhaps it was in the past that the essential inquiry is not whether relief from forfeiture should be granted, but whether specific performance should be granted of the contract for the sale of land, in spite of the

68 (1987) 162 CLR 221.
69 AS Burrows, 'Free Acceptance & the Law of Restitution', 104 (1988) *LQR* 576.
70 As occurred in *Romanos*, above n 26; see also above n 57.

purchaser's breach of the time stipulation, and, if so, on what terms. But even if the equitable question is formulated as one of performance, and not of forfeiture of interest, the unjust enrichment question remains the same: in what circumstances will the purchaser be entitled to the return of money paid under the contract, or to payment for valuable services performed for the vendor? The equitable characterisation of the issue does not alter the nature of the unjust enrichment inquiry.

The final argument made in this paper is that the law of unjust enrichment has an important role to play in reinforcing equity's prophylactic aims. It is well known that the law of fiduciary obligations prophylactically attempts to prevent unauthorised conflicts and profit-making by visiting drastic sanctions on the delinquent fiduciary, but this is not the only example of equitable prophylaxis. The principles of equitable relief from penalties are intended to prevent overcompensation by avoiding the penalty clause *ex ante*. But what if prophylaxis fails? Equity has at its disposal a flexible array of responses, including compensation (though in Australia not exemplary damages[71]) and profit disgorgement. One of the responses is restitution for unjust enrichment. Indeed, prophylaxis in private law would be seriously deficient if the commission of the proscribed conduct in equity did not attract restitution for unjust enrichment.

71 *Harris v Digital Pulse* (2003) 56 NSWLR 298.

Index

www.ingramcontent.com/pod-product-compliance
Ingram Content Group UK Ltd.
Pitfield, Milton Keynes, MK11 3LW, UK
UKHW020230290926
15470UKWH00002B/447

9 781841 138145